The Greatest Ode to Lord Ram

Pavan K. Varma is a writer-diplomat and was till recently an MP in the Rajya Sabha. He was earlier Advisor to the Chief Minister of Bihar, with the rank of Cabinet minister. He has been India's Ambassador in several countries, also Director of the Nehru Centre in London, Official Spokesperson of the Ministry of External Affairs, and Press Secretary to the President of India.

Author of over a dozen successful books, Pavan K. Varma was conferred an Honorary Doctoral Degree for his contribution to the fields of diplomacy, literature, culture and aesthetics by the University of Indianapolis in 2005.

He was also conferred the Druk Thuksey, Bhutan's highest civilian award, in 2012.

Books by the Same Author

Adi Shankaracharya: Hinduism's Greatest Thinker
Chanakya's View: India in Transition

The Great Hindu Civilisation: Achievement, Neglect, Bias and the Way Forward

PAVAN K. VARMA

The Greatest Ode to Lord Ram

Tulsidas's Ramcharitmanas
Selections & Commentaries

WESTLAND
NON-FICTION

WESTLAND
NON-FICTION

First published in hardback by Westland Publications Private Limited in 2020

Published by Westland Non-Fiction, an imprint of Westland Books, a division of Nasadiya Technologies Private Limited, in 2023

No. 269/2B, First Floor, 'Irai Arul', Vimalraj Street, Nethaji Nagar, Alapakkam Main Road, Maduravoyal, Chennai 600095

ISBN: 9789357764742

10 9 8 7 6 5 4 3 2 1

Typeset by Digiultrabooks Pvt. Ltd.

Printed at Manipal Technologies Limited, Manipal

For my mother, Shakuntala, and my father, Badrinath Varma, who were great devotees of maryada purushottam Ram.

Contents

Introduction

Maryada purushottam Ram is one of the most beloved and revered deities of the Hindu faith. He is the epitome of rectitude, the touchstone of impeccable behaviour, the role model of the perfect human being, and a personal God, whose very remembrance elevates a devotee to truth, integrity, and devotion.

Tulsidas's Ramcharitmanas, which literally translates into 'the splendid lake of Ram's exploits', is arguably the greatest ode to Lord Ram. Based on the much earlier Sanskrit epic Ramayana (dated variously between the fifth century BCE to the first century BCE), written by Valmiki, the Manas is a shorter version of the same story, but with the inimitable stamp of Tulsi's loftiness of mind and poetic genius. Although shorter, it is nevertheless an epic, consisting of 12,800 lines divided into 1,073 stanzas, and seven *kands* or sections.

Goswami Tulsidas's work is a lyrical outpouring of the greatest devotion—bhakti—to Ram. The poet is well-versed in the philosophical intricacies of Hinduism, including the dichotomy between a nirguna (attributeless Absolute) and a saguna (attribute-full) deity, but while displaying deep insight into these arguments, of which he gives great evidence, his personal preference is to overarch them, and posit the argument of unblemished and unalloyed devotion to the fount of grace and compassion—Lord Ram.

Mahatma Gandhi regarded the Ramcharitmanas 'as the greatest book in all devotional literature.' In north India, in particular, the Manas is equivalent to the Bible for most Hindus. The book also ranks among the greatest works of literature in the world. The work is noteworthy not only for its scintillating poetic skills, but also its philosophical sophistication, its earthy wisdom and, above all, its great devotional fervour.

It is significant that Tulsi decided to write the work in Awadhi, not Sanskrit. It is believed that Shiva and Parvati once appeared to him in a dream and asked him to write the Manas in Awadhi, the spoken and understood language of the masses. Whatever the veracity of the legend, Tulsi's decision to write in Awadhi was a continuation of a historical trend wherein bhakti literature was removed from the classical pedestal of Sanskrit to embrace the ordinary person in his or her own language. From the fourteenth to the sixteenth centuries, a host of poets wrote in the language spoken by the common man. Chandidasa, who lived in the confluence of the fourteenth and fifteenth centuries, wrote in his native Bengali and is regarded by many as the founder of modern Bengali literature. Vidyapati (1352–1448), a younger contemporary of Chandidasa, lived in Mithila, Bihar, and wrote in the language he knew best, Maithili. Surdas in the sixteenth century wrote in Braj, as did Bihari (1595–1664), and Govindadasa, a contemporary of Surdas, wrote in Brajboli, a local dialect having elements of both Bengali and Maithili.

Tulsidas (1532–1623) was only continuing this tradition of linguistically democratising devotional literature. The difference between him and the other poets cited above is that while their deity of devotion was Lord Krishna, Tulsi's was Ram. In fact, it would not be an exaggeration to say, that because of the phenomenal popularity of the Ramcharitmanas, Tulsi single-handedly made Ram—the subject of his devotional ardour—the greatest object of personal veneration in the popular mindset.

Even so, there appears to have been opposition to Tulsi's choice of Awadhi rather than Sanskrit. Many Brahmins in Varanasi felt that he should not have renounced Sanskrit. According to a popular legend, they decided to test the worth of the book. A copy of the Ramcharitmanas was kept at the bottom of a pile of Sanskrit texts in the sanctum sanctorum of the Kashi Vishwanath temple in Varanasi, and the doors were locked. In the morning when the doors were opened, the Ramcharitmanas was found at the top of the pile. The words *'Satyam, Shivam, Sundaram'*—

truth, auspiciousness and beauty—were inscribed on the Manas, with the signature of Shiva. Attempts were also made to steal the manuscript, but it was miraculously protected. Tulsidas sent one copy of the manuscript for safeguarding to his friend, Todar Mal, the finance minister of the Mughal emperor, Akbar.

No exhaustive or complete account is available of Tulsi's life. Although views vary, the generally accepted version is that he was born in 1532 at Rajapur in UP situated on the banks of the Ganga. It is believed that due to the inauspicious astrological configuration of his birth, he was abandoned by his parents. At the age of five, the orphan was adopted by Narharidasa, a Vaishnava ascetic of Ramananda's monastic order. It was from him that Tulsi repeatedly heard the story of Ramayana. Apparently, his marriage played an important role in his becoming a renunciate. The story goes that he was greatly in love with his wife. Once, without asking him, she went to her father's home. Tulsi was so bereft without her that he followed her there. This angered his wife, who said: 'Have you no love for Ram? My body, to which you are so attached, is just a collection of skin and bone.' This reproach greatly affected Tulsi, and he promptly left her and returned, taking a vow to renounce domestic life, and adopt the life of an ascetic.

Tulsi spent the early years of his life in Ayodhya, the birthplace of Ram. He began to write the Manas in 1574, on Ram Navami, the birth date of Ram. After writing the first three sections of the book, he wrote the other four in Kashi, for which he had to depart because of a dispute with one of the religious sects in Ayodhya. During his lifetime, there are many stories of how Ram and Lakshman, and Hanuman, appeared before him and blessed him. He died in Kashi in 1623, at the age of ninety-one. The Tulsi Ghat in Varanasi is named after his long association with the city. By then he had acquired great fame for his unwavering dedication to Ram, and his remarkable literary skills. The historian Vincent Smith has called him the greatest man of his age in India, greater than even Akbar himself. The linguist Sir George Griffith has described him as 'the greatest leader of the people after the Buddha.'

The sincere attempt of my book is to bring selections of Tulsidas's great ode to Ram to the largest numbers of readers in a readable, accessible and enjoyable form. The Ramcharitmanas is an epic. It is a remarkable literary work, scintillating from beginning till end. However, since it is an epic, and is written in Awadhi, not everybody may be able to—in spite of their best intentions—read it from beginning to end, or to comprehend the full meaning of the stanzas. Yet, it is too great a work of literary and spiritual value, not to be read at all. The attempt, therefore, is to present a briefer version of the epic, with carefully chosen selections which reflect the best examples—from my point of view—of the greatness of Tulsi's writing, and the inspiring profile of Lord Ram. Given the enormous richness of the material, the selection itself was a very onerous task. Along with the selection, translations in both Hindi and English are provided. These have been taken from the Gita Press, which stand out for their fidelity and linguistic quality compared with other such publications. Finally, a commentary has been appended to each selection, so that the reader can assimilate not only the actual text, but also the context, background, characters, reasoning, and meaning of the poet's narrative. My hope is to thus take the greatness of the Manas to the largest number of readers, helping them to enrich their lives, understand the real value of maryada purushottam Ram, and realise the exquisite quality of one of the greatest literary works in the world.

I would like to express my deep gratitude to Sudha Sadhanand, my editor at Westland Publications, for her constant encouragement and support. I have also no words to sufficiently thank Mani Shankar Dwivedi, an exceptionally talented doctorate scholar from Jawaharlal Nehru University, who helped me in making the selection of the stanzas, and was always available to provide advice and guidance. A salute too to my secretary, Manish Tiwari who ensured that I meet deadlines amidst my many other preoccupations, and helped organise my work and schedule. Finally, I must record my debt to my wife, Renuka, who—as with all my books—was a part of my journey as a writer.

1. Characteristics of Saints and Salutations to Them

साधु चरित सुभ चरित कपासू।
निरस बिसद गुनमय फल जासू ॥
जो सहि दुख परछिद्र दुरावा।
बंदनीय जेहिं जग जस पावा ॥[1]

sādhu carita subha carita kapāsū ।
nirasa bisada gunamaya phala jāsū ।।
jo sahi dukha parachidra durāvā ।
baṃdanīya jehiṃ jaga jasa pāvā ।।

The conduct of holy men is noble as the career of the cotton plant, the fruit whereof is tasteless, white and fibrous (even as the doings of saints yield results which are free from attachment, stainless and full of goodness). Even by suffering hardships (in the form of ginning, spinning and weaving) the cotton covers others' faults and has thereby earned in the world a renown which is worthy of adoration.

बिनु सतसंग बिबेक न होई।
राम कृपा बिन सुलभ न सोई ॥
सतसंगत मुद मंगल मूला।
सोइ फल सिधि सब साधन फूला ॥[2]

binu satasaṅga bibeka na hoī ।
Rāma kṛpā binu sulabha na soī ।।

satasaṃgata muda maṃgala mūlā ।
soi phala sidhi saba sādhana phūlā ।।

Wisdom dawns not without association with saints and such association cannot be easily had without the grace of Shri Ram. Contact with noble souls is the root of joy and blessings; it constitutes the very fruit and fulfilment of all endeavours, whereas all other practices are blossoms as it were.

सठ सुधरहिं सतसंगति पाई।
पारस परस कुधात सुहाई॥
बिधि बस सुजन कुसंगत परहीं।
फनि मनि सम निज गुन अनुसरहीं॥[3]

saṭha sudharahiṃ satasaṃgati pāī ।
pārasa parasa kudhāta suhāī ।।
bidhi basa sujana kusaṃgata parahīṃ ।
phani mani sama nija guna anusarahīṃ ।।

Through contact with the virtuous even the wicked get reformed, just as a base metal is transmuted by the touch of the philosopher's stone. On the other hand, if by mischance good men fall into evil company, they maintain their noble character like the gem on the hood of a serpent.

बंदऊँ संत समान चित हित अनहित नहिं कोइ।
अंजलि गत सुभ सुमन जिमि सम सुगंध कर दोइ॥[4]

bandauun santa samāna cita hita anahita nahiṃ koi ।
añjali gata subha sumana jimi sama sugandha kara doi ।।

I bow to the saints, who are even-minded towards all and have no friend or foe, just as a flower of good quality placed in the palm of one's hands communicates its fragrance alike to both the hands (the one which plucked it and that which held and preserved it).

Tulsidas begins the Ramcharitmanas by a fulsome tribute to sages, saints, and good people, and the substantial benefits their company imparts to ordinary people. This is a recurring refrain throughout the Manas, but is particularly emphasised in the opening stanzas, since he considers the blessings of evolved and saintly people important to his project of writing a magnum opus like the one he has in mind.

The analogies he employs in paying this tribute are remarkable. Saints, he says, are like cotton, which in spite of going through great hardships in the making of cloth, readily undergoes this suffering, so as to benefit people by covering their nakedness. In the last stanza of this section, he also underlines a distinguishing quality of sages which is that they are always dispassionate, rising transcendentally above both friendship and enmity. The illustrative example he gives is that of beautiful flowers, which leave their fragrance both in the hands of those who break them and the crucible where they are put.

Tulsidas also underlines the great importance of satsang, the organised congregational meetings with sages. In fact, he says that without this as an essential part of our lives, *viveka,* or discrimination, is not possible, nor is the possibility of happiness and joy.

And finally, it is worth noting that right in the beginning, he makes clear what will be the most fundamental ideological underpinning of his Ramayana, which is the importance of absolute bhakti or devotion to Ram. Even the company of good people, he says, is not possible unless there is the blessings and grace of Lord Ram—*Ram kripa bina sulabha na soi.*

2. Characteristics of the Wicked and Salutations to Them

बहुरि बंदि खल गन सतिभाएँ।
जे बिनु काज दाहिनेहु बाएँ।।
पर हित हानि लाभ जिन्ह केरें।
उजरें हरष बिषाद बसेरें।।[5]

bahuri bandi khala gana satibhāen ।
je binu kāja dāhinehu bāen ।।
para hita hāni lābha jinha keren ।
ujaren haraṣa biṣāda baseren ।।

Again, I greet with a sincere heart the malevolent class, who are hostile without purpose even to the friendly, to whom others' loss is their own gain, and who delight in others' desolation and wail over their prosperity.

हरि हर जस राकेस राहु से।
पर अकाज भट सहसबाहु से।।
जे पर दोष लखहिं सहसाखी।
पर हित घृत जिन्ह के मन माखी।।[6]

Hari Hara jasa rākesa Rāhu se ।
para akāja bhaṭa Sahasabāhu se ।।
je para doṣa lakhahin sahasākhī ।
para hita ghṛta jinha ke mana mākhī ।।

They try to eclipse the glory of Vishnu and Shiva even as the demon Rahu intercepts the light of the full moon (during what is known as the lunar eclipse); and they are valiant like the reputed king Sahasrabahu (so-called because of his possessing a thousand arms) in working others' woe. They detect others' faults as if with a thousand eyes and their (designing) mind mars others' interests even as a fly spoils clarified butter.

तेज कृसानु रोष महिषेसा।
अघ अवगुन धन धनी धनेसा॥
उदय केत सम हित सबही के।
कुंभकरन सम सोवत नीके॥[7]

teja kṛsānu roṣa Mahiṣesā ।
agha avaguna dhana dhanī dhanesā ।।
udaya keta sama hita sabahī ke ।
Kuṃbhakarana sama sovata nīke ।।

In splendour they emulate the god of fire and in anger they vie with the god of death, who rides a buffalo. They are rich in crime and vice as Kubera, the god of riches, is in gold. Like the rise of a comet, their advancement augurs ill for others' interests; like the slumber of Kumbhakarana their decline alone is propitious for the world.

पर अकाजु लगि तनु परिहरहीं।
जिमि हिम उपल कृषी दलि गरहीं॥
बंदउँ खल जस सेष सरोषा।
सहस बदन बरनइ पर दोषा॥[8]

para akāju lagi tanu pariharahīn ।
jimi hima upala kṛṣī dali garahīn ।।
baṃdaun khala jasa Seṣa saroṣā ।
sahasa badana baranai para doṣā ।।

They lay down their very life in order to be able to harm others, even as hailstones dissolve after destroying the crop. I revere a wicked soul as the fiery (thousand-tongued) serpent-god Shesha, in so far as he eagerly expatiates on others' faults with a thousand tongues as it were.

Tulsidas is at his best in saluting the wicked too. With folded hands and with true conviction, he says that it is important to greet such people. There is more than a hint of sarcasm in this display of humility. Tulsi is aware that the evil, driven by envy and by the desire to find and magnify faults, will cast a baneful eye on his writings, and he preempts their proclivity by acknowledging—even paying tribute—to them.

These stanzas must be understood in the specific context in which Tulsi wrote the Manas. He was aware that his decision to write in the vernacular—Awadhi—and not in the classical language—Sanskrit— that scholars normally used, would be a cause for criticism and opposition. He must have also been aware that in the fraternity of scholars on the Ramayana, and in the priestly class, there was a great deal of envy and competitiveness. He must have decided, therefore, to take this opposition head on, and to disarm his critics through these verses, while simultaneously conveying to them that he was aware of what they were likely to do.

Although he begins these stanzas as a salutation, his subsequent description of those of a wicked dispensation is nothing short of devastating. Such people congenitally do bad even to those who do good to them; they delight in the misfortunes of others; they lack piety and devotion; they are forever in the forefront in pulling others down; they are prone to anger; they lack all redeeming qualities, and revel in undoing the constructive endeavours of others.

A significant feature of the bad, Tulsi says, is that they are even willing to destroy themselves in pursuing their hostility against others. Two images he conjures in explicating this point are noteworthy. The evil, he says, are like the fly that will fall into ghee to spoil it, even though it knows that in doing so it will die itself. The other image he invokes is that of hailstones, which will destroy a standing crop, even if in so doing they are aware that they will melt away (cease to exist) themselves.

3. The Creation of Brahma and Its Form

भलेउ पोच सब बिधि उपजाए।
गनि गुन दोष बेद बिलगाए॥
कहहिं बेद इतिहास पुराना।
बिधि प्रपंचु गुन अवगुन साना॥[9]

bhaleu poca saba bidhi upajāe ।
gani guna doṣa Beda bilagāe ।।
kahahin Beda Itihāsa Purānā ।
bidhi prapañcu guna avaguna sānā ।।

The good as well as the vile, all have been brought into being by the Creator; it is the Vedas that have differentiated them by reckoning the merits of the former class and the demerits of the other. The Vedas, the Itihasas (such as the Ramayana and the Mahabharat) and the Puranas unanimously declare that the creation of Brahma (the Creator) is an intermixture of good and evil.

दुख सुख पाप पुन्य दिन राती।
साधु असाधु सुजाति कुजाती॥
दानव देव ऊँच अरु नीचू।
अमिअ सुजीवनु माहुरु मीचू॥
माया ब्रह्म जीव जगदीसा।
लच्छि अलच्छि रंक अवनीसा॥
कासी मग सुरसरि क्रमनासा।
मरु मारव महिदेव गवासा॥

सरग नरक अनुराग बिरागा।
निगमागम गुन दोष बिभागा ।।[10]

dukha sukha pāpa punya dina rātī ।
sādhu asādhu sujāti kujātī ।।
dānava deva ūñca aru nīcū ।
amia sujīvanu māhuru mīcū ।।
Māyā Brahma jīva jagadīsā ।
lacchi alacchi raṅka avanīsā ।।
Kāsī Maga surasari kramnāsā ।
maru mārava mahideva gavāsā ।।
saraga naraka anurāga birāgā ।
nigamāgama guna doṣa bibhāgā ।।

It is characterised by pairs of opposites such as pain and pleasure, sin and merit, day and night, the good and the wicked, good birth and vile birth, demons and gods, the high and the low, nectar and poison, a happy life and death, Maya and Brahma, i.e., Matter and Spirit, the soul and God (the Lord of the universe), plenty and poverty, the pauper and the king, the sacred Kashi or Varanasi and Magadha or North Bihar (the accursed land), the holy Ganga the river of the celestial and the unholy Karmanasha (in Bihar), the desert land of Maravara (Western Rajaputana and Sindha) and the rich soil of Malava, the Brahma—who is a veritable god on earth—and the barbarian who feeds on the cow, heaven and hell, attachment and dispassion. The Vedas and other sacred books have sifted good from evil.

These two stanzas have been selected to indicate that while Tulsi is exceptionally hard-hitting against the wicked, at another level he recognises that both the good and the bad have validity as part of the unified reality of creation. Good and bad—and, indeed, all opposites—are entwined together in the matrix of this cosmos, and must, therefore, be accepted with equanimity. They exist as a unity that is the essence of the empirical world, but it is the Vedas that have segregated them as part of one cluster or the other.

In the second stanza, he uses his full poetic genius to describe a series of opposites, including sorrow and joy, virtue and sin, the saintly and the wicked, the high and the low, nectar and poison—all these seemingly opposed entities are the reality of life. In fact, he goes so far as to say that even the illusory powers of Maya—that compel us to mistake the unreal for the Real—and Godhood itself—Ishwara—is part of this creation, as is Brahman, that transcendent, attributeless, omnipotent, omniscient, unchanging cosmic energy. The important takeaway is that Tulsi, while resolutely ranging himself on the side of the good, has the philosophical detachment to accept that the ultimate reality is complex and composite, and we must have the insight to accept it for what it is, because the world in its entirety is the creation of Brahma.

4. The Form of Shri Ram-Sita and Salutations to Them

गिरा अरथ जल बीचि सम कहिअत भिन्न न भिन्न ।
बंदउँ सीता राम पद जिन्हहि परम प्रिय खिन्न ॥[11]

girā aratha jala bīci sama kahiata bhinna na bhinna ।
badaun Sītā Rāma pada jinhahi param priya khinna ।।

I revere the feet of Sita and Ram, who though stated to be different are yet identical just like a word and its meaning or like water and the waves on its surface, and to whom the afflicted are most dear.

बंदउँ नाम राम रघुबर को ।
हेतु कृसानु भानु हिमकर को ॥
बिधि हरि हरमय बेद प्रान सो ।
अगुन अनूपम गुन निधान सो ॥[12]

baṃdaun nāma Rāma Raghuvara ko ।
hetu kṛsānu bhānu himakara ko ।।
bidhi hari haramya Beda prāna so ।
aguna anūpama guna nidhāna so ।।

I greet the name 'Ram' of the Chief of Raghus, which is composed of seed letters representing the fire god, the sun god and the moon god (viz., Ra, A and Ma respectively). It is the same as Brahma (the creative aspect of God), Vishnu (His preservative aspect) and Shiva (His disintegrating aspect), and the vital breath of the Vedas; it is attributeless, peerless and a mine of virtues.

These two stanzas are pivotally important in delineating the vision of Tulsi to Lord Ram. He asserts that at the surface level what appears as diversified, is essentially a unity, and Ram alone can bridge this apparent contradiction. A difference can be posited between the articulation of words, and their meaning, or between water and the waves interred in it. But, this difference is superficial and misleading, because at the core it is a transcendent unity. In the first verse selected here, Tulsi says that Ram and Sita, although two different persons, represent that joint unity, and it is only through surrender at their lotus-feet—unmindful of any polarity—that salvation is possible, especially for those who are unhappy or in suffering.

In the second stanza, Tulsi elaborates on this idea further. Paying obeisance to Ram, he says that the alphabets of his name are an amalgam of three basic elements represented by fire, the sun, and moon. Ram, as the very essence of the Vedas, is also the divine combination of the trinity—Brahma, Vishnu and Mahadeva.

Then Tulsi touches upon what is one of his favourite themes, namely that Ram is both nirguna—attributeless, sans all descriptive or qualifying qualities—and the ultimate collation of all qualities—saguna. How can this basic contradiction be synthesised? For Tulsi, this is simply done, because of the element of bhakti, or devotional surrender. At the ontological level, Ram is Brahman, to which no quality can be ascribed because any attempt to do so would circumscribe the plenitude of this undifferentiated consciousness—*nirvishesh chin matram*—pervading the cosmos. But, for the devotee, that very nirguna Brahman, becomes saguna, assuming all beneficent qualities, and in so doing, neither of the two attributions is negated.

Tulsi's audacious conflation of nirguna and saguna takes us to the very core of Hindu philosophy and metaphysics. The great Adi Shankaracharya, basing himself on the verities of the Upanishad, propounded in the eighth century CE the doctrine of absolute monism—Advaita—where there could be no other reality other than the unqualified supra-consciousness of Brahman. Later philosophers, especially Ramanuja in the ninth century CE, articulated the concept of Vishishta Advaita, or qualified monism, whereby, while Brahman is, indeed, the foundational reality, it could manifest itself with qualities. This thought was taken much further by other thinkers, namely Madhava in the twelfth century CE, Nimbarkar around the same time who propounded the theory of Dvait Advaita or dual monism, and Vallabha in the fifteenth century CE, who spoke of Shuddha Advaita. All of these were devotional—and Vaishnava—derogations from Shankaracharya's rigid monism, and were adopted primarily because the attributeless Brahman was much too dry a concept for devotees craving for a personal deity with verifiable and visible qualities that they could surrender to and revere. This desire was taken to new heights by the absolute Vaishnava devotionalism of Chaitanya, and it is this mood which appears to be the primary influencing factor on Tulsi. The poet, like the philosophers before him, could actually claim legitimacy for their preference of a personal god by invoking—ironically—Shankaracharya himself, who, while remaining unyielding in his assertion of the primacy of Brahman, conceded that at the level of intermediate knowledge—*apara vidya,* as contrasted with absolute knowledge, *para vidya*—that very Brahman could be worshipped in the form of a personal deity, but only so long as this concession was a means to finally understand that Brahman alone is the only reality.

Tulsi intervenes in this debate by preferring the piety of devotees to the quibbling of philosophers. Just like water and the waves that emanate from it are—in the final analysis—indistinguishable, so Ram is both the attributeless Brahman, and the attributeful saguna form of that Brahman. For the simple devotee of Ram, this dialectic overarching was far easier to comprehend than the finer points of philosophy and metaphysics. As we shall see, this assertion of Tulsi is a pervasive theme of the Manas, where, without ever compromising on the primacy of Ram, which for him is an article of faith, he sometimes describes the Lord as nirguna, at other times as saguna, and often as both.

5. Glory of the Name and Character of Shri Ram

अगुन सगुन दुइ ब्रह्म सरूपा।
अकथ अगाध अनादि अनूपा॥
मोरें मत बड़ नामु दुहू तें।
किए जेहिं जुग निज बस निज बूतें॥[13]

aguna saguna dui Brahma sarūpā ।
akatha agādha anādi anūpā ॥
moren mata baḍanāmu duhū ten ।
kie jehin juga nija basa nija būten ॥

There are two aspects of God—the one unqualified and the other qualified. Both these aspects are unspeakable, unfathomable, without beginning and without parallel. To my mind, greater than both is the Name, that has established its rule over both by its might.

ब्रह्म राम तें नामु बड़ बर दायक बर दानि।
रामचरित सत कोटि महँ लिय महेस जियँ जानि॥[14]

Brahma Rāma ten nāmu baḍabara dāyaka bara dāni ।
Rāmacarita sata koṭi mahaṁ liya Mahesa jiyan jāni ॥

The Name is thus greater than Brahma and Shri Ram both and confers blessings even on the bestowers of boons. Knowing this in His heart, the great Lord Shiva chose this word (Ram) for Himself out of Shri Ram's story comprising a hundred crore verses.

राम नाम नरकेसरी कनककसिपु कलिकाल ।
जापक जन प्रहलाद जिमि पालिहि दलि सुरसाल ॥[15]

Rāma nāma narakesarī kanakakasipu kalikāla ।
jāpaka jana Prahalāda jimi pālihi dali surasāla ।।

The Name of Ram is, as it were, the Lord manifested as a man-lion and the age of Kali; the demon Hiranyakashipu. Crushing this enemy of gods, the Name will protect the devotees repeating it, even as the man-lion protected Prahlada.

भायँ कुभायँ अनख आलसहूँ ।
नाम जपत मंगल दिसि दसहूँ ॥
सुमिरि सो नाम राम गुन गाथा ।
करउँ नाइ रघुनाथहि माथा ॥[16]

bhāyan kubhāyan anakha ālasahūn ।
nāma japata maṅgala disi dasahūn ।।
sumiri so nāma Rāma guna gāthā ।
karaun nāi Raghunāthahi māthā ।।

The Name repeated either with good or evil intentions, in an angry mood or even while yawning, diffuses joy in all the ten directions. Remembering that Name and bowing my head to the Lord of Raghus, I proceed to recount the virtues of Shri Ram.

राम कथा मंदाकिनी चित्रकूट चित चारु ।
तुलसी सुभग सनेह बन सिय रघुबीर बिहारु ॥[17]

Rāma kathā Mandākinī Citrakūṭa cita cāru ।
Tulsī subhaga saneha bana Siya Raghubī ra bihāru ।।

The story of Shri Ram is the river Mandakini (which washes the foot of Chitrakuta); a guileless heart is Mount Chitrakuta (one of the happy resorts of Shri Ram during his wanderings in the forest); while pure love, says Tulsidas, is the woodland in which Sita and Ram carry on their divine pastimes.

Having established that the powerful influence of Ram cannot be constrained by the debate on whether he is nirguna or saguna—because he could be both—Tulsi proceeds to emphasise that the very name Ram is by itself a cause of definitive redemption. Following the philosophical line of Ramanuja's Vishishta Advaita, he says that the all-pervading Brahman could be both nirguna or saguna, but the name of Ram is bigger than both these categories. It is greater than those who grant boons, because it can grant a boon even to them. Drawing from Hindu mythology, Tulsi says that the name Ram is like Narasimha, the avatar of Vishnu. In mythology, Narasimha was part man, part lion, who came to earth to destroy evil and restore dharma. In this form, he is also known as the Great Protector, which is exactly like the protection the mere enunciation of the name Ram bestows. Carrying the theme of mythology further, Tulsi compares the demon Hiranyakashipu as the representative of Kaliyuga, the era of evil in the Hindu cosmic time cycle. Hiranyakashipu had acquired a boon from Lord Brahma that he cannot be killed by god, man or animal, in the day or the night, inside or outside his residence, or on the ground or on the sky. Narasimha—whom Tulsi compares with the power that comes from Ramajapa, the chanting of the name of Ram—then kills Hiranyakashipu, because as Narasimha he is neither entirely man or animal nor god, and does so at twilight which is neither day or night, pinning him down on his lap so that he is neither on the ground nor in the sky, and at the threshold of the courtyard so that he is neither at his residence or outside. Moreover, he does so by disemboweling the demon, using his lion's claws to rip his stomach apart.

The fact that Tulsi compares the power of Ramajapa to Narasimha is not happenstance. Narasimha, the man-lion is one of the most powerful—even overwhelming—images in Hindu mythology, of the powerful manner in which good can triumph over evil, and graphic images in stone and terracotta of the man-lion have been found dating back to the beginning of the Common Era. By saying that the name Ram is like Narasimha, Tulsi was actually using this image of tremendous strength, and of invincibility and goodness, to project the power that chanting the name of Ram provides. It was meant to leave the devotee in no doubt about the efficacy of this power. Those who recite this name, Tulsi says, are like Prahlada who—continuing the mythological comparison—is the good son of Hiranyakashipu. Prahlad is a great devotee of Lord Vishnu, and refuses to be intimidated by his father, who even attempts to kill him, but ultimately, with the help of Narasimha, it is Prahlada who emerges victorious.

It is interesting that Tulsi deliberately states that the benefits of reciting the name of Ram is available to all, even those who recite it out of ill will, or in anger, or in a mood of indolence. In other words, the name itself is so powerful that it neutralises the intention of the reciter, and is thus a source of universal benevolence.

Tulsi seals the argument by asserting that the katha of Ram is like the pure, beautiful river Mandakini, which originating from a glacier near Kedarnath, the ethereal Himalayan abode of Lord Shiva, merges with the river Alaknanda at Rudraprayag, and ultimately, along with the Bhagirathi river, becomes the holy Ganga. The noble spirit animating the story of Ram is like Chitrakoot, a place in current UP held in great reverence, where Ram, Sita and Lakshman spent six and eleven months of their fourteen-year banishment, and which was visited—according to lore—by the Hindu trinity, Brahma, Vishnu and Shiva, and also was the place where renowned saints like Atri, Sati Anusuya, Dattatreya and Valmiki meditated. The lush and green forest around Chitrakoot, Tulsi says, is symbolic of the deep love and affection in the midst of which Ram and Sita reside.

6. The Glory, Creator and Form of Shri Ramcharitmanas

रामचरितमानस एहि नामा।
सुनत श्रवन पाइअ बिश्रामा।
मन करि बिषय अनल बन जरई।
होइ सुखी जौं एहिं सर परई ॥[18]

Rāmacaritamānasa ehi nāmā ।
sunata śravana pāia biśrāmā ।।
mana kari viṣaya anala bana jaraī ।
hōi sukhī jaun ehin sara paraī ।।

One derives solace by hearing its very name, Ramcharitmanas (the Manasa lake of Shri Ram's exploits). The elephant of our mind, which is being scorched by the wild fire of sensuous enjoyments, is sure to get relief, should it drop into this lake.

रामचरितमानस मुनि भावन।
बिरचेउ संभु सुहावन पावन ॥
त्रिबिध दोष दुख दारिद दावन।
कलि कुचालि कुलि कलुष नसावन ॥[19]

Rāmacaritamānasa muni bhāvana ।
biracēu saṃbhu suhāvana pāvana ।।
tribidha dōṣa dukha dārida dāvana ।
kali kucāli kuli kaluṣa nasāvana ।।

The holy and beautiful Ramcharitmanas is the delight of sages; it was conceived by Shambhu (Lord Shiva). It puts down the three kinds of error, sorrow and indigence and uproots all evil practices and impurities of the Kali age.

रचि महेस निज मानस राखा ।
पाइ सुसमउ सिवा सन भाषा ॥
तातें रामचरितमानस बर ।
धरेउ नाम हियँ हेरि हरषि हर ॥[20]

raci Mahēsa nija mānasa rākhā ।
pāi susamau sivā sana bhāṣā ॥
tātēṃ Rāmacaritamānasa bara ।
dharēu nāma hiyaom hēri harași Hara ॥

Having conceived it, the great Lord Shiva treasured it in His mind till, when a favourable opportunity presented itself, He communicated it to His consort, Parvati. Therefore, after due consideration Lord Hara joyously gave it the excellent title of Ramcharitmanas.

जस मानस जेहि बिधि भयउ जग प्रचार जेहि हेतु ।
अब सोइ कहउँ प्रसंग सब सुमिरि उमा बृषकेतु ॥[21]

jasa Mānasa jehi bidhi bhayau jaga pracāra jehi hetu ।
aba soi kahauon prasaṅga saba sumiri Umā bṛṣaketu ॥

Invoking Uma (Goddess Parvati) and Lord Shiva (who has a bull emblazoned on His standard), I now proceed to give a full account as to what this Ramcharitmanas is like, how it came to be and what led to its popularity in the world.

संभु प्रसाद सुमति हियँ हुलसी ।
रामचरितमानस कबि तुलसी ॥
करइ मनोहर मति अनुहारी ।
सुजन सुचित सुनि लेहु सुधारी ॥[22]

Saṃbhu prasāda sumati hiyan hulasī ।
Rāmacaritamānasa kabi Tulsī ।।
karai manōhara mati anuhārī ।
sujana sucita suni lēhu sudhārī ।।

By the grace of Shambhu (Lord Shiva), a blessed idea inspired the mind of Tulsidas, which made him the author of the Ramcharitmanas. The author has polished his composition to the best of his intellect; yet listen to it with a sympathetic mind, O noble souls, and correct it.

सुमति भूमि थल हृदय अगाधू।
बेद पुरान उदधि घन साधू॥
बरषहिं राम सुजस बर बारी।
मधुर मनोहर मंगलकारी॥[23]

sumati bhūmi thala hṛdaya agādhū ।
Beda Purāna udadhi ghana sādhū ।।
baraṣahiṃ Rāma sujasa bara bārī ।
madhura manōhara maṅgalakārī ।।

A refined (sattvika) intellect is the catchment area, heart is the fathomless cavity, the Vedas and Puranas constitute the ocean; while holy men represent the clouds which rain down pure, sweet, agreeable and blessed water in the form of Shri Ram's excellent glory.

सुठि सुंदर संबाद बर बिरचे बुद्धि बिचारि।
तेइ एहि पावन सुभग सर घाट मनोहर चारि॥[24]

suṭhi suṃdara saṃbāda bara biracē buddhi bicāri ।
tei ehi pāvana subhaga sara ghāṭa manōhara cāri ।।

The four most beautiful and excellent dialogues (viz., those between (i) Bhushundi and Garuda, (ii) Shiva and Parvati (iii) Yajnavalkya and Bharadwaj and (iv) between Tulsidas and other saints) that have been cleverly woven into this narrative are the four lovely *ghats* of this holy and charming lake.

सप्त प्रबन्ध सुभग सोपाना ।
ग्यान नयन निरखत मन माना ।
रघुपति महिमा अगुन अबाधा ।
बरनब सोइ बर बारि अगाधा ।।[25]

sapta prabandha subhaga sopānā ।
gyāna nayana nirakhata mana mānā ।।
Raghupati mahimā aguna abādhā ।
baranaba soi bara bāri agādhā ।।

The seven books are the seven beautiful flights of steps, which the soul delights to look upon with the eyes of wisdom; the unqualified and unbounded greatness of Shri Ram, which will be presently discussed, represents the unfathomable depth of this holy water.

राम सीय जस सलिल सुधासम ।
उपमा बिच बिलास मनोरम ।।
पुरइनि सघन चारु चौपाई ।
जुगुति मंजु मनि सीप सुहाई ।।[26]

Rāma Sīya jasa salila sudhāsama ।
upamā bīci bilāsa manōram ।।
puraini saghana cāru caupaī ।
juguti manju mani sīpa suhāi ।।

The glory of Shri Ram and Sita constitutes the nectar in water; the similes represent the soul-ravishing sport of its wavelets. The beautiful *chaupais,* four-line stanzas, represent the thick growth of lotus-plants; the various poetic devices constitute the lovely shells that yield beautiful pearls.

छंद सोरठा सुंदर दोहा ।
सोइ बहुरंग कमल कुल सोहा ।
अरथ अनूप सुभाव सुभासा ।
सोइ पराग मकरंद सुबासा ।।[27]

chaṃda sōraṭhā sundara dohā ।
sōi bahuranga kamala kula sohā ।।
aratha anūpa sumāva subhāsā ।
soi parāga makaranda subāsā ।।

The other metres, viz., *chhandas, sorthas* and *dohas,* are the cluster of charming many-coloured lotuses. The incomparable sense, the beautiful ideas and the elegant expression represent the pollen, honey and fragrance of those flowers respectively.

In this stanza, Tulsi speaks about the Ramcharitmanas itself, and although he makes an effort to bring in an element of humility, his poetic genius is largely devoted to bringing out the greatness and glory of the work. In one chaupai, he says that the poet has tried to make the work as beautiful as possible, but those who in the right spirit believe that it can be improved are welcome to do so. However, apart from this passing concession conceding the possibility of improvement, for the rest Tulsi is euphoric about the Manas, and given the remarkable quality of the work, his lack of modesty can, indeed, be forgiven.

The analogy, which he uses with great dexterity, is that of a lake. Unlike Valmiki, who around the fifth century CE gave the straightforward title of Ramayana to his historic work, Tulsi chose the title of Ramcharitmanas, which literally translates into the 'lake of the character (or deeds) of Ram'. Since this is his title, he uses the analogy of the lake to profile the nature of his work. The bedrock of this lake, he says, is pure intellect, while its deepest spot is the heart, and the Vedas and the Puranas are the vast ocean beyond. Saintly people are like the clouds that hover over this lake, and the rainfall drenches the reader in the beautiful, enchanting and beneficent character of Ram. The four principal dialogues of the work (between Bhushundi and Garuda, Shiva and Parvati, Yajnavalkya and Bharadwaj, and Tulsi and saints) are the four ghats of the lake. The seven *kands,* or sections, of the work are the seven steps leading to the lake. The glory of Ram and Sita are the ambrosia like waters of the lake, the analogies are like the waves in the water, the chaupais are like beautiful creepers adorning the lake, and the finer aspects of the poetry are like rare pearls found in its waters. The chhands, sorthas, and dohas in the work are like lotuses, and their meanings and emotion are like the pollen, nectar and fragrance of the flowers.

At one point, Tulsi says that the depth of the lake reflects the nirguna form of Ram. This categorical assertion is in direct conflict with Tulsi's worship of Ram in His saguna form, and his argument that the Lord is actually above the philosophical contradictions between nirguna and saguna. Such statements appear to be an attempt by Tulsi to appease those for whom the Absolute, following the powerful Advaita tradition, is omnipotent but attributeless. While himself being a convinced votary of the saguna bhakti school of thought, he makes these statements both to deflect criticism from those thinking otherwise, and to make the point that even if Ram is, at one level nirguna, this does not in any way prevent him from being a saguna symbol, who invokes devotion and worship of a personal god as the only saviour.

Tulsi also claims divine sanction for the Manas. He makes the statement that the work is the creation of Shiva, and he (Tulsi) is only the medium to put it on paper. The work was created keeping Shiva-Parvati always in mind, and it is because of the blessings of Shiva that the poet was able to write it. The association of Shiva with the creation of the Manas, was a powerful means of conveying to his critics (if any) that he was only an instrument in the fulfilment of a divine purpose, and that, therefore, to attack the work would be tantamount to attacking its prime inspiration and motivator—Shiva.

Tulsi gives concrete reasons too why reading the Manas is personally beneficial for the reader. Firstly, the mere hearing of the narration of the content of the work gives peace to the mind. It soothes the nerves, and calms mental agitations. Tulsi gives a very telling analogy to make this point. The ceaseless activity of the mind is like an elephant, he says, that is burning in the fire of different categories of thought—*vishayarupi,* the perennial subject-object seductions of our thinking processes. The moment this elephant bathes in the cooling waters of the Manas, all tensions and distress cease, and there is the experience of unalloyed joy. Secondly, the Manas is the reason for the end of all sin, sorrow and deprivation. Here, Tulsi dips again into philosophy, by speaking of human pain as a result of *dosha,* or error or perception, where the unreal is given primacy whereas the Real is ignored. The Manas, Tulsi says, corrects this dosha, and in doing so rids the devotee of the pain that is the normal companion of human life.

7. Dialogue Between Shiva and Sati

बड़ अधिकार दच्छ जब पावा।
अति अभिमानु हृदयँ तब आवा॥
नहिं कोउ अस जनमा जग माहीं।
प्रभुता पाइ जाहि मद नाहीं॥[28]

baḍa adhikāra Daccha jaba pāvā ।
ati abhimānu hṛdayan taba āvā ।।
nahiṃ kou asa janamā jaga māhīṃ ।
prabhutā pāi jāhi mada nāhīṃ ।।

On careful consideration, the Creator (Brahma) found Daksha qualified in every way and appointed him as the supreme lord of created beings. When Daksha attained this high position, the pride of his heart knew no bounds. Never was a creature born in this world, whom power did not intoxicate.

जदपि मित्र प्रभु पितु गुर गेहा।
जाइअ बिनु बोलेहुँ न सँदेहा॥
तदपि बिरोध मान जहँ कोई।
तहाँगएँ कल्यानु न होई॥[29]

jadapi mitra prabhu pitu gura gehā ।
jāia binu bolehun na saondehā ।।
tadapi birodha māna jahaṁ koī ।
tahāṁ gaeṁ kalyānu na hoī ।।

It is no doubt true that one should call on one who is friend, master, father or teacher without waiting for a formal invitation; yet where someone nurses a grudge against you, you reap no good by going there.

मातु पिता गुर प्रभु कै बानी।
बिनहिं बिचार करिअ सुभ जानी॥
तुम्ह सब भाँति परम हितकारी।
अग्या सिर पर नाथ तुम्हारी॥[30]

mātu pitā gura prabhu kai bānī ।
binahiṃ bicāra karia subha jānī ।।
tumha saba bhānti param hitakārī ।
agyā sira para nātha tumhārī ।।

The words of one's parents, teacher and master must be unquestionably obeyed as conducive to bliss. You are my supreme benefactor in every way; therefore, my Lord, I bow to Your commands.

These stanzas are important for some very important practical advice given by Tulsi. In fact, throughout the Manas, he introduces in his dialogues between different characters, apparent obiter dicta, that is actually the essence of what is sought to be conveyed. We thus have examples of practical wisdom on a great variety of matters that pertain to life, and our own behaviour within its circle.

Here, Tulsi uses the dialogue between Shiva and Sati, to introduce two remarkable insights. Firstly, he says that no one has yet been born who on obtaining power is able to resist arrogance. Secondly, he emphasises that even to the home of one's parents, a friend, one's guru, or one's master, one should not go uninvited if there is the least possibility that the visit is unwelcome, or the respect due to you is not assured.

These lines have acquired the status of proverbs, especially in north India, and have been included to demonstrate that for Tulsi, the Manas, apart from being above all a devotional text par excellence, was also a vehicle to elaborate on a wide range of issues pertaining to earthly wisdom, and we shall see more examples of this in the pages ahead.

In the mythological context, as narrated in various Puranas, these lines refer to Daksha, the father of Sati or Uma. Daksha was the son of Lord Brahma, and on obtaining power, became unacceptably arrogant. Sati was married to Shiva, but Daksha did not approve of the marriage. In order to insult Shiva and Sati, he organised a big yagna, but did not invite them. Sati insisted on attending the yagna nevertheless, against the advice of Shiva. She believed that as the favourite daughter of Daksha, and since it was her parents' home, she could go even if not invited. Shiva felt that in the absence of an invitation it would be wrong to attend, but Sati was adamant, and Shiva relented, although he did not go himself. At the yagna, Daksha insulted Sati, and also Shiva in absentia. Unable to bear the humiliation any more, Sati committed suicide by jumping into the sacrificial fire. When Shiva learnt of this, his wrath was unbearable. He forthwith sent his army of *bhutanagas* to wreak vengeance on Daksha. The yagna was destroyed, and Daksha himself was decapitated. Shiva was, however, inconsolable at the death of Sati. He took her half-burnt body, and traversed the universe. As he did so, parts of her body fell in different places. These fifty-one places, representing fifty-one Sanskrit alphabets, have now become revered Shakti peethas. Ultimately, Sati was born again as Parvati, and Shiva, recognising her as such, married her.

8. The Spring Form of Kamadeva (the God of Love) and His Immolation by Shiva

सुरन्ह कही निज बिपति सब सुनि मन कीन्ह बिचार ।
संभु बिरोध न कुसल मोहि बिहसि कहेउ अस मार ॥ [31]

suranha kahī nija bipati saba suni mana kīnha bicāra ।
Saṃbhu birodha na kusala mohi bihasi kaheu asa māra ।।

The gods told him all their distress; hearing their tale, the God of Love pondered and spoke thus with a smile: I expect no good results for myself from hostility to Shambhu.

तदपि करब मैं काजु तुम्हारा ।
श्रुति कह परम धरम उपकारा ॥
पर हित लागि तजइ जो देही ।
संतत संत प्रसंसहिं तेही ॥[32]

tadapi karaba maiṃ kāju tumhārā ।
śruti kaha param dharam upakārā ।।
para hita lāgi tajai jo dehī ।
santata santa prasaṃsahiṃ tehī ।।

However, I shall do your work; for the Vedas say benevolence is the highest virtue. The saints ever praise him who lays down his life in the service of others.

अस कहि चलेउ सबहि सिरु नाई ।
सुमन धनुष कर सहित सहाई ।
चलत मार अस हृदयँ बिचारा ।
सिव बिरोध ध्रुव मरनु हमारा ॥[33]

asa kahi caleu sabahi siru nāī ।
sumana dhanuṣa kara sahita sahāī ॥
calata māra asa hṛdayan bicārā ।
Siva birōdha dhruva maranu hamārā ॥

So saying, the God of Love bowed his head to all and departed with his associates, the bow of flowers in hand. While leaving, the God of Love thought within himself that hostility to Shiva would mean sure death to him.

तब आपन प्रभाउ बिस्तारा ।
निज बस कीन्ह सकल संसारा ॥
कोपेउ जबहिं बारिचरकेतू ।
छन महुँ मिटे सकल श्रुति सेतू ॥[34]

taba āpana prabhāu bistārā ।
nija basa kīnha sakala saṃsārā ॥
kōpeu jabahiṁ bāricaraketū ।
chana mahuṁ miṭē sakala śruti setū ॥

He then exhibited his power and brought the whole world under his sway. When the God of Love (who bears a fish for his emblem) betrayed his anger, all the barriers imposed by the Vedas were swept away in a moment.

ब्रह्मचर्ज ब्रत संजम नाना ।
धीरज धरम ग्यान बिग्याना ॥
सदाचार जप जोग बिरागा ।
सभय बिबेक कटकु सबु भागा ॥[35]

brahmacarja brata saṃjama nānā ।
dhīraja dharam gyāna bigyānā ।।
sadācāra japa joga birāgā ।
sabhaya bibēka kaṭaku saba bhāgā ।।

The whole army of viveka (discriminating knowledge), continence, religious vows, self-restraint of many kinds, fortitude, piety, spiritual wisdom and the knowledge of qualified divinity both with form and without form, morality, muttering of prayers, Yoga (contemplative union with god), dispassion and so on, fled in panic.

भागेउ बिबेकु सहाय सहित सो सुभट संजुग महि मुरे ।
सदग्रंथ पर्बत कंदरन्हि महुँ जाई तेहि अवसर दुरे ॥
होनिहार का करतार को रखवार जग खरभरु परा ।
दुइ माथ केहि रतिनाथ जेहि कहुँ कोपि कर धनु सरु धरा ॥[36]

bhāgeu bibeka sahāya sahita so subhaṭa saṃjuga mahi mure ।
sadagrantha parbata kandaranhi mahuṁ jāi tēhi avasara dure ।।
honihāra kā karatāra ko rakhavāra jaga kharabharu parā ।
dui mātha kehi ratinātha jēhi kahṁ kopi kara dhanu saru dharā ।।

Viveka took to flight with his associates; his great warriors turned their back on the field of battle. They all went and hid themselves in mountain-caves in the form of sacred books at that time. There was commotion in the world and everybody said, 'My goodness, what is going to happen? What power will save us? Who is that superhuman being with two heads to conquer whom the lord of Rati, Love, has lifted his bow and arrows in rage?'

जे सजीव जग अचर चर नारि पुरुष अस नाम ।
ते निज निज मरजाद तजि भए सकल बस काम ॥[37]

je sajīva jaga acara cara nāri puruṣa asa nāma ।
tē nija nija marajāda taji bhae sakala basa kāma ।।

Whatever creatures existed in the world, whether animate or inanimate and bearing masculine or feminine appellations transgressed their natural bounds and were completely possessed by lust.

सब के हृदयँ मदन अभिलाषा।
लता निहारि नवहिं तरु साखा॥
नदीं उमगि अंबुधि कहुँ धाई।
संगम करहिं तलाव तलाई॥[38]

saba ke hṛdayan madana abhilāṣā ।
latā nihāri navahiṃ taru sākhā ।।
nadīṃ umagi aṃbudhi kahuṁ dhāī ।
saṅgama karahiṃ talāva talāīn ।।

The minds of all were seized with lust; the boughs of trees bent low at the sight of creepers. Rivers in spate rushed to meet the ocean; lakes and ponds united in love with one another.

जहँ असि दसा जड़न्य कै बरनी।
को कहि सकइ सचेतन करनी॥
पसु पच्छी नभ जल थल चारी।
भए काम बस समय बिसारी॥[39]

jahaṁ asi dasā jaḍanya kai baranī ।
ko kahi sakai sacētana karanī ।।
pasu pacchī nabha jala thalacārī ।
bhaē kāmabasa samaya bisārī ।।

Where such was reported to be the case with the inanimate creation, who can relate the doings of sentient beings? Beasts that walk on land and birds traversing the air, and water, lost all sense of time and became victims of lust.

मदन अंध ब्याकुल सब लोका।
निसि दिनु नहिं अवलोकहिं कोका।

देव दनुज नर किंनर ब्याला।
प्रेत पिसाच भूत बेताला॥
इन्ह कै दसा न कहेउँ बखानी।
सदा काम के चेरे जानी॥
सिद्ध बिरक्त महामुनि जोगी।
तेपि कामबश भए बियोगी॥[40]

madana andha byākula saba lokā ।
nisi dinu nahiṃ avalōkahiṃ kōkā ।।
deva danuja nara Kinnara byālā ।
preta pisāca bhūta betālā ।।
inha kai dasā na kaheuṁ bakhānī ।
sadā kāma ke cere jānī ।।
siddha birakta mahāmuni jogī ।
tepi kāmabasa bhae biyogī ।।

The whole world was blinded with passion and agitated. The Chakravaka birds (ruddy goose) regarded neither day nor night. Gods, demons, human beings, Kinnaras (a class of demigods), serpents, evil spirits, fiends, ghosts and vampires—I have refrained from dwelling on the condition of these, knowing them to be eternal slaves of passion. Even siddhas (spiritual adepts), great sages who had no attraction for the world and yogis (mystics) gave up their Yoga (contemplative union with god) under the influence of lust.

भए कामबस जोगीस तापस पावँरन्हि की को कहै।
देखहिं चराचर नारिमय जे ब्रह्ममय देखत रहे॥
अबला बिलोकहिं पुरुषमय जगु पुरुष सब अबलामयं।
दुइ दंड भरि ब्रह्मांड भीतर कामकृत कौतुक अयं॥[41]

bhae kāmabasa jogīsa tāpasa pāvanranhi kī ko kahai ।
dekhahiṃ carācara nārimaya je Brahmamaya dekhata rahe ।।
abalā bilokahiṃ puruṣamaya jagu puruṣa saba abalāmayaṃ ।
dui daṇḍa bhari brahmāṇḍa bhītara kāmakṛta kautuka ayaṃ ।।

Even great yogis and ascetics were completely possessed by lust, to say nothing of low-minded people? Those who till lately looked upon the animate and inanimate creation as full of Brahma (God) now saw it as full of the fair sex. Women perceived the whole world as full of men; while the latter beheld it as full of women. For nearly an hour this wonderful game of love lasted in the universe.

धरी न काहूँ धीर सब के मन मनसिज हरे।
जे राखे रघुबीर ते उबरे तेहि काल महुँ ॥[42]

dharī na kāhūn dhira sabake mana manasija harē ।
jē rākhē Raghubīra te ubare tehi kāla mahuoṁ ।।

Nobody could remain self-possessed; the hearts of all were stolen by the God of Love. They alone could hold their own against him, to whom the Hero of Raghu's race extended His protection.

उभय घरी अस कौतुक भयऊ।
जौ लगि कामु संभु पहिं गयऊ॥
सिवहि बिलोकि ससंकेउ मारू।
भयउ जथाथिति सबु संसारू ॥[43]

ubhaya gharī asa kautuka bhayaū ।
jau lagi kāmu Saṃbhu pahiṃ gayaū ॥
Sivahi biloki sasaṅkeu mārū ।
bhayau jathāthiti sabu saṃsārū ॥

The wonder lasted for an hour or so till the God of Love reached Shambhu. Cupid trembled at the sight of Shiva; the whole world returned to itself.

भए तुरत सब जीव सुखारे।
जिमि मद उतरि गएँ मतवारे॥
रुद्रहि देखि मदन भय माना।
दुराधरष दुर्गम भगवाना ॥[44]

bhae turata saba jīva sukhārē ।
jimi mada utari gaeṁ matavāre ।।
Rudrahi dekhi madana bhaya mānā ।
durādharaṣa durgama Bhagavānā ।।

All living beings regained their peace of mind at once, even as the intoxicated feel relieved when their spell of drunkenness is over. The God of Love was struck with terror at the sight of Bhagawan Rudra (Shiva), who is so difficult to conquer and so hard to comprehend.

फिरत लाज कछु करि नहिं जाई।
मरनु ठानि मन रचेसि उपाई॥
प्रगटेसि तुरत रुचिर रितुराजा।
कुसुमित नव तरु राजि बिराजा॥[45]

phirata lāja kachu kari nahiṃ jāī ।
maranu ṭhāni mana racesi upāī ।।
pragaṭēsi turata rucira riturājā ।
kusumita nava taru rāji birājā ।।

He felt shy in retreating and was incapable of doing anything; ultimately he resolved upon death and devised a plan. He forthwith manifested the lovely spring, the king of all seasons; rows of young trees laden with flowers appeared so charming.

बन उपबन बापिका तड़ागा।
परम सुभग सब दिसा बिभागा॥
जहँ तहँ जनु उमगत अनुरागा।
देखि मुएहुँ मन मनसिज जागा॥[46]

bana upabana bāpikā taḍaāgā ।
param subhaga saba disā bibhāgā ।।
jahaṁ tahaṁ janu umagata anurāgā ।
dēkhi muehun mana manasija jāgā ।।

Woods and groves, wells and ponds and all the quarters of heaven assumed a most delightful aspect. Everywhere nature overflowed with love as it were; the sight aroused passion even in dead souls.

जागइ मनोभव मुएहुँ मन बन सुभगता न परै कही ।
सीतल सुगंध सुमंद मारुत मदन अनल सखा सही ॥
बिकसे सरन्हि बहु कंज गुंजत पुंज मंजुल मधुकरा ।
कलहंस पिक सुक सरस रव करि गान नाचहिं अपछरा ॥[47]

jāgai manōbhava muehun mana bana subhagatā na parai kahī ।
sītala sugandha sumanda māruta madana anala sakhā sahī ।।
bikasē saranhi bahu kaṃja guṃjata puṃja maṃjula madhukarā ।
kalahaṃsa pika suka sarasa rava kari gāna nācahiṃ apacharā ।।

Passion was aroused even in dead souls and the beauty of the forest beggared description. A cool, gentle and fragrant breeze fanned the fire of passion as a faithful companion. Rows of lotuses blossomed in lakes and swarms of charming bees hummed on them. Swans, cuckoos and parrots uttered their sweet notes; while celestial damsels sang and danced.

सकल कला करि कोटि बिधि हारेउ सेन समेत ।
चली न अचल समाधि सिव कोपेउ हृदयनिकेत ॥[48]

sakala kalā kari koṭi bidhi hāreu sena sameta ।
call na acala samādhi Siva kōpēu hṛdayanikēta ॥

The God of Love with his army of followers exhausted all his numberless stratagems; Shiva in unbroken trance, however, could not be disturbed. This made Cupid angry.

देखि रसाल बिटप बर साखा ।
तेहि पर चढ़ेउ मदनु मन माखा ॥
सुमन चाप निज सर संधाने ।
अति रिस ताकि श्रवन लगि ताने ॥[49]

dekhi rasāla biṭapa bara sākhā ।
tehi para caḍhaēu madanu mana mākhā ।।
sumana cāpa nija sara sandhānē ।
ati risa tāki śravana lagi tānē ।।

Seeing a beautiful bough of a mango tree, the God of Love climbed up to it in a mood of frustration. He joined his five arrows to his bow of flowers and, casting an angry look, drew the string home to his very ears.

छाड़े बिषम बिसिख उर लागे।
छूटि समाधि संभु तब जागे॥
भयउ ईस मन छोभु बिसेषी।
नयन उघारि सकल दिसि देखी॥[50]

chāḍe biṣama bisikha ura lāge ।
chūṭi samādhi Saṃbhu taba jāge ।।
bhayau īsa mana chōbhu biseṣī ।
nayana ughāri sakala disi dekhī ।।

He discharged the five sharp arrows, which smote the breast of Shiva. The trance was now broken and Shambhu awoke. The Lord's mind was much agitated. Opening His eyes He looked all round.

सौरभ पल्लव मदनु बिलोका।
भयउ कोपु कंपेउ त्रैलोका॥
तब सिवँ तीसर नयन उघारा।
चितवत कामु भयउ जरि छाया॥[51]

saurabha pallava Madanu bilokā ।
bhayau kopu kaṃpeu trailōkā ।।
taba Sivan tīsara nayana ughārā ।
citavata Kāmu bhayau jari chārā ।।

When He saw Cupid hiding behind mango leaves, He flew into a rage, which made all the three spheres tremble. Shiva then uncovered His third eye; the moment He looked at the God of Love, the latter was reduced to ashes.

हाहाकार भयउ जग भारी ।
डरपे सुर भए असुर सुखारी ॥
समुझि कामसुख सोचहिं भोगी ।
भय अकंटक साधक जोगी ॥[52]

hāhākāra bhayau jaga bhārī ।
ḍarape sura bhae asura sukhārī ।।
samujhi kāmasukhu socahiṃ bhogī ।
bhaya akanṭaka sādhaka jōgī ।।

A loud wail went up through the universe. The gods were alarmed, while the demons were gratified. The thought of (loss of) sense-delights made the voluptuary sad; while the striving yogis were relieved of a thorn as it were.

जोगी अकंटक भए पति गति सुनत रति मुरुछित भई ।
रोदति बदति बहु भाँति करुना करति संकर पहिं गई ॥
अति प्रेम करि बिनति बिबिध बिधि जोरी कर सम्मुख रही ।
प्रभु आसुतोष कृपाल सिव अबला निरखि बोले सही ॥[53]

Jōgī akaṃṭaka bhae pati gati sunata Rati muruchita bhaī ।
rodati badati bahu bhānti karunā karati Saṅkara pahiṃ gaī ।।
ati prēma kari binatī bibidha bidhi jori kara sanmukha rahī ।
prabhu āsutoṣa kṛpāla Siva abalā nirakhi bole sahī ।।

The yogis were freed from torment; while Rati (wife of the God of Love) fainted as soon as she heard of the fate of her lord. Weeping and wailing and mourning in various ways, she approached Shankara; and making loving entreaties in divergent ways, she stood before the Lord with clasped hands. Seeing the helpless woman, the benevolent Lord Shiva, who is so easy to placate, prophesied as follows:

अब तें रति तव नाथ कर होइहि नाम अनंगु ।
बिनु बपु ब्यापिहि सबहि पुनि सुनु निज मिलन प्रसंगु ॥[54]

aba teṃ Rati tava nātha kara hoihi nāmu Anaṅgu ।
binu bapu byāpihi sabahi puni sunu nija milana prasaṅgu ।।

'Henceforth, O Rati, your husband shall be called by the name of Ananga (bodiless); he shall dominate all even without a body Now hear how you will meet him again.'

जब जदुबंस कृष्न अवतारा ।
होइहि हरन महा महिभारा ।
कृष्ण तनय होइहि पति तोरा ।
बचनु अन्यथा होइ न मोरा ॥[55]

jaba Jadubansa Kṛṣna avatārā ।
hōihi harana mahā mahibhārā ।।
Kṛṣna tanaya hoihi pati torā ।
bacanu anyathā hoi na morā ।।

When Shri Krishna will descend in the line of Yadu to relieve the earth of its heavy burden, your lord will be born again as His son (Pradyumna); this prediction of mine can never be untrue.

These lines on the overwhelming impact of Kamadeva, or the God of Love, shows Tulsi at his poetic best. Kama's journey to Shiva, whom he has been tasked by the gods to awake from his unending and deep meditation, provides Tulsi the template to describe the power of the sensual God. Such is the power of Kama that what to speak of human beings, even the gods could not resist his influence. All animate beings and all inanimate objects, became a prey to his beguiling stimulus. Tulsi goes so far to say that the very Vedas lost their *maryada,* or established code of conduct; laws, dharma, restraint, patience, yoga, detachment, and viveka or discrimination, were all thrown to the winds; even the deeply spiritually evolved, great saints and yogis, were suffused by the emotions invoked by the irrepressible God of Love.

Why did Tulsi accord so much power to Kama? Firstly, Kamadeva is a very important divinity in the Hindu pantheon. The *Vishnu Purana* and the *Bhagawata Purana* say that he is the son of Vishnu and Lakshmi. The *Shiva Purana* considers him to be the creation of the creator of the world, Lord Brahma. The *Atharva Veda* exalts Kama as a supreme god and creator. 'Kama was born the first. Him neither gods, nor fathers, nor men have equalled.' The *Rig Veda* pays similar homage, commending him for worship since he is unequalled by the gods. 'May Kama, having well directed his arrow, which is winged with pain, barbed with longing, and has desire for its shaft, pierce thee in the heart.'

Kama's other names are Manmatha (the churner of the mind or the heart), and Madana (the intoxicating one). His weapons are a sugarcane bow and a floral arrow, and the attributes associated with him are a cuckoo, a parrot, humming bees, the season of spring, and the gentle breeze. Depicted, predictably, as a young and handsome man, he is married to Rati, the sister of Parvati.

The comparison of Kama with Cupid, the God of Love in western classical mythology are evident. Like Kama, Cupid too has an important place in western mythological tradition, and is regarded as the son of the goddess Venus and the war god, Mars. Cupid's Greek counterpart is Eros.

Apart from the great importance of Kama in Hindu mythology, the second reason why Tulsi wrote so eloquently about the power of the erotic god, was because he was evidently fully aware of the acceptance of Kama, or the role of the sensual, in the Hindu world view This is clearly brought out by Vatsyayana in his *Kama Sutra*. This book opens with a learned contemplation on the legitimacy of desire. There are four goals that should animate the intelligent man, argues Vatsyayana. These are dharma, or right conduct, artha, or the acquisition of wealth, and kama, the pursuit of desire. If dharma, artha and kama are pursued in proportion, as the manifestation of a balanced life, then moksha, or salvation, the fourth and final goal, is the natural consequence.

Hence, Tulsi was only reiterating the philosophical validity given to kama, or desire, in the Hindu scheme of things. His poetic exegesis in lauding the power of kama, must be understood in this context. It should, however, not be misinterpreted to mean that Tulsi himself was a votary of sensuality or hedonism. His limited point in these beautifully crafted lines is to explicate that when kama takes a grip of people, they are, more often than not, swept off their feet, and lose their restraint and wisdom.

When Kamadeva shoots his arrow at Shiva, and breaks his meditation, the Mahadeva's third eye opens in anger, and reduces Kama to cinders. It is significant that, such is the importance of Kama, that Parvati herself requests Shiva to revive him. Shiva says that he cannot revive him in the form that he existed, but that, henceforth, he would be bodiless, invisible but potent, Ananga. In this form, he would continue to pervade the cosmos, and animate both human and inanimate life. Kamadeva, thus, was seen as indispensable in Hindu mythology, and Tulsi's tribute to his prowess, is a reiteration of this pragmatic acceptance in the Hindu world view.

9. Dialogue Between Shiva and Parvati About Saguna-Nirguna

सगुणसगुनहि अगुनहि नहिं कछु भेदा।
गावहिं मुनि पुरान बुध बेदा ॥
अगुन अरूप अलख अज जोई।
भगत प्रेम बस सगुन सो होई ॥[56]

sagunahi agunahi nahiṃ kachu bhedā ।
gāvahiṃ muni Purāna budha Bedā ।।
aguna arupa alakha aja joī ।
bhagata prēma basa saguna so hoī ।।

There is no difference between qualified Divinity and the unqualified Brahma: so declare the sages and men of wisdom, the Vedas and the Puranas. That which is attributeless and formless, imperceptible and unborn, becomes qualified under the influence of the devotee's love.

जो गुन रहित सगुन सोइ कैसें।
जलु हिम उपल बिलग नहिं जैसें ॥
जासु नाम भ्रम तिमिर पतंगा।
तेहि किमि कहिअ बिमोह प्रसंगा ॥[57]

jo guna rahita saguna soi kaiseṃ ।
jalu hima upala bilaga nahiṃ jaiseṃ ।।
jāsū nāma bhram timira pataṇgā ।
tehi kimi kahia bimoha prasaṇgā ।।

How can the Absolute become qualified? In the same way as water and the hailstone are non-different in substance. Infatuation is out of the question for Him whose very name is like the sun to the darkness of error.

राम सच्चिदानंद दिनेसा।
नहिं तहँ मोह निसा लवलेसा॥
सहज प्रकासरूप भगवाना।
नहिं तहँ पुनि बिग्यान बिहाना॥[58]

Rāma Saccidānaṃda Dinesā ।
nahiṃ tahaṁ moha nisā lavalesā ।।
sahaja prakāsarupa bhagavānā ।
nahiṃ tahaṁ puni bigyāna bihānā ।।

Shri Ram, who is truth, consciousness and bliss combined, is like the sun; the night of ignorance cannot subsist in Him even to the smallest degree. He is the Lord whose very being is light; there is no dawn of understanding in His case (for the dawn pre-supposes night and night there is none in the sunlight of Shri Ram).

हरष बिषाद ग्यान अग्याना।
जीव धर्म अहमिति अभिमाना॥
राम ब्रह्म ब्यापक जग जाना।
परमानंद परेस पुराना॥[59]

haraṣa biṣāda gyāna agyānā ।
jīva dharma ahamiti abhimānā ।।
Rāma Brahma byāpaka jaga jānā ।
paramānanda paresa purānā ।।

Joy and grief, knowledge and ignorance, egoism and pride—these are the characteristics of a jiva (finite being). Shri Ram is the all-pervading Brahma; He is supreme bliss personified, the highest Lord and the most ancient Being. The whole world knows it.

बिनु पद चलइ सुनइ बिनु काना।
कर बिनु करम करइ बिधि नाना॥
आनन रहित सकल रस भोगी।
बिनु बानी बकता बड़ जोगी॥[60]

binu pada calai sunai binu kānā ।
kara binu karam karai bidhi nānā ॥
ānana rahita sakala rasa bhōgī ।
binu bānī bakatā baḍa jōgī ॥

He walks without feet, hears without ears and performs actions of various kinds even without hands. He enjoys all tastes without a mouth (palate) and is a most clever speaker even though devoid of speech.

तन बिनु परस नयन बिनु देखा।
ग्रहइ बिनु बास असेषा॥
असि सब भाँति अलौकिक करनी।
महिमा जासु जाइ नहिं बरनी॥[61]

tanu binu parasa nayana binu dekhā ।
grahai ghrāna binu bāsa aseṣā ॥
asi saba bhāṁti alaukika karanī ।
mahimā jāsu jāi nahiṃ baranī ॥

He touches without a body (the tactile sense), sees without eyes and catches all odours even without a nose (the olfactory sense). His ways are thus supernatural in every respect and His glory is beyond description.

In these lines, taken from the dialogue between Shiva and Parvati, the central theme—once again is the dialectic between nirguna—the unqualified, attributeless supreme—and saguna, the qualified divine, accessible with all attributes to the devotee. Tulsi uses Shiva to pronounce the verity that there is no difference between nirguna and saguna. This stratagem is significant, because if Shiva makes this claim, then Tulsi gets divine sanction for his own belief. For Shiva to obliterate the difference between nirguna and saguna, is particularly significant. In many traditions, including most influentially the Kashmir Shaivite philosophy, Shiva is the very manifestation of the unchallenged supremacy of the nirguna and omnipotent Brahman. Adi Shankaracharya, the strongest and most convincing proponent of the absolute and uncompromising monism of the nirguna Brahman, was himself partial to Shiva, as the one god who symbolised the nirguna spirit. Here, Tulsi, in order to add legitimacy to his own belief, uses Shiva himself to say that nirguna and saguna are essentially the same.

Tulsi uses a very important argument to support his viewpoint. He says that the nirguna Brahman becomes the personal god to fulfill the love of devotees. In other words, unlike other philosophers, cited earlier, such as Ramanuja, he does not resort to metaphysical arguments to argue that the supreme Brahman can have qualifications that sanction a personal god. His argument is direct in its simplicity. It is in response to the love of bhakts, that the nirguna Brahman has no option but to adopt attributes with which devotees can identify. This devotional love for the Absolute, which is the key aspect of the bhakti school, and which fully animates Tulsi himself, is what, in one instance, conflates the nirguna and the saguna. Shri Ram is both the inexpressible Brahman, and the highly expressible personal God, always available for the succour of his devotees. He is both the all-pervasive Brahman, and the devotees' Prabhu, or personal saviour.

Having made this pivotal point, Tulsi typically, bends backwards not to devalue the validity of the nirguna concept, and adds some beautifully crafted chaupais in praise of Brahman.

10. Incarnation of Shri Ram

जोग लगन ग्रह बार तिथि सकल भए अनुकूल।
चर अरु अचर हर्षजुत राम जनम सुखमूल ॥[62]

joga lagana graha bāra tithi sakala bhae anukūla ।
cara aru acara harṣajuta rāma janama sukhamūla ।।

The position of the sun and the moon, the zodiacal sign into which the sun had entered, the position of the seven other planets, the day of the week as well as the day of the lunar month, yoga, lagna, planet, day, lunar day *(tithi)* all these turned out to be propitious. And full of delight was all creation, animate and inanimate; for the birth of Shri Ram is the source of joy.

नौमी तिथि मधु मास पुनीता।
सुकल पच्छ अभिजित हरिप्रीता॥
मध्यदिवस अति सीत न घामा।
पावन काल लोक बिश्रामा॥[63]

naumī tithi madhu māsa punītā ।
sukala paccha Abhijita Haripritā ।।
madhyadivasa ati sīta na ghāmā ।
pāvana kāla loka biśrāmā ।।

It was the ninth day of the bright half of the sacred month of Chaitra; the moon had entered the asterism named Abhijit, which is so dear to Shri Hari. The sun was at its meridian; the day was neither cold nor hot. It was a holy time which gave rest to the whole world.

सीतल मंद सुरभि बह बाऊ ।
हरषित सुर संतन मन चाऊ ॥
बन कुसुमित गिरिगन मनिआरा ।
स्रवहिं सकल सरिताऽमृतधारा ॥[64]

sītala maṃda surabhi baha bāū ।
harașita sura saṃtana mana cāū ॥
bana kusumita girigana maniārā ।
stravahiṃ sakala saritā'mṛtadhārā ॥

A cool, soft and fragrant breeze was blowing. The gods were feeling exhilarated and the saints were bubbling with enthusiasm. The woods were full of blossoms, the mountains were resplendent with gems and every river flowed a stream of nectar.

सो अवसर बिरंचि जब जाना ।
चले सकल सुर साजि बिमाना ॥
गगन बिमल संकुल सुर जूथा ।
गावहिं गुन गंधर्ब बरूथा ॥
बरषहिं सुमन सुअंजुलि साजी ।
गहगहि गगन दुंदुभी बाजी ॥
अस्तुति करहिं नाग मुनि देवा ।
बहुबिधि लावहिं निज निज सेवा ॥[65]

so avasara biraṃci jaba jānā ।
cale sakala sura sāji bimānā ॥
gagana bimala samkula sura jūthā ।
gāvahiṃ guna gaṃdharba barūthā ॥
barașahiṃ sumana suaṃjali sājī ।
gahagahi gagana duṃdubhī bājī ॥
astuti karahiṃ nāga muni devā ।
bahubidhi lāvahiṃ nija nija sevā ॥

When Brahma perceived that the time of Shri Ram's birth had approached, all the gods came out with their aerial cars duly equipped. The bright heaven was crowded with their hosts and troops of Gandharvas chanted praises and rained down flowers placing them in their beautiful palms. The sky resounded with the beat of kettledrums. Nagas, sages and gods offered praises and tendered their services in manifold ways.

सुर समूह बिनती करि पहुँचे निज निज धाम ।
जगनिवास प्रभु प्रगटे अखिल लोक बिश्राम ।। 66

sura samūha binatī kari pahumce nija nija dhāma ।
jaganivāsa prabhu pragaṭe akhila loka biśrāma ।।

Having offered their praises, the gods returned to their several abodes, when the Lord, and abode of the universe and the solace of all creation, manifested Himself.

भए प्रगट कृपाला दीनदयाला कौसल्या हितकारी ।
हरषित महतारी मुनि मन हारी अद्भुत रूप बिचारी ।।
लोचन अभिरामा तनु घनस्यामा निज आयुध भुज चारी ।
भूषन बनमाला नयन बिसाला सोभासिंधु खरारी ।।[67]

bhaye pragaṭa kṛpālā dīnadayālā Kausalyā hitakārī ।
haraṣita mahatārī muni mana hārī adbhuta rūpa bicārī ।।
locana abhirāmā tanu ghanasyāmā nija āyudha bhuja cārī ।
bhūṣana vanamālā nayana bisālā sobhāsindhu Kharārī ।।

The gracious Lord, who is compassionate to the lowly and the benefactor of Kaushalya appeared. The thought of His marvellous form, which stole the heart of sages, filled the mother with joy. His body was dark as a cloud, the delight of all eyes; in His four arms He bore His characteristic emblems (a conch-shell, a discus, a club and a lotus). Adorned with jewels and a garland of sylvan flowers and endowed with large eyes, the slayer of the demon Khara was an ocean of beauty.

कह दुइ कर जोरी अस्तुति तोरी केहि बिधि करौं अनंता ।
माया गुन ग्यानातीत अमाना बेद पुरान भनंता ।।

करुना सुख सागर सब गुन अगर जेहि गावहिं श्रुति संता।
सो मम हित लागी जन अनुरागी भयउ प्रगट श्रीकंता ॥[68]

kaha dui kara jorī astuti torī kehi bidhi karauṃ anaṃtā ।
māyā guana gyānātīta amānā Beda Purāna bhanaṃtā ॥
karunā sukha sāgara saba guna āgara jehi gāvahiṃ śruti saṃtā ।
so mama hita lāgī jana anurāgī bhayau prakaṭa śrīkaṃtā ॥

Joining both her palms, the mother said, 'O infinite Lord, how can I praise You! The Vedas as well as the Puranas declare You as transcending Maya, Guna (made of prakati) and beyond all measure. He who is sung by the Vedas and holy men as an ocean of mercy and bliss and the repository of all virtues, the same Lord of Lakshmi, the lover of His devotees, has revealed Himself for my good.'

ब्रह्मांड निकाया निर्मित माया रोम रोम प्रति बेद कहै।
मम उर सो बसी यह उपहासी सुनत धीर मति थिर न रहै ॥
उपजा जब ग्याना प्रभु मुसुकाना चरित बहुत बिधि कीन्ह चहै।
कहि कथा सुहाई मातु बुझाई जेहि प्रकार सुत प्रेम लहै ॥[69]

brahmāṃḍa nikāyā nirmita māyā roma roma prati Beda kahai ।
mama ura so bāsī yaha upahāsī sunata dhīra mati thira na rahai ॥
upajā jaba gyānā prabhu musukānā carita bahuta bidhi kīnha cahai ।
kahi kathā suhāī mātu bujhāī jehi prakāra suta prema lahai ॥

The Vedas proclaim that every pore of Your body contains multitudes of universes brought forth by Maya. 'That such a Lord stayed in my womb, this amusing story staggers the mind of even men of wisdom.' When the revelation came upon the mother, the Lord smiled; He would perform many a sportive act. Therefore, He exhorted her by telling her the charming account of her previous birth so that she might love Him as her own child.

माता पुनि बोली सो मति डोली तजहु तात यह रूपा।
कीजे सिसुलीला अति प्रियसीला यह सुख परम अनूपा ॥

सुनि बचन सुजाना रोदन ठाना होइ बालक सुरभूपा।
यह चरित जे गावहिं हरिपद पावहिं ते न परहिं भवकूपा॥[70]

mātā puni bolī so mati ḍolī tajahu tāta yaha rūpā ।
kīje sisulīlā ati priyasīlā yaha sukha param anūpā ॥
suni bacana sujānā rodana ṭhānā hoi bālaka surabhūpā ।
yaha carita je gāvahi Haripada pāvahi te na parahiṃ bhavakūpā ॥

The mother's mind was changed; she spoke again: 'Give up this superhuman form and indulge in childish sports, which are so dear to a mother's heart; the joy that comes from such sports is unequalled in everyway.' Hearing these words the all-wise Lord of immortals became an infant and began to cry. Those who sing this (says Tulsidas) attain to the abode of Shri Hari and never fall into the well of mundane existence.

बिप्र धेनु सुर संत हित लीन्ह मनुज अवतार।
निज इच्छा निर्मित तनु माया गुन गो पार॥[71]

bipra dhenu sura saṃta hita līnha manuja avatāra ।
nija icchā nirmita tanu māyā guna go pāra ॥

For the sake of Brahmins, cows, gods and saints, the Lord, who transcends Maya and is beyond the three modes of prakati (sattva, rajas and tamas) as well as beyond the reach of the senses, took birth as a man assuming a form which is a product of His own will.

These famous stanzas on the birth of Ram gives Tulsi, the dexterous poet, an opportunity to weave in several complex thoughts and emotions, apart from merely describing the advent of Ram in this mortal world. The poet begins by setting the mood, elaborating on how the time of the birth was the most auspicious, and had the blessings of all the gods. The atmosphere was one of joy and celebration, and the entire cosmos was vibrating with the imminence of the emergence of the Lord. When the Lord is born, the first two qualities that Tulsi ascribes to him is one of mercy—*kripala*—and that of the saviour of the weak and vulnerable—*deen dayala.* These qualities, depicting Ram as the righteous crusader for those dependent on his benediction is a recurring theme in Tulsi's veneration of Ram.

Tulsi then plays upon Kaushalya's incredulity at the fact that she had given birth to the Lord of the universe. When Ram is born, he appears in the full regalia of his divine splendour, with his four arms bearing arms, and his body adorned with all the symbols of divinity. Tulsi brings out Kaushalya's sense of amazement at how she—an ordinary lady—could be the mother of one who is the master and ruler of the world. She greets him with reverence, recalling that according to the Vedas, Ram was beyond the limitations of any qualifying attributes, knowledge, and the seductions of Maya. In apparent contradiction, she also exclaims that this supremely unqualified Being, was simultaneously the home of all virtuous qualities.

Kaushalya says that for the Lord—in whose every pore of the body reside several universe—to be born to her is a matter of disbelief, even laughter. In a gesture of humaneness, Ram smiles to see her puzzlement, and sets her at ease by narrating many stories of the past explicating how he has come to be born and how she is his mother. Significantly, he does so, so Tulsi says, to invoke in her the love of a mother towards her child, *vatsalya.*

As the emotion of vatsalya rises in her, Kaushalya asks Ram to shed his divine form, and adopt that of a normal child. These are the most moving lines of this section: a mother asking the Lord to be her child, rather than the Supreme Being. Her request is for Ram to play the role of a child, leela, for the joys of a mother are unparalleled. On hearing her request, the Lord complies, and all of a sudden the divine form disappears and he becomes a child crying in the arms of his mother. Tulsi rightly says that those who internalise this sequence of events—a mother's plea, and Ram, in response to her request, giving up his divine form to become a newborn baby—attain the eternal blessings of the Lord.

Tulsi ends by making the philosophically important point that Ram took the avatar of a mortal out of his own free will, which is an aspect of his unfettered powers, since by definition he is not bound by the conventional limitations of mortality—the senses, the three gunas, rajas, tamas and sattva, or the shackles of Maya.

11. A Visit to Janak's Garden by Shri Ram-Lakshman When Shri Ram-Sita Catch Sight of Each Other

भूप बागु बर देखेउ जाई।
जहँ बसंत रितु रही लोभाई॥
लागे बिटप मनोहर नाना।
बरन बरन बर बेलि बिताना॥[72]

bhūpa bāgu bara dekheu jāī ।
jahaṁ basaṃta ritu rahī lobhāī ।।
lāge biṭapa manohara nānā ।
barana barana bara beli bitānā ।।

When the time came, the two brothers took leave of the preceptor and went out to gather flowers. Having gone out, they saw the lovely royal garden, enamoured of whose beauty the vernal season had taken its permanent abode there. It was planted with charming trees of various kinds and overhung with beautiful creepers of different colours.

नव पल्लव फल सुमन सुहाए।
निज संपति सुर रूख लजाए॥
चातक कोकिल कीर चकोरा।
कूजत बिहग नटत कल मोरा॥[73]

nava pallava phala sumāna suhāe ।
nija saṃpati sura rūkha lajāe ।।

cātaka kokila kīra cakorā ।
kūjata bihaga naṭata kala morā ।।

Rich in fresh leaf, fruit and flower they put to shame even Kalpavriksha trees by their affluence. The feathered choir of the Chatakas, cuckoos, parrots and Chakoras warbled and peacocks beautifully danced.

मध्य बाग सरु सोह सुहावा।
मनि सोपान बिचित्र बनावा॥
बिमल सलिलु सरसिज बहुरंगा।
जलखग कूजत गुंजत भृंगा॥[74]

madhya bāga saru soha suhāvā ।
mani sopāna bicitra banāvā ।।
bimala salilu sarasija bahuraṃgā ।
jalakhaga kūjata guṃjata bhṛṃgā ।।

In the centre of the garden, a lovely lake shone bright with flights of steps made of many-coloured gems. Its limpid water contained lotuses of various colours and was vocal with the cooing of aquatic birds and the humming of bees.

बागु तड़ागु बिलोकि प्रभु हरषे बंधु समेत।
परम रम्य आरामु यहु जो रामहि सुख देत॥[75]

bāgu taḍaāgu biloki prabhu haraṣe baṃdhu sameta ।
param ramya ārāmu yahu jo Rāmahi sukha deta ।।

Both the Lord and His brother were delighted to behold the garden with its lake. Most lovely must have been that garden which delighted even Shri Ram (lit., the delighter of all)!

चहुँ दिसि चितइ पूँछि मालीगन।
लगे लेन दल फूल मुदित मन॥

तेहि अवसर सीता तहँ आई।
गिरिजा पूजन जननि पठाई॥[76]

cahuṁ disi citai pūṁchi māligana ।
lage lena dala phūla mudita mana ।।
tehi avasara Sītā tahaṁ āī ।
Girijā pūjana janani paṭhāī ।।

After looking all about, and with the consent of the gardeners, the two brothers began in high glee to gather leaves and flowers. On that very occasion Sita too arrived there, having been sent by Her mother to worship Girija.

संग सखीं सब सुभग सयानीं।
गावहिं गीत मनोहर बानीं॥
सर समीप गिरिजा गृह सोहा।
बरनि न जाइ देखि मनु मोहा॥[77]

saṃga sakhīṃ saba subhaga sayānī ।
gāvahiṃ gīta manohara bānīṃ ।।
sara samīpa Girijā gṛha sohā ।
barani na jāi dekhi manu mohā ।।

She was accompanied by Her girl-companions, who were all lovely and intelligent. They sang melodies in an enchanting voice. Close to the lake stood a temple, sacred to Girija, which was beautiful beyond description, and captivated the minds of those who looked at it.

मज्जनु करि सर सखिन्ह समेता।
गई मुदित मन गौरि निकेता॥
पूजा कीन्हि अधिक अनुरागा।
निज अनुरूप सुभग बरु मागा॥[78]

majjanu kari sara sakhinha sametā ।
gaī mudita mana Gauri niketā ।।

pūjā kinhi adhika anurāgā ।
nija anurūpa subhaga baru māgā ।।

Having taken a dip into the lake with Her companions, Sita went with a glad heart to Girija's temple. She offered worship with great devotion and begged of the Goddess a handsome match worthy of Her.

एक सखी सिय संगु बिहाई।
गई रही देखन फुलवाई॥
तेहिं दोउ बंधु बिलोके जाई।
प्रेम बिबस सीता पहिं आई॥[79]

eka sakhī siya saṃgu bihāī ।
gaī rahī dekhana phulavāī ।।
tehiṁ dou baṃdhu biloke jāī ।
prema bibasa Sītā pahiṃ āī ।।

One of Her companions had strayed away from Her in order to have a look at the garden. She chanced to behold the two brothers and returned to Sita overwhelmed with love.

तासु दसा देखी सखिन्ह पुलक गात जलु नैन।
कहु कारनु निज हरष कर पूछहिं सब मृदु बैन॥[80]

tāsu dasā dekhi sakhinha pulaka gāta jalu naina ।
kahu kāranu nija haraṣa kara pūchahi saba mṛdu baina ।।

When her companions saw her condition, her body thrilling all over and her eyes full of tears, they all asked her in gentle tones, Tell us what gladdens your heart.'

देखन बागु कुअँर दुइ आए।
बय किसोर सब भाँति सुहाए॥
स्याम गौर किमि कहौं बखानी।
गिरा अनयन नयन बिनु बानी॥[81]

dekhana bāgu kuaṁra dui āe ।
baya kisora saba bhāṁti suhāe ।।
syāma gaura kimi kahauṃ bakhānī ।
girā anayana nayana binu bānī ।।

Two princes have come to see the garden, both of tender age and charming in every way, one dark of hue and the other fair; how shall I describe them? For speech is sightless, while the eyes are mute.'

सुनि हरषीं सब सखीं सयानी ।
सिय हियँ अति उतकंठा जानी ॥
एक कहइ नृपसुत तेइ आली ।
सुने जे मुनि सँग आए काली ॥[82]

suni haraṣīṁ saba sakhīṃ sayānī ।
Siya hiyaṁ ati utakaṃthā jānī ।।
eka kahai nṛpasuta tei ālī ।
sune je muni saṁga āe kālī ।।

All the clever maidens were delighted to hear this. Perceiving the intense longing in Sita's bosom, one of them said, They must be the two princes, my dear, who, I was told, arrived yesterday with the sage (Vishwamitra).'

सुमिरि सीय नारद बचन उपजी प्रीति पुनीत ।
चकित बिलोकति सकल दिसि जनु सिसु मृगी सभीत ॥[83]

sumiri Sīya Nārada bacana upajī prīti punīta ।।
cakita bilokati sakala disi janu sisu mṛgī sabhīta ।।

Recollecting Narada's words, She was filled with innocent love; and with anxious eyes She gazed all around like a startled fawn.

कंकन किंकिनि नूपुर धुनि सुनि ।
कहत लखन सन रामु हृदयँ सुनि ॥

मानहुँ मदन दुंदुभी दीन्ही ।
मनसा बिस्व बिजय कहँ कीन्ही ॥[84]

kaṃkana kiṃkini nūpura dhuni suni ।
kahata lakhana sana rāmu hṛdayaṃ guni ।।
mānahuṃ madana duṃdubhī dīnhī ।।
manasā bisva bijaya kahaṃ kīnhī ।।

Hearing the tinkling of bangles, the small bells tied round the waist and the anklets, Shri Ram thought within Himself and then said to Lakshman, 'It seems as if Cupid has sounded his kettledrum with the intent to conquer the universe.'

अस कहि फिरि चितए तेहि ओरा ।
सिय मुख ससि फए नयन चकोरा ॥
भए बिलोचन चारु अचंचल ।
मनहुँ सकुचि निमि तजे दिगंचल ॥[85]

asa kahi phiri citae tehi orā ।
Siya mukha sasi bhae nayana cakorā ।।
bhae bilocana cāru acaṃcala ।
manahuṁ sakuci nimi taje digaṃcala ।।

So saying, He looked once again in the same direction (whence the sound came); and lo! His eyes feasted themselves on Sita's countenance even as the Chakora bird gazes on the moon. His charming eyes became motionless, as if Nimi (the god of winking) had left the eyelids out of shyness.

देखि सीय सोभा सुख पावा ।
हृदयँ सराहत बचनु न आवा ॥
जनु बिरंचि सब निज निपुनाई ।
बिरचि बिस्व कहँ प्रगटि देखाई ॥[86]

dekhi Sīya sobhā sukhu pāvā ।
hṛdayaṁ sarāhata bacanu na āvā ।।
janu biraṃci saba nija nipunāī ।
biraci bisva kahaṁ pragaṭi dekhāī ।।

Shri Ram was filled with rapture to behold Sita's beauty; He admired it in His heart, but utterance failed Him. He felt as if the Creator had put his whole creative skill in visible form and demonstrated it to the world at large.

सुंदरता कहुँ सुंदर करई।
छबिगृहँ दीपसिखा जनु बरई॥
सब उपमा कबि रहे जुठारी।
केहिं पटतरौं बिदेहकुमारी॥[87]

suṃdaratā kahuṁ suṃdara karaī ।
chabigṛhaṁ dīpasikhā janu baraī ।।
saba upamā kabi rahe juṭhārī ।
kehiṃ paṭataraumi Bidehakumārī ।।

'She lends charm to charm itself,' He said to Himself, 'and looks as if a flame of light is burning in a house of beauty. The similes already employed by the poets are all stale and hackneyed; to whom shall I liken the daughter of Videha?'

सिय शोभा हियँ बरनि प्रभु आपनि दसा बिचारि।
बोले सुचि मन अनुज सन बचन समय अनुहार॥[88]

Siya śobhā hiyaṁ barani prabhu āpani dasā bicāri ।
bole suci mana anuja sana bacana samaya anuhāri ।।

Thus describing to Himself Sita's loveliness and reflecting on His own condition the Lord innocently spoke to His younger brother in terms appropriate to the occasion:-

तात जनकतनया यह सोई।
धनुषजग्य जेहि कारन होई॥
पूजन गौरि सखीं लै आई।
करत प्रकासु फिरइ फुलवाई॥[89]

tāta Janakatanayā yaha soī ।
dhanuṣajagya jehi kārana hoī ।।
pūjana Gauri sakhīṃ lai āīṁ ।
karata prakāsu phirai phulavāī ।।

'Brother, she is no other than the daughter of King Janak, for whom the bow sacrifice is being arranged. She has been escorted by her girh-companions to worship Goddess Gauri and is moving about in the garden diffusing light all about her.'

जासु बिलोकि अलौकिक सोभा।
सहज पुनीत मोर मनु छोभा॥
सो सबु कारन जान बिधाता।
फरकहिं सुभद अंग सुनु भ्राता॥[90]

jāsu biloki alokika sobhā ।
sahaja punīta mora manu chobhā ।।
so sabu kārana jāna bidhātā ।
pharakahiṃ subhada aṃga sunu bhrātā ।।

'My heart which is naturally pure, is agitated by the sight of Her transcendent beauty. The reason of all this is known to god alone; but I tell you, brother, my right limbs are throbbing, which is an index of coming good fortune.'

रघुबंसिन्ह कर सहज सुभाऊ।
मनु कुपंथ पगु धरइ न काऊ॥
मोहि अतिसय प्रतीति मन केरी।
जेहिं सपनेहुँ परनारि न हेरी॥[91]

Raghubaṃsinha kara sahaja subhāū ।
manu kupaṃtha pagu dharai na kāū ।।
mohi atisaya pratīti mana kerī ।
jehiṃ sapanehuṁ paranāri na herī ।।

It is a natural trait with the race of Raghu that they never set their heart on evil courses. As for myself, I am fully confident of my mind, which has never sought another's wife even in a dream.

जिन्ह कै लहहिं न रिपु रन पीठी।
नहिं पावहिं परतिय मनु डीठी ॥
मंगन लहहिं न जिन्ह कै नाहीं ।
ते नरबर थोरे जग माही ॥[92]

jinha kai lahahiṃ na ripu rana pīṭhī ।
nahiṃ pāvahiṃ paratiya manu ḍīṭhī ।।
maṃgana lahahi na jinha kai nāhīṃ ।
te narabara thore jaga māhīṃ ।।

Rare in this world are those noble men who never turn their back on the foe in battle nor give their heart to or cast an amorous glance on another's wife, and from whom no beggar meets with a rebuff.

करत बतकही अनुज सन मन सिय रूप लोभान।
मुख सरोज मकरंद छबि करइ मधुप इव पान ॥[93]

karata batakahī anuja sana mana Siya rūpa lobhāna ।
mukha saroja makaraṃda chabi karai madhupa iva pāna ।।

While Shri Ram was talking to His younger brother in this strain, His mind, which was enamoured of Sita's beauty, was all the time drinking in the loveliness of Her countenance, like a bee sucking the nectar from a lotus.

चितवति चकित चहूँ दिसि सीता।
कहँ गए नृप किसोर मनु चिंता॥
जहँ बिलोक मृग सावक नैनी।
जनु तहँ बरिस कमल सित श्रेनी॥[94]

citavahi cakita cahūṁ disi Sītā ।
kahaṁ gae nṛpakisora manu ciṃtā ।।
jahaṁ biloka mṛga sāvaka nainī ।
janu tahaṁ barisa kamala Sita śrenī ।।

Sita looked surprisingly all round; Her mind was at a loss as to where the princes had gone. Wherever the fawn-eyed princess cast Her glance, a continuous stream of white lotuses seemed to rain there.

लताभवन तें प्रगट भे तेहि अवसर दोउ भाइ।
तकिसे जनु जुग बिमल बिधु जलद पटल बिलगाई॥[95]

latābhavana teṃ pragaṭa bhe tehi avasara dou bhāi ।
takise janu juga bimala bidhu jalada paṭala bilagāi ।।

At that very moment the two brothers emerged from a bower. It looked as if a pair of spotless moons had shone forth tearing the veil of a cloud.

सोभा सीवँ सुभग दोउ बीरा।
नील पीत जलजाभ सरीरा॥
मोरपंख सिर सोहत नीके।
गुच्छ बीच बिच कुसुम कली के॥[96]

sobhā sīvaṁ subhaga dou bīrā ।
nīla pīta jalajābha sarīrā ।।
morapaṃkha sira sohata nīke ।
guccha bīca bica kusuma kalī ke ।।

The two gallant heroes were the very perfection of beauty; their bodies resembled in hue a blue and a yellow lotus respectively. Charming peacock feathers adorned their head, which had bunches of flower-buds stuck here and there.

भाल तिलक श्रमबिंदु सुहाए।
श्रवन सुभग भूषन छबि छाए॥
विकट भृकुटि कच घूघरवारे।
नव सरोज लोचन रतनारे॥
चारु चिबुक नासिका कपोला।
हास बिलास लेत मनु मोला॥
मुखछबि कहि न जाइ मोहि पाहीं।
जो बिलोकि बहु काम लजाहीं॥[97]

bhāla tilaka śrambiṃdu suhāe ।
śravana subhaga bhūṣana chabi chāe ।।
bikaṭa bhṛkuṭi kaca ghūgharavāre ।
nava saroja locana ratanāre ।।
cāru cibuka nāsikā kapolā ।
hāsa bilāsa leta manu molā ।।
mukhachabi kahi na jāi mohi pāhīṃ ।
jo biloki bahu kāma lajāhīṃ ।।

A sectarian mark and beads of perspiration glistened on their brow; while graceful pendants shed their lustre on their ears. With arched eyebrows and curly locks, eyes red as a lotus-bud and a lovely chin, nose and cheeks their gracious smile was soul-enthralling. The beauty of their countenance was more than I can describe; it would put to shame a myriad Cupids.

उर मनि माल कंबु कल गीवा।
काम कलभ कर भुज बलसींवा॥
सुमन समेत बाम कर दोना।
सावँर कुअँर सखी सुठि लोना॥ [98]

ura mani māla kaṃbu kala gīvā ।
kāma kalabha kara bhuja balasīṃvā ।।

sumana sameta bāma kara donā ।
sāvaṁra kuaṁra sakhī suṭhi lonā ।।

They had a string of jewels on their breast; their lovely neck resembled a conch-shell in its spiral shape; while their mighty arms vied with the trunk of a young elephant, who was the very incarnation of Cupid. With a cup of leaves full of flowers in His left hand, the dark-hued prince, my dear, is most charming.

जानि कठिन सिवचाप बिसूरति ।
चली राखि उर स्यामल मूरति ॥
प्रभु जब जात जानकी जानी ।
सुख सनेह सोभा गुन खानी ॥[99]

jāni kaṭhina sivacāpa bisūrati ।
calī rākhi ura syāmala mūrati ।।
prabhu jaba jāta jānakī jānī ।
sukha saneha sobhā guna khānī ।।

Drooping at the thought of the unyielding bow of Shiva, She proceeded with the image of the swarthy form in Her heart.

परम प्रेममय मृदु मसि कीन्ही ।
चारु चित्त भीतीं लिखि लीन्ही ॥
गई भवानी भवन बहोरी ।
बंदि चरन बोली कर जोरी ॥[100]

param premamaya mṛdu masi kīnhī ।
cāru cita bhītīṃ likhi līnhī ।।
gaī Bhavānī bhavana bahorī ।
baṃdi carana bolī kara jorī ।।

When the Lord perceived that Janak's daughter, a fountain of bliss, affection, grace and goodness, was going, He sketched Her on the sheet of His heart with the soft ink of supreme love. Sita then sought Bhavani's temple and, adoring Her feet, prayed to Her with joined palms:

जय जय गिरिबरराज किसोरी ।
जय महेस मुख चंद चकोरी ॥
जय गजबदन षडानन माता ।
जगत जननि दामिनि दुति गातो ॥[101]

jaya jaya Giribararāja kisorī ।
jaya Mahesa mukha caṃda cakorī ।।
jaya Gaja badana ṣaḍaānana mātā ।
jagata janani dāmini duti gātā ।।

'Glory, all glory to You, O Daughter of the mountain-king! Glory to You, who gaze on the countenance of the great Lord Shiva as a Chakora bird on the moon. Glory to You, O Mother of the elephant-headed Ganesh and the six-faced Kartikeya and mother of the universe with limbs shining as lightning.'

नहिं तव आदि मध्य अवसाना।
अमित प्रभाउ बेदु नहिं जाना ॥
भव भव बिभव पराभव कारिनि ।
बिस्व बिमोहनि स्वबस बिहारिनि ॥[102]

nahiṃ tava ādi madhya avasānā ।
amita prabhāu Bedu nahiṃ jānā ।।
bhava bhava bibhava parābhava kārini ।
bisva bimohani svabasa bihārini ।।

You have no beginning, middle or end; Your infinite glory is a mystery even to the Vedas. You are responsible for the birth, maintenance and destruction of the universe; You enchant the whole universe and carry on Your sports independently of others.

The first meeting of Ram and Sita is described most evocatively by Tulsi. In conformity with Indian aesthetics, the setting for the meeting has to be beautiful. Vatsyayana in his *Kama Sutra* writes at length on the importance of the aesthetic setting for a lover's tryst, and although this is not the context of the first meeting between Ram and Sita, the emotions of love and longing are very much there. The meeting thus takes place in Sita's father, Raja Janak's beautiful garden, and Tulsi writes several chaupais to describe its features, the flowers, the season of spring, the enticing waters of the pool, the seductive chatter of birds, and the fruit-laden trees. In Tulsi's description, the script of romance is very much there. Ram and Lakshman are in the garden, as is Sita with her friends. That first meeting, where Ram and Sita get a glimpse of each other is waiting to happen, and the dramatic tension is built up, carrying the reader along.

Ram and Sita see each other, but do not exchange a single word. In this combination of love and attraction, and shyness and restraint, lies the beauty of this *prasang* (context). Their first meeting has the passion of longing; indeed, Tulsi writes that the situation was so suffused with love that Ram tells Lakshman that it seems that the God of Love, Kama, had himself blown his trumpet to proclaim his resolve to conquer the world. But, this painfully burgeoning love was untainted by the slightest notion of lust or any base emotion, the aim being clearly to bring out the sheer enticement of pure love. Ram becomes aware of Sita's presence by just the sound of anklets, bracelets and the adornment worn around the waist. Tulsi's description has itself a poetic phonetic quality: *Kankan, kinkini, nupur dhuni suni.* Then follows a description of Sita's beauty, and Ram's handsomeness. Tulsi says that Sita's beauty is such that no comparison can be given to describe it. In a remarkable line, he says that her beauty adds lustre even to beauty itself: *sundarta kahun sundar karayin.* To illustrate his point, he gives the example of a beautiful home that suddenly becomes even more beautiful by the glow that illumines it when a lamp is lit within it: *chhabigraha deepshika janu barayin.*

Ram's attraction is irresistible. Tulsi uses a charming analogy to describe it. One of Sita's friends, who is completely taken up by Ram's persona, says she cannot narrate its impact, because speech cannot see, nor can the eyes speak: *gira anayan nayan binu bani*. Of course, Sita too comes fully under the spell of Ram. For Tulsi to acknowledge that a woman could so completely be swept off her feet by the physical attributes of a man, would add an unwarranted physicality to this encounter, but there is a definite innocence woven into Tulsi's narrative. For both Sita and Ram it is their first brush with love. Tulsi takes pains to clarify that Ram would not even dream of looking at other women, *parayi stri*. Thus, their mutual love has an inherent innocence that combines nobility, respect and dignity.

Such is Sita's love for Ram that she irrationally worries about whether he would be able to break the great bow to win her hand. Driven by this concern, she returns to pray again to Girija, in the temple within the garden dedicated to the goddess. Girija is another name for Parvati, Shiva's consort. The lines of her prayer make for two stanzas of the most compelling poetry, powerful, passionate and resounding with the grace of rhyme and metre. It is significant that Sita prays to Girija, and not to Lakshmi, Vishnu's consort. It is precisely by these stratagems that Tulsi overarches the schism between the Shaivite and Vaishnavite schools, and projects a harmony where Hinduism is seen as a holistic unity, undivided by the acrimonies that often became very virulent in southern India.

12. Description of Sita's Unique Beauty by Shri Ram

प्राची दिसि ससि उयउ सुहावा।
सिय मुख सरिस देखि सुख पावा ॥
बहुरि बिचारु कीन्ह मन माहीं।
सीय बदन सम हिमकर नाहीं ॥[103]

prācī disi sasi uyau suhāvā ।
Siya mukha sarisa dekhi sukhu pāvā ।।
bahuri bicāru kīnha mana māhīṃ ।
Sīya badana sama himakara nāhīṃ ।।

In the meantime, the charming moon rose in the eastern horizon; perceiving that her orb resembled Sita's face, Shri Ram felt happy. The Lord then reasoned within Himself. The queen of night bears no resemblance to Sita.

जनमु सिंधु पुनि बंधु बिषु दिन मलीन सकलंक।
सिय मुख समता पाव किमि चंदु बापुरो रंक ॥[104]

janamu siṃdhu puni baṃdhu biṣu dina malīna sakalaṃka ।
Siya mukha samatā pāva kimi caṃdu bāpuro raṃka ।।

'Born of the ocean (with its salt water), with poison for her brother, dim and obscure by the day and with a dark spot in her orb, how can the poor and wretched moon be matched with Sita's countenance?'

घटइ बढ़इ बिरहिनि दुखदाई।
ग्रसर राहु निज संधिहिं पाई॥
कोक सोकप्रद पंकज द्रोही।
अवगुन बहुत चंद्रमा तोही॥[105]

ghaṭai baḍhai birahani dukhadāī ।
grasai Rāhu nija saṃdhihiṃ pāī ॥
koka sikaprada paṃkaja drohī ।
avaguna bahuta caṃdramā tohī ॥

Again, the moon waxes and wanes; she is the curse of lovesick damsels and is devoured by Rahu when she crosses the latter's orbit. She causes anguish to the Chakravaka (the ruddy goose) and withers the lotus. O moon, there are numerous faults in you.

बैदेही मुख पटतर दीन्हे।
होइ दोषु बड़ अनुचित कीन्हे॥
सिय मुख छबि बिधु ब्याज बखानी।
गुर पहिं चले निसा बड़ि जानी॥[106]

Baidehī mukha paṭatara dīnhe ।
hoi doṣa baḍaanucita kīnhe ॥
Siya mukha chabi bidhu byāja bakhānī ।
guru pahiṃ cale nisā baḍai jānī ॥

One would incur the blame of having done a highly improper act by comparing you with the countenance of Videha's daughter. Thus finding in the moon a pretext for extolling the beauty of Sita's countenance and perceiving that the night had far advanced, Shri Ram returned to His Guru.

There are occasions when Tulsi deliberately chooses a creative diversion to give a larger canvas to his poetic imagination. These lines are an illustration of that. Ram initially compares Sita's beauty to that of the moon, but then finds all the reasons to negate this comparison. The moon has too many blemishes, too many limitations, too many drawbacks to be compared to the unblemished Sita. The significant takeaway from this evocative prasang is that it serves to illustrate how, literally, Ram was 'moon-struck' in his love for Sita. The stanza is meant to show that having once seen Sita, Ram could not stop thinking about her. In describing the pathways of his overactive mind—where he first compares her to the moon and then finds the reasons against this comparison—Tulsi also very cleverly brings out the state of a besotted lover. When someone is in love, the mind is unstable, forever agitated, seeking solace, trying to find assurance, and looking for new and newer ways to recollect and treasure the image of the object of his love. Tulsi's little poetic rumination on the moon is meant to profile Ram in love, and this ability to humanise the divine is precisely why the Manas invokes among its readers such devotion and affection.

13. Shri Ram-Lakshman in Sita's Svayamwara

रंगभूमि आए दोउ भाई।
असि सुधि सब पुरबासिन्ह पाई॥
चले सकल गृह काज बिसारी।
बाल जुबान जरठ नर नारी॥[107]

raṃgabhūmi āe dou bhāī ।
asi sudhi saba purabāsinha pāī ।।
cale sakala gṛha kāja bisārī ।
bāla jubāna jaraṭha nara nārī ।।

When the inhabitants of the town got the news that the two brothers had reached the arena, they all sallied forth, oblivious of their homes and duties—men and women, young and old, and even children.

राजकुअँर तेहि अवसर आए।
मनहुँ मनोहरता तन छाए॥
गुन सागर नागर बर बीरा।
सुंदर स्यामल गौर सरीरा॥[108]

rājakuaṁra tehi avasara āe ।
manahuṁ manoharatā tana chāe ।।
guna sāgara nāgara bara bīrā ।
suṃdara syāmala gaura sarīrā ।।

Meanwhile there arrived the two princes, the very abodes of beauty as it were, both ocean of goodness, polished in manners and gallant heroes, charming of forms, the one dark and the other fair.

> राज समाज बिराजत रुरे।
> उडगन महुँ जनु जुग बिधु पूरे॥
> जिन्ह कें रही भावना जैसी।
> प्रभु मूरति तिन्ह देखी तैसी॥[109]

> rāja samāja birājata rūre ।
> uḍagana mahuṁ janu juga bidhu pūre ।।
> jinha keṃ rahī bhāvanā jaisī ।
> prabhu mūrati tinha dekhī taisī ।।

Shining bright in the galaxy of princes, they looked like two full moons in a circle of stars. Everyone looked on the Lord's form according to the conception each had about Him.

> देखहिं रूप महा रनधीरा।
> मनहुँ बीर रसु धरें सरीरा॥
> डरे कुटिल नृप प्रभुहि निहारी।
> मनहुँ भयानक मूरति भारी॥[110]

> dekhahiṃ rūpa mahā ranadhīrā ।
> manahuṁ bīra rasu dhareṃ sarīrā ।।
> ḍare kuṭila nṛpa prabhuhi nihārī ।
> manahuṁ bhayānaka mūrati bhārī ।।

Those who were surpassingly staunch in battle gazed on His form as though He was the heroic sentiment personified. The wicked kings trembled at the sight of the Lord as if He had a most terrible form.

> रहे असुर छल छोनिप बेषा।
> तिन्ह प्रभु प्रगट कालसम देखा।

पुरबासिन्ह देखे दोउ भाई।
नरभूषन लोचन सुखदाई ॥[111]

rahe asura chala chonipa beṣā ।
tinha prabhu pragaṭa kālasama dekhā ।।
purabāsinha dekhe dou bhāī ।
narabhūṣana locana sukhadāī ।।

The demons, who were cunningly disguised as princes, beheld the Lord as Death in visible form, while the citizens regarded the two brothers as the ornaments of humanity and the delight of their eyes.

नारि बिलोकहिं हरषि हियँ निज-निज रुचि अनुरूप।
जनु सोहत सिंगार धरि मूरति परम अनूप ॥[112]

nāri bilokahiṃ harași hiyaṁ nija nija ruci anurūpa ।
janu sohata siṃgāra dhari mūrati param anūpa ।।

With joy in their heart, the women saw Him according to the attitude of mind each had towards Him, as if the erotic sentiment itself had appeared in an utterly incomparable form.

बिदुषन्ह प्रभु बिराटमय दीसा।
बहु मुख कर पग लोचन सीसा।
जनक जाति अवलोकहिं कैसें।
सजन सगे प्रिय लागहिं जैसें ॥[113]

biduṣanha prabhu birāṭamaya dīsā ।
bahu mukha kara paga locana sīsā ।।
Janak jāti avalokahiṃ kaisaiṃ ।
sajana sage priya lāgahiṃ jaiseṃ ।।

The wise saw the Lord in His cosmic form, with many faces, hands, feet, eyes and heads. And how did He appear to Janak's kinsmen? Like one's own beloved relation.

सहित बिदेह बिलोकहिं रानी।
सिसु सम प्रीति न जाति बखानी॥
जोगिन्ह परम तत्वमय भासा।
सांत सुद्ध सम सहज प्रकासा॥[114]

sahita bideha bilokahiṃ rānī ।
sisu sama prīti na jāti bakhānī ।।
joginha param tatvamaya bhāsā ।
sāṃta suddha sama sahaja prakāsā ।।

The queen, no less than the king, regarded Him with unspeakable love like a dear child. To the yogis (those ever united with god), He shone forth as no other than the highest truth, placid, unsullied, equipoised, and resplendent by its very nature.

हरिभगतन्ह देखे दोउ भ्राता।
इष्टदेव इव सब सुख दाता॥
रामहि चितव भायँ जेहि सीया।
सो सनेहु सुख नहिं कथनीया॥[115]

Haribhagatanha dekhe dou bhrātā ।
iṣṭadeva iva saba sukha dātā ।।
Rāmahi citava bhāyaṁ jehi Sīyā ।
so sanehu sukhu nahiṃ kathanīyā ।।

The devotees of Shri Hari beheld the two brothers as their beloved deity, the fountain of all joy. The emotion of love and joy with which Sita gazed on Shri Ram was ineffable.

उर अनुभवति न कहि सक सोऊ।
कवन प्रकार कहै कबि कोऊ॥
एहि बिधि रहा जाहि जस भाऊ।
तेहिं तस देखेउ कोसलराऊ॥[116]

ura anubhavati na kahi saka soū ।
kavana prakāra kahai kabi koū ।।
ehi bidhi rahā jāhi jasa bhāū ।
tehiṃ tasa dekheu kosalarāū ।।

She felt the emotion in Her heart, but could not utter it; how, then, can a poet describe it? In this way, everyone regarded the Lord of Ayodhya according to the attitude of mind each had towards Him.

सिय सोभा नहिं जाइ बखानी ।
जगदंबिका रूप गुन खानी ॥
उपमा सकल मोहि लघु लागीं ।
प्राकृत नारि अंग अनुरागी ॥[117]

Siya sobhā nahiṃ jāi bakhānī ।
Jagadaṃbikā rūpa guna khānī ।।
upamā sakala mohi laghu lāgīṃ ।
prākṛta nāri aṃga anurāgīṃ ।।

Sita's beauty defies all description, Mother of the universe that She is and an embodiment of charm and excellence. All comparisons seem to me too poor; for they have affinity with the limbs of mortal women.

सिय बरनिअ तेइ उपमा देई ।
कुकबि कहाइ अजसु को लेई ॥
जौं पटतरिअ तीय सम सीया ।
जग असि जुबति कहाँ कमनीया ॥[118]

Siya barania tei upamā deī ।
kukabi kahāi ajasu ko leī ।।
jau paṭataria tīya sama sīyā ।
jaga asi jubati kahāṁ kamanīyā ।।

Proceeding to depict Sita with the help of those very similes why should one earn the title of an unworthy poet and court ill-repute? Should Sita be likened to any woman of this material creation, where in this world shall one come across such a lovely damsel?

गिरा मुखर तन अरध भवानी।
रति अति दुखित अतनु पति जानी॥
बिष बारुनी बंधु प्रिय जेही।
कहिअ रमासम किमि बैदेही॥[119]

girā mukhara tana aradha Bhavānī ।
Rati ati dukhita atanu pati jānī ।।
biṣa bāruṇī baṃdhu priya jehī ।
kahia Ramāsama kimi Baidehī ।।

The Goddess of Speech (Saraswati), for instance, is a chatterer; while Bhavani possesses only half a body (the other half being represented by her lord, Shiva). And Rati (God of Love's consort) is extremely distressed by the thought of her husband being without a form. And it is quite out of the question to compare Videha's daughter with Ram (Lakshmi), who has poison and spirituous liquor for her dear brothers.

जौं छबि सुधा पयोनिधि होई।
परम रूपमय कच्छपु सोई॥
सोभा रजु मंदरु सिंगारू।
मथै पानि पंकज निज मारू॥[120]

jau chabi sudhā payonidhi hoī ।
param rūpamaya kacchapa soī ।।
sobhā raju Maṃdaru siṃgārū ।
mathai pāni paṃkaja nija mārū ।।

Supposing there was an ocean of nectar in the form of loveliness and the tortoise serving as a base for churning it was an embodiment of consummate beauty, and if splendour itself were to take the form of a cord, the erotic sentiment should crystallise and assume the shape of

Mount Mandara and the God of Love himself were to churn this ocean with his own hands.

एहि बिधि उपजै लच्छि जब सुंदरता सुख मूल।
तदपि सकोच समेत कबि कहहिं सीय समतूल ॥[121]

ehi bidhi upajai lacchi jaba suṃdaratā sukha mūla ।
tadapi sakoca sameta kabi kahahiṃ Sīya samatūla ।।

And if from such churning were to be born a Lakshmi, who was the source of all loveliness and joy, the poet would even then hesitatingly declare her as analogous to Sita.

गिरा अलिनि मुख पंकज रोकी।
प्रगट न लाज निसा अवलोकी ॥
लोचन जलु रह लोचन कोना।
जैसें परम कृपन कर सोना ॥[122]

girā alini mukha paṃkaja rokī ।
pragaṭa na lāja nisā avalokī ।।
locana jalu raha locana konā ।
jaise param kṛpana kara sonā ।।

Held captive within Her lotus-like mouth, Her bee-like speech did not stir out for fear of the night of modesty Tears remained confined within the corner of Her eyes, just as the gold of a stingy miser remains buried in a nook of his house.

सकुची ब्याकुलता बड़ि जानी।
धरि धीरजु प्रतीति उर आनी ॥
तन मन बचन मोर पनु साचा।
रघुपति पद सरोज चितु राचा ॥
तौ भगवानु सकल उर बासी।
करिहिं मोहि रघुबर कै दासी ॥

जेहि कें जेहि पर सत्य सनेहू।
सो तेहि मिलइ न कछु संदेहू॥[123]

sakucī byākulatā baḍi jānī ।
dhari dhīraju pratīti ura ānī ।।
tana mana bacana mora panu sācā ।
Raghupati pada saroja citu rācā ।।
tau bhagavānu sakala ura bāsī ।
karihiṃ mohi Raghubara kai dāsī ।।
jehi keṃ jehi para satya sanehū ।
so tehi milai na kachu saṃhehū ।।

Sita felt abashed when She perceived Her great agitation of mind; summoning up courage in Her heart, therefore, She confidently said to Herself, if I am true to my vow in thought, word and deed, and if my mind is really attached to the lotus-feet of Shri Ram, I am sure God, who dwells in the hearts of all, will make me Shri Ram's bond-slave; for one gets united without doubt with him for whom one cherishes true love.

प्रभु तन चितइ प्रेम तन ठाना।
कृपानिधान राम सबु जाना॥
सियहि बिलोकि तकेउ धनु कैसें।
चितव गरुरु लघु ब्यालहि जैसें॥[124]

prabhu tana citai prema tana ṭhānā ।
kṛpānidhāna Rāma sabu jānā ।।
Siyahi biloki takeu dhanu kaise ।
citava garuru laghu byālahi jaise ।।

Casting a glance at the Lord, She resolved to love Him even at the cost of Her life. Shri Ram, the embodiment of compassion, understood it all; looking at Sita, He glanced at the bow as Garuda (the king of birds) would gaze on a poor little snake.

का बरषा सब कृषी सुखानें।
समय चुकें पुनि का पछितानें ॥
अस जियँ जानि जानकी देखी।
प्रभु पुल के लखि प्रीति बिसेषी ॥[125]

kā baraṣā saba kṛṣī sukhāneṃ ।
samaya cukeṃ puni kā pachitāneṃ ॥
asa jiya— jāni Jānakī dekhī ।
prabhu pulake lakhi prīti biseṣī ॥

What good is a shower when the whole crop is dried up; what use repenting over an opportunity lost? Thinking thus within Himself the Lord looked at Janak's daughter and thrilled all over to perceive Her singular devotion.

Tulsi's description of the scene of the svayamwara (the practice of choosing a husband from a list of suitors), where Ram and Lakshman are present along with other powerful kings and princes to vie for Sita's hand on condition that they can break the great bow, is devoted almost wholly to the description of Ram and Sita. Where Ram is concerned, the key lines are: *jinh ke rahi bhavna jaisi, prabhu murati tinh dekhi taisi.* In other words, Ram appears to different people present at the svayamwara depending on how they wish to see him. With these two lines as a pivot, Tulsi describes how the brave, the wicked, the demons in disguise, ordinary citizens, women, the learned, the family members of Janak and his queens, the renunciates, and devotees see Ram. The bad see him with anger, arrogance and envy, and the good with love and reverence.

Where Sita is concerned, Tulsi makes an open declaration that to use any comparison to describe her would be grossly inadequate and, therefore, as a poet, he would not commit this unpardonable error. But then he goes a step further, and rates her above all the other goddesses in the Hindu pantheon. Saraswati, he says, speaks too much; Parvati is Ardhanarishwara, half-man half-woman, and thus only half a woman; Kamadeva's wife, Rati, is perennially unhappy because her husband has no corporeal form.

Tulsi goes so far to say that Sita was even superior to Lakshmi. His reasons for this is that while Lakshmi was born from the churning of the primordial ocean, *samudra manthan,* Sita was self-born. This comparison is based on the fact that according to many ancient scriptures, including Valmiki's Ramayana, Lakshmi springs forth with other precious things from the foam of the ocean of milk when it is churned by the gods and demons for the recovery of *amrita,* or divine nectar. Tulsi was being audacious in placing Sita above Lakshmi, since Sita is herself considered to be an avatar of Lakshmi and, as the shakti of Vishnu, enjoys universal reverence of Hindus as the goddess of wealth, fortune and prosperity. Ram is himself the incarnation of Vishnu, whose consort, Lakshmi is considered the Supreme Being in the Vaishnavite tradition. But such is the poet's unwavering commitment to the glorification of Ram and Sita, that he does not hesitate to put both on a pedestal where they are above all other divine rivals.

The incomparable Sita awaits the proceedings of the svayamwara, and Tulsi has a beautiful analogy to describe her bashfulness. Her heart is brimming with love for Ram, but she hesitates from showing it, as though she is unwilling to penetrate the night of shy restraint that envelopes her. Ram, the all-knowing, is aware of her love for him, and draws strength and joy from this. The formidable bow that has to be broken is for him, Tulsi says, but a small snake eyed by the mythical bird Garuda, the formidable serpent hunter. He resolves then to rise to the occasion, for a call not taken when the moment comes is, in the words of Tulsi, like the rains after the harvest has shrivelled. What is the use of regret when the moment is not ceased when it should be.

14. The Ceremony of Jaimala and Marriage of Shri Ram-Sita

बंदी मागध सूतगन बिरुद बदहिं मतिधीर।
करहिं निछावरि लोग सब हय गय धन मनि चीर ॥[126]

baṃdī māgadha sūtagana biruda badahiṃ matidhīra ।
karahiṃ nichāvari loga saba haya gaya dhana mani cīra ।।

Talented bards, minstrels and panegyrists sang praises; and everybody gave away horses, elephants, riches, jewels and raiments as an act of invocation of God's blessings on the youthful champion.

झाँझि मृदंग संख सहनाई।
भेरि ढोल दुंदुभी सुहाई ॥
बाजहिं बहु बाजने सुहाए।
जहँ तहँ जुबतिन्ह मंगल गाए ॥[127]

jhāṁjhi mṛdaṃga saṃkha sahanāī ।
bheri ḍhola duṃdubhī suhāī ।।
bājahiṃ bahu bājane suhāe ।
jahaṁ tahaṁ jubatinha maṃgala gāe ।।

There was a crash of cymbals and tabors, conches and clarionets, drums and sweet-sounding kettledrums, both large and small; and many other charming instruments also played. Everywhere young women sang auspicious strains.

सखिन्ह सहित हरषी अति रानी।
सूखत धान परा जनु पानी॥
जनक लहेउ सुखु सोचु बिहाई।
तैरत थकें थाह जनु पाई॥[128]

sakhinha sahita haraṣī ati rānī ।
sūkhata dhāna parā janu pānī ।।
Janak laheu sukhu socu bihāī ।
tairata thakeṃ thāha janu pāī ।।

The queen with her companions was much delighted, as though a withering crop of paddy had been refreshed by a shower. King Janak was now carefree and felt gratified, as if a tired swimmer had reached a shallow.

श्रीहत भए भूप धनु टूटे।
जैसें दिवस दीप छबि छूटें॥
सीय सुखहि बरनिअ केहि भाँती।
जनु चातकी पाइ जलु स्वातीं॥[129]

śrīhata bhae bhūpa dhanu ṭūṭe ।
jaiseṃ divasa dīpa chabi chūṭe ।।
Sīya sukhahi barania kehi bhāṁtī ।
janu cātakī pāi jalu svātī ।।

The kings' countenance fell at the breaking of the bow, just as a lamp is dimmed at dawn of day. Sita's delight could only be compared to that of a female Chataka bird on receiving a raindrop when the sun is in the same longitude as the constellation named Swati (Arcturus).

रामहि लखनु बिलोकत कैसें।
ससिहि चकोर किसोरकु जैसें॥
सतानंद तब आयसु दीन्हा।
सीताँ गमनु राम पहिं कीन्हा॥[130]

Rāmahi Lakhanu bilokata kaiseṃ ।
sasihi cakora kisoraku jaiseṃ ।।
Satānaṃda taba āyasu dīnhā ।
Sītāṁ gamanu Rāma pahiṃ kīnhā ।।

Lakshman fixed his eyes on Ram as the young of a Chakora bird gazes on the moon. Shatananda then gave the word and Sita advanced towards Ram.

संग सखीं सुंदर चतुर गावहिं मंगलचार ।
गवनी बाल मराल गति सुषमा अंग अपार ॥[131]

saṃga sakhīṃ sudaṃra catura gāvahiṃ maṃgalacāra ।
gavanī bāla marāla gati suṣamā aṃga apāra ।।

Accompanied by Her fair and talented companions, who were singing festal songs, She paced like a cygnet, Her limbs possessing infinite charm.

सखिन्ह मध्य सिय सोहति कैसें ।
छबिगन मध्य महाछबि जैसें ॥
कर सरोज जयमाल सुहाई ।
बिस्व बिजय सोभा जेहिं छाई ॥[132]

sakhinha madhya siya sohati kaise ।
chabigana madhya mahāchabi jaiseṃ ।।
kara saroja jayamāla suhāī ।
bisva bijaya sobhā jehiṃ chāī ।।

In the midst of Her companions, Sita shone as a personification of supreme beauty among other embodiments of beauty. She held in Her lotus-hands the fair wreath of victory, resplendent with the glory of triumph over the whole universe.

तन सकोचु मन परम उछाहू ।
गूढ़ प्रेमु लखि परइ न काहू ॥

जाइ समीप राम छबि देखी ।
रहि जनु कुअँरि चित्र अवरेखी ॥[133]

tana sakocu mana param uchāhū ।
gūḍhapremu lakhi parai na kāhū ॥
jāi samīpa Rāma chabi dekhī ।
rahi janu kuṁari citra avarekhī ॥

While Her body shrank with modesty, Her heart was full of rapture; Her hidden love could not be perceived by others. As She drew near and beheld Shri Ram's beauty, Princess Sita stood motionless as a portrait.

चतुर सखीं लखि कहा बुझाई।
पहिरावहु जयमाल सुहाई ॥
सुनत जुगल कर माल उठाई।
प्रेम बिबस पहिराइ न जाई ॥[134]

catura sakhīṃ lakhi kahā bujhāī ।
pahirāvahu jayamāla suhāī ॥
sunata jugala kara māla uṭhāī ।
prema bibasa pahirāi na jāī ॥

A clever companion, who perceived Her in this condition, exhorted Her saying, 'Invest the bridegroom with the beautiful wreath of victory.' At this, She raised the wreath with both of Her hands, but was too overwhelmed with emotion to garland Him.

सोहत जनु जुग जलज सनाला ।
ससिहि सभीत देत जयमाला ॥
गावहिं छबि अवलोकि सहेली।
सियँ जयमाल राम उर मेली ॥[135]

sohata janu juga jalaja sanālā ।
sasihi sabhīta deta jayamālā ॥

gāvahiṃ chabi avaloki sahelī ।
Siyaṁ jayamāla Rāma ura melī ।।

In this act, Her uplifted hands shone as if a pair of lotuses with their stalks which were timidly investing the moon with a wreath of victory. At this charming sight, Her companions broke into a song, while Sita placed the wreath of victory round Shri Ram's neck so as to adorn His breast.

रघुबर उर जयमाल देखि देव बरिसहिं सुमन ।
सकुचे सकल भुआल जनु बिलोकि रबि कुमुदगन ।।[136]

Raghubara ura jayamāla dekhi deva barisahiṃ sumana ।
sakuce sakala bhuāla janu biloki rabi kumudagana ।।

Witnessing the wreath of victory resting on Shri Ram's bosom, gods rained down flowers; while the kings all shrank in confusion like lillies at the rising of the sun.

पुर अरु ब्योम बाजने बाजे ।
खल भए मलिन साधु सब राजे ।।
सुर किंनर नर नाग मुनीसा ।
जय जय जय कहि देहिं असीसा ।।[137]

pura aru byoma bājane bāje ।
khala bhae malina sādhu saba rāje ।।
sura Kinnara nara nāga munīsā ।
jaya jaya jaya kahi dehiṃ asīsā ।।

There was music both in the city and in the heavens; while the wicked were downcast, the virtuous beamed with joy. Gods, Kinnaras, men, Nagas and great sages uttered blessings with shouts of victory.

नाचहिं गावहिं बिबुध बधूटीं ।
बार बार कुसुमांजलि छूटीं ।।

जहँ तहँ बिप्र बेदधुनि करहीं ।
बंदी बिरिदावलि उच्चरहीं ।।[138]

nācahiṃ gāvahiṃ bibudha badhūṭīṃ ।
bāra bāra kusumāṃjali chūṭīṃ ।।
jahaṁ tahaṁ bipra Bedadhuni karahīṃ ।
baṃdī biradāvali uccarahīṃ ।।

Celestial dames danced and sang and handfuls of flowers were showered again and again. Here and there the Brahmins recited the Vedas, while panegyrists sang praises.

महिं पाताल नाक जसु ब्यापा ।
राम बरी सिय भंजेउ चापा ।
करहिं आरती पुर नर नारी ।
देहिं निछावरि बित्त बिसारी ।।[139]

mahiṁ pātāla nāka jasu byāpā ।
Rāma barī Siya bhaṃjeu cāpā ।।
karahiṃ āratī pura nara nārī ।
dehiṃ nichāvari bitta bisārī ।।

The glad tidings spread throughout the earth, the subterranean regions and heaven that Shri Ram had broken the bow and won the hand of Sita. The people of the city waved lights round the pair in order to ward off evil; and regardless of their means they scattered gifts in profusion as an act of invocation of divine blessings on the couple.

सोहति सीय राम कै जोरी।
छबि सिंगारु मनहुँ एक ठोरी ।।
सखीं कहहिं प्रभु पद गहु सीता ।
करति न चरन परस अति भीता ।।[140]

sohati Sīya Rāma kai jorī ।
chabi siṃgāru manahuṁ eka ṭhorī ।।

sakhīṃ kahahiṃ prabhupada gahu Sītā ।
karati na carana parasa ati bhītā ।।

The pair of Shri Ram and Sita shone as if beauty and the sentiment of love had met together in human form. Her companions urged Her, 'Sita, clasp your Lord's feet.' But Sita was much too afraid to touch His feet.

गौतम तिय गति सुरति करि नहिं परसति पग पानि ।
मन बिहसे रघुबंसमनि प्रीति अलौकिक जानि ॥[141]

Gautama tiya gati surati kari nahiṃ parasati paga pāni ।
mana bihase Raghubaṃsamani prīti alaukika jāni ।।

Remembering the fate of the sage Gautama's wife, Ahalya, She would not touch His feet with Her hands; the Jewel of Raghu's race inwardly smiled to perceive Her transcendent love.

रामहि देखि बरात जुड़ानी ।
प्रीति कि रीति न जाति बखानी ॥
नृप समीप सोहहिं सुत चारी ।
जनु धन धरमादिक तनुधारी ॥ 142

Rāmahi dekhi barāta juḍānī ।
prīti ki rīti na jāti bakhānī ।।
nṛpa samīpa sohahiṃ suta cārī ।
janu dhana dharamādika tanudhārī ।।

The sight of Shri Ram was so soothing to the guests; the ways of love are beyond description. Beside the king, his four sons looked like incarnations as it were, of the four ends of human endeavour, viz., riches, religious merit etc. The people of the city were delighted beyond measure to see King Dasharath with his sons.

The wedding of Ram and Sita, especially the jayamala, where the bride and bridegroom exchange garlands, is described with poetic verve by Tulsi. Celebrations resound, and Tulsi uses two beautiful analogies to describe the feelings of the mothers of Sita, and that of her father, Janak. He says that the queen mothers felt the joy of a dying crop that suddenly receives the benediction of rain. Janak, he says, is like someone who, exhausted when swimming, finds the shore.

Our poet is at his dexterous best when describing the jayamala. Surrounded by her friends, Sita stands out like a stunning picture amidst many other beautiful pictures. Her mind is soaring with love, but her body, out of shyness, is withdrawing into itself: *tana sakochu mana param uchahu.* This is such an evocative way of describing a bashful bride. The exuberance of joy and expectation, counterbalanced with the natural diffidence of a bride, is profiled so sensitively. If there is exuberance, there is also reticence; if there is anticipation, there is also coyness. The combination of the two is what engages the poet. Sita is unable to express her deep love for Ram, and when she comes close to him for the jayamala, she is transfixed, stilled, as Tulsi says, like a lovely picture in a frame.

Her friends nudge her to garland Ram, but overpowered by her love for him, she is unable to move her hands. Tulsi's description of the jayamala still resonates in traditional marriages across India, especially arranged ones. The bride does not yet know the groom, apart from a possible chance meeting or perfunctory acquaintance, if that; she is suffused with happiness, but that happiness is mixed with shyness and trepidation and sometimes anxiety, and the tension of ensuring that her emotions within are not seen outside. She can look radiant, but is also restrained in the midst of so many relatives and guests. When Sita finally picks up courage to garland Ram, her hands, Tulsi writes, are like the stems of two lotuses raised to garland the moon.

Once the jayamala is over, Ram and Sita stand together, and the couple is so magnetic, that it is, as though, unblemished beauty and the mood of sensuality—*shringara rasa*—have merged. Tulsi's reference to shringara rasa is interesting, because he is usually reticent to touch this emotion in his description of the divine duo. His mentioning of sensuality is the concession he makes to a fundamental aspect in the projection of a newly married couple, and fits in with his earlier literary gusto in enumerating the power of Kamadeva, the God of Love and the erotic mood. In fact, Sita is reluctant to even touch the feet of her husband—which seen outside contemporary notions of gender equality—was a ritual performed by the bride. Apart from her reticence to the physical touch—in fact, the beauty of Tulsi's description of the meeting of Ram and Sita and the love that burgeons between them is that it is entirely at the emotional level, where their physical appearance is a factor but there is not even remotely any physical contact between them—she is also influenced, Tulsi writes, by the powerful transformative *sparsh* (or touch)—of Ram's body, as illustrated by the story of Ahalya. In mythology, Ahalya is the wife of the great sage, Gautama Maharishi. She was a great beauty and was seduced by Lord Indra, the king of gods. For this act of infidelity, her husband curses her and turns her to stone. She regains her human form only when Ram's feet brush past her.

15. Dialogue Between Dashrath and Kaikeyi

बिपति बीजु बरषा रितु चेरी ।
भुइँ भइ कुमति कैकई केरी ।
पाइ कपट जलु अंकुर जामा ।
बर दोउ दल दुख फल परिनामा ॥[143]

bipati bīju baraṣā ritu cerī ।
bhuiṁ bhai kumati Kaikeī kerī ।।
pāi kapaṭa jalu aṃkura jāmā ।
bara dou dala dukha phala parināmā ।।

Discord was the seed and the servant-girl (Manthara) the rainy season; while the evil mind of Kaikeyi served as the soil. Fed by the water of wiliness the seed took root and sprouted with the two boons as its leaves and will eventually bear the fruit of adversity.

केहि हेतु रानि रिसानि परसत पानि पतिहि नेवारई ।
मानहुँ सरोष भुअंग भामिनि बिषम भाँति निहारई ॥
दोउ बासना रसना दसन बर मरम ठाहरु देखई ।
तुलसी नृपति भवतब्यता बस काम कौतुक लेखई ॥[144]

kehi hetu rāni risāni parasata pāni patihi nevāraī ।
mānahuṁ saroṣa bhuaṃga bhāmini biṣama bhāṁti nihāraī ।।
dou bāsanā rasanā dasana bara maram ṭhāharu dekhaī ।
Tulsī nṛpati bhavatabyatā basa kāma kautuka lekhaī ।।

As the king touched her with his hand saying, 'Why are you angry, my queen?' Kaikeyi threw it aside and flashed upon him a furious glance like an enraged serpent with the two (above-mentioned) cravings of her heart for its bifurcated tongue and the boons (that had been promised to her by the king) for its fangs, spying out a vital part. As fate would have it, says Tulsi, the king took it all as an amorous sport.

दोउ बर कूल कठिन हठ धारा।
भवँर कूबरी बचन प्रचारा॥
ढाहत भूपरूप तरु मूला।
चली बिपति बारिधि अनुकूला॥[145]

dou bara kūla kaṭhina haṭha dhārā ।
bhavaṁra kūbarī bacana pracārā ।।
ḍhāhata bhūparūpa taru mūlā ।
calī bipati bāridhi anukūlā ।।

The two boons she had asked for represented its banks, her inexorable obstinacy corresponded to its (swift) current and the impelling force of Manthara's words stood for its eddies; uprooting the king like a tree the river headed towards the ocean of adversity.

This prasang of the meeting between Dashrath and Kaikeyi has been primarily selected to illustrate the remarkable powers of analogy of Tulsi. His ability to chisel the scene using poetic comparisons brings out clearly his unparalleled genius as a poet. The setting is ominous. Kaikeyi is in high dudgeon, waiting to extract from her husband, Dashrath, the fulfilment of the two boons he had promised her. Her mind is made up, her intent is evil, she is going to ask firstly, for the banishment of Ram from Ayodhya for fourteen years, and secondly, for her own son, Bharat, to be declared the heir apparent.

In this backdrop, Tulsi says that acrimony is the seed, Kaikeyi's maid Manthara (who poisons the mind of Kaikeyi) is the rainfall, and Kaikeyi's own convoluted mind is the fertile ground for the seed to germinate. From the soil will spring a plant whose two leaves are the boons Kaikeyi will ask for, and the fruit of the plant will ultimately be sorrow.

Dashrath is unsuspecting. Seeing Kaikeyi angry he tries to placate her, but she spurns his advances. In describing Kaikeyi's demeanour, the poet is in his elements again. He writes that she is like an angry serpent *(nagin)*. The desire to ask for the two boons from Dashrath are like the two tongues of that serpent, while the boons themselves are the serpent's two sharp teeth. Kaikeyi is looking for a soft spot to dig in the two teeth. In sheer contrast, Dashrath interprets Kaikeyi's behaviour as though it is the effect of Kamadeva, or the play of desire.

From the invocation of a ferocious serpent, Tulsi suddenly moves to a gentler analogy, in which there is the element of fatalism, and of the ebb and flow of destiny. Kaikeyi's two boons, he says, are the two shores of a river, her adamancy is the fast flow of that river, and the incendiary promptings of Manthara the whirlpools that lurk in the river. That furious river will uproot from its roots the tree that is Dashrath, and ultimately flow towards a sea of unmitigated conflict.

16. Dialogue Between Shri Ram and Kaikeyi

जाइ दीख रघुबंसमनि नरपति निपट कुसाजु।
सहमि परेउ लखि सिंघिनिहि मनहुँ बृद्ध गजराजु ॥[146]

jāi dīkha Raghubaṃsamani narapati nipaṭa kusāju ।।
sahami pareu lakhi siṃghinihi manahuṃ bṛddha gajarāju ।।

The Jewel of Raghu's race went and saw the king in an utterly wretched state, like an aged elephant who had dropped down in terror at the sight of a lioness.

सूखहिं अधर जरइ सबु अंगू।
मनहुँ दीन मनिहीन भुअंगू ॥
सरुष समीप दीखि कैकेई।
मानहुँ मीचु घरीं गनि लेई ॥[147]

sūkhahiṃ adhara jarai sabu aṃgū ।
manahuṁ dīna manihīna bhuaṃgū ।।
saruṣa samīpa dīkhi kaikeī ।
mānahuṁ mīcu gharī gani leī ।।

His lips got parched and his whole frame burned; he looked like a helpless snake bereft of the gem. The Lord beheld by the side of His father angry Kaikeyi, who stood there like Death personified counting the last minutes of his life.

करुनामय मृदु राम सुभाऊ।
प्रथम दीख दुख सुना न काऊ॥
तदपि धीर धरि समउ बिचारी।
पूँछी मधुर बचन महतारी॥[148]

karunāmaya mṛdu Rāma subhāū ।
prathama dīkha dukhu sunā na kāū ।।
tadapi dhīra dhari samau bicārī ।
pūṁchī madhura bacana mahatārī ।।

Shri Ram was compassionate and soft by nature; He witnessed sorrow for the first time in His life, He had never heard of it before. Yet, recovering Himself as the occasion demanded, addressed His stepmother in the following sweet words:

मोहि कहु मातु तात दुख कारन।
करिअ जतन जेहिं होइ निवारन॥
सुनहु राम सबु कारनु एहू।
राजहि तुम्ह पर बहुत सनेहू॥
देन कहेन्हि मोहि दुइ बरदाना।
मागेउँ जो कछु मोहि सोहाना॥
सो सुनि भयउ भूप उर सोचू।
छाड़ि न सकहिं तुम्हार सँकोचू॥[149]

mohi kahu mātu tāta dukha kārana ।
karia jatana jehiṃ hoi nivārana ।।
sunahu Rāma sabu kārana ehū ।
rājahi tuma para bahuta sanehū ।।
dena kahenhi mohi dui baradānā ।
māgeuṁ jo kachu mohi sohānā ।
so suni bhayau bhūpa ura socū ।
chāḍai na sakahiṃ tumhāra saṁkocū ।।

'Tell me, dear mother, the cause of my father's distress, so that an attempt may be made to remove it.' 'Listen, Ram; the sole cause is this: the king is very fond of you. He had promised me two boons of my choice and I asked whatever I liked. The king, however, was stricken with grief to hear my requests; for he cannot shake off the hesitation on your score.'

सुत सनेहु इत बचनु उत संकट परेउ नरेसु।
सकहु त आयसु धरहु सिर मेटहु कठिन कलेसु॥[150]

suta saneha ita bacanu uta saṃkaṭa pareu naresu ।
sakahu na āyasu dharahu sira meṭahu kaṭhina kalesu ।।

'Love for his son on one side and his plighted word on the other: the king is placed on the horns of a dilemma. Obey his command if you can, and rid him of a severe mental torture.'

निधरक बैठि कहइ कटु बानी।
सुनत कठिनता अति अकुलानी॥
जीभ कमान बचन सर नाना।
मनहुँ महिप मृदु लच्छ समाना॥
जनु कठोरपनु धरें सरीरू।
सिखइ धनुषबिद्या बर बीरू॥
सबु प्रसंगु रघुपतिहि सुनाई।
बैठि मनहुँ तनु धरि निठुराई॥[151]

nidharaka baiṭhi kahai kaṭu bānī ।
sunata kaṭhinatā ati akulānī ।।
jībha kamāna bacana sara nānā ।
manahuṁ mahipa mṛdu laccha samānā ।।
janu kaṭhorapanu dhareṃ sarīrū ।
sikhai dhanuṣabidyā bara bīrū ।।
saba prasaṃgu Raghupatihi sunāī ।
baiṭhi manahuṁ tanu dhari niṭhurāī ।।

Kaikeyi unhesitatingly spoke these pungent words, which callousness itself was sore distressed to hear. With the tongue for a bow, and words for so many shafts and with the king for a delicate target as it were, it looked as hard-heartedness had assumed the form of a great hero and practised bowmanship. Having communicated the whole incident to the Lord of Raghus (Shri Ram), she sat like the very incarnation of heartlessness.

मन मुसुकाइ भानुकुल भानू ।
रामु सहज आनंद निधानू ॥
बोले बचन बिगत सब दूषन ।
मृदु मंजुल जनु बाग बिभूषन ॥
सुनु जननी सोइ सुतु बड़भागी।
जो पितु मातु बचन अनुरागी ॥
तनय मातु पितु तोषनिहारा ।
दुर्लभ जननि सकल संसारा ॥[152]

mana musakāi bhānukula bhānu ।
Rāmu sahaja ānaṃda nidhānū ।।
bole bacana bigata saba dūṣana ।
mṛdu maṃjula janu bāga bibhūṣana ।।
sunu jananī soi sutu baḍabhāgī ।
jo pitu mātu bacana anurāgī ।।
tanaya mātu pitu toṣanihārā ।
durlabha janani sakala saṃsārā ।।

The Sun of the solar dynasty, Shri Ram, the natural fountain of joy, smiled within Himself and spoke words which were free from all blemish and were so sweet and agreeable that they seemed to be the very ornaments of speech; 'Listen, mother: that son alone is blessed, who is devoted to the words of his parents. A son who gratifies his father and mother is rare in this whole world, mother.'

मुनिगन मिलनु बिसेषि बन सबहि भाँति हित मोर ।
तेहि महँ पितु आयसु बहुरि संमत जननी तोर ॥[153]

munigana milanu biseṣi bana sabahi bhāṃti hita mora ।
tehi mahaṃ pitu āyasu bahuri saṃmata jananī tora ।।

'In the forest I shall get more opportunities of meeting hermits, which will be beneficial to me in everyway. On top of it, I have my father's command and your approval to boot, mother.'

भरतु प्रानप्रिय पावहिं राजू ।
बिधि सब बिधि मोहि सनमुख आजू ।।
जौं न जाउँ बन ऐसेहु काजा ।
प्रथम गनिअ मोहि मूढ़समाजा ।।[154]

Bharat prānapriya pāvahiṃ rājū ।
bidhi saba bidhi mohi sanamukha āju ।।
joṃ na jāuṃ bana aisehu kājā ।
prathama gania mohi mūḍhasamājā ।।

'Again, Bharat, who is dear to me as life, will get the sovereignty: God is propitious to me in every respect today. If I refuse to proceed to the woods even under such circumstances, I should be reckoned foremost in an assembly of fools.'

सेवहिं अरँडु कलपतरु त्यागी ।
परिहरि अमृत लेहिं बिषु मागी ।।
तेउ न पाइ अस समउ चुकाहीं ।
देखु बिचारि मातु मन माहीं ।।[155]

sevahiṃ araṃḍu kalapataru tyāgī ।
parihari amṛta lehiṃ biṣu māgī ।।
teu na pāi asa samau cukāhīṃ ।
dekhu bicāri mātu mana māhīṃ ।।

'Those who nurture a castor oil plant leaving the tree of paradise and barter away nectar for poison, they too will not lose an opportunity like this should they ever get it: ponder this fact in your mind and realise it, mother.'

अंब एक दुखु मोहि बिसेषी।
निपट बिकल नरनायकु देखी ॥
थोरिहिं बात पितहि दुख भारी ।
होति प्रतीति न मोहि महतारी ॥[156]

aṃba eka dukhu mohi biseṣī ।
nipaṭa bikala naranāyaku dekhī ।।
thorihiṃ bāta pitahi dukha bhārī ।
hoti pratīti na mohi mahatārī ।।

'Only one thing pains me most, mother; I am grieved to see the king sore distressed. That my father should be so overwhelmed with grief over a trifling matter is more than I can believe, dear mother.'

राउ धीर गुन उदधि अगाधू ।
भा मोहि तें कछु बड़अपराधू ॥
जातें मोहि न कहत कछु राऊ ।
मोरि सपथ तोहि कहु सतिभाऊ ॥[157]

rāu dhīra guna udadhi agādhū ।
bhā mohi te kachu baḍaaparādhū ।।
jāteṃ mohi na kahata kachu rāū ।
mori sapatha tohi kahu satibhāū ।।

'The king is stout of heart and a fathomless ocean of goodness; I must have committed some great offence, which prevents the king from speaking out his mind to me. I adjure you, therefore, to tell me the truth.'

सहज सकल रघुबर बचन कुमति कुटिल करि जान ।
चलइ जोंक जल बक्रगति जद्यपि सलिलु समान ॥[158]

sahaja sakala Raghubara bacana kumati kuṭila kari jāna ।
calai joṃka jala bakragati jadyapi salilu samāna ।।

The words of Shri Ram were artless and straight-forward, yet the evil-minded Kaikeyi took them to be otherwise. A leech must always move obliquely even though the water on which it moves has a smooth surface.

रहसी रानि राम रुख पाई ।
बोली कपट सनेहु जनाई ॥
सपथ तुम्हार भरत कै आना।
हेतु न दूसर मैं कछु जाना ॥[159]

rahasī rāni Rāma rukha pāī ।
bolī kapaṭa sanehu janāī ।।
sapatha tumhāra Bharat kai ānā ।
hetu na dūsara mai kachu jānā ।।

The queen rejoiced to find Shri Ram acquiescing to her proposal and said with a false show of affection, 'I swear by yourself and Bharat that no other cause of the king's affliction is known to me.'

तुम्ह अपराध जोगु नहिं ताता।
जननी जनक बंधु सुखदाता ॥
राम सत्य सबु जो कछु कहहू ।
तुम्ह पितु मातु बचन रत अहहू ॥[160]

tumha aparādha jogu nahiṃ tātā ।
jananī janaka baṃdhu sukhadātā ।।
Rāma satya sabu jo kachu kahahū ।
tumha pitu mātu bacana rata ahahū ।।

'You are not supposed to do any offence, dear son, a source of delight that you are to your parents and brothers. What you say is all true; you are devoted to the words of your father and mother.'

पितहि बुझाइ कहहु बलि सोई।
चौथेंपन जेहिं अजसु न होई॥
तुम्ह सम सुअन सुकृत जेहिं दीन्हे।
उचित न तासु निरादरु कीन्हे॥[161]

pitahi bujhāi kahahu bali soī ।
cauthempana jehiṃ ajasu na hoī ।।
tumha sama suana sukṛta jehiṃ dīnhe ।
ucita na tāsu nirādaru kīnhe ।।

'I adjure you to argue with your father that he may not incur opprobrium in the evening of his life. It is hardly desirable for him to disregard the virtues (truthfulness etc.) that have fetched him a son like you.'

लागहिं कुमुख बचन सुभ कैसे।
मगहँ गयादिक तीरथ जैसे॥
रामहि मातु बचन सब भाए।
जिमि सुरसरि गत सलिल सुहाए॥[162]

lāgahiṃ kumukha bacana subha kaise ।
Magahaṃ Gayādika tīratha jaise ।।
Rāmahi mātu bacana saba bhāe ।
jimi surasari gata salila suhāe ।।

These polite words adorned her detestable mouth even as sacred spots just as Gaya is situated in the accursed land of Magadha (south Bihar). All these words from His stepmother sounded pleasant to Ram in the same way as waters of all kinds are hallowed through their confluence with the holy Ganga.

The meeting between Kaikeyi and Ram is primarily important for demonstrating the *maryada purushottam* character of Ram, wherein he is portrayed as the very epitome of rectitude. The scene is dramatic in its setting: Kaikeyi viciously adamant in obtaining her desire for the banishment of Ram and the anointment of her own son, Bharat, on the throne of Ayodhya, and Ram, by stark contrast, calm and serene, soft-spoken, polite, free of rancour and obedient. Tulsi plays on this contrast most adeptly. The stronger is his description of the evil-minded and angry Kaikeyi—his exact words are that even cruelty itself would be outmatched by her, her tongue is a bow, her words arrows, and the target is Dashrath—the greater is his emphasis on Ram being the direct opposite. Kaikeyi is agitated, Ram is composed; Kaikeyi is wilful, Ram is, as is befitting a son, compliant; Kaikeyi is furious, Ram is tranquil and unruffled. In this depiction of contrasting personas, skillfully interwoven by Tulsi, he brings in another element, which is that of leela, or the play of the divine. Ram, as the omnipotent divinity, is aware of what is unfolding, but he participates in the drama as part of leela, the volitional circumscribing of the Almighty to be part of a temporal drama, without being in any way effected by it. To bring this element in, Tulsi says that Ram, the repose of unblemished and permanent joy—*anand nidhana*—smiles to himself in anticipation of Kaikeyi's onslaught, as proof that he is aware of it, above it, and free of any mortal emotions of anger or vengeance or conflict.

The maryada purushottam aspect of Ram's personality comes out best in the exchange between Kaikeyi and him. He asks her why Dashrath is so grief-stricken, and Kaikeyi says that the root problem is that Dashrath is much too partial to him—*sunahu Ram sab karana ehu, raju tumha par bohat sanehu.* To this, Ram's famous reply is: *sun janani soi sut bada bhagi, jo pitu maat bachan anuragi:* O mother, that son is blessed who has a chance to fulfil the wishes of his parents. In responding in this manner, Ram is at once elevated to another ethical dimension. He emerges as one who will do the correct thing, irrespective of the circumstances, or the consequences of such an action. Although he is being deprived of his rightful claim to the throne, and being punished with banishment to the forests for fourteen years, he will not waver from his ordained duty as a son to obey his parents. Nor will he bear any ill will towards his brother, Bharat. His behaviour and response will be solely guided by what should be done, and for this reason he is willing—notwithstanding the conspiracy of which he is a victim—to not only carry out the command of his parents, but also bear unmitigated love for his brother—an example of transcendental filial love—Bharat, whom, in Tulsi's words, he describes as *prana priya,* as beloved as his own life.

It is important to remember that Ram is venerated with such fervour by millions of devotees, precisely for his being maryada purushottam, and Tulsi has played a pivotal role in profiling and projecting this aspect of the Lord's character.

17. Dialogue Between Lakshman and Nishadraja

बोले लखन मधुर मृदु बानी।
ग्यान बिराग भगति रस सानी ॥
काहु न कोउ सुख दुख कर दाता।
निज कृत करम भोग सबु भ्राता ॥[163]

bole Lakhana madhura mṛdu bānī ।
gyāna birāga bhagati rasa sānī ।।
kāhu na kou sukha dukha kara dātā ।
nija kṛta karam bhoga sabu bhrātā ।।

Lakshman spoke to him sweet and gentle words imbued with the nectar of wisdom, dispassion and devotion: no one is a source of delight or pain to another; everyone reaps the fruit of one's own actions, brother.

जोग बियोग भोग भल मंदा।
हित अनहित मध्यम भ्रम फंदा ॥
जनमु मरनु जहँ लगि जग जालू।
संपति बिपति करमु अरु कालू ॥
धरनि धामु धनु पुर परिवारू।
सरगु नरकु जहँ लगि व्यवहारू ॥
देखिअ सुनिअ गुनिअ मन माहीं।
मोह मूल परमारथु नाहीं ॥[164]

joga biyoga bhoga bhala maṃdā ।
hita anahita madhyama bhram phaṃdā ।।
janamu maranu jahaṃ lagi jaga jālū ।
saṃpatī bipati karamu am kālū ।।
dharani dhāmu dhanu pura parivārū ।
saragu naraku jahaṃ lagi byavahārū ।।
dekhia sunia gunia mana māhīṃ ।
moha mūla paramārathu nāhīṃ ।।

Union and separation, pleasurable and painful experiences, friends and foes, are all snares of delusion. Even so birth and death, prosperity and adversity, destiny and time and all the illusion of the world; lands, houses, wealth, town and family, heaven and hell, and all the phenomena of the world; nay, whatever is seen, heard or thought of with the mind has its root in ignorance: nothing exists in reality.

सपनें होइ भिखारि नृपु रंकु नाकपति होइ।
जागें लाभु न हानि कछु तिमि प्रपंच जियँ जोइ॥[165]

sapanēṃ hoi bhikhāri nṛpa raṃku nākapati hoi ।
jāgeṃ lābhu na hāni kachu timi prapaṃca jiyaṃ joi ।।

Suppose in a dream a king becomes a pauper and a pauper becomes lord of paradise; on waking, the one does not gain nor does the other lose anything. So must you look upon this world.

अस बिचारि नहिं कीजिअ रोसू।
काहुहि बादि न देइअ दोसू।
मोह निसाँ सबु सोवनिहारा।
देखिअ सपन अनेक प्रकारा॥[166]

asa bicāri nahiṃ kījā rosū ।
kāhuhi bādi na deia dosū ।।
moha nisāṃ sabu sovanihārā ।
dekhia sapana aneka prakārā ।।

Reasoning thus, be not angry nor blame anyone in vain. Everyone is slumbering in the night of delusion, and while asleep one sees dreams of various kinds.

एहिं जग जामिनि जागहिं जोगी ।
परमारथी प्रपंच बियोगी ।।
जानिअ तबहिं जीव जग जागा ।
जब सब बिषय बिलास बिरागा ।।[167]

ehiṃ jaga jāmini jāgahiṃ jogī ।
paramārathī prapaṃca biyogī ।।
jānia tabahiṃ jīva jaga jāgā ।
jaba jaba biṣaya bilāsa birāgā ।।

In this night of mundane existence, it is yogis alone who keep awake—yogis who are in the quest of the highest truth and remain aloof from the world. A soul should be deemed as having awoke from the night of the world only when he develops an aversion for the enjoyments of the world of sense.

होइ बिबेकु मोह भ्रम भागा ।
तब रघुनाथ चरन अनुरागा ।।
सखा परम पमारथु एहू ।
मन क्रम बचन राम पद नेहू ।।[168]

hoi bibeku moha bhram bhāgā ।
taba Raghunātha carana anurāgā ।।
sakhā param paramārathu ehū ।
mana kram bacana Rāma pada nehū ।।

It is only when right understanding comes that the error of delusion disappears and then alone one develops love for the feet of Shri Ram (the Lord of Raghus). O friend, the highest spiritual goal is this: to be devoted to the feet of Shri Ram in thought, word and deed.

राम ब्रह्म परमारथ रूपा ।
अबिगत अलख अनादि अनूपा ।।
सकल बिकार रहित गतभेदा ।
कहि नित नेति निरूपहिं बेदा ।।[169]

Rāma Brahma paramāratha rūpā ।
abigata alakha anādi anūpā ।।
sakala bikāra rahita gatabhedā ।
kahi nita neti nirūpahiṃ Bedā ।

Shri Ram is no other than Brahma (God), the supreme Reality, unknown, imperceptible, beginningless, incomparable, free from all change and beyond all diversity. The Vedas ever speak of Him in negative terms (not this).

भगत भूमि भूसुर सुरभि सुर हित लागि कृपाल ।
करत चरित धरि मनुज तनु सुनत मिटहिं जग जाल ।।[170]

bhagat bhumi bhusur sur hit laagi kripala ।
karat carit dhari manuj tanu sunat mitaheen jan jaal ।।

For the sake of His devotees, Earth, the Brahmins, cows and gods, the gracious Lord takes the form of a man and performs actions by hearing of which the snares of the world are broken asunder.

This is an extremely important dialogue between Nishadraja and Lakshman. Nishadraja was the King of the boatmen, who ruled over the kingdom of Shringverpur (near Gorakhpur). He helped Ram, Sita and Lakshman to cross the Ganga. On exile, Ram spent the first night with the Nishadraja. The Nishadraja expressed his deep sorrow to see Ram and Sita sleeping on the ground in exile. To this lament, Tulsi chooses Lakshman to reply. Lakshman's reply is noteworthy for its transcendental detachment, *vairagya,* deep spiritual knowledge, *jnana,* and unqualified devotion to Ram, bhakti.

It is a little surprising that Tulsi chooses Lakshman to express these remarkably philosophical lines. In fact, the conventional and popular perception of Lakshman is that of a somewhat impulsive person—a counterpoint to the ever composed Ram—quick to take umbrage, forever ready for action, but not especially partial to such profound contemplative sermons. It is Lakshman who becomes unnecessarily agitated when news comes in that his half-brother, Bharat, is coming at the head of a large congregation to meet Ram in the forests. Lakshman is quick to come to the conclusion that Bharat's intentions are suspect, until Ram counsels him about Bharat's sterling character. He is also the person who in anger cuts off the nose of Ravana's sister, Surpanakha, when she tries to seduce Ram and insult Sita.

In mythology, the Puranas describe Lakshman as the incarnation of Shesha, the multi-headed naga upon whom Lord Vishnu rests in the primordial ocean of milk, kshirsagara. He is seen as a great warrior, who during the battle with Ravana, killed the demon's sons, Indrajit and Atikaya. The essential point is that Lakshman is notable for his unwavering devotion to Ram; he is seen as a mighty warrior quick to action, but is not particularly known for deep philosophical sermons. It is curious, therefore, that Tulsi chooses Lakshman to voice the thoughts expressed in these lines. Perhaps, his intention was to show that conventional images apart, those close to Ram—and Lakshman along with Sita were the closest—were spiritually very evolved and capable of speaking in the same language as Ram.

To Nishadraja's sadness at the suffering being endured by Ram and Sita, Lakshman says that nobody can be blamed for what others suffer because each of us is undergoing the consequences of our own karma. Worldly joys and tribulations—union and parting, good and bad experiences, wealth and deprivation, friends and enemies, birth and death—are but an illusion, shadows on the veil of Maya. We give undue importance to the normal paraphernalia of our ephemeral existence—land, home, money, family, town, heaven, hell—because of ignorance—*avidya* or *ajnana.* This avidya gives rise to incorrect appraisal, or an inaccuracy or dosha of perception. The world of objects is like a dream, and in that dream a king can become a beggar, and a beggar can become Indra—the King of the universe. When the dream ends, so does the charade of such conceptions. The great poet Mirza Ghalib expressed a similar thought in one of his couplets where he says: *Tha khwab mein khayal ko tujh se muamla, jab aankh khul gayi toh ziya tha na sood tha:* in dreams did my thoughts have a connect with you, when my eyes opened I was back where I was. At the ontological level there is only absolute Reality, which is above the *jagat prapancha*— the transient, unsubstantial distractions of the world. Once, through correct discrimination—viveka—we understand this truth, nothing else matters, the dosha of our perception is rectified, the *moha* or entanglement with worldly desires ends, and there is no reason left to resent what someone else has done.

It is then that with complete devotion we can surrender ourselves to the lotus-feet of Lord Ram. In decidedly Vedantic terms, Tulsi says that Ram is Brahman, the Ultimate Reality—*paramartha*—all-pervasive, beyond thought, sight, duality, comparison or time, whom the Vedas describe only as *'Neti, Neti'* (Not this, Not this). Here we see Tulsi reverting to the nirguna concept of Ram, when elsewhere he is emphatic in saying that Ram is saguna, the repository of all auspicious attributes. Either way, Lakshman's conclusion is to advocate the undisputed primacy of Ram, and the absolute importance of total surrender to him. This, he tells Nishadraja, is the only thing that matters, and the only means that can provide redemption from the sea of sorrows of this world. That is Tulsi's belief too, and after Lakshman's remarkable philosophical peroration—he uses him to unequivocally make this point.

18. The Form of Shri Ram-Sita and Lakshman in the Woods

आगें रामु लखनु बने पाछें।
तापस बेष बिराजत काछें॥
उभय बीच सिय सोहति कैसें।
ब्रह्म जीव बिच माया जैसें॥[171]

āge Rāmu Lakhanu bane pācheṃ ।
tāpasa beṣa birājata kācheṃ ।।
ubhaya bīca Siya sohati kaise ।
Brahma jīva bica māyā jaise ।।

Shri Ram walked in front while Lakshman followed in the rear, both conspicuous in the robes of ascetics. Between the two, Sita shone like Maya (the divine energy) that stands between Brahma (God), on the one hand, and the individual soul on the other.

बहुरि कहउँ छबि जसि मन बसई।
जनु मधु मदन मध्य रति लसई॥
उपमा बहुरि कहउँ जियँ जोही।
जनु बुध बिच रोहिनि सोही॥[172]

bahuri kahauṃ chabi jasi mana basaī ।
janu madhu Madana madhya Rati lasaī ।।
upamā bahuri kahauṃ jiyaṃ johī ।
janu Budha bidhu bica Rohini sohī ।।

To illustrate Her beauty as it exists in my mind in another way, She looked like Rati (the wife of the God of Love) shining between madhu (the spirit presiding over the vernal season) and the God of Love. Beating my brains for another illustration, let me say She shone like Rohini between Buddha and the Moon God.

An iconic image hugely popular with the ordinary Hindu is that of Ram, Sita and Lakshman, in the forests in exile, dressed in the clothes of ascetics. It is this image that Tulsi captures in these lines. The analogies that he gives to describe them are exceptionally important, not only for the visual image they conjure up, but also for their deep philosophical content.

In the first—and most significant—analogy, he says that the three of them are like Brahman, Maya, and the Jiva. Ram is Brahman; Sita is Maya; and Lakshman is Jiva. As Brahman, Ram is the omnipotent, omnipresent, omniscient cosmic consciousness. In Advaitic terms, he is *akhanda* (indivisible), *adrishta* (unseen), *achintya* (beyond thought), *kevala jnana* (infinite knowledge), *sarvapratyaya darshananin* (all-knowing intelligence), *nirvisheshchinmatram* (undifferentiated consciousness), nirguna (attributeless), and the supreme repository of *chid* (absolute awareness) and anand (absolute bliss). Avidya, or ignorance, at the individual level, is Maya at the cosmic level. But, Tulsi, in equating Sita to Maya, is not seeking to highlight the avidya aspect of Maya. In his mind it is Maya's description as the power inherent in Brahman. In fact, Adi Shankaracharya himself regards Maya—that mysterious but cosmic veil of illusion—as the *bija shakti*—the seed power—of Brahman. It is Brahman that empowers this creative power, much like a spider weaves a web from its own body. The ground for the distortion created by Maya, remains Brahman. As the Jagad Guru writes: 'Even when a snake, a silver, a mirage appears to rise, all these appearances are invariably found to be supported, in each case, by a sustaining ground on which they appear, viz., a rope, a shell, and the surface of the desert, unsupported by which these appearances cannot for a moment stand.'

The philosophical premise that Maya is the shakti inherent in Brahman, is the fundamental premise of Kashmir Shaivism, in particular.

If in Kashmir, Shiva is Brahman incarnate, for Tulsi, Ram is. Whether it is Shiva or Ram, both agree that the potentiality to create the phenomenal world was due to the shakti or Maya within Brahman.

Chaitanya Mahaprabhu (1486–1534), the Hindu mystic from Bengal who took Vaishnava bhakti to new heights, argued that divinity was characterised by several shaktis, the three principal ones being: jiva shakti, maya shakti and swarupa shakti. Individual souls were the emanations of the Lord's jiva shakti; the manifest world was a creation of his maya shakti; the expression of his own bliss was swarupa shakti. The relation between these shaktis or energies was one of *achintyabhedabheda*—inconceivable oneness and difference—wherein each was different, but all were one with Krishna, or in the case of Tulsi, with Ram. The jiva is the *bhokta,* who undergoes the cycle of karma, lives under the spell of avidya, mistaking the unreal for the Real, until it realises that it is actually one with Brahman, and is separated only due to an error of perception—*adhyasha.* In this way, it is, as Chaitanya postulates, an intrinsic part of the divinely supreme Brahman.

Apart from Advaita philosophy, Tulsi must have also been greatly influenced by Chaitanya, since they were near contemporaries, as Tulsi was born two years before the death of the Mahaprabhu. Thus, in this important analogy, Tulsi, in describing Ram as Brahman, Lakshman as Jiva, and Sita, in between, as Maya, is making the foundational point that although appearing different, they are all one with Brahman incarnate as Ram, and Sita is the philosophically causal link between the essential source, Brahman, and the Jiva. It is a beautiful analogy founded on profound metaphysical knowledge.

Compared to this analogy, Tulsi's other two descriptions are on a lighter level. In one he says that Sita is like Rati between Kamadeva and spring; and, in the other he compares Sita to Rohini (Chandram or the moon's wife) and Chandram's son Budha. In both cases, the attempt of the poet is to invoke an image of the threesome in exile in celestial terms, with a common thread connecting all three.

19. Dialogue Between Shri Ram and Valmiki

देखत बन सर सैल सुहाए।
बालमीकि आश्रम प्रभु आए॥
राम दीख मुनि बासु सुहावन।
सुंदर गिरि काननु जलु पावन॥[173]

dekhata bana sara saila suhāe ।
Bālamīki āśram prabhu āe ।।
rāma dīkha muni bāsu suhāvana ।
suṃdara giri kānanu jalu pāvana ।।

Beholding lovely woods, lakes and hills, the Lord reached the hermitage of Valmiki. Shri Ram saw the sage in beautiful dwelling with its charming hills and forest and its sacred waters.

सरनि सरोज बिटप बन फूले।
गुंजत मंजु मधुप रस भूले॥
खग मृग बिपुल कोलाहल करहीं।
बिरहित बैर मुदित मन चरहीं॥[174]

sarani saroja biṭapa bana phūle ।
guṃjata maṃju madhupa rasa bhūle ।।
khaga mṛga bipula kolāhala karahīṃ ।
birahita baira mudita mana carahīṃ ।।

The lotuses in the ponds and the trees in the woods were in blossom; intoxicated with their honey bees sweetly hummed over them. Birds and beasts made a tumultuous noise and moved about in joy free from all animosities.

सुचि सुंदर आश्रमु निरखि हरषे राजिवनेन ।
सुनि रघुबर आगमन मुनि आगें आयउ लेन ॥[175]

suci suṃdara āśramu nirakhi haraṣe rājivanena ।
suni Raghubara āgamanu muni āgeṃ āyau lena ।।

The lotus-eyed Ram rejoiced to behold the sacred and lovely hermitage; and hearing of the arrival of Shri Ram (the Chief of Raghu's line) the sage came forth to receive Him.

मुनि कहुँ राम दंडवत कीन्हा ।
आसिरबादु बिप्रबर दीन्हा ॥
देखि राम छबि नयन जुड़ाने ।
करि सनमानु आश्रमहिं आने ॥[176]

muni kahuṃ Rāma daṃḍavata kīnhā ।
āsirabādu biprabara dīnhā ।।
dekhi Rāma chabi nayana juḍaāne ।
kari sanamānu āśramhiṃ āne ।।

Shri Ram fell prostrate before the sage and the holy Brahmin blessed Him in return. The sight of Shri Rains beauty gladdened his eyes and with due honour he took the Lord into the hermitage.

मुनिबर अतिथि प्रानप्रिय पाए ।
कंद मूल फल मधुर मँगाए ॥
सिय सौमित्रि राम फल खाए ।
तब मुनि आश्रम दिए सुहाए ॥[177]

munibara atithi prānapriya pāe ।
kaṃda mūla phala madhura magāe ।।

Siya Saumitri Rāma phala khāe ।
taba muni āśRam die suhāe ।।

Finding a guest as dear to him as life itself, the holy sage sent for delicious bulbs, roots and fruits. Sita, Lakshman (Saumitra's son) and Ram partook of those fruits and the sage then assigned them beautiful quarters.

बालमीकि मन आनँदु भारी ।
मंगल मूरति नयन निहारी ॥
तब कर कमल जोरि रघुराई ।
बोले बचन श्रवन सुखदाई ॥[178]

Bālamīki mana ānaṃdu bhārī ।
maṃgala mūrati nayana nihārī ।।
taba kara kamala jori Raghurāī ।
bole bacana śravana sukhadāī ।।

Great was the joy of Valmiki's heart as he beheld with his own eyes Shri Ram, who was bliss personified. Joining His lotus palms the Lord of Raghus then spoke to him in words which were delightful to the ears.

तुम्ह त्रिकाल दरसी मुनिनाथा ।
बिस्व बदर जिमि तुम्हरें हाथा ॥
अस कहि प्रभु सब कथा बखानी ।
जेहि जेहि भाँति दीन्ह बनु रानी ॥[179]

tumha trikāla darasī munināthā ।
bisva badara jimi tumhareṃ hāthā ।।
asa kahi prabhu saba kathā bakhānī ।
jehi jehi bhāṃti dīnha banu rānī ।।

You directly perceive everything relating to the past, present and future, O lord of sages; the whole universe is as if berry in the palm of your hand. Saying so, the Lord related to him the whole story as to how the queen (Kaikeyi) had exiled Him into the woods.

तात बचन पुनि मातु हित भाइ भरत अस राउ ।
मो कहुँ दरस तुम्हार प्रभु सबु मम पुन्य प्रभाउ ।।[180]

tāta bacana puni mātu hita bhāi Bharat asa rāu ।
mo kahuṃ darasa tumhāra prabhu sabu mama punya prabhāu ।।

Compliance with my father's commands, gratification of my stepmother (Kaikeyi), the installation of a brother like Bharat to the throne and my seeing you all this, my lord, is the result of my meritorious acts.

देखि पाय मुनिराय तुम्हारे ।
भए सुकृत सब सुफल हमारे ।।
अब जहँ राउर आयसु होई ।
मुनि उदबेगु न पावै कोई ।।[181]

dekhi pāya munirāya tumhāre ।
bhae sukṛta saba suphala hamāre ।।
aba jahaṃ rāura āyasu hoī ।
muni udabegu na pāvai koī ।।

In beholding your feet, O king of sages, all my good deeds have been rewarded. Now I intend to go wherever you command me to go and where no anchorite may feel disturbed.

मुनि तापस जिन्ह तें दुखु लहहीं ।
ते नरेस बिनु पावक दहहीं ।।
मंगल मूल बिप्र परितोषू ।
दहइ कोटि कुल भूसुर रोषू ।।[182]

muni tāpasa jinha teṃ dukhu lahahīṃ ।
te naresa binu pāvaka dahahīṃ ।।
maṃgala mūla bipra paritoṣū ।
dahai koṭi kula bhūsura roṣū ।।

For such monarchs as prove a source of annoyance to hermits and ascetics are consumed without fire. While the satisfaction of Brahmins is the root of happiness, their wrath consumes millions of generations.

अस जियँ जानि कहिअ सोइ ठाऊँ ।
सिय सौमित्रि सहित जहँ जाऊँ ॥
तहँ रचि रुचिर परन तृन साला ।
बासु करौं कछु काल कृपाला ॥[183]

asa jiyaṃ jāni kahia soi ṭhāūṃ ।
Siya Saumitri sahita jahaṃ jāūṃ ।।
tahaṃ raci rucira parana tṛna sālā ।
bāsu karau kachu kāla kṛpālā ।।

Bearing this in mind, pray tell me a place to which I may proceed with Sita and Lakshman, and building a charming hut of leaves and grass may spend some time there, O good sir.

सहज सरल सुनि रघुबर बानी ।
साधु साधु बोले मुनि ग्यानी ॥
कस न कहहु अस रघुकुलकेतू ।
तुम्ह पालक संतत श्रुति सेतू ॥[184]

sahaja sarala suni Raghubara bānī ।
sādhu sādhu bole muni gyānī ।।
kasa na kahahu asa Raghukulaketū ।
tumha pālaka saṃtata śruti setū ।।

Hearing these guileless and unsophisticated words of Shri Ram (the Chief of Raghu's line) the enlightened sage exclaimed, 'Quite so, right You are. Why should You not speak thus, O Glory of Raghu's line, ever busy as You are in maintaining the laws laid down by the Vedas?'

श्रुति सेतु पालक राम तुम्ह जगदीस माया जानकी ।
जो सृजति जगु पालति हरति रुख पाइ कृपानिधान की ॥

जो सहससीसु अहीसु महिधरु लखनु सचराचर धनी ।
सुर काज धरि नरराज तनु चले दलन खल निसिचर अनी ॥[185]

śruti setu pālaka Rāma tumha jagadīsa māyā Jānakī ।
jo sṛjati jagu pālati harati rūkha pāi kṛpānidhāna kī ।।
jo sahasasīsu ahīsu mahidharu Lakhanu sacarācara dhanī ।
sura kāja dhari nararāja tanu cale dalana khala nisicara anī ।।

'While You are the custodian of the Vedic laws and the Lord of the universe, Sita (Janak's daughter) is Your Maya (divine energy) who creates, preserves and dissolves the universe on receiving the tacit approval of Your gracious Self. As for Lakshman, he is no other than the thousand-headed Shesha (the lord of serpents), the supporter of the globe and the lord of the entire creation, both animate and inanimate. Having assumed the form of a king for the sake of the gods, You are out to crush the host of wicked demons.'

राम सरूप तुम्हार बचन अगोचर बुद्धिपर ।
अबिगत अकथ अपार नेति नेति नित निगम कह ॥[186]

Rāma sarupa tumhāra bacana agocara buddhipara ।
abigata akatha apāra neti nita nigama kaha ।।

'Tour Being, O Ram, is beyond the range of speech and beyond conception, unknown, unutterable and infinite; the Vedas ever speak of It as "Not that, Not that".'

जगु पेखन तुम्ह देखनिहारे ।
बिधि हरि संभु नचावनिहारे ॥
तेउ न जानहिं मरमु तुम्हारा ।
और तुम्हहि को जाननिहारा ॥[187]

jagu pekhana tumha dekhanihāre ।
bidhi Hari Saṃbhu nacāvanihāre ।।

teu na jānahiṃ maramu tumhārā ।
auru tumhahi ko jānanihārā ।।

This world is a spectacle and You are its spectator; nay, You make even Brahma (the Creator), Vishnu (the Preserver) and Shambhu (the Destroyer) dance to Your tune. Even these latter know not Your secret; who else can know You?

सोइ जानइ जेहि देहु जनाई।
जानत तुम्हहि तुम्हइ होइ जाई।।
तुम्हरिहि कृपाँ तुम्हहि रघुनंदन।
जानहिं भगत भगत उर चंदन।।[188]

soi jānai jehi dehu janāī ।
jānata tumhahi tumhai hoi jāī ।।
tumharihi kṛpāṃ tumhahi Raghunaṃdana ।
jānahiṃ bhagata bhagata ura caṃdana ।।

In fact, he alone can know You, to whom You make Yourself known; and the moment he knows You, he becomes one with You. It is by Your grace, O Delighter of Raghus, that Your votaries come to know You, O comforter of the heart of devotees.

चिदानंदमय देह तुम्हारी।
बिगत बिकार जान अधिकारी।।
नर तनु धरेहु संत सुर काजा।
कहहु करहु जस प्राकृत राजा।। 189

cidānaṃdamaya deha tumhārī ।
bigata bikāra jāna adhikārī ।।
nara tanu dharehu saṃta sura kājā ।
kahahu karahu jasa prākṛta rājā ।।

Your body is all consciousness and bliss and is devoid of change; it is the competent alone who realise this. It is for the sake of saints and gods that

You have assumed a human semblance and speak and act even as worldly monarchs do.

राम देखि सुनि चरित तुम्हारे।
जड़मोहहिं बुध होहिं सुखारे॥
तुम्ह जो कहहु करहु सबु साँचा।
जस काछिअ तस चाहिअ नाचा॥ [190]

Rāma dekhi suni carita tumhāre ।
jaḍamohahiṃ budha hohiṃ sukhāre ।।
tumha jo kahahu karahu sabu sāṃcā ।
jasa kāchia tasa cāhia nācā ।।

The stupid get puzzled while the wise feel delighted when they see or hear of Your doings. All that You say or do is true; for one should play the role one has assumed on the stage.

पूँछेहु मोहि कि रहौं कहँ मैं पूँछत सकुचाउँ।
जहँ न होहु तहँ देहु कहि तुम्हहि देखावौं ठाउँ॥[191]

pūṃchehu mohi ki rahauṃ kahaṃ maim pūṃchata sakucāuṃ ।
jahaṃ na hohu tahaṃ dehu kahi tumhahi dekhāvauṃ ṭhāuṃ ।।

'You ask me: "Where should I take up my residence?" But I ask You with diffidence: tell me first the place where You are not; then alone I can show You a suitable place.'

सुनि मुनि बचन प्रेम रस साने।
सकुचि राम मन महुँ मुसुकाने॥
बालमीकि हँसि कहहिं बहोरी।
बानी मधुर अमिअ रस बोरी॥[192]

suni muni bacana prema rasa sāne ।
sakuci Rāma mana mahuṃ musukāne ।।

Bālamīki haṃsi kahahiṃ bahorī ।
bānī madhura amia rasa borī ।।

On hearing the sage's words, imbued as they were with love, Shri Ram felt abashed and smiled within Himself. Valmiki too smiled and spoke to Him again in words as sweet as though they were steeped in nectar:

सुनहु राम अब कहउँ निकेता ।
जहाँ बसहु सिय लखन समेता ॥
जिन्ह के श्रवन समुद्र समाना ।
कथा तुम्हारि सुभग सरि नाना ॥
भरहिं निरंतर होहिं न पूरे ।
तिन्ह के हिय तुम्ह कहुँ गुह रूरे ॥
लोचन चातक जिन्ह करि राखे ।
रहहिं दरस जलधर अभिलाषे ॥
निदरहिं सरित सिंधु सर भारी ।
रूप बिंदु जल होहिं सुखारी ॥
तिन्ह के हृदय सदन सुखदायक ।
बसहु बंधु सिय सह रघुनायक ॥[193]

sunahu Rāma aba kahauṃ niketā ।
jahāṃ basahu Siya Lakhana sametā ।।
jinha ke śravana samudra samānā ।
kathā tumhāri subhaga sari nānā ।।
bharahiṃ niraṃtara hohiṃ na pūre ।
tinha ke hiya tumha kahuṃ gṛha rūre ।।
locana cātaka jinha kari rākhe ।
rahahiṃ darasa jaladhara abhilāṣe ।।
nidarahiṃ sarita siṃdhu sara bhārī ।
rūpa biṃdu jala hohiṃ sukhārī ।।
tinha ke hṛdaya sadana sukhadāyaka ।
basahu baṃdhu Siya saha Raghunāyaka ।।

'Listen, Ram: I tell You now the places where You should abide with Sita and Lakshman. The heart of those whose ears are like the ocean, constantly replenished with a number of lovely streams in the shape of Your stories but know no surfeit, shall be Your charming abode. Just as Chataka always longs to see the rain clouds, disdaining all big rivers, oceans and lakes and prefers only drops of rain clouds. Similarly, those whose eyes are always laying for Your beautiful vision disdain all worldly comforts and always lay for a glimpse of Your beauty in their hearts, there is a comfortable abode for You to live in alongwith Lakshman and Sita.'

जसु तुम्हार मानस बिमल हंसिनि जीहा जासु।
मुकताहल गुन गन चुनइ राम बसहु हियँ तासु ॥[194]

jasu tumhāra Mānasa bimala haṃsini jīhā jāsu ।
mukutāhala guna gana cunai rāma basahu hiyaṃ tāsu ।।

'Nay, You should dwell in the heart of him whose swan-like tongue picks up pearls in the shape of Your virtues in the holy Manasarovara lake of Your fame.'

प्रभु प्रसाद सुचि सुभग सुबासा।
सादर जासु लहइ नित नासा ॥
तुम्हहि निबेदित भोजन करहीं।
प्रभु प्रसाद पट भूषन धरहीं ॥[195]

सीस नवहिं सुर गुरु द्विज देखी।
प्रीति सहित करि बिनय बिसेषी ॥
कर नित करहिं राम पद पूजा।
राम भरोस हृदयँ नहिं दूजा ॥[196]

चरन राम तीरथ चलि जाहीं।
राम बसहु तिन्ह के मन माहीं ॥
मंत्रराजु नित जपहिं तुम्हारा।
पूजहि तुम्हहि सहित परिवारा ॥[197]
तरपन होम करहिं बिधि नाना।
बिप्र जेवाँइदेहिं बहु दाना ॥

तुम्ह तें अधिक गुरहि जियँ जानी ।
सकल भायँ सेवहिं सनमानी ॥[198]

prabhu prasāda suci subhaga subāsā ।
sādara jāsu lahai nita nāsā ।।
tumhahi nibedita bhojana karahīṃ ।
prabhu prasāda paṭa bhūṣana dharahīṃ ।।

sīsa navahiṃ sura guru dvija dekhī ।
prīti sahita kari binaya biseṣī ।।
kara nita karahiṃ Rāma pada pūjā ।
Rāma bharosa hṛdayaṃ nahi dūjā ।।

carana Rāma tīratha cali jāhīṃ ।
Rāma basahu tinha ke mana māhīṃ ।।
maṃtrarāju nita japahiṃ tumhārā ।
pūjahiṃ tumhahi sahita parivārā ।।

tarapana homa karahiṃ bidhi nānā ।
bipra jevāṃi dehiṃ bahu dānā ।।
tumha teṃ adhika gurahi jiyaṃ jānī ।
sakala bhāyaṃ sevahiṃ sanamānī ।।

'Abide, O Ram, in the mind of those whose nose devoutly inhales everyday the fragrance of sacred and lovely offerings (in the shape of flowers, sandal-paste, etc.,) made to their Lord (Yourself), who eat only that which has been offered to You and put on clothes and ornaments first dedicated to You, whose heads bow down most submissively and lovingly at the sight of a god, preceptor or Brahmin, whose hands adore Shri Ram's feet everyday, who cherish in their heart faith in Ram and none else, and whose feet take them to holy places sacred to Ram. Again, those who are ever engaged in muttering the Ram mantra *(Shri Ramya Namah),* the king of all sacred formulas, and worship You alongwith Your associates; who offer water to the manes and pour oblations into the sacred fire in diverse ways, who feed the Brahmins and bestow liberal gifts on them and who look upon their preceptor as greater than Yourself and wait upon him with due honour and entire devotion.'

सबु करि मागहिं एक फलु राम चरन रति होउ।
तिन्ह कें मन मंदिर बसहु सिय रघुनंदन दोउ ॥[199]

sabu kari māgahiṃ eka phalu rāma carana rati hou ।
tinha keṃ mana maṃdira basahu Siya Raghunaṃdana dou ॥

And who having done all this ask only one boon as their reward: 'Let me have devotion to Shri Ram's feet!'—enthrone Yourself in the temple of their heart, both Sita and the Delighter of Raghus (Yourself).

काम कोह मद मान न मोहा।
लोभ न छोभ न राग न द्रोहा ॥
जिन्ह कें कपट दंभ नहिं माया।
तिन्ह के हृदय बसहु रघुराया ॥[200]

kāma koha mada māna na mohā ।
lobha na chobha na rāga na drohā ॥
jinha keṃ kapaṭa daṃbha nahiṃ māyā ।
tinha keṃ hṛdaya basahu Raghurāyā ॥

Those who have no lust, anger, arrogance, pride or infatuation, are without greed, excitement, attraction or aversion and who are free from fraud, hypocrisy and deceit, it is in their heart that You should abide, O Chief of Raghus.

सब के प्रिय सब के हितकारी।
दुख सुख सरिस प्रसंसा गारी ॥
कहहिं सत्य प्रिय बचन बिचारी।
जागत सोवत सरन तुम्हारी ॥
तुम्हहि छाड़ि गति दूसरि नाहीं।
राम बसहु तिन्ह के मन माहीं ॥

जननी सम जानहिं परनारी।
धनु पराव बिष तें बिष भारी ॥
जे हरषहिं पर संपति देखी।
दुखित होहिं पर बिपति बिसेषी ॥
जिन्हहि राम तुम्ह प्रानपिआरे।
तिन्ह के मन सुभ सदन तुम्हारे ॥[201]

saba ke priya saba ke hitakārī ।
dukha sukha sarisa prasaṃsā gārī ।।
kahahiṃ satya priya bacana bicārī ।
jāgata sovata sarana tumhārī ।।
tumhahi chāḍi gati dūsari nāhīṃ ।
Rāma basahu tinha ke mana māhīṃ ।।
jananī sama jānahiṃ paranārī ।
dhanu parāva biṣa teṃ biṣa bhārī ।।
je haraṣahiṃ para saṃpati dekhī ।
dukhita hohiṃ para bipati biseṣī ।।
jinhahi Rāma tumha prānapiāre ।
tinha ke mana subha sadana tumhāre ।।

Again, those who are beloved of all and friendly to all, to whom joy and sorrow, applause and abuse are alike and who scrupulously utter truthful and polite words, nay, who are resigned to You whether awake or asleep and who have no support other than Yourself—it is in their mind, O Ram, that You should dwell. Again, those who look upon another's wife as their own mother and to whom another's wealth is the deadliest of all poisons, who rejoice to see others' prosperity and are particularly grieved to see another's distress, and to whom, O Ram, You are dear as their own life—their minds are Your blessed abodes.

स्वामि सखा पितु मातु गुर जिन्ह के सब तुम्ह तात।
मन मंदिर तिन्ह कें बसहु सीय सहित दोउ भ्रात ॥[202]

svāmi sakhā pitu mātu gura jinha ke saba tumha tāta ।
mana maṃdira tinha keṃ basahu Sīya sahita dou bhrāta ।।

'Nay, those to whom, my dear, You are at once master and companion, father and mother, preceptor and everything else—it is in the temple of their mind that Sita and you two brothers should reside.'

अवगुन तजि सब के गुन गहहीं।
बिप्र धेनु हित संकट सहहीं॥
नीति निपुन जिन्ह कइ जग लीका॥
घर तुम्हार तिन्ह कर मनु नीका॥[203]

avaguna taji saba ke guna gahahīṃ ।
bipra dhenu hita saṃkaṭa sahahīṃ ।।
nīti nipuna jinha kai jaga līkā ।
ghara tumhāra tinha kara manu nīkā ।।

Those who overlook others' faults and pick out their virtues and endure hardships for the sake of the Brahmins and cows, nay, who have established their reputation in the world as well-versed in the laws of propriety, their mind is Your excellent abode.

गुन तुम्हार समुझइ निज दोसा।
जेहि सब भाँति तुम्हार भरोसा॥
राम भगत प्रिय लागहिं जेही।
तेहि उर बसहु सहित बैदेही॥[204]

guna tumhāra samujhai nija dosā ।
jehi saba bhāṃti tumhāra bharosā ।।
Rāma bhagata priya lāgahiṃ jehī ।
tehi ura basahu sahita Baidehī ।।

Again, he who attributes his virtues to You and holds himself responsible for his faults, nay, who entirely depends on You and loves Shri Ram's (Your) devotees, it is in his heart that You should stay alongwith Videha's daughter (Sita).

जाति पाँति धनु धरमु बड़ाई।
प्रिय परिवार सदन सुखदाई॥
सब तजि तुम्हहि रहइ उर लाई।
तेहि के हृदयँ रहहु रघुराई॥[205]

jāti pāṃti dhanu dharam baḍāī ।
priya parivāra sadana sukhadāī ॥
saba taji tumhahi rahai ura lāī ।
tehi ke hṛdayaṃ rahahu Raghurāī ॥

He who, renouncing his caste and kinsmen, wealth, faith and glory, his near and dear ones, his happy home and everything else, cherishes You in his bosom—in his heart, You should take up Your residence, O Lord of the Raghus.

सरगु नरकु अपबरगु समाना।
जहँ तहँ देख धरें धनु बाना॥
करम बचन मन राउर चेरा।
राम करहु तेहि कें उर डेरा॥[206]

saragu naraku apabaragu samānā ।
jahaṃ tahaṃ dekha dhareṃ dhanu bānā ॥
karam bacana mana rāura cerā ।
Rāma karahu tehi keṃ ura ḍerā ॥

Again, he to whom heaven and hell and even freedom from birth and death are the same in as much as he beholds You armed with a bow and arrow here, there and everywhere, and who is Your servant in thought, word and deed, make his heart, O Ram, Your permanent abode.

जाहि न चाहिअ कबहुँ कछु तुम्ह सन सहज सनेहु।
बसहु निरंतर तासु मन सो राउर निज गेहु॥[207]

jāhi na cāhia kabahuṃ kachu tumha sana sahaja sanehu ।
basahu niraṃtara tāsu mana so rāura nija gehu ॥

'Lastly, he who never wants anything and bears natural affinity to You, incessantly dwell in his mind; for that is Your own home.'

This dialogue between Ram and Valmiki must rank as one of the most evocative expressions of devotion and surrender to the Lord. Valmiki is not only a revered sage, but is recognised as the Adi Kavi, the first Sanskrit poet who wrote the epic Ramayana, dated around the fifth century BCE, with the blessings, it is believed, of Lord Brahma. Ram meets him in exile in the forests, and Valmiki with great love and devotion welcomes him to his ashram. It is Valmiki too, who much later, gives refuge to Sita when she is banished by Ram from Ayodhya. Sita gives birth to her twin sons— Lava and Kusha—in the ashram of Valmiki. Many people regard Tulsi as the reincarnation of Valmiki.

As maryada purushottam, Ram greets Valmiki with every correct and appropriate salutation, including prostrating himself at the sage's feet. Tulsi describes Valmiki's great joy in Ram visiting his ashram. The sub-text of this entire meeting is that Valmiki knows that Ram is the Almighty incarnate, and Ram knows that Valmiki knows. In fact, at one point of the narrative, Ram smiles to himself, wondering whether Valmiki who knows the truth behind this entire human charade, may not reveal it. In a sense then, this dialogue is between two people who don't need to speak at all, but Tulsi needs them to because they are instruments in the poet's hand to articulate Tulsi's own devotional ardour.

The dramatic content of this exchange lies in Ram asking Valmiki's advice on where he could build a small hut—*kuti*—to live while in exile. This question, of the Lord of the universe asking where he should stay, is a part of the leela or play of divinity, where the omnipotent too has to act a part of want and seeking, when, in fact, the earth itself is his emanation, and there is nothing that he needs to seek.

Valmiki's answer to this question—laughable at one level but seriously asked at another—is the distinguishing feature of this prasang. As is normal with Tulsi, he first makes Valmiki pay tribute to Ram in his nirguna form. To acknowledge Ram as Brahman— beyond speech, beyond intellect, inexpressible, beyond description, immeasurable, and describable only by the label—Not this, Not this, Neti, Neti—was a ploy Tulsi uses often, before he opens the floodgates of the worship of Ram as saguna, a personal and accessible god with all his divine attributes.

Valmiki then asks a series of questions which play on the request of Ram for guidance as to where he should build his kuti. What is the place, Valmiki asks Ram, where you are not present for me to tell you where you should reside? For the god, for whom the entire world is like a fruit on his palm, there is no dearth of place, but Valmiki says that he will still try and indicate where it should be: in the heart and mind of his devotees. Valmiki then takes this argument forward. What kind of devotee should it be whose heart and mind can provide the place for Ram to reside? In describing such a devotee, Tulsi gives full vent to his absolute devotion to Ram. The devotee who in sleep or while awake thinks only of Ram, who has no other refuge but Ram, whose friend, guru, father and mother is Ram, who rises above caste, creed, wealth, faith, praise, family and home to only keep Ram in his heart, who asks for nothing for himself and has a natural love only for Ram—that is the kind of devotee in whose heart and mind Ram must reside.

To this outpouring of complete devotion, Tulsi, through Valmiki, adds an ethical dimension too. Devotion, although pivotal, is not enough. The devotee must also have some qualities. He should rejoice at the well-being of others, and be pained by the affliction of others, he should reject all that is unethical and adopt all good qualities, and he should be recognised for his 'maryada', correct behaviour, in all matters of law and social interaction—*niti.* In other words, maryada purushottam Ram, the epitome of rectitude, must also have devotees who strive to emulate his qualities, for only then do devotion and right conduct combine to create the ideal place for the Lord to reside. This emphasis on ethicality is also Tulsi's way of paying obeisance to Ram, who is ethics personified.

20. Dialogue Between Sumantra and Dashrath

जनम मरन सब दुख सुख भोगा ।
हानि लाभु प्रिय मिलन बियोगा ॥
काल करम बस होहिं गोसाईं ।
बरबस राति दिवस की नाई ॥[208]

janama marana saba dukha sukha bhogā ।
hāni lābha priya milana biyogā ।।
kāla karam basa hauhiṃ gosāīṃ ।
barabasa rāti divasa kī nāīṃ ।।

Birth and death, all painful and pleasurable experiences, loss and gain, union with and separation from friends—all these, my lord, take place under the unalterable laws of time and destiny like the succession of night and day.

सुख हरषहिं जड़ दुख बिलखाहीं ।
दोउ सम धीर धरहिं मन माहीं ॥
धीरज धरहु बिबेकु बिचारी ।
छाड़िअ सोच सकल हितकारी ॥[209]

sukha haraṣahiṃ jaḍadukha bilakhāhīṃ ।
dou sama dhīra dharahiṃ mana māhīṃ ।।
dhīraja dharahu bibeku bicārī ।
chāḍia soca sakala hitakārī ।।

Fools rejoice in prosperity and mourn in adversity; while the wise account both alike. Therefore, exercising your mature judgement take up courage and cease sorrowing, O friend of all.

This nugget of just two chaupais is included to provide a window to the profound philosophical insights that are a constant sub-text to Tulsi's narrative of Ram. Here, the context is a grieving Dashrath, whose eldest son and heir, Ram, has just been banished from the kingdom on a fourteen-year exile, due to the vow redeemed by Kaikeyi, Dashrath's second queen, who wants her own son, Bharat, to succeed to the throne. Sumantra, Dashrath's minister and chief counsellor, is seeking to console his king. It was Sumantra who had tried to convince Kaikeyi not to carry out her vicious plan, but in vain. It was he who then drove Ram, Sita and Lakshman out of Ayodhya in the royal chariot, to begin their period of exile.

Sumantra, in a deeply contemplative note, advises Dashrath that the vicissitudes and achievements of life are but a factor of the play of time and karma—our previous actions and their consequences. Birth-death, happiness-sorrow, profit-loss, union-parting—all of these must inevitably be linked to each other even as night is linked with day. Only the foolish become uncontrollably happy when the going is good, or hopelessly cry when things go wrong. Those with fortitude, understanding the root cause behind such happenings, face the ups and downs of life with enlightened stoicism. Thus, Sumantra advises Dashrath that the king should abstain from sorrow, and retain his fortitude.

Tulsi's purpose in bringing in different dramatic personae like Sumantra to propound such eternal verities is to demonstrate the philosophical roots that are the sub-stratum of the Hindu world view. He also wishes to indicate the high intellectual and ethical quality of the kingdom of Koshala, whose ministers are of such high calibre. If the ministers are of such integrity and wisdom, it can only be imagined what must be the quality of the royal family itself and, at its very centre, that of Ram.

21. Dialogue Between Sage Vasishtha and Bharat

सुनहु भरत भावी प्रबल बिलखि कहेउ मुनिनाथ।
हानि लाभु जीवनु मरनु जसु अपजसु बिधि हाथ॥[210]

sunahu Bharat bhāvī prabala bilakhi kaheu muninātha ।
hāni lābhu jīvana maranu jasu apajasu bidhi hātha ।।

'Listen, Bharat: formidable is fate!' the lord of sages sorrowfully exclaimed. 'Loss and gain, life and death, glory and infamy—all these lie in the hands of Providence.'

सोचिअ बिप्र जो बेद बिहीना।
तजि निज धरमु बिषय लयलीना॥
सोचिअ नृपति जो नीति न जाना।
जेहि न प्रजा प्रिय प्रान समाना॥
सोचिअ बयसु कृपन धनवानू।
जो न अतिथि सिव भगति सुजानू॥
सोचिअ सूद्रु बिप्र अवमानी।
मुखर मानप्रिय ग्यान गुमानी॥
सोचिअ पुनि पति बंचक नारी।
कुटिल कलहप्रिय इच्छाचारी॥
सोचिअ बटु निज ब्रत परिहरई।
जो नहिं गुर आयसु अनुसरई॥[211]

socia bipra jo Beda bihīnā ।
taji nija dharamu biṣaya layalīnā ।।
socia nṛpati jo nīti na jānā ।
jehi na prajā priya prāna samānā ।।
socia bayasu kṛpana dhanavānū ।
jo na atithi Siva bhagati sujānū ।।
socia sūdru bipra avamānī ।
mukhara mānapriya gyāna gumānī ।।
socia puni pati baṃcaka nārī ।
kuṭila kalahapriya icchācārī ।।
socia baṭu nija bratu pariharaī ।
jo nahiṃ gura āyasu anusaraī ।।

'Pitiable is the Brahmin who is ignorant of the Vedas, and who has abandoned his own duty and is engrossed in the pleasures of sense; pitiable the king who has no knowledge of polity and who does not love his people as his own life: pitiable the Vaishya (a member of the trading class) who is niggardly though rich, and who is not perfect in hospitality nor in devotion to Lord Shiva; pitiable the Shudra (a member of the labouring or artisan class) who is disrespectful towards the Brahmins, loquacious and proud of his knowledge and loves to be honoured. Pitiable, again, is the woman who deceives her husband, is crooked and quarrelsome and follows her own will; pitiable the religious student who breaks his vow and obeys not the orders of his preceptor.'

सोचिअ गृही जो मोह बस करइ करम पथ त्याग।
सोचिअ जती प्रपंच रत बिगत बिबेक बिराग॥[212]

socia gṛhī jo moha basa karai karam patha tyāga ।
socia jati praṃpaca rata bigata bibeka birāga ।।

Nay, pitiable is the householder who out of ignorance forsakes the path of duty, and pitiable the recluse who is attached to the world and lacks discretion and dispassion.

बैखानस सोइ सोचौ जोगू ।
तपु बिहाइ जेहि भावइ भोगू ॥
सोचिअ पिसुन अकारन क्रोधी ।
जननि जनक गुर बंधु बिरोधी ॥[213]

baikhānasa soi socai jogu ।
tapu bihāi jehi bhāvai bhogū ।।
socia pisuna akārana krodhī ।
janani janaka gura baṃdhu birodhī ।।

Pitiable is the anchorite who has given up penance and developed a liking for luxuries; pitiable the backbiter who is angry without cause and an enemy of his own parents, preceptor and brothers.

सब बिधि सोचिअ पर अपकारी ।
निज तनु पोषक निरदय भारी ॥
सोचनीय सबहीं बिधि सोई ।
जो न छाड़ि छलु हरि जन होई ॥[214]

saba bidhi socia para apakārī ।
nija tanu poṣaka niradaya bhārī ।।
socanīya sabahi bidhi soī ।
jo na chāḍi chalu Hari jana hoī ।।

Pitiable in every way is he who harms others, cherishes his own body and is exceedingly heartless. And pitiable in every respect is he who is not sincerely devoted to Shri Hari.

सोचनीय नहिं कोसलराऊ ।
भुवन चारिदस प्रगट प्रभाऊ ॥
भयउ न अहइ न अब होनिहारा ।
भूप भरत जस पिता तुम्हारा ॥[215]

socanīya nahiṃ Kosalarāū ।
bhuvana cāridasa pragaṭa prabhāū ।।

bhayau na ahai na aba honihārā ।
bhūpa Bharat jasa pitā tumhārā ।।

The lord of Kosala is not worth grieving for, his glory being manifest through all the fourteen spheres. There never was, nor is, nor shall be hereafter, a monarch like your father, Bharat.

बिधि हरि हरु सुरपति दिसिनाथा ।
बरनहिं सब दसरथ गुन गाथा ।।[216]

Bidhi Hari Haru surapati disināthā ।
baranahiṃ saba dasaratha guna gāthā ।।

Brahma, Vishnu, Shiva, Indra (the lord of celestials) and the guardians of the quarters, all sing praises of King Dashrath.

अनुचित उचित बिचारु तजि ते पालहिं पितु बैन ।
ते भाजन सुख सुजस के बसहिं अमरपति ऐन ।। [217]

anucita ucita bicāru taji je pālahiṃ pitu baina ।
te bhājana sukha sujasa ke basahiṃ amarapati aina ।।

Those who cherish their father's word, minding not whether it is reasonable or otherwise, attain happiness and fair renown and dwell in the abode of Indra (the lord of immortals).

अवसि नरेस बचन फुर करहू ।
पालहु प्रजा सोकु परिहरहू ।।
सुरपुर नृपु पाइहि परितोषू ।
तुम्ह कहुँ सुकृतु सुजसु नहिं दोषू ।।[218]

avasi naresa bacana phura karahū ।
pālahu prajā soku pariharahū ।।
surapura nṛpa pāihi paritoṣū ।
tumha kahuṃ sukṛta sujasu nahiṃ doṣū ।।

Therefore, you must redeem the king's word; cherish your subjects and cease to grieve. The king in heaven will derive solace, while you will earn merit and good fame and shall incur no blame.

बेद बिदित संमत सबही का।
जेहि पितु देइ सो पावर टीका॥
करहु राजु परिहरहु गलानी।
मानहु मोर बचन हित जानी॥[219]

Beda bidita saṃmata sabahī kā ।
jehi pitu dei so pāvai ṭīkā ।।
karahu rāju pariharahu galānī ।
mānahu mora bacana hita jānī ।।

It is well known in the Vedas and has the sanction of all that the crown goes to him on whom the father bestows it. Therefore, rule the kingdom, feel no remorse and accept my advice as salutary.

सुनि सुख लहब राम बैदेहीं।
अनुचित कहब न पंडित केहीं॥
कौसल्यादि सकल महतारीं।
तेउ प्रजा सुख होहिं सुखारीं॥[220]

suni sukhu lahaba Rāma Baidehīṃ ।
anucita kahaba na paṃḍita kehīṃ ।।
Kausalyādi sakala mahatārīṃ ।
teu prajā sukha hohiṃ sukhārīṃ ।।

Ram and Videha's daughter (Sita) will be gratified when they hear of it and no wise man will call it wrong. Kaushalya and all the other mothers too will be happy in the happiness of the people.

Vasishtha was one of the oldest and most revered Vedic saints or rishis. He is one of the saptarishis of India. He is credited with having written the seventh book of the *Rig Veda,* and is mentioned in the *Rig*

Veda, and several other Vedic texts. In mythology, he is known too for his long-standing rivalry with another sage, Vishwamitra, who, it is said, coveted Nandini, Vasishtha's divine cow that could grant any material request made to it.

Vasishtha was also the teacher of the Ikshvaku clan, to which Ram belonged. He was thus one of the preceptors of Dashrath's court. Following the demise of Dashrath, Vasishtha arrives at Ayodhya to counsel and advise Bharat, who is disconsolate at the exile of Ram, and the death of his father. In these lines the sage advises Bharat to give up his grief, and to rise above loss and gain, birth and death, and fame and ignominy. He then tells Bharat to look beyond his own sorrows, and as one now in charge of the kingdom of Kosala assume his duties, focusing on the things that are not right, and which, befitting a king, need rectification. This was an intelligent way to divert Bharat's fixation with his own grief, and to draw his attention to the wider world, and some of the distortions that unfold therein.

The examples Vasishtha cites are interesting for the light they throw on the social and political priorities of that time. Think about that Brahmin or priest, Vasishtha tells Bharat, who does not know the Vedas, and is argumentative for the sake of argument. Think of that king, who is oblivious to the demands of law and correct behaviour, and does not hold his subjects close to his heart. Think of that businessman, who in spite of his wealth, is tight-fisted, and does not know how to treat guests or worship Shiva. Think of the woman, who creates discord and is self-willed and selfish. Think of that renunciate who repudiates his vows, and deliberately flouts the instructions of his guru.

Think also of that Shudra who insults Brahmins, talks too big, and is excessively proud of his own wisdom. Since this advice specifically cites Shudras, the question does arise as to what Tulsi's approach was to the caste system. Certainly, there are more than one occasion when Tulsi expresses his veneration for the Brahmins, and appears to deride Shudras. The real issue is whether he does so as a consequence of the acceptance of the inflexibly hierarchical nature of the caste system, and the inequities inherent in such an acceptance, or he refers to Brahmins and Shudras on the basis of their learning and wisdom or the lack of it. In other words, is Tulsi guided by the caste system based on its prescriptive discrimination on the basis of birth, or does he refer to the varnas within it on the basis of the competence or vocation or the qualities pursued or possessed by individuals in a society? No definitive answer can be given to this question, and a great deal depends on the interpretation that an individual would wish to give, but there are several instances where Tulsi cites with approval the closeness and affection with which Ram, who is of the higher Kshatriya or warrior class, interacts with those conventionally below him in the social order.

22. Dialogue Between Bharat and the People of Ayodhya

मोहि उपदेसु दीन्ह गुरु नीका ।
प्रजा सचिव संमत सबही का ।।
मातु उचित धरि आयसु दीन्हा ।
अवसि सीस धरि चाहऊँ कीन्हा ।।[221]

mohi upadesu dīnha gura nīkā ।
prajā saciva saṃmata sabahī kā ।।
mātu ucita dhari āyasu dīnhā ।
avasi sīsa dhari cāhauṃ kīnhā ।।

My preceptor has given me excellent advice, which has been endorsed by my subjects, ministers and all. Mother (Kaushalya) too has enjoined on me what she has thought fit and which I certainly wish to carry out with reverence.

गुरु पितु मातु स्वामि हित बानी ।
सुनि मन मुदित करिअ भलि जानी ।।
उचित कि अनुचित किएँ बिचारू ।
धरमु जाइ सिर पातक भारू ।।[222]

gura pitu mātu svāmi hita bānī ।
suni mana mudita karia bhali jānī ।।
ucita ki anucita kieṃ bicārū ।
dharamu jāi sira pātaka bhārū ।।

The advice of one's preceptor, parents, master and friend ought to be acted upon with a cheerful heart as conducive to one's good. By pausing to think whether it is right or wrong, one fails in one's duty and incurs a load of sin.

सरुज सरीर बादि बहु भोगा।
बिनु हरिभगति जायँ जप जोगा॥
जायँ जीव बिनु देह सुहाई।
बादि मोर सबु बिनु रघुराई॥[223]

saruja sarīra bādi bahu bhogā ।
binu Haribhagati jāyaṃ japa jogā ।।
jāyaṃ jīva binu deha suhāī ।
bādi mora sabu binu Raghurāī ।।

Abundant enjoyments are of no use to a diseased body; of little use are *japa* (muttering of prayers) and Yoga (exercises of mind-control) without devotion to Shri Hari. A handsome body is of no use without life and all I have is naught without the Lord of Raghus.

Bharat is one of the most respected and loved characters in the Ramayana. His love for Ram was immeasurable. Not for a moment was he seduced by the fact that the throne of Ayodhya was his. His only concern was to persuade Ram to return from his exile. As an example of filial love, the story of Bharat's love for Ram, and that of Ram for him, has captured the imagination of devotees.

Ram holds Bharat as a symbol of dharma and idealism. For Bharat, Ram is the ideal for which there could be no substitute. When Ram refuses to accede to Bharat's request to return—for he cannot dishonour the word given by his father—Bharat asks for his *padukas* (slippers) and places them on the royal throne of Ayodhya, thereby making it clear that Ram would—notwithstanding his exile—be the de jure ruler of the kingdom, and Bharat would only rule in his name. In the fourteen years of Ram's exile, Bharat lived like an ascetic. He spent most of his time in

Nandigram (a forest near Ayodhya), living in austere conditions, and wearing the clothes of rishis and munis, or renunciates.

It is interesting that Bharat was married to Sita's cousin, Mandavi, who was the daughter of Kushadhwaja, Janak's younger brother. He had two sons, Taksha and Pushkala. According to mythology, on his death Bharat merged with Ram's Mahavishnu form.

The lines above provide a window to Bharat's character, and the nature of the kingdom of Ayodhya, where apart from the advice of sages and seers, there were also consultations directly with the people. Here, Bharat is in a dialogue with the citizens of Ayodhya. He confides with them that the advice of the guru, parents, and friend must surely be beneficial, and he would, thus, proceed on that basis and, giving up his grief, tend to the affairs of state. But, he also makes clear that the throne of Ayodhya holds not the slightest charm for him. In fact, it is something that he would most happily give up, if only Ram would return. Tulsi employs several powerful analogies to illustrate this. In one he says that Ayodhya without Ram and Sita is like a body adorned with jewellery but sans clothes. In the other he says that for a diseased body delicious foods are futile; without total surrender to Shri Ram, japa and yoga are to no avail; and, a body which has no jiva, or living being, is as good as being dead. Ayodhya in the absence of Ram is precisely like that.

Having definitively made his point, Bharat tells the citizens that he has resolved to go to the forests to persuade Ram to return to Ayodhya.

23. A Meeting Between Shri Ram and Janak in the Woods

आश्रम सागर सांत रस पूरन पावन पाथु।
सेन मनहुँ करुना सरित लिएँ जाहिं रघुनाथु ॥[224]

āśram sāgara sāṃta rasa pūrana pāvana pāthu ।
sena manahuṃ karunā sarita lieṃ jāhiṃ Raghunāthu ।।

Shri Ram's hermitage was an ocean as it were, overflowing with the sacred water of quietism; while the host that accompanied Janak was as it were, a river of pathos, which the Lord of Raghus was now conducting (to the ocean of His hermitage).

बिषई साधक सिद्ध सयाने।
त्रिबिध जीव जग बेद बखाने ॥
राम सनेह सरस मन जासू।
साधु सभाँ बड़ आदर तासू ॥ 225

biṣaī sādhaka siddha sayāne ।
tribidha jīva jaga Beda bakhāne ।।
Rāma saneha sarasa mana jāsū ।
sādhu sabhāṃ baḍaādara tāsū ।।

According to the Vedas, there are three types of embodied souls (human beings) in the world—the sensual, the seeker and the wise who have attained perfection (in the form of God—Realisation). Of all these, he alone is highly honoured in an assembly of holy men, whose heart is sweetened by the love for Shri Ram.

आगम निगम प्रसिद्ध पुराना।
सेवाधरमु कठिन जगु जाना॥
स्वामि धरम स्वारथहि बिरोधू।
बैरु अंध प्रेमहि न प्रबोधू॥[226]

āgama nigama prasiddha Purānā ।
sevādharamu kaṭhina jagu jānā ।।
svāmi dharam svārathahi birodhū ।
bairu aṃdha premahi na prabodhū ।।

It is fully recognised in the Tantras, Vedas and Puranas, and all the world knows, that the duty of a servant is hard indeed. Duty to a master is incompatible with selfishness. Hatred is blind and love is not discreet.

दुचित कतहुँ परितोषु न लहहीं।
एक एक मन मरमु न कहहीं॥
लखि हियँ हँसि कह कृपानिधानू।
सरिस स्वान मघवान जुबानु॥ 227

ducita katahuṃ paritoṣu na lahahīṃ ।
eka eka sana maramu na kahahīṃ ।।
lakhi hiyaṃ haṃsi kaha kṛpānidhānū ।
sarisa svāna maghavāna jubānū ।।

Wavering in mind, they did not derive solace anywhere, nor did they disclose their heart to one another. Observing this, the all-compassionate Lord smiled within Himself and said, The canine race, Indra and reckless youth are alike in nature.'

These lines are important for the emphasis they place on duty. Ram is aware of the deep love that Bharat bears for him, and for the intense desire in his mind—and in the minds of the public of Ayodhya and of

Mithilanchal which has accompanied Bharat and Janak to the forest to persuade Ram to return to Ayodhya. Yet, his advice to Bharat, so lyrically expressed here, is that both of them should do only that which is in conformity with what is right and what is expected from them, which is to follow the obligations prescribed by royal custom and tradition. To do so—and this alone—creates the confluence between righteous conduct, fame, and valour.

In view of the above, Ram instructs Bharat that although he is aware of the affliction he will go through, his duty is to return and look to the good of the people of Ayodhya, and take care of the members of the royal family. Ram makes light of his own suffering, saying that it has been shared by all the people. His concern is that Bharat should be fortified to assume the responsibilities of taking care of Ayodhya for the fourteen years that he will be away. Ram accepts that Bharat will find this advice very difficult to accept, but he urges him to rise to the occasion, for only a good brother is there to help when the need arises. Tulsi's analogy is that in such circumstances, even a mighty celestial weapon must be repelled by one's bare hands.

Finally, Ram gives authority to his advice. He tells Bharat that one who serves is like the hands, feet and eyes of a body. But the master is like the mouth, giving instructions to all the subordinate limbs and faculties. In other words, Ram conveys to Bharat that what he is saying must be complied with, but does so with infinite gentleness and love and compassion.

24. Description of Spiritual Wisdom, Dispassion and Illusion Through Dialogu Between Shri Ram and Lakshman

एक बार प्रभु सुख आसीना।
लछिमन बचन कहे छलहीना॥
सुर नर मुनि सचराचर साईं।
मैं पूछउँ निज प्रभु की नाई॥[228]

eka bāra prabhu sukha āsīnā ।
Lachimana bacana kahe chalahīnā ॥
sura nara muni sacarācara sāīṃ ।
maiṃ pūchauṃ nija prabhu kī nāī ॥

Once upon a time, as the Lord was sitting at ease, Lakshman addressed Him in guileless words: 'O Lord of gods, human beings, sages and all animate and inanimate creation! I ask of You as of my own master.

मोहि समुझाइ कहहु सोइ देवा।
सब तजि करौं चरन रज सेवा॥
कहहु ग्यान बिराग अरु माया।
कहहु सो भगति करहु जेहिं दाया॥[229]

mohi samujhāi kahahu soi devā ।
saba taji karauṃ carana raja sevā ॥
kahahu gyāna birāga aru māyā ।
kahahu so bhagati karahu jehiṃ dāyā ॥

'Instruct me, my lord, how I may be able to adore the dust of Your feet to the exclusion of everything else. Discourse to me on spiritual wisdom and dispassion as well as on Maya (Illusion); and also speak to me about bhakti due to which you shower Your grace.

ईस्वर जीव भेद प्रभु सकल कहौ समुझाइ।
जातें होइ चरन रति सोक मोह भ्रम जाइ ।।[230]

Isvara jīva bheda prabhu sakala kahau samujhāī ।।
jāteṃ hoi carana rati soka moha bhram jāi ।।

'Also explain to me all the difference between God and the individual soul, so that I may be devoted to Your feet and my sorrow, infatuation and delusion may disappear.'

थोरेहि महँ सब कहउँ बुझाई।
सुनहु तात मति मन चित लाई ।।
मैं अरु मोर तोर तैं माया।
जेहिं बस कीन्हे जीव निकाया ।।[231]

thorehi mahaṃ saba kahauṃ bujhāī ।
sunahu tāta mati mana cita lāī ।।
maiṃ aru mora tora taiṃ Māyā ।
jehiṃ basa kīnhe jīva nikāyā ।।

'I will explain everything in a nutshell; listen, dear brother, with your mind, intellect and reason fully absorbed. The feeling of "I" and "mine" and "you" and "yours" is Maya (Illusion), which holds sway over all created beings.

गो गोचर जहँ लगि मन जाई।
सो सब माया जानेहु भाई ।।
तेहि कर भेद सुनहु तुम्ह सोऊ।
बिद्या अपर अबिद्या दोऊ ।।[232]

go gocara jahaṃ lagi mana jāī ।
so saba māyā jānehu bhāī ।।
tehi kara bheda sunahu tumha soū ।
bidyā apara abidyā doū ।।

'Whatever is perceived by the senses and that which lies within the reach of the mind, know it all to be Maya. And hear of its divisions too: they are two, viz., knowledge and ignorance.

एक दुष्ट अतिसय दुखरूपा ।
जा बस जीव परा भवकूपा ॥
एक रचइ जग गुन बस जाकें ।
प्रभु प्रेरित नहिं निज बल ताकें ॥[233]

eka duṣṭa atisaya dukharūpā ।
jā basa jīva parā bhavakūpā ।।
eka racai jaga guna basa jākeṃ ।
prabhu prerita nahiṃ nija bala tākeṃ ।।

'The one (ignorance) is vile and extremely painful, and has cast the jiva into metempsychosis. The other (knowledge), which brings forth the creation and which holds sway over the three gunas (sattva, rajas and tamas) is directed by the Lord and has no strength of its own.

ग्यान मान जहँ एकउ नाहीं ।
देख ब्रह्म समान सब माहीं ॥
कहिअ तात सो परम बिरागी ।
तृन सम सिद्धि तीनि गुन त्यागी ॥[234]

gyāna māna jahaṃ ekau nāhīṃ ।
dekha brahma samāna saba māhī ।।
kahia tāta so param birāgī ।
tṛna sama siddhi tīni guna tyāgī ।।

'Spiritual wisdom is that which is free from all blemishes in the shape of pride etc., and which sees the Supreme Spirit equally in all. He alone, dear brother, should be called a man of supreme dispassion, who has spurned all supernatural powers as well as the three gunas (of which the universe is composed) as if of no more account than a blade of grass.

माया ईस न आपु कहुँ जान कहिअ सो जीव।
बंध मोच्छ प्रद सर्बपर माया प्रेरक सीव ॥[235]

Māyā īsa na āpu kahuṃ jāna kahia so jīva ।
baṃdha moccha prada sarbapara Māyā preraka Sīva ।।

That alone deserves to be called a jiva (individual soul), which knows not Maya nor God nor one's own self. And Shiva (God) is He who awards bondage and liberation (according to one's deserts), transcends all and is the motivator of Maya.

धर्म तें बिरति जोग तें ग्याना।
ग्यान मोच्छप्रद बेद बखाना ॥
जातें बेगि द्रवउँ मैं भाई।
सो मम भगति भगत सुखदाई ॥[236]

dharma teṃ birati joga teṃ gyānā ।
gyāna mocchaprada Beda bakhānā ।।
jāteṃ begi dravauṃ maiṃ bhāī ।
so mama bhagati bhagata sukhadāī ।।

'Dispassion results from the practice of virtue, while spiritual wisdom comes of the practice of Yoga (concentration of mind); and wisdom is the bestower of liberation: so declare the Vedas. And that which melts my heart quickly, dear brother, is devotion, which is the delight of my devotees.

सो सुतंत्र अवलंब न आना।
तेहि आधीन ग्यान बिग्याना ॥

भगति तात अनुपम सुखमूला।
मिलइ जो संत होइँ अनुकूला ।।[237]

so sutaṃtra avalaṃba na ānā ।
tehi ādhīna gyāna bigyānā ।।
bhagati tāta anupama sukhamūlā ।
milai jo saṃta hoiṃ anukūlā ।।

'It stands by itself and requires no other prop; whereas jnana (knowledge of God in His absolute formless aspect) and *vijnana* (knowledge of the qualified aspect of God, both with and without form) depend on it. Devotion, dear brother, is incomparable and the very root of bliss; it can be acquired only by the favour of saints.

भगति कि साधन कहउँ बखानी।
सुगम पंथ मोहि पावहिं प्रानी ।।
प्रथमहिं बिप्र चरन अति प्रीती।
निज निज कर्म निरत श्रुति रीती ।।[238]

bhagati ki sādhana kahauṃ bakhānī ।
sugama paṃtha mohi pāvahiṃ prānī ।।
prathamahiṃ bipra carana ati prītī ।
nija nija karma nirata śruti rītī ।।

'I now proceed to tell you at some length the means of acquiring devotion, an easy path by which men find me. In the first place, a man should cultivate excessive devotion to the feet of the Brahmins and secondly he should remain engaged in his own duty according to the lines laid down by the Vedas.

एहि कर फल पुनि बिषय बिरागा।
तब मम धर्म उपज अनुरागा ।।
श्रवनादिक नव भक्ति दृढ़ाहीं।
मम लीला रति अति मन माहीं ।।[239]

ehi kara phala puni biṣaya birāgā ।
taba mama dharma upaja anurāgā ।।
śravanādika nava bhakti dṛḍhaāhīṃ ।
mama līlā rati ati mana māhīṃ ।।

'This induces an aversion to the pleasures of sense and dispassion in its turn engenders a love for my cult (the Cult of Devotion). This will bring steadfastness in the nine forms of devotion such as *shravana* (hearing of the Lord's praises etc.,) and the mind will develop an excessive fondness for my sports.

संत चरन पंकज अति प्रेमा ।
मन क्रम बचन भजन दृढ़ नेमा ।।
गुरु पितु मातु बंधु पति देवा ।
सब मोहि कहँ जानै दृढ़ सेवा ।।[240]

saṃta carana paṃkaja ati premā ।
mana kram bacana bhajana dṛḍhanemā ।।
guru pitu mātu baṃdhu pati devā ।
saba mohi kahaṃ jāne dṛḍhasevā ।।

'Again, one should be extremely devoted to the lotus-feet of saints and should be persistent in the practice of adoration through mind, speech and action. He should recognise me as his preceptor, father, mother, kinsman, lord, deity and all and should be steadfast in my service.

मम गुन गावत पुलक सरीरा ।
गदगद गिरा नयन बह नीरा ।।
काम आदि मद दंभ न जाकें ।
तात निरंतर बस मैं ताकें ।।[241]

mama guna gāvata pulaka sarīrā ।
gadagada girā nayana baha nīrā ।।
kāma ādi mada daṃbha na jākeṃ ।
tāta niraṃtara basa maiṃ tākeṃ ।।

'A thrill runs through his body as he sings my praises; his voice gets choked and his eyes flow with tears; he is free from lust and other vices, pride and hypocrisy. I am ever at the beck and call of such a devotee.

बचन कर्म मन मोरि गति भजन करहिं नि:काम ।
तिन्ह के हृदय कमल महुँ करउँ सदा बिश्राम ।।[242]

bacana karma mana mori gati bhajanu karahiṃ niḥkāma ।।
tinha ke hṛdaya kamala mahuṃ karauṃ sadā biśrāma ।।

'Nay, I ever repose in the lotus-heart of those who depend on me in thought, word and deed and who worship me in a selfless way.'

भगति जोग सुनि अति सुख पावा ।
लछिमन प्रभु चरनन्हि सिरु नावा ।।
एहि बिधि गए कछुक दिन बीती ।
कहत बिराग ग्यान गुन नीती ।।[243]

bhagati joga suni ati sukha pāvā ।
Lachimana prabhu carananhi siru nāvā ।।
ehi bidhi gae kachuka dina bītī ।
kahata birāga gyāna guna nītī ।।

Lakshman was greatly delighted to hear the above discourse on the discipline of bhakti and bowed his head at the feet of the Lord. In this way, some days were spent in discoursing on dispassion, spiritual wisdom, goodness and morality.

Tulsi, the adept dramatist, creates a situation in the Manas, which is in the nature of a philosophical pause. During exile, deep in the forest, when Ram is relaxed, Lakshman takes the opportunity to ask him about some foundational concepts in Hindu philosophy. These relate to Maya, jnana, jiva, Ishwara and bhakti. Like a student would ask his teacher, Lakshman requests Ram to elaborate on them, thus providing Tulsi the opportunity to speak about these seminal issues, and bring in also his own point of view.

In a single line that stands out for its brilliant brevity, Ram says that Maya is simply about the notions of me, mine and yours: *mai aur mor, taur tai maya.* In an ephemeral world, where a life is just like a momentary bubble afloat on the river of time, the ordinary human being builds an entirely false paraphernalia relating to a sense of I-ness, the futile assertion of the individual self, and to the dialectics of mine and yours. This illusionary and transient world, and the immense importance we give to it, is the consequence of the veil of ignorance that is Maya. Maya is natural *(naisargika)*, *anadi* (timeless) and *anant* (eternal). It operates in two ways: *avarana,* or masking the truth, and *vikshepa,* the distortion of the truth. A mere mortal is unable to resist its influence. This leads to a dosha or error of perception. We take the impermanent world of the ego, and all its appurtenances, including pride in the ownership of possessions, and of family and friends, as the sole reality of this world, and ignore the essence of our beings, which is unalloyed and unending bliss and joy, as a part of Brahman.

Jnana or knowledge is, Ram says, the correction in the error of perception. When that rectification happens, and we begin to see everything as the emanation and expression of Brahman, we are possessed of the right knowledge. Through the pursuit of the right knowledge, when an individual understands what is the essence of his real self (atman), he goes beyond the sterile ego of personal accomplishments, and the three gunas—sattva, rajas and tamas—which are the creation of Maya, and infest in varying proportions and degrees in all aspects of life.

Ishwara, Ram explains, is the divine derogation of the all-pervading cosmic, omnipotent and omniscient consciousness that is Brahman. The Upanishads proclaimed: *Tat tvam asi:* that thou art: you are that, which is Brahman. They declared: *Aham Brahmasi:* I am Brahman: atman and Brahman are one and the same. This unyielding non-duality was in the eighth century CE developed by the great Advaita thinker, Adi Shankaracharya. However, later philosophers, such as Ramanuja and Nimbarkar, diluted this extreme monism, to include the concept of Ishwara, a personal god, to whom a devotee could surrender to find succour. Tulsi believed in the concept of Ishwara, which was the distinguishing feature of the devotionalism of the Vaishnava school Accordingly, Ram tells Lakshman that Ishwara, although transcendental, is available to grant moksha to a devotee, and is the director of the operation of Maya.

The jiva, which is the individual self, is one caught in the seductive snare of Maya, but does not know what Maya is or how it operates, and thus does not recognise his own essential self, which is the same as Brahman.

Bhakti—or total and complete devotional surrender—is the greatest and easiest path to redemption for an ordinary mortal. Since this so fully conforms to Tulsi's own beliefs, he is in his elements explaining the redeeming features of bhakti. Bhakti, he says, is a complete and independent path to salvation; it is above the dialectics of jnana or vijnana, above knowledge or reasoning. Indeed, knowledge is subordinate to bhakti. The path of bhakti is easily accessible, where the grace of the Lord is effortlessly obtained. Bhakti creates detachment to worldly things, and fills the devotee with divine love. In that love, the devotee sees his guru, parents, siblings, spouse and even godhood in Ram, and Ram alone. In a beautiful chaupai, Tulsi says that when a devotee's body vibrates with joy in singing the praises of Ram, when his speech quivers with ecstasy, and his eyes brim over with tears in surrendering to Ram, and he is completely free from pride, desire and ego, then Ram is entirely accessible to him. Who in action, speech and thought surrenders to me, and worships me with no ulterior motive of reward, in their lotus-heart does Ram reside.

This important philosophical interlude projects Ram as a sublime philosopher, not only an object of devotion, but a fount of knowledge based on deep insight and contemplation. Tulsi's Ram had to be possessed of every virtue, and here he adroitly brings in Ram as the metaphysician, clinically analysing the essential elements of Hindu philosophy. This prasang also enables Tulsi to elaborate upon his own philosophical belief, which is unalloyed, total and complete bhakti. Ram is the object of that bhakti, and Tulsi is the ideal devotee.

25. Shri Ram's Lament in the Disassociation of Sita

जेहि बिधि कपट कुरंग सँग धाइ चले श्रीराम ।
सो छबि सीता राखि उर रटति रहति हरिनाम ॥[244]

jehi bidhi kapaṭa kuraṃga saṃga dhāi cale Srīrāma ।
so chabi Sītā rākhi ura raṭati rahati Harināma ।।

Having impressed on Her heart the beautiful image of Shri Ram as He appeared while running in pursuit of the false deer, Sita incessantly repeated Shri Han's name.

रघुपति अनुजहि आवत देखी।
बाहिज चिंता कीन्हि बिसेषी ॥
जनकसुता परिहरिहु अकेली ।
आयहु तात बचन मम पेली ॥
निसिचर निकर फिरहिं बन माहीं ।
मम मन सीता आश्रम नाहीं ॥
गहि पद कमल अनुज कर जोरी।
कहेउ नाथ कछु मोहि न खोरी ॥[245]

Raghupati anujahi āvata dekhī ।
bāhija ciṃtā kīnhi bisesị ।।
Janakasutā pariharihu akelī ।
āyahu tāta bacana mama pelī ।।
nisicara nikara phirahiṃ bana māhīṃ ।
mama mana Sītā āśram nāhīṃ ।।

gahi pada kamala anuja kara jorī ।
kaheu nātha kachu mohi na khorī ।।

When the Lord of Raghus saw His younger brother coming, He outwardly expressed much concern. Alas! You have left Janak's daughter alone and come here against my instructions. Hosts of demons are roaming about in the forest; I, therefore, suspect Sita is not at the hermitage.' Lakshman clasped Shri Ram's lotus-feet and replied with joined palms, 'Lord, it is no fault of mine.'

अनुज समेत गए प्रभु तहवाँ।
गोदावरि तट आश्रम जहवाँ॥
आश्रम देखि जानकी हीना।
भए बिकल जस प्राकृत दीना॥[246]

anuja sameta gae prabhu tahavāṃ ।
Godāvari taṭa āśram jahavāṃ ।।
āśram dekhi Jānakī hīnā ।
bhae bikala jasa prākṛta dīnā ।।

Accompanied by His younger brother, the Lord went back to His hermitage on the bank of the Godavari. When He saw the hermitage bereft of Janak's daughter, He felt as perturbed and afflicted as any common man.

हा गुन खानि जानकी सीता।
रूप सील ब्रत नेम पुनीता॥
लछिमन समुझाए बहु भाँति।
पूछत चले लता तरु पाँती॥[247]

hā guna khāni Jānaki Sītā ।
rūpa sīla brata nema punītā ।।
Lachimana samujhāe bahu bhāṃtī ।
pūchata cale latā taru pāṃtī ।।

'Alas! Sita, Janak's daughter, the very mine of virtues, of such flawless beauty, character, austerity and devotion!' Lakshman consoled Him in many ways. He questioned all the creepers and trees (that stood on the way) as He went along (in search of Her):

हे खग मृग हे मधुकर श्रेनी।
तुम्ह देखी सीता मृगनैनी॥
खंजन सुक कपोत मृग मीना।
मधुप निकर कोकिला प्रबीना॥
कुंद कली दाड़िम दामिनी।
कमल सरद ससि अहिभामिनी॥
बरुन पास मनोज धनु हंसा।
गज केहरि निज सुनत प्रसंसा॥[248]

he khaga mṛga he madhukara śrenī ।
tumha dekhī Sītā mṛganainī ।।
khaṃjana suka kapota mṛga mīnā ।
madhupa nikara kokilā prabīnā ।।
kuṃda kalī dāḍima dāminī ।
kamala sarada sasi ahibhāminī ।।
Baruna pāsa manoja dhanu haṃsā ।
gaja kehari nija sunata prasaṃsā ।।

'O birds and deer, O string of bees, have you seen the fawn-eyed Sita?' The wagtail, the parrot, the pigeon, the deer, the fish, the swarms of bees, the clever cuckoo, the jasmine buds, the pomegranate, the lightning, the lotus, the autumnal moon, the gliding serpent, the noose of Varuna (the god of water), the bow of Cupid, the swan, the elephant and the lion now hear themselves praised.

श्रीफल कनक कदलि हरषाहीं।
नेकु न संक सकुच मन माहीं॥
सुनु जानकी तोहि बिनु आजू।
हरषे सकल पाइ जनु राजू॥[249]

śrīphala kanaka kadali haraṣāhīṃ ।
neku na saṃka sakuca mana māhīṃ ।।
sunu Jānakī tohi binu ājū ।
haraṣe sakala pāi janu rājū ।।

'The bilva fruit and the gold banana rejoice and do not feel the least misgiving or bashfulness. Listen, Janak's daughter: in your absence today they are all glad as if they have got a kingdom.

किमि सहि जात अनख तोहि पाहीं।
प्रिया बेगि प्रगटसि कस नाहीं॥
एहि बिधि खोजत बिलपत स्वामी।
मनहुँ महा बिरही अति कामी॥[250]

kimi sahi jāta anakha tohi pāhīṃ ।
priyā begi pragaṭasi kasa nāhīṃ ।।
ehi bidhi khaujata bilapata svāmī ।
manahuṃ mahā birahī ati kāmī ।।

'How can you bear such rivalry? Why do you not reveal yourself quickly, my darling?' In this way, the Lord searched and lamented like an uxorious husband sore smitten with pangs of separation.

पूरकनाम राम सुख रासी।
मनुज चरित कर अज अबिनासी॥[251]

pūranakāma Rāma sukha rāsī ।
manuja carita kara aja abināsī ।।

Shri Ram, who is bliss personified and has all His wishes accomplished, and who is both unborn and immortal, behaved like a mortal.

These lines must be understood by the last comment of the selection. Therein Tulsi marvels at the fact that Ram, who is omnipotence personified, unruffled joy incarnate, and invincible and eternal, is acting out the role of a sorrowful husband whose wife, Sita, cannot be traced. This sense of marvel is the essence of leela, the play that the Almighty indulges in for his own pleasure, as a natural outpouring of his undiminished abundance, a volitional concession to the demands of reducing himself to mortality.

Ram's torment at Sita's absence is depicted by Tulsi both dramatically and realistically. He portrays him as an ordinary mortal, torn by grief at his wife's disappearance, seeking desperately to find her. He cries out for her, and almost like a man possessed, asks the trees and flowers, the birds, bees and beasts if they have seen her. In his anguish, he praises her and, in spite of the attempts of Lakshman to assuage him, remains inconsolable.

But, in all of this, Tulsi sustains the essential contradiction, between Ram, behaving like an ordinary mortal, and Ram, the all-powerful divine. What is at one level the grief of a mortal, is at another but the charade of the Almighty in order to fulfil the requirements of his human avatar.

There are but few occasions in the Ramayana when Ram becomes so completely human. In other situations, where he is part of the drama of ordinary mortals, he is shown as always composed, playing his part, but with equanimity and equilibrium, in control of his senses and faculties. However, Sita's disappearance is one moment when Tulsi lowers the bar, and Ram is portrayed—deliberately—as quintessentially human, subject to the same doubts, fears, anxiety and sorrow, as ordinary mortals would feel.

Why does Tulsi use this occasion to show Ram in such a human form? Perhaps, it is because the occasion demands it. A man's attachment to his wife is self-evident. More importantly, Sita is no ordinary wife. She is, at the philosophical level, Ram's shakti, or inherent power. In his grief, Ram recalls her human qualities—her beauty, her self-restraint, her purity, her dutifulness. It is obvious, that for Tulsi, Sita is worthy of divine reverence. Both Ram and Sita are conjointly part of his cosmic piety. Sita's separation from Ram is for Tulsi a sufficient reason to show Ram losing his composure. But still, he creates for his readers a sense of detachment from the drama of the proceedings by indicating that Ram, as God, is only playing the part of a human being.

26. Dialogue Between Shri Ram and Shabari

ताहि देइ गतिराम उदारा।
सबरी कें आश्रम पगु धारा ।।
सबरी देखि राम गृहँ आए।
मुनि के बचन समुझि जियँ भाए ।।[252]

tāhi dei gati Rāma udārā ।
Sabarī keṃ āśram pagu dhārā ।।
Sabarī dekhi Rāma gṛham āe ।
muni ke bacana samujhi jiyam bhāe ।।

Having conferred on him his own (Gandharva) state, the beneficent Ram repaired to the hermitage of Shabari. When Shabari saw that Shri Ram had called at her abode, she recalled the words of the sage (Matanga) and was glad of heart.

सरसिज लोचन बाहु बिसाला।
जटा मुकुट सिर उर बनमाला ।।
स्याम गौर सुंदर दोउ भाई।
सबरी परी चरन लपटाई ।।[253]

sarasija locana bāhu bisālā ।
jaṭā mukuṭa sira ura banamālā ।।
syāma gaura suṃdara dou bhāī ।
Sabarī parī carana lapaṭāī ।।

With lotus-like eyes, long arms, a tuft of matted hair adorning their head like a crown and a garland of wild flowers hanging upon their breast, the two brothers looked most charming, the one dark of hue and the other fair; Shabari fell prostrate and embraced their feet.

प्रेम मगन मुख बचन न आवा।
पुनि पुनि पद सरोज सिर नावा ॥
सादर जल लै चरन पखारे।
पुनि सुंदर आसन बैठारे ॥[254]

premа magana mukha bacana na āvā ।
puni puni pada saroja sira nāvā ।।
sādara jala lai carana pakhāre ।
puni suṃdara āsana baiṭhāre ।।

She was so overwhelmed with love that no words came to her lips. Again and again she bowed her head at their lotus-feet. Presently, she took some water and reverently laved their feet and then conducted them to a seat of honour.

कंद मूल फल सुरस अति दिए राम कहुँ आनि।
प्रेम सहित प्रभु खाए बारंबार बखानि ॥[255]

kaṃda mūla phala surasa ati die Rāma kahum āni ।
prema sahita prabhu khāe bāraṃbāra bakhāni ।।

She brought and offered to Shri Ram the most delicious bulbs, roots and fruits. The Lord partook of them appreciating again and again.

पानि जोरि आगें भइ ठाढ़ी।
प्रभुहि बिलोकि प्रीति अति बढ़ी ॥
केहि बिधि अस्तुति करौं तुम्हारी।
अधम जाति मैं जड़मति भारी ॥[256]

pāni jori āgeṃ bhai ṭhāḍhī ।
prabhuhi biloki prīti ati bāḍhī ।।

kehi bidhi astuti karauṃ tumhārī ।
adhama jāti maiṃ jaḍamati bhārī ।।

Joining her palms she stood before Him; as she gazed upon the Lord her love waxed yet more ardent. How can I extol You, lowest in descent and the dullest of wit as I am?

अधम ते अधम अधम अति नारी ।
तिन्ह महँ मैं मतिमंद अघारी ।
कह रघुपति सुनु भामिनि बाता ।
मानउँ एक भगति कर नाता ॥[257]

adhama te adhama adhama ati nārī ।
tinha mahaṃ maiṃ matimaṃda aghārī ।।
kaha Raghupati sunu bhāmini bātā ।
mānauṃ eka bhagati kara nātā ।।

A woman is the lowest of those who rank as the lowest of the low. Of women again I am the most dull-headed, O Destroyer of sins. Answered the Lord of Raghus: 'Listen, O good lady, to my words I recognise no other kinship except that of devotion.'

जाति पाँति कुल धर्म बड़ाई ।
धन बल परिजन गुन चतुराई ॥
भगति हीन नर सोहइ कैसा ।
बिनु जल बारिद देखिअ जैसा ॥[258]

jāti pāṃti kula dharma baḍaāī ।
dhana bala parijana guna caturāī ।।
bhagati hīna nara sohai kaisā ।
binu jala bārida dekhia jaisā ।।

Despite caste, kinship, lineage, dharma, reputation, wealth, physical strength, numerical strength of his family, accomplishments and ability, a man lacking in devotion is of no more worth than a cloud without water.

नवधा भगति कहउँ तोहि पाहीं ।
सावधान सुनु धरु मन माहीं ॥
प्रथम भगति संतन्ह कर संगा ।
दूसरि रति मम कथा प्रसंगा ॥[259]

navadhā bhagati kahauṃ tohi pāhīṃ ।
sāvadhāna sunu dharu mana māhīṃ ।।
prathama bhagati saṃtanha kara saṃgā ।
dūsari rati mama kathā prasaṃgā ।।

'Now I tell you the nine forms of devotion; please listen attentively and cherish them in your mind. The first in order is company with the saints and the second is marked by a fondness for my stories.

गुर पद पंकज सेवा तीसरि भगति अमान ।
चौथि भगति मम गुन गन करइ कपट तजि गान ॥[260]

gura pada paṃkaja sevā tīsari bhagati amāna ।
cauthi bhagati mama guna gana karai kapaṭa taji gāna ।।

'Humble service of the lotus-feet of one's preceptor is the third form of devotion, while the fourth type of devotion consists in singing my praises with a guileless heart.

मंत्र जाप मम दृढ़बिस्वासा ।
पंचम भजन सो बेद प्रकासा ॥
छठ दम सील बिरति बहु करमा ।
निरत निरंतर सज्जन धरमा ॥[261]

mantra jāpa mama dṛḍhabisvāsā ।
paṃcama bhajana so beda prakāsā ।।

chaṭha dama sīla birati bahu karamā ।
nirata niraṃtara sajjana dharamā ।।

'Muttering my name with unwavering faith constitutes the fifth form of adoration revealed in the Vedas. The sixth variety consists in the practice of self-control and virtue, desisting from manifold activities and ever pursuing the course of conduct prescribed for saints.

सातवँ सम मोहि मय जग देखा।
मोतें संत अधिक करि लेखा ॥
आठवँ जथालाभ संतोषा ।
सपनेहुँ नहिं देखइ परदोषा ॥[262]

sātavaṃ sama mohi maya jaga dekhā ।
moteṃ saṃta adhika kari lekhā ।।
āṭhavaṃ jathālābha saṃtoṣā ।
sapanehuṃ nahiṃ dekhai paradoṣā ।।

'He who practices the seventh type sees the world full of me without distinction and reckons the saints as even greater than myself. He who cultivates the eighth type of devotion remains contented with whatever he gets and never thinks of detecting others' faults.

नवम सरल सब सन छलहीना ।
मम भरोस हियँ हरष न दीना ॥
नव महुँ एकउ जिन्ह कें होई ।
नारि पुरुष सचराचर कोई ॥[263]

navama sarala saba sana chalahīnā ।
mama bharosa hiyaṃ haraṣa na dīnā ।।
nava mahuṃ ekau jinha keṃ hoī ।
nāri puruṣa sacarācara koī ।।

'The ninth form of devotion demands that one should be guileless and straight in one's dealings with everybody, and should in his heart cherish implicit faith in me without either exultation or depression. Whoever possesses any one of these nine forms of devotion, be the man or woman or any other creature—sentient or insentient—is most dear to me, O good lady.

सोइ अतिसय प्रिय भामिनि मोरें।
सकल प्रकार भगति दृढ़तारें ॥
जोगि बृंद दुरलभ गति जोई।
तो कहुँ आजु सुलभ भइ सोई ॥[264]

soi atisaya priya bhāmini more ।
sakala prakāra bhagati dṛḍhatoreṃ ॥
jogi bṛṃda duralabha gati joī ।
to kahuṃ āju sulabha bhai soī ॥

'As for yourself, you are blessed with unflinching devotion of all these types. The prize which is hardly won by the yogis is within your easy reach today.

मम दरसन फल परम अनूपा।
जीव पाव निज सहज सरूपा ॥
जनकसुता कइ सुधि भामिनी।
जानहि कहु करिबरगामिनी ॥[265]

mama darasana phala param anūpā ।
jīva pāva nija sahaja sarūpā ॥
Janakasutā kai sudhi bhāminī ।
jānahi kahu karibaragāminī ॥

'The most incomparable fruit of seeing me is that the soul attains its natural state. If you know anything about Janak's daughter, my good lady, tell me her news, O fair dame.'

पंपा सरहि जाहु रघुराई।
तहँ होइहि सुग्रीव मिताई॥
सो सब कहिहि देव रघुबीरा।
जानतहूँ पूछहु मतिधीरा॥
बार बार प्रभु पद सिरु नाई।
प्रेम सहित सब कथा सुनाई॥[266]

paṃpā sarahi jāhu Raghurāī ।
tahaṃ hoihi Sugrīva mitāī ।।
so saba kahihi deva Raghubīrā ।
jānatahūṃ pūchahu matidhīrā ।।
bāra bāra prabhu pada siru nāī ।
prema sahita saba kathā sunāī ।।

'Go to the Pampa lake, O Lord of Raghus; there You will make friends with Sugriva. He will tell You everything, my Lord Ram, hero of Raghu's line; You are of steady resolve and know everything; nevertheless You ask me!' Bowing her head at the Lord's feet again and again, she lovingly related the whole story (of what the sage Matanga had told her and how eagerly she had watched His approach all the time).

कहि कथा सकल बिलोकि हरि मुख हृदयँ पद पंकज धरे।
तजि जोग पावक देह हरि पद लीन भइ जहँ नहिं फिरे॥
नर बिबिध कर्म अधर्म बहु मत सोकप्रद सब त्यागहू।
बिस्वास करि कह दास तुलसी राम पद अनुरागहू॥[267]

kahi kathā sakala biloki Hari mukha hṛdayaṃ pada paṃkaja dhare ।
taji joga pāvaka deha Hari pada līna bhai jahaṃ nahiṃ phire ।।
nara bibidha karma adharma bahu mata sokaprada saba tyāgahū ।
bisvāsa kari kaha dāsa Tulsī Rāma pada anurāgahū ।।

After telling the whole story she gazed on the Lord's countenance and imprinted the image of His lotus-feet on her heart; and casting her body in the fire of Yoga she entered Shri Hari's state where from there is no return. 'O men, abandon your varied activities, sins and diverse creeds, which all give birth to sorrow, and with genuine faith,' I say Tulsidas, 'be devoted to the feet of Shri Ram.'

> जाति हीन अघ जन्म महि मुक्त कीन्हि असि नारि ।
> महामंद मन सुख चहसि ऐसे प्रभुहि बिसारि ॥[268]

> jāti hīna agha janma mahi mukta kīnhi asi nāri ।
> mahāmaṃda mana sukha cahasi aise prabhuhi bisāri ॥

The Lord conferred final beatitude even on a woman who was not only an outcaste but a very mine of sin; you seek happiness, my most foolish mind, by forgetting such a master!

The meeting between Ram and Shabari is a very important episode in the Ramayana. It is believed that Shabari was a queen in her previous life, but because of her qualities of detachment, simplicity and spiritual devotion, gave up her life while standing meditating in the Ganga. She was reborn as the extremely pious and righteous daughter of a tribal (Bhil) hunter, at the lowest scale of the social ladder. At a young age, she left her home and became a disciple of sage Matanga, accepting him as her guru. She served her guru for many years with exceptional dedication, notwithstanding her low caste, which was looked at askance by some of the other rishis. When sage Matanga was about to die, Shabari, by now an old lady, sought to accompany him to the final 'abode of peace' where he would go after his mortal death. But Matanga told her that as a reward for her *seva* (service), Lord Ram would one day give her his darshan. Saying this the sage, sitting in the lotus posture, attained *mahasamadhi.*

Shabari spent the rest of her life waiting for Ram to come. Every day she would lovingly collect the humble *ber* (berry) for Ram. The wait was long, but one day Ram and Lakshman did fulfil her wish. The Lord was crystal clear in his purpose. Although all the rishis in the forest wanted him to visit their ashram, he came first to Shabari, because of her selfless and complete devotion for him.

Tulsi describes evocatively the long-awaited meeting between Ram and Shabari. She can hardly believe that the event for which she has waited so eagerly for so many years has at last happened. She lovingly offers to the Lord the berries she has especially collected for him. To ensure that he eats only the sweetest among them, she first tastes them herself. Ram accepts her offerings, completely oblivious to the prevailing norms of ritual defilement, particularly from someone of such a low caste. In fact, Lakshman does object. But Ram says to Lakshman that nothing could equal these berries offered with so much devotion. A true devotee's offering is in a class by itself, he says, and urges Lakshman to eat them.

If Shabari is seen as the very symbol of patient, steadfast, pure and persevering devotion, Ram, emerges through this incident as the ever compassionate Lord, totally at the disposal of his selfless devotees, without any notion of social hierarchy or extraneous considerations of caste, creed or material prosperity. There may have been competing priorities for Ram's attention, and other causes for his divine mercy, but his overarching concern is to fulfil the wishes of that person who is his true and unwavering devotee. Shabari was, indeed, such a person. In the conventional hierarchy, she was the last person in the scale of importance; she had neither wealth nor social status. But, for Ram, she had the one really important quality of faith, and that was more important for him than any other worldly-wise consideration.

It is not surprising, therefore, that it is to Shabari that Ram explains the *navdha* bhakti, the nine ways of devotion. The first is satsang, or association with righteous people. The second is to develop a taste for hearing the nectar-like stories of the Lord. The third is complete devotion to the guru. The fourth is kirtan, or the love-intoxicated communal singing in praise of the Lord. Japa, or the repetition of the name of the Lord is the fifth. The sixth is to endeavour to become a better human being, through following the scriptural injunctions, controlling the senses, practicing selfless service and cultivating nobility of character. The seventh is to see the Lord manifested in everything. To be content with one's lot and to find no fault in anyone is the eighth. Unreserved faith and total surrender to the Lord is the ninth.

The incident of Shabari, as described by Tulsi, allows the poet to revel in the importance of devotion and surrender, irrespective of any other spiritual practice or sadhana. Bhakti is Tulsi's favourite theme, and is the recurring refrain throughout the Manas. Shabari achieves moksha through her pure and selfless devotion to the Lord. In Hindu spiritualism, she has become the metaphor for the endless wait of a true devotee for the benediction of the Lord.

27. Dialogue Between Shri Ram and Lakshman

लछिमन देखु बिपिन कै सोभा ।
देखत केहि कर मन नहिं छोभा ॥
नारि सहित सब खग मृग बृंदा ।
मानहुँ मोरि करत हहिं निंदा ॥[269]

Lachimana dekhu bipina kai sobhā ।
dekhata kehi kara mana nahiṃ chobhā ।।
nāri sahita saba khaga mṛga bṛṃdā ।
mānahuṃ mori karata hahiṃ niṃdā ।।

'Lakshman, mark the beauty of the forest; whose heart will not be stirred at its sight? United with their mates all the swarms of birds and herds of deer are reproaching me as it were.'

संग लाइ करिनीं करि लेहीं ।
मानहुँ मोहि सिखावनु देहीं ॥
सास्त्र सुचिंतित पुनि पुनि देखिअ ।
भूप सुसेवित बस नहिं लेखिअ ॥
राखिअ नारि जदपि उर माहीं ।
जुबती सास्त्र नृपति बस नाहीं ॥
देखहु तात बसंत सुहावा ।
प्रिया हीन मोहि भय उपजावा ॥[270]

saṃga lāi karinīṃ kari lehīṃ ।
mānahuṃ mohi sikhāvanu dehīṃ ।।
sāstra suciṃtita puni puni dekhia ।
bhūpa susevita basa nahiṃ lekhia ।।
rākhia nāri jadapi ura māhīṃ ।
jubatī sāstra nṛpati basa nāhīṃ ।।
dekhahu tāta basaṃta suhāvā ।
priyā hīna mohi bhaya upajāvā ।।

'The elephants would take their mates along with them as if to teach me a lesson (that a man should never leave his wife alone). The sacred lore, however thoroughly studied, must be gone through over and over again; a king, however well served, should never be depended upon; and a woman, weapon, and king, even though you may cherish her in your bosom, is never thoroughly mastered. See, brother, how pleasant the spring is; yet to me, bereft of my beloved, it is frightful.'

These lines have been selected for a thought of considerable interest embedded in them, which needs analysis. Ram is still inconsolable at the disappearance of Sita. He is envious of the birds and animals of the forest, who are happy in conjugal bliss. Then, Tulsi, brings in a thought of his own. He says that a young woman, a weapon, and a king, can never be controlled: *jubati, sastra, nripati bas nahin.*

Is this statement about a young woman an example of Tulsi's misogyny, or is it a tribute to feminine power? At one level, it can be argued that Tulsi is being sexist—as he is indeed on many other occasions in the Ramayana—by seeing young women as so sensually inclined that they cannot be restrained. Why is this aspect not applicable to young men? In fact, there are far more instances, including due to the in-built inequity between the sexes, for young men to be out of control. At another level, though, it is the acknowledgement of the prowess of youthful women, that come what may their ability—and desire—to achieve their purpose cannot be stopped. Such is their explosive potential, that to try and circumscribe it is futile. Which of the two interpretations to accept is left to the reader, but it may be contextual to add that Tulsi himself often sees women in general, apart from his veneration of Sita, in a derogatory light, and even goes so far as to believe that they can be the source for all the misfortunes that can befall a man. No doubt, such a jaundiced view was based on his own alleged experience with his wife, but one would have expected a poet of his eminence to rise above his personal predilections. In this specific case, however, what Tulsi says can be given the benefit of doubt.

Such an interpretation, must be juxtaposed to the other two examples he cites. A weapon—*shastra*—is never only subordinate to the person who owns it. It can, should the opportunity present itself, be used against him, or anyone else, and hence is not really an object that moulds itself to monopolistic control. Similarly, a king is entirely a creature of his own will. A supplicant may think that his service or sycophancy has curbed this proclivity, but, by the nature of his supreme office and the power that he wields, a king is inherently subject to no one's control or direction.

Such nuggets of thought occur frequently in the Ramayana. Tulsi uses one or the other characters in the epic—in this case Ram himself—to voice these thoughts, and they are an indication of the poet's views on various aspects of life, as he has internalised and experienced them.

28. Dialogue Between Shri Ram and Sugriva

जे न मित्र दुख होहिं दुखारी।
तिन्हहि बिलोकत पातक भारी।।
निज दुख गिरि सम रज करि जाना।
मित्रक दुख रज मेरु समाना।।[271]

je na mitra dukha hohiṃ dukhārī ।
tinhahi bilokata pātaka bhārī ।।
nija dukha giri sama raja kari jānā ।
mitraka dukha raja meru samānā ।।

One would incur great sin by the very sight of those who are not distressed to see the distress of a friend. A man should regard his own mountain-like troubles as of no more account than a mere grain of sand, while the troubles of a friend should appear to him like Mount Sumeru, though really they may be as trifling as a grain of sand.

जिन्ह कें असि मति सहज न आई।
ते सठ कत हठि करत मिताई।।
कुपथ निवारि सुपंथ चलावा।
गुन प्रगटै अवगुनन्हि दुरावा।।
देत लेत मन संक न धरई।
बल अनुमान सदा हित करई।।
बिपति काल कर सतगुन नेहा।
श्रुति कह संत मित्र गुन एहा।।[272]

jinha keṃ asi mati sahaja na āī ।
te saṭha kata haṭhi karata mitāī ।।
kupatha nivāri supaṃtha calāvā ।
guna pragaṭe avagunanhi durāvā ।।
deta leta mana saṃka na dharaī ।
bala anumāna sadā hita karaī ।।
bipati kāla kara sataguna nehā ।
śruti kaha saṃta mitra guna ehā ।।

Those fools who are not of such a temperament presume in vain to make friends with anybody. A friend should restrain his companion from the evil path and lead him on the path of virtue; he should proclaim the latter's good points and screen his faults, should give and take things without any scruple and serve his friend's interest to the best of his ability and finding him in distress love him a hundred times more than ever. The Vedas declare these to be the qualities of a noble friend.

आगें कह मृदु बचन बनाई ।
पाछें अनहित मन कुटिलाई ॥
जाकर चित अहि गति सम भाई ।
अस कुमित्र परिहरेहिं भलाई ॥[273]

āgeṃ kaha mṛdu bacana banāī ।
pācheṃ anahita mana kuṭilāī ।।
jā kara cita ahi gati sama bhāī ।
asa kumitra pariharehi bhalāī ।।

He, however, who contrives to speak bland words to your face and harms you behind your back and harbours some evil design in his heart, and whose mind is as tortuous as the movements of a snake is an unworthy friend and one had better bid goodbye to such a friend.

सेवक सठ नृप कृपन कुनारी ।
कपटी मित्र सूल सम चारी ॥

सखा सोच त्यागहु बल मोरें।
सब बिधि घटब काज मैं तोरे ॥[274]

sevaka saṭha nṛpa kṛpana kunārī ।
kapaṭī mitra sūla sama cārī ।।
sakhā soca tyāgahu bala moreṃ ।
saba bidhi ghaṭaba kāja maiṃ toreṃ ।।

A stupid servant, a stingy monarch, a bad wife and a false friend—these four are tormenting like a pike. Relying on my strength, dear friend, grieve no more; I will serve your cause in everyway possible.

Kishkinda is the kingdom of Bali and Sugriva, the *vanara* martials that Ram meets in exile. Sugriva is Bali's younger brother. He is considered to be the avatar of Surya, the sun god. The legend of Bali and Sugriva caught the imagination of people wide and large, and is well known in Java and Bali in Indonesia, Laos, Cambodia and Myanmar.

The story goes that Bali ostracised his younger brother from the kingdom on the suspicion that he had betrayed him. Bali was caught in a battle of life and death with a demon. Both had entered a cave, from which volumes of blood flowed out as a consequence of their fierce battle. When none of them emerged for a very long time, Sugriva thought that his elder brother had not survived, and assumed the kingdom in good faith. However, Bali finally defeated the demon and returned to his kingdom, only to find that Sugriva had assumed the throne. Sugriva tried to explain the reasons for his doing so, but Bali was unforgiving. He banished Sugriva, and what was worse, took his wife, Ruma, as his own.

When Sugriva was banished, he met Ram in the forest. Ram befriended Sugriva, and promised to kill Bali, not the least for him having cast an evil eye over his younger brother's wife. Sugriva, on his part, agreed to assist Ram in every possible way to rescue Sita from Ravana. Ram assured Sugriva that henceforth he has nothing to worry, and can leave everything to him, his friend.

These lines are important for Ram's emphasis on the importance of a good friend, which he has promised to be to Sugriva. It is a sin to even look at a person who is not grieved at his friend's afflictions, says Ram. For a true friend, his own sorrows are like the dust on the ground, while his friend's grief is higher than Mount Sumeru. A friend's duty is to guide his friend to the path of righteousness, and away from the path of evil. A good friend gives of his own without the slightest sense of reservation or doubt. He always works for the good of his friend to the best of his ability, especially if his friend is in difficulty. That person who speaks sweetly before you, and badly behind your back, is like a snake. It is best to give him up.

As a sermon on friendship, these are very evocative lines. In addition, and in the same context, there is also one of Tulsi's personal nuggets of wisdom. A foolish subordinate, a miserly king, an acrimonious wife, and a wicked friend, are like four painful shafts that pierce your body. This advice, voiced by Ram, reflect the sturdy common sense and insight that was Tulsi's forte.

29. Dialogue Between Shri Ram and Bali

धर्म हेतु अवतरेहु गोसाईं।
मारेहु मोहि ब्याध की नाईं॥
मैं बैरी सुग्रीव पिआरा।
अवगुन कवन नाथ मोहि मारा॥[275]

dharma hetu avatarehu Gosāī ।
mārehu mohi byādha kī nāī ॥
maiṃ bairī Sugrīva piārā ।
avaguna kabana nātha mohi mārā ॥

'Even though, my lord, You descended on earth for upholding righteousness, You have killed me as a hunter would. I, Your enemy and Sugriva, Your dear friend! For what fault did You take my life, my lord?'

अनुज बधू भगिनी सुत नारी।
सुनु सठ कन्या सम ए चारी॥
इन्हहि कुदृष्टि बिलोकइ जोई।
ताहि बधें कछु पाप न होई॥[276]

anuja badhū bhaginī suta nārī ।
sunu saṭha kanyā sama e cārī ॥
inhahi kuddaṣṭi bilokai joī ।
tāhi badheṃ kachu pāpa na hoī ॥

'Listen, O wretch: a younger brother's wife, a sister, a daughter-in-law and one's own daughter these four are alike. One would incur no sin by killing him who looks upon these with an evil eye.'

तारा बिकल देखि रघुराया।
दीन्ह ग्यान हरि लीन्ही माया॥
छिति जल पावक गगन समीरा।
पंच रचित अति अधम सरीरा॥[277]

Tārā bikala dekhi Raghurāyā ।
dīnha gyāna hari līnhī māyā ।।
chiti jala pāvaka gagana samīrā ।
paṃca racita ati adhama sarīrā ।।

When the Lord of Raghus saw her (Tara) distress, He imparted to her wisdom and dispelled her delusion. Made up of the five elements, viz., earth, water, fire, ether and air, this body is extremely vile.

प्रगट सो तनु तव आगें सोवा।
जीव नित्य केहि लगि तुम्ह रोवा॥
उपजा ग्यान चरन तब लागी।
लीन्हेसि परम भगति बर मागी।[278]

pragaṭa so tanu tava āgeṃ sovā ।
jīva nitya kehi lagi tumha rovā ।।
upajā gyāna carana taba lāgī ।
līnhesi param bhagati bara māgī ।।

The mortal frame lies, buried in eternal sleep before your eyes, while the soul is everlasting. For whom, then, do you lament? The light of wisdom dawned on her and now she embraced His feet and asked of Him the boon of supreme Devotion.

उमा दारु जोषित की नाईं।
सबहि नचावत रामु गोसाईं॥

तब सुग्रीवहि आयसु दीन्हा ।
मृतक कर्म बिधिवत सब कीन्हा ॥[279]

Umā dāru joṣita kī nāī ।
sabahi nacāvata Rāmu Gosāī ।।
taba Sugrīvahi āyasu dīnhā ।
mṛtaka karma bidhibata saba kīnhā ।।

The almighty Shri Ram, O Uma (says Bhagawan Shankar) makes us all dance like so many marionettes. Shri Ram then gave orders to Sugriva, who performed all the funeral rites with due ceremony.

उमा राम सम हत जग माहीं ।
गुरु पितु मातु बंधु प्रभु नाहीं ॥
सुर नर मुनि सब कै यह रीती ।
स्वारथ लागि करहिं सब प्रीति ॥[280]

Umā Rāma sama hita jaga māhīṃ ।
guru pitu mātu baṃdhu prabhu nāhīṃ ।।
sura nara muni saba kai yaha rītī ।
svāratha lāgi karahiṃ saba prītī ।।

Uma, there is no such friend as Shri Ram in this world neither preceptor, nor father, nor mother, nor brother, nor master. Gods, men and sages, all as a rule have some selfish motive behind their love.

This conversation between Bali and Ram is an important part of the Kishkinda section. The scene is dramatic. Ram has just shot Bali through his heart. A dying Bali remonstrates with Ram on why he has befriended his brother, Sugriva, and gone against him, shooting the fatal arrow not in frontal battle but from behind.

Ram's reply is very significant. He says that any man who casts an evil eye on a brother's wife, a sister, a daughter-in-law, or any parayi (other) woman, is worthy of the worst punishment, and he who puts him to death, in whatever way, incurs no sin. This stern message to Bali is entirely in keeping with Ram's essence as maryada purushottam, the epitome of rectitude. It is not surprising then that Ram voices this opinion without the slightest ambivalence, and with the guarantee that such evil conduct is not only punishable, but is punishable with death.

When Bali dies, having attained to moksha for having been killed at the hands of Ram, his wife, Tara, is inconsolable. Ram, the merciful, then gives her wisdom and, in the lines of Tulsi, removes the veil of ignorance generated by Maya from her mind. This role of Ram is important. He not only dispenses justice swiftly, but is also the giver of enlightenment, an act of divine grace. Our body, Ram says, is composed of the five elements of the earth, water, fire, ether *(akash)* and wind. The body of Bali is no longer alive, and has rejoined the five elements, *panch tattva.* But, the soul is eternal. It does not die. For whom then, Ram asks, is Tara weeping? As knowledge dawns on Tara, she sheds her grief, and embraces the lotus-feet of the Lord.

This incident is being narrated by Shiva to Parvati. Shiva, praising Ram, says something very interesting: like puppets, everyone dances to the command of Ram. The analogy of the universe being but a puppet in the hands of all-powerful Ram, is a tribute to Ram's omnipotence. That it comes from Shiva, who is himself Mahadeva, the greatest god, is Tulsi's way of emphasising Ram's primacy, and, at the same time bridging the divide between Shaivites and Vaishnavites.

Shiva further tells Parvati that there is none like Ram in the universe who is devoted only to the well-being of all. He is, for his devotees, a guru, a father, a mother, a friend and a master. It is, therefore, in the self-interest of a devotee to completely and totally surrender himself to Ram. In this context, Tulsi slips in one of his remarkably pragmatic—and oft-quoted—verities: *sur, nara, muni sab kai yeh riti, svarath lagi karahin sab priti:* gods, men and saints, for all of them, self-interest motivates adoration. The line must be read in two ways. First, it is only an extension of what Shiva is saying, which is that since Ram is the well-wisher of all, it is in everybody's self-interest to worship him. But, Tulsi is also making a comment on the ways of the world. Love, affection, devotion and suchlike emotions are, in the real world, driven more by self-interest than selfless devotion. Affairs in real life are far more transactional. People may profess to the contrary, but, in reality, they are driven by self-interest alone. This is Tulsi's vital obiter dicta, his way of slipping in his own commentary on life and matters.

30. A Description of the Rainy Season

प्रथमहिं देवन्ह गिरि गुहा राखेउ रुचिर बनाइ ।
राम कृपानिधि कछु दिन बास करहिंगे आइ ॥[281]

prathamahiṃ devanha giri guhā rākheu rucira banāi ।
Rāma kṛpānidhi kachu dina bāsa karahiṃge āi ॥

The gods had already kept ready for Him a charming cave in the mountain in the hope that the all-merciful Shri Ram would come and stay there for some time.

सुंदर बन कुसुमित अति सोभा ।
गुंजत मधुप निकर मधु लोभा ॥
कंद मूल फल पत्र सुहाए।
भए बहुत जब ते प्रभु आए ॥[282]

suṃdara bana kusumita ati sobhā ।
guṃjata madhupa nikara madhu lobhā ॥
kaṃda mūla phala patra suhāe ।
bhae bahuta jaba te prabhuāye ॥

The lovely forest, rich in flowers, presented a most splendid sight with its swarms of bees humming in greed of honey. Delightful bulbs, roots, fruits and leaves grew in abundance from the time the Lord came there.

देखि मनोहर सैल अनूपा।
रहे तहँ अनुज सहित सुरभूपा॥
मधुकर खग मृग तनु धरि देवा।
करहिं सिद्ध मुनि प्रभु कै सेवा॥[283]

dekhi manohara saila anūpā ।
rahe tahaṃ anuja sahita surabhūpā ।।
madhukara khaga mṛga tanu dhari devā ।
karahiṃ siddha muni prabhu kai sevā ।।

Seeing the mountain incomparable in its charms, Shri Ram, the suzerain Lord of gods, stayed there with His younger brother. Taking the form of bees, birds and beasts, gods, siddhas and hermits did service to the Lord.

मंगलरूप भयउ बन तब ते।
कीन्ह निवास रमापति जब ते॥
फटिक सिला अति सुभ्र सुहाई।
सुख आसीन तहाँ द्वौ भाई॥[284]

maṅgalarūpa bhayau bana taba te
kīnha nivāsa Ramāpati jaba te ।।
phaṭika silā ati subhra suhāī ।
sukha āsīna tahāṃ dvau bhāī ।।

The forest became a picture of felicity from the time Shri Ram, the Lord of Lakshmi (the goddess of prosperity), took up His residence there. There was a delightful and glistening rock of crystal, on which the two brothers sat at ease.

कहत अनुज सन कथा अनेका।
भगति बिरत नृपनीति बिबेका॥
बरषा काल मेघ नभ छाए।
गरजत लागत परम सुहाए॥[285]

kahata anuja sana kathā anekā ।
bhagati birati nṛpanīti bibekā ।।
barașā kāla megha nabha chāe ।
garajata lāgata param suhāe ।।

Shri Ram gave a discourse to His younger brother on many a topic such as devotion, dispassion, statecraft and spiritual wisdom. As the rains had set in, the sky was overcast with clouds, which made a delightful rumbling noise.

लछिमन देखु मोर गन नाचत बारिद पेखि।
गृही बिरति रत हरष जस बिष्नुभगत कहुँ देखि ॥[286]

Lachimana dekhu mora gana nācata bārida pekhi ।
gṛhī birati rata harașa jasa Bișnu bhagata kahuṃ dekhi ।।

'Look here, Lakshman: the peacocks dance at the sight of the clouds, even as a householder having a leaning towards dispassion would rejoice to see a devotee of Bhagawan Vishnu.'

घन घमंड नभ गरजत घोरा।
प्रिया हीन डरपत मन मोरा ॥
दामिनि दमक रह नघन माहीं।
खल कै प्रीति जथा थिर नाहीं ॥[287]

ghana ghamaṃḍa nabha garajata ghorā ।
priyā hīna ḍarapata mana morā ।।
dāmini damaka raha naghana māhīṃ ।
khala kai prīti jathā thira nāhīṃ ।।

The roaming clouds are terribly thundering in the sky. Bereft as I am, of my darling (Sita), my heart trembles to see all this. The lightning flashes fitfully amid the clouds, like the friendship of the wicked, never endures.

बरषहिं जलद भूमि निअराएँ।
जथा नवहिं बुध बिद्या पाएँ॥
बूँद अघात सहहिं गिरि कैसे।
खल के बचन संत सह जैसें॥[288]

baraṣahiṃ jalada bhūmi niarāeṃ ।
jathā navahiṃ budha bidyā pāeṃ ।।
būṃda aghāta sahahiṃ giri kaiṃseṃ ।
khala ke bacana saṃta saha jaiseṃ ।।

The pouring clouds cleave close to the ground even as the learned stoop beneath accumulated lore. The mountains endure the buffeting of showers even as a saint would put up with the taunts of the wicked.

छुद्र नदीं भरि चलीं तोराई।
जस थोरेहुँ धन खल इतराई॥
भूमि परत भा ढाबर पानी।
जनु जीवहि माया लपटानी॥[289]

chudra nadīṃ bhari calīṃ torāī ।
jasa thorehuṃ dhana khala itarāī ।।
bhūmi parata bhā ḍābara pānī ।
janu jīvahi māyā lapaṭānī ।।

The swelling streamlets rush with great speed just as the wicked would feel elated even with a small fortune. The water becomes turbid the moment it descends on earth, even as the jiva (an embodied soul) is enveloped in Maya as soon as it is born.

समिटि समिटि जल भरहिं तलावा।
जिमि सदगुन सज्जन पहिं आवा॥
सरिता जल जलनिधि महुँ जोई।
होई अचल जिमि जिव हरि पाई॥[290]

samiṭi samiṭi jala bharahiṃ talāvā ।
jimi sadaguna sajjana pahiṃ āvā ।।
saritā jala jalanidhi mahuṃ jāī ।
hoī acala jimi jiva Hari pāī ।।

The water coming from various directions gathers into a pool even as commendable virtues find their way into the heart of a noble soul. The water of the stream becomes still once it enters into the ocean, just as the ego finds eternal rest on attaining union with Shri Hari.

हरित भूमि तृन संकुल समुझि परहिं नहिं पंथ।
जिमि पाखंड बाद तें गुप्त होहिं सदग्रंथ॥[291]

harita bhūmi tṛna saṃkula samujhi parahiṃ nahiṃ paṃtha ।
jimi pākhaṃḍa bāda teṃ gupta hohiṃ sadagraṃtha ।।

The green earth is so choked with grass that the tracks cannot be distinguished, just as holy books are obscured by heretic doctrines.

दादुर धुनि चहु दिसा सुहाई।
बेद पढ़हिं जनु बटु समुदाई॥
नव पल्लव भए बिटप अनेका।
साधक मन जस मिलें बिबेका॥[292]

dādura dhuni cahu disā suhāī ।
Beda paḍhahiṃ janu baṭu samudāī ।।
nava pallava bhae biṭapa anekā ।
sādhaka mana jasa mileṃ bibekā ।।

On all sides one hears the delightful croaking of frogs, which reminds one of a batch of religious students chanting the Vedas. Clothed with new leaves, the trees of different species look as green and cheerful as the mind of a striving soul who has attained spiritual wisdom.

अर्क जवास पात बिनु भयऊ।
जस सुराज खल उद्यम गयऊ ।।
खोजत कतहुँ मिलइ नहिं धूरी
करइ क्रोध जिमि धरमहि दूरी ।।[293]

arka jabāsa pāta binu bhayaū ।
jasa surāja khala udyama gayaū ।।
khojata katahuṃ milai nahiṃ dhūrī ।
karai krodha jimi dhaRamhi dūrī ।।

The leaves of the arka and javasa plants have fallen off even as under a good government the plans of the wicked come to naught. Dust cannot be found even if one searches for it, just as piety is scared away by anger.

ससि संपन्न सोह महि कैसी ।
उपकारी के संपति जैसी ॥
निसि तम घन खद्योत बिराजा ।
जनु दंभिन्ह कर मिला समाजा ।।[294]

sasi saṃpanna soha mahi kaisī ।
upakārī kai saṃpati jaisī ।।
nisi tama ghana khadyota birājā ।
janu daṃbhinha kara milā samājā ।।

The earth rich with crops appears as delightful as the wealth of a generous man. In the thick darkness of the night fireflies gleam like a mustered band of hypocrites.

महाबृष्टि चलि फूटि किआरीं ।
जिमि सुतंत्र भएँ बिगरहिं नारीं ।।
कृषी निरावहिं चतुर किसाना ।
जिमि बुध तजहिं मोह मद माना ।।[295]

mahābṛṣṭi cali phūṭi kiārīṃ ।
jimi sutaṃtra bhaeṃ bigarahiṃ nārīṃ ।।

kṛṣī nirāvahiṃ catura kisānā ।
jimi budha tajahiṃ moha mada mānā ॥

The embankments of the fields have been breached by torrential rains just as women get spoiled by freedom. Clever farmers weed out the grass from their crops, just as the wise discard infatuation, vanity and pride.

देखिअत चक्रबाक खग नाहीं।
कलिहि पाइ जिमि धर्म पराहीं॥
ऊषर बरषइ तृन नहिं जामा।
जिमि हरिजन हियँ उपज न कामा॥[296]

dekhiata cakrabāka khaga nāhīṃ ।
kalihi pāi jimi dharma parāhīṃ ॥
ūṣara baraṣai tṛna nahiṃ jāmā ।
jimi Harijana hiyaṃ upaja na kāmā ॥

The Chakravaka birds are no more to be seen, just as virtues disappear with the Kali age. Even though it rains on the barren lands as well, not a blade of grass sprouts on it, just as concupiscence takes no root in the heart of a servant of Shri Hari.

बिबिध जंतु संकुल महि भ्राजा।
प्रजा बाढ़ जिमि पाइ सुराजा॥
जहँ तहँ रहे पथिक थकि नाना।
जिमि इंद्रिय गन उपजें ग्याना॥[297]

bibidha jaṃtu saṃkula mahi bhrājā ।
prajā bāḍhajimi pāi surājā ॥
jahaṃ tahaṃ rahe pathika thaki nānā ।
jimi iṃdriya gana upajeṃ gyānā ॥

The earth looks charming with the swarms of various living creatures even as the population grows under a good government. Many a weary traveller has stopped here and there, just as with the dawning of wisdom the senses become still.

कबहुँ प्रबल बह मारुत जहँ तहँ मेघ बिलाहिं।
जिमि कपूत के उपजें कुल सद्धर्म नसाहिं ॥[298]

kabahuṃ prabala baha māruta jahaṃ tahaṃ megha bilāhiṃ ।
jimi kapūta ke upajeṃ kula saddharma nasāhiṃ ।।

Sometimes a strong wind would blow and disperse the clouds in various directions, just as with the birth of an unworthy son the noble traditions of a family get extinct.

कबहु दिवस महँ निबिड़ तम कबहुँक प्रगट पतंग।
बिनसइ उपजइ ग्यान जिमि पाइ कुसंग सुसंग ॥[299]

kabahuṃ divasa mahaṃ nibiḍatama kabahuṃka pragaṭa pataṃga ।
binasai upajai gyāna jimi pāi kusaṃga susaṃga ।।

No wit becomes pitch-dark even during the day, while at other times the sun would shine brightly, just as the light of wisdom is obscured in the company of the vile and manifests itself in the company of the good.

Tulsidas has a deep love for nature. The poet gets a full canvas to portray the monsoons, as Ram and Lakshman find a cave on a mountain deep in the jungles to spend some time during the glorious rainy season. What is, however, amazing, is how Tulsi describes each aspect of the rains with an analogy relating to life, philosophy, and the conduct of people. This poetic imagination is nothing short of remarkable.

Thus, peacocks dancing in abandon on seeing the clouds are, for the poet, like a detached householder delighted to see devotees of Vishnu. The inability of the clouds to contain lightning, is like the instability of a wicked man's affections. The low hanging raining clouds, are like a shower of knowledge that renders humble the learned. The piercing impact of the rain on the mountain, is like the words of the wicked borne stoically by saints. Tiny rivulets enjoying their brimful expanse of water, are like a miser preening himself with a little bit of wealth. The way in which the pristine rain becomes muddy on touching the ground, is like what the jiva becomes when wrapped up in the veil of Maya. The manner in which water collects in ponds, is like how noble qualities accumulate in the persona of a good man. Just as a river becomes still on merging with the ocean, so does a jiva become stable on finding Shri Hari. The earth is lush and verdant, overwhelming the pathways, just like in the false projection of untruth, holy books are overcome. The sound of frogs resounding everywhere is enchanting, just like a group of students chanting verses from the Vedas. New leaves have sprouted on trees, just like enlightenment comes to a student when he acquires knowledge. Some trees have shed their leaves, just as in a righteous kingdom the wicked fall away. Not a speck of dust can be found anywhere, just like anger disappears in the presence of dharma. The fields are ripe with crop, just like a good man's coffers. Fireflies enticingly illuminate the dark, as though a group of egoists has gathered to have a conversation. Clever farmers are weeding out the overflowing grass from the carries, just like the learned remove greed, arrogance and pride from their beings. The Chakravaka bird can nowhere be seen, just as dharma disappears during Kaliyuga. The earth is replete with all kinds of creatures, just as in a well governed kingdom the population increases. Here and there, travellers are marooned, just as in the presence of knowledge our senses are stranded. Sometimes the wind blows powerfully, driving the clouds away, just as righteous conduct is driven out of a home when an evil son is born. When clouds gather it becomes dark, and sometimes the sun peeps through, just as in bad company knowledge is destroyed, and in good company knowledge appears.

These series of remarkable analogies serve a dual purpose. They describe the many moods of the monsoon, and also give the poet a full palette to revel in his poetic imagery. Only a poet of Tulsi's abilities could achieve this feat.

In Tulsi's poetry, the magic of the monsoons comes alive, and with it Ram and Lakshman's enjoyment of it, safely ensconced in the comfort of their cave. There is a tremendously human quality to the duo's delight with the rains. In Indian tradition, the monsoons are the season of the anguish and union of love. When, after the terribly hot summer, the first drops of the rains cool the hot earth, and the sweltering weather is replaced by moist breezes, it invokes in every lover the intense desire to be united with the beloved, and if the beloved is away or separate, it causes unbearable anguish. Ram was not immune to this tradition. One line, in particular, brings this out beautifully. Ram says to Lakshman: *ghan ghamand nabh garjat ghora, priya heen darpat man mora:* in the sky the clouds thunder and roll, but without my beloved I feel afraid. For the Lord of the universe to admit the emotion of fear, and of longing for his beloved, adds a very human quality to Ram, who is always composed, restrained and correct in his behaviour, and unlike leela purushottam Krishna, is not inclined to show his human emotions. It is interesting, too, that Ram admits how incomplete he is without Sita. She is his shakti, his power, his energy, the secret of his prowess. In Hinduism, the adulation of the female goddess is directly correlated to the acceptance of the power of Shakti, and it is no coincidence that there is no major god in the Hindu pantheon who does not have his divine consort. As the clouds thunder, and lightning strikes, with the skies pouring down, Ram confesses that without Sita he is afraid. Perhaps, he is also afraid for Sita, who is untraceable. Either way, for Tulsi to portray Ram as subject to this emotion, is both a tribute to the many moods of the monsoons, and an acknowledgement—not very often projected—of the human profile of Ram.

31. A Description of the Winter Season

बरषा बिगत सरद रितु आई।
लछिमन देखहु परम सुहाई॥
फूलें कास सकल महि छाई।
जनु बरषाँ कृत प्रगट बुढ़ाई॥[300]

baraṣā bigata sarada ritu āī ।
Lachimana dekhahu param suhāī ।।
phūleṃ kāsa sakala mahi chāī ।
janu baraṣāṃ kṛta pragaṭa buḍhāī ।।

Look here, Lakshman: the rains are over now and the most charming autumn has arrived. The whole earth is covered by the kasa grass with its white flowers as if the rainy season has exposed its old age.

उदित अगस्ति पंथ जल सोषा।
जिमि लोभहिं सोषइ संतोषा॥
सरिता सर निर्मल जल सोहा।
संत हृदय जस गत मद मोहा॥[301]

udita Agasti paṃtha jala soṣā ।
jimi lobhahi soṣai saṃtoṣā ।।
saritā sara nirmala jala sohā ।
saṃta hṛdaya jasa gata mada mohā ।।

The constellation known by the name of Agastya (Canopus) has appeared and dried up the water on the roads even as contentment swallows greed.

The limpid water of the rivers and lakes looks charming as a saint's heart devoid of pride and infatuation.

रस रस सूख सरित सर पानी।
ममता त्याग करहिं जिमि ग्यानी ॥
जानि सरद रितु खंजन आए।
पाइ समय जिमि सुकृत सुहाए ॥[302]

rasa rasa sūkha sarita sara pānī ।
mamatā tyāga karahiṃ jimi gyānī ॥
jāni sarada ritu Khaṃjana āe ।
pāi samaya jimi sukṛta suhāe ॥

Slowly but gradually, the water of the streams and lakes is drying up even as the wise shake off the possessive instinct. Knowing that the autumn had set in, the Khanjana bird has made its appearance, just as the welcome fruit of one's meritorious deeds appears at the appointed time (neither sooner nor later).

पंक न रेनु सोह असि धरनी।
नीति निपुन नृप कै जसि करनी ॥
जल संकोच बिकल भइँ मीना।
अबुध कुटुंबी जिमि धनहीना ॥[303]

paṃka na renu soha asi dharanī ।
nīti nipuna nṛpa kai jasi karanī ॥
jala saṃkoca bikala bhaiṃ mīnā ।
abudha kuṭuṃbī jimi dhanahīnā ॥

Devoid of mud and dust the earth has assumed a lovely aspect, just like the administration of a monarch well-versed in politics. The fish are distressed on account of the diminishing waters, even as an improvident householder suffering from want of money.

बिनु घन निर्मल सोह अकासा।
हरिजन इव परिहरि सब आसा॥
कहुँ कहुँ बृष्टि सारदी थोरी।
कोउ एक भाव भगति जिमि मोरी॥[304]

binu dhana nirmala soha akāsā ।
Harijana iva parihari saba āsā ।।
kahuṃ kahuṃ bṛṣṭi sāradī thorī ।
kou eka pāva bhagati jimi morī ।।

The cloudless sky is shining as bright as a devotee of Shri Hari, who has abandoned all desires. Here and there we have light autumnal showers, just as a rare soul comes to develop devotion to me.

चले हरषि तजि नगर नृप तापस बनिक भिखारि।
जिमि हरिभगति पाइ श्रम तजहिं आश्रमी चारि॥[305]

cale harași taji nagara nṛpa tāpasa banika bhikhāri ।
jimi Haribhagata pāi śram tajahi āśramī cāri ।।

'Kings and ascetics, merchants and mendicants are gladly leaving the city (kings for extending their dominions, ascetics in search of a suitable place for practicing penance, merchants for carrying on their trade and mendicants for begging alms), just as men in any of the four stages of life cease to toil (for perfection) once they have acquired devotion to Shri Hari.'

सुखी मीन जे नीर अगाधा।
जिमि हरि सरन न एकऊ बाधा॥
फूलें कमल सोह सर कैसा।
निर्गुन ब्रह्म सगुन भएँ जैसा॥[306]

sukhī mīna je nīra agādhā ।
jimi Hari sarana na ekau bādhā ।।

phūleṃ kamala soha sara kaisā ।
nirguna Brahman saguna bhaeṃ jaisā ।।

In deep waters, the fish are as happy as ever, just as those who have taken refuge in Shri Hari (i.e., myself) never to fall into trouble of any kind. With full-blown lotuses, the lake appears as charming as when the absolute Brahma appears with form.

गुंजत मधुकर मुखर अनूपा।
सुंदर खग रव नाना रूपा॥
चक्रबाक मन दुख निसि पेखी।
जिमि दुर्जन पर संपति देखी॥[307]

guṃjata madhukara mukhara anūpā ।
suṃdara khaga rava nānā rūpā ।।
cakrabāka mana dukha nisi paikhī ।
jimi durjana para saṃpati dekhī ।।

The bees are making a humming sound which possesses a unique melody of its own, and the birds a charming concert of diverse sounds. The Chakravaka bird is sad at heart to see the night, just as a villain is grieved at the sight of another's fortune.

चातक रटत तृषा अति ओही।
जिमि सुख लहइ न संकर द्रोही॥
सरदातप निसि ससि अपहरई।
संत दरस जिमि पातक टरई॥[308]

cātaka raṭata tṛṣā ati ohī ।
jimi sukha lahai na Saṃkaradrohī ।।
saradātapa nisi sasi apaharaī ।
saṃta darasa jimi pātaka ṭaraī ।।

The Chataka cries out in its agony of excessive thirst just as an enemy of Shankara knows no rest. The moon by night relieves the heat of the autumnal sun, just as the sight of a holy man drives away sin.

देखि इंदु चकोर समुदाई।
चितवहिं जिमि हरिजन हरि पाई॥
मसक दंस बीते हिम त्रासा।
जिमि द्विज द्रोह किएँ कुल नासा॥[309]

dekhi iṃdu cakora samudāī ।
citavatahiṃ jimi Harijana hari pāī ।।
masaka daṃsa bīte hima trāsā ।
jimi dvija droha kieṃ kula nāsā ।।

Flocks of Chakora birds fix their gaze on the moon as soon as she comes to their view, even as the votaries of Shri Hari on meeting Him. Mosquitoes and gadflies have perished due to fear of cold, just as hostility to the Brahmins brings ruin to the entire family.

भूमि जीव संकुल रहे गए सरद रितु पाइ।
सदगुर मिलें जाहिं जिमि संसय भ्रम समुदाइ॥[310]

bhūmi jīva saṃkula rahe gae sarada ritu pāi ।
sadagura mile jāhiṃ jimi saṃsaya bhram samudāi ।।

The insects that teemed on the earth have perished with the advent of the autumn, just as a man who has found a teacher in the real sense of the term, is rid of all doubt and error.

Like with his evocation of the monsoons, Tulsi is at his poetic best in describing the coming of autumn—the *sharad ritu.* As he does with the monsoons, the poet waxes eloquent on the elements of sharad, replete with analogies, displaying both his love of nature, and the joy of Ram and Lakshman at the change of season.

In the Indian aesthetic tradition, sharad is the time of fulfilment and of plenty. The rains have left the earth lush and green. The rivers and ponds are full of water. The crops are ripe. Trees are full of fruit, the skies are clear, the stars shine bright, there is a cool breeze, the nights are pleasant, the days balmy, the granaries full and the cows with plenty to eat. It is no coincidence that Krishna enacts his raas leela—the celestial and sensual dance with the gopis on the banks of the Yamuna in Vrindavan—at this time. When all the elements of weather and season and human need are in place, and to this is added the music of the magical flute of Krishna, the sringara mood—of intense and poignant sensuality—is born, and the raas leela takes place spontaneously.

Ram is not Krishna. One is maryada purushottam, the other is leela purushottam. Krishna is considered the *purna avatar,* possessing all of the sixteen elements that constitute complete divinity, while Ram has thirteen, the three not there relating to sringara. He is, nevertheless, one of Hinduism's most revered deities, and even without the sringara element, is portrayed by Tulsi—as we have seen—with human emotions of love and longing. The onset of sharad only increases Ram's anguish at the absence of Sita, and he tells Lakshman that he must at any cost find her.

There is one analogy that Tulsi uses which requires our special attention. In one chaupai, the four-line stanza, he says that fully bloomed lotuses have appeared in the lakes, as though the nirguna Brahman has become saguna: *nirguna Brahman saguna bhain jaisa.* Here we find Tulsi return to his oft-repeated belief, that the undifferentiated nirguna Absolute, which is Brahman, manifests itself, for the needs of devotees, as saguna. Ram is Brahman reincarnate in saguna form, accessible to his devotees, and a fount of mercy and redemption. In this beautifully crafted analogy, the waters of the lake are the attributeless Absolute, but they contain within them the potentiality to give rise to the personal divinity, which are the lotuses emerging from within them. The impersonal divine then becomes a personal god. For Tulsi, Ram is that perfect personal god, detached and transcendent like Brahman, but human in form as an object of complete reverence for his devotees.

32. A Description of Shri Hanuman

जासु नाम जपि सुनहु भवानी।
भव बंधन काटहिं नर ग्यानी॥
तासु दूत कि बंध तरु आवा।
प्रभु कारज लगि कपिहिं बँधावा॥[311]

jāsu nāma japi sunahu Bhavānī ।
bhava baṃdhana kāṭahiṃ nara gyānī ।।
tāsu dūta ki baṃdha taru āvā ।
prabhu kāraja lagi kapihiṃ baṃdhāvā ।।

Now, Parvati, is it conceivable that the envoy of the Lord whose very name enables the wise to cut asunder the bonds of mundane existence should come under bondage? No, it was in the service of the Lord that Hanuman allowed himself to be bound.

राम नाम बिनु गिरा न सोहा।
देखु बिचारि त्यागि मद मोहा॥
बसन हीन नहिं सोह सुरारी।
सब भूषन भूषित बर नारी॥[312]

Rāma nāma binu girā na sohā ।
dekhu bicāri tyāgi mada mohā ।।
basana hīna nahiṃ soha surārī ।
saba bhūṣaṇa bhūṣita bara nārī ।।

Speech is charmless without Shri Ram's name. Ponder and see for yourself, casting aside arrogance and infatuation. A fair lady without clothes, O enemy of gods, does not a look herself even though adorned with all kinds of jewels.

> ता कहुँ प्रभु कछु अगम नहिं जा पर तुम्ह अनुकूल।
> तव प्रभावँ बड़वानलहिं जारि सकइ खलु तूल ॥[313]

> tā kahuṃ prabhu kachu agama nahiṃ jā para tumha anukula ।
> taba prabhāvaṃ baḍavānalahiṃ jāri sakai khalu tūla ।।

'Nothing is unattainable, my lord, to him who enjoys Your grace. Through Your might a mere shred of cotton can surely burn a submarine fire (the impossible can be made possible).'

Hanuman is one of the central and most loved characters of the Ramayana. Son of Kesari and Anjana, he is known by many names, including Mahavira, Kesarinandan, Pavansuta, Anjaniputra, Bajrangbali, Anjaneya, and Pavan Kumar. According to mythology, he is the son of the wind, hence Pavansuta. He is also regarded as the son of fire, Anjaniputra.

Hanuman stands for complete devotion to Ram. This selfless devotion or bhakti for his Lord, which he pursues with single-minded focus, is his foremost and most endearing quality. But, he is also considered to be endowed with many other qualities, which is one reason why his worship is both highly popular and widespread. He is the quintessential brahmachari or celibate, in eternal control over his senses, a yogi incarnate, with no other personal cause to pursue except the bhakti of Ram. He stands for great strength and valour, with the mace or *gada* as his weapon. He is the embodiment of knowledge and scholarship—*gyan guna sagar,* the ocean of jnana and of all auspicious qualities. According to Tulsi, he is learned in Vedantic philosophy, a master of the Vedas, a poet, a polymath, a grammarian, a singer and a musician par excellence. He is the remover of dangers, *sankata mochana.* The seventeenth century Maharashtrian saint and poet, Samartha Ramdasa, saw him as a symbol of nationalism and resistance to persecution. In later literature, he is also seen as the patron god of the martial arts.

The three passages taken here illustrate different facets of Hanuman. In the first, Shiva himself tells Parvati, that as the envoy or *duta* of the all-powerful and omnipotent Ram, Hanuman's strength knows no bounds. In the literal sense, Shiva is referring to the futile attempts by Ravana's soldiers to tie up Hanuman, but in the larger sense this is a tribute to his legendary might, of which examples abound in the Ramayana. The most famous of these is when Lakshman is mortally wounded in the battle with Ravana, and was likely to die without treatment of a herb from a Himalayan mountain. Hanuman, who could move with the speed of the wind, is sent to bring that herb. Upon reaching the Himalayas, he finds that the mountain has a variety of herbs and he cannot recognise the specific one required. So, the story goes, he rips the entire mountain from the earth, and flies back with it to the wounded Lakshman. This legendary act is one of the most popular stories of Hanuman, and has been widely illustrated over the centuries, showing Hanuman flying through the skies with the entire mountain perched on his shoulder.

The second stanza depicts Hanuman advising Ravana to give up his hubris and pride, and accept the servitude of Ram. No amount of boastful talk by Ravana is to any avail, just as a woman adorned with jewellery but without clothes is still considered naked. Here, Hanuman is the sage, giving counsel to Ravana, displaying both his devotion to Ram, and his virtues of a scholar and yogi. Ravana has enough opportunities to see the great valour of Hanuman. In spite of his efforts to stop him, the mighty monkey god has met with the incarcerated Sita, and almost set the entire city of Lanka ablaze when soldiers tried to set fire to his tail. Failing to convince Ravana to surrender to the omnipotence of Ram, Hanuman manages to escape and rejoin Ram.

The third stanza illustrates Hanuman's total and complete devotion to Ram. Nothing is unattainable for him who enjoys your favour, Hanuman tells Ram. The analogy that follows is most interesting. Ram may appear to be soft like cotton, but this cotton has the power to reduce to cinders everything, even the fire burning below the sea, in the very underbelly of the earth. This tremendous bhakti of Ram has become an inevitable part of any iconography of Hanuman. After Ram defeats

Ravana, and returns victorious to Ayodhya, he wishes to give Hanuman a gift by which he could remember him. Hanuman refuses to accept this gift, saying that it is redundant, since Ram and Sita were enshrined forever in his heart. As proof of this, he tears open his chest to reveal his heart, which shows an image of Ram and Sita. Ram then wants to bless Hanuman with immortality, but again Hanuman refuses, asking only for a place at the feet of Ram so that he could worship him. Both these incidents have been illustrated in countless drawings and paintings, and constitute the popular image of devotion and surrender that symbolises the character of Hanuman.

33. Dialogue Between Ravana and Vibhishana

सचिव बैद गुर तीनि जौं प्रिय बोलहिं भय आस।
राज धर्म तन तीनि कर होइ बेगिहीं नास ॥[314]

saciva baida gura tīni jauṃ priya bolahiṃ bhaya āsa ।
rāja dharma tana tīni kara hoi begihīṃ nāsa ।।

When a minister, a physician and a religious preceptor—these three use pleasing words from fear or hope of reward, the result is that dominion, health and faith, all the three forthwith go to the dogs.

जो आपन चाहै कल्याना।
सुजसु सुमति सुभ गति सुख नाना॥
सो परनारि लिलार गोसाईं।
तजउ चउथि के चंद कि नाईं॥[315]

jo āpana cāhai kalyānā ।
sujasu sumati subha gati sukha nānā ।।
so paranāri lilāra gosāīṃ ।
tajau cauthi ke caṃda ki nāṃ ।।

Let him who seeks after his welfare, good reputation, wisdom, a good destiny after his death and joys of various kinds, turn his eyes away from the brow of another's wife even as one should refuse to see the moon on the fourth night (of the bright half) of a lunar month.

काम क्रोध मद लोभ सब नाथ नरक के पंथ।
सब परिहरि रघुबीरहि भजहु भजहिं जेहि संत ॥[316]

kāma krodha mada lobha saba nātha naraka ke paṃtha ।
saba parihari Raghubīrahi bhajahu bhajahiṃ jehi saṃta ।।

Lust, anger, vanity and covetousness are all paths leading to hell. Abjuring all these adore the Hero of Raghu's line, whom saints worship.

गो द्विज धेनु देव हितकारी।
कृपासिंधु मानुष तनुधारी ॥
जन रंजन भंजन खल ब्राता।
बेद धर्म रच्छक सुनु भ्राता ॥[317]

go dvija dhenu deva hitakārī ।
kṛpāsiṃdhu mānuṣa tanudhārī ।।
jana Raṃjana bhaṃjana khala brātā ।
Beda dharma racchaka sunu bhrātā ।।

'An ocean of compassion, He has assumed the form of a human being for the good of Earth, the Brahmin, the cow and the gods. Listen, brother: He delights His devotees and breaks the ranks of the impious and is the champion of the Vedas and true religion.'

सुमति कुमति सब कें उर रहहीं।
नाथ पुरान निगम अस कहहीं ॥
जहाँ सुमति तहँ संपति नाना।
जहाँ कुमति तहँ बिपति निदाना ॥[318]

sumati kumati saba keṃ ura rahahīṃ ।
nātha Purāna nigama asa kahahīṃ ।।
jahāṃ sumati tahaṃ saṃpati nānā ।
jahāṃ kumati tahaṃ bipati nidānā ।।

Rightful intellect and the perverted one dwell in the heart of all: so declare the Puranas and Vedas, my lord. Where there is right type of intellect, prosperity of every kind reigns; and where there is unwisdom, misfortune is the inevitable end.

Vibhishana is a very interesting character in the Ramayana. He is Ravana, and Kumbhkaran's younger brother, the youngest son of Sage Vishrava and Kaikeshi, and the grandson of Sage Putsalya, one of the heavenly guardians. By birth, he belonged to the family of 'rakshasas', but in contrast to what should have been his ingrained evil mindset, he is of noble character, with a sattvik mind and the heart of a bhakt of the Lord. It is said that as a child he became a devotee of Lord Vishnu. Pleased with his dedicated devotion, Brahma appeared before him, and offered him any boon he wanted. Vibhishana said that all he wanted was to have his mind fixed on the lotus-feet of the Lord, and receive a darshan of Vishnu. This prayer was fulfilled, and Vibhishana gave up all his wealth, renounced his family, and lived a life of piety and devotion.

Naturally, Vibhishana was against Ravana's abduction of Sita, and berated his arrogance and hubris. He urged his elder brother to return Sita forthwith to Ram, and to change his ways, but to no avail When Ravana refused to listen to him, Vibhishana joined Ram, who embraced him as we shall see in the following prasang. Vibhishana played a key role in Ram's victory over Ravana, divulging the secrets of the demon king's army. In fact, when Ram was unable to kill Ravana, because a new head would come up for every head Ram severed, it is Vibhishana who tells Ram to shoot an arrow at Ravana's navel, for that is where his 'nectar' of immortality lies.

After the defeat of Ravana, Ram, appearing in his original form of Vishnu, anointed Vibhishana as the king of Lanka. In this role, he is considered as one of the 'seven immortals or Chiranjeevis'.

Vibhishana is also associated with a very interesting lore relating to the famous Sri Ranganathaswamy temple at Srirangam in Tamil Nadu, considered the abode of Vishnu on earth. The story goes that Vibhishana, as the king of Lanka, was presented with the sacred Sri Ranga Vimana.

While carrying it to his kingdom in Lanka, Vibhishana stopped to rest midway on the banks of the Kaveri. After his rest, when he wanted to leave, he found that he could not lift the Vimana, however much he tried. Mahavishnu then appeared to him, and said that he wished to stay as Ranganath in this very place, which went on to become the famous holy city of Srirangam.

Vibhishana's dialogue with Ravana is significant for its ethical intensity, and some remarkable words of practical wisdom. The most important of these is Tulsi's pronouncement that in a kingdom, if a minister *(sachiv),* doctor (vaidya) and guru, do not give good and correct advice to the ruler out of either fear or anticipation of personal gain, then the kingdom, the body, and dharma will be soon destroyed. The efficacy of these words is time-tested, as contextual today as when they were then written. Tulsi uses his characters to introduce certain verities, and in so doing also reveals what was the dominant ethic or traditional wisdom prevailing in his times. A ruler must be given correct and impartial advice by his subordinates. This was stated in the *Shanti Parva* of the Mahabharat, as also by Chanakya in the *Arthashastra.* The three key figures in a ruler's court were the minister or principal secular counsellor, the guru or spiritual preceptor, and the vaidya or one who administered to the personal health of the king. They were conjoined to always speak the truth, for the consequences of their not doing so could be disastrous for the well-being of the kingdom. Tulsi could find no more apt character than Vibhishana to state this truth to Ravana.

While urging Ravana to give up his greed and pride, and to surrender to Ram, Vibhishana says that the Lord—who is the ocean of mercy—has taken human avatar for the benefit of the gods, and the protection of the cow and of Brahmins. This valorisation of Brahmins is an oft-repeated sentiment in Tulsidas. The question is whether he is referring to Brahmins as a caste based on the prescriptive entitlement of birth, or to people who are learned and have the qualities of a Brahmin. It would be useful to remember that Tulsi was himself a Brahmin, and, therefore, there would be, prima facie, a reason to believe that he may have been predisposed to posit a privileged position for members of his own caste. However, Tulsi was also a learned person, well versed in all the Shastras, and would be entitled, on the basis of his vocation as a writer, poet, and his vast knowledge—apart from his saintliness and piety—to qualify to be a Brahmin on the basis of personal achievement rather than birth. This then is a question that must be raised but left without a definitive answer, leaving it to the predilections of the reader to give our poet the benefit of doubt, or accuse him of being partial to the prescriptive hierarchies of the caste system.

34. Dialogue Between Shri Ram and Vibhishana

बरु भल बास नरक कर ताता।
दुष्ट संग जनि देइ बिधाता॥
अब पद देखि कुसल रघुराया।
जौं तुम्ह कीन्हि जानि जन दाया॥[319]

baru bhala bāsa naraka kara tātā ।
duṣṭa saṃga jani dei bidhātā ।।
aba pada dekhi kusala Raghurāyā ।
jauṃ tumha kīnha jāni jana dāyā ।।

'It is much better to live in hell, dear Vibhishna; but may Providence never place us in the company of the wicked. All is well with me now that I have beheld Your feet, O Lord of the Raghus, and since You have shown Your mercy to me, recognising me as Your servant.'

तजि मद मोह कपट छल नाना।
करउँ सद्य तेहि साधु समाना॥
जननी जनक बंधु सुत दारा।
तनु धनु भवन सुहृद परिवारा॥
सब कै ममता ताग बटोरी।
मम पद मनहिं बाँध बरि डोरी॥
समदरसी इच्छा कछु नाहीं।
हरष सोक भय नहिं मन माहीं॥[320]

taji mada moha kapaṭa chala nānā ।
karauṃ sadya tehi sādhu samānā ।।
jananī Janaka baṃdhu suta dārā ।
tanu dhanu bhavana suhrada parivārā ।।
saba kai mamatā tāga baṭorī ।
mama pada manahi bāṃdha bari ḍorī ।।
samadarasī icchā kachu nāhīṃ ।
harasa soka bhaya nahiṃ mana māhīṃ ।।

'Listen, my friend: I tell you my nature, which is known to Bhushundi, Shambhu (Lord Shiva) and Girija (Parvati) too. If a man, even though he has been an enemy of the whole animate and inanimate creation, comes terror-stricken to me, seeking my protection and discarding vanity, infatuation, hypocrisy and trickeries of various kinds, I speedily make him the very like of a saint. The ties of affection that bind a man to his mother, father, brother, son, wife, body, wealth, house, friends and relations are like so many threads which a pious soul gathers up and twists into a string where with he binds his soul to my feet. Nay, he looks upon all with the same eye and has no craving and his mind is free from joy, grief and fear.

अस सज्जन मम उर बस कैसें ।
लोभी हृदयँ बसइ धनु जैसें ॥
तुम्ह सारिखे संत प्रिय मोरें ।
धरउँ देह नहिं आन निहोरें ॥[321]

asa sajjana mama ura basa kaiseṃ ।
lobhī hṛdayaṃ basai dhanu jaiseṃ ।।
tumha sārikhe saṃta priya moreṃ ।
dharauṃ deha nahiṃ āna nihoreṃ ।।

'A saint of this description abides in my heart even as mammon resides in the heart of a covetous man. Only saints of your type are dear to me; for the sake of none else do I body myself forth.'

The manner in which Ram welcomes Vibhishana is important both for the big heartedness of the Lord, and for delineating the qualities which he seeks in a devotee. Firstly, he lauds Vibhishana for the discrimination he has shown in shunning the company of the wicked. It is better to be confined to hell, he says, than to be in the wrong company. Secondly, he emphasises that absolute surrender is the key to redemption, and this applies even to those who have sinned against both animate and inanimate creation. Thirdly, he elaborates upon the qualities of a true bhakt. That person is worthy of being a real devotee who abjures vanity, infatuation, guile and hypocrisy. The true bhakt must also take the separate threads of attachment that bind him to his parents, brother, son, wife, friends, wealth, home and family, and entwine them into a single rope that is bound to the feet of the Lord. Once he has done that, and is no longer driven by craving, fear or joy and grief, he is accepted by the Lord like a saint, and abides in the Lord's heart 'like riches do in the heart of a covetous man'. The analogy is a bit awkward, but the intent is crystal clear, that for Ram a bhakt who has transcended worldly attachments and acquired the equanimity of the detached, has a permanent place in his heart.

Here, Tulsi appears to be elaborating upon his own firm belief in the importance of surrendering to the Almighty, but also echoing the most vital aspects of the prevailing Vaishnava ideology, which expects a devotee to unconditionally surrender to the Lord, while simultaneously purifying himself internally so as to be free from all worldly attachments. The simple point that Tulsi is making is that unconditional devotion to Ram is not possible for the person who is entangled in the conventional seductions of the temporal world, and since Vibhishana has given up conventional attachments in preference to the bhakti of the Lord, he is a devotee that Ram welcomed with open arms.

35. Dialogue Between Ravana and Mandodari

पद पाताल सीस अज धामा ।
अपर लोक अँग अँग बिश्रामा ॥
भृकुटि बिलास भयंकर काला ।
नयन दिवाकर कच घन माला ॥[322]

pada pātāla sīsa aja dhāmā ।
apara loka aṃga aṃga biśrāmā ।।
bhṛkuṭi bilāsa bhayaṃkara kālā ।
nayana divākara kaca ghana mālā ।।

The subterranean regions *(patala)* are His feet and the abode of Brahma His head; while the other (intermediate) spheres are located in His other limbs. Terrible Death is the mere contraction of His eyebrows, the sun is His eye and the mass of clouds His locks.

जासु घ्रान अस्वनीकुमारा ।
निसि अरु दिवस निमेष अपारा ॥
श्रवन दिसा दस बेद बखानी ।
मारुत स्वास निगम निज बानी ॥[323]

jāsu ghrāna Asvinīkumārā ।
nisi aru divasa nimeṣa apārā ।।
śravana disā dasa Beda bakhānī ।
māruta svāsa nigama nija bānī ।।

The twin-born gods Ashvinikumaras (the celestial physicians) are His nostrils and the alternating days and nights constitute the repeated twinkling of His eyelids; while the ten quarters of the heavens are His ears: so declare the Vedas. The winds are His breath and the Vedas, His own speech.

अधर लोभ जम दसन कराला।
माया हास बाहु दिगपाला॥
आनन अनल अंबुपति जीहा।
उतपति पालन प्रलय समीहा॥[324]

adhara lobha jama dasana karālā ।
Māyā hāsa bāhu digapālā ।।
ānana anala aṃbupati jīhā ।
utapati pālana pralaya samīhā ।।

Greed is His lower lip and Yama (the god who sits in judgement on the dead), His dreadful teeth; Maya (cosmic illusion) is His laughter and the regents of the ten quarters, His arms; fire is His mouth and Varuna (the god presiding over the waters), His tongue; while the creation, preservation and destruction of the universe are His gestures.

रोम राजि अष्टादस भारा।
अस्थि सैल सरिता नस जारा॥
उदर उदधि अधगो जातना।
जगमय प्रभु का बहु कलपना॥[325]

roma rāji aṣṭādasa bhārā ।
asthi saila saritā nasa jārā ।।
udara udadhi adhago jātanā ।
jagamaya prabhu kā bahu kalapanā ।।

The eighteen principal species of the vegetable kingdom constitute the line of hair on His belly, the mountains are His bones and the rivers represent the network of His veins. The ocean is His belly and the inferno, His organs of urination and excretion. In short, the universe is a manifestation of the Lord and it is no use going into further details.

Hindu mythology revels in contradictions. There are no definitive black and white polarities. In a landscape rich in greys there is no one absolutely bad, nor no one absolutely good. Ravana's family is a case in point. Although he himself was a rakshasa, his brother, Vibhishana, as we have seen, was an upright, honest and righteous worshipper of Shri Vishnu, and a devoted follower of Ram. This was the case with Ravana's chief queen, Mandodari, too. She was the daughter of Mayasura, king of the asuras or demons, but notwithstanding this lineage, was herself beautiful, pious and moral. Mandodari is extolled as one of the five '*panchkanyas*' (or five virgins, the other four being Ahalya, Draupadi, Tara and Kunti), the recital of whose name dispels sin. In mythology, Mandodari represents the element of water, turbulent on the surface but deep and silent in her spiritual quest.

Mandodari was a good wife to Ravana. She bore him three sons—Meghnada, Atikaya and Akshayakumara. Fully aware of Ravana's evil disposition, her role was to try and persuade him to desist from doing the wrong thing, a task in which she failed in spite of her persistence. However, on her part, she was very good to Sita, and fully accepted her fidelity to Ram. When Ravana died, she lamented his demise, not only as any good wife would do at the death of her husband, but also because she loved him in spite of his wicked traits. According to many traditions, after the war, and the death of Ravana, she married, on Ram's advice, Vibhishana, who had been crowned as the new king of Lanka.

These lines in which Mandodari describes the grandeur, power, omnipotence and omniscience of Ram from head to toe, must rank as one of the most powerful and compelling praises of the Lord in the Manas. It is significant that she has the courage to convey this tribute to Ravana directly, whose undying hostility to Ram is known. Predictably, Ravana scoffs at her and her eulogy for his arch enemy.

36. Dialogue Between Angad and Ravana

प्रीति बिरोध समान सन करिअ नीति असि आहि।
जौं मृगपति बध मेडुकन्हि भल कि कहइ कोउ ताहि ॥[326]

prīti birodha samāna sana karia nīti asi āhi ।
jauṃ mṛgapati badha meḍukanhi bhala ki kahai kou tāhi ॥

Make friends or enter into hostilities only with your equals: this is a sound maxim to follow. If a lion were to kill frogs, will anyone speak well of him?

कौल कामबस कृपिन बिमूढा।
अति दरिद्र अजसी अति बूढा॥
सदा रोगबस संतत क्रोधी।
बिष्नु बिमुखश्रुति संत बिरोधी॥
तनु पोषक निंदक अघ खानी।
जीवत सव सम चौदह प्रानी॥[327]

kaula kāmabasa kṛpina bimūḍhā ।
ati daridra ajasī ati būḍhaā ॥
sadā rogabasa saṃtata krodhī ।
Biṣnu bimūkha śruti saṃta birodhī ॥
tanu poṣaka niṃdaka agha khānī ।
jīvata sava sama caudaha prānī ॥

A follower of the Vanamarga (a sect of Shakti-worshippers indulging in certain prohibited practices as a part of their worship), a man given over to lust, a miser, a grossly stupid fellow, an utterly destitute person, a man suffering from disrepute, an extremely old man, an ever sick person, one who is always angry, he who is hostile to Lord Vishnu, an enemy of the Vedas and saints, he who exclusively nourishes his own body, he who is given to slandering others, and he who is a storehouse of sins of these fourteen types of persons are no better than corpses, even while they live.

Ram's army of vanaras had many members of great valour and strength. One of them was Angad, son of Bali and Tara, and nephew of Sugriva. According to legend, Angad's strength was such that none could lift his leg if he planted it firmly on the ground. Angad demonstrated this in Ravana's court, where he had gone as Ram's envoy to give diplomacy a last chance. Angad issued a challenge to those present to try and move his leg. Everyone, including Ravana tried, but failed.

Angad was very close to Ram. He played a key role in reconciling Ram and Lakshman with Sugriva, whom Ram had helped against his brother Bali. Sugriva had offered to help Ram in return, but reneged on his promise and got busy in drink and merriment. This greatly incensed Ram and Lakshman, but Angad intervened and made Sugriva realise his mistake, after which the entire vanara sena worked with devotion and dedication for Ram. In the war, Angad killed many of Ravana's key warriors, including Ravana's son, Narantaka, and his chief general, Mahaparshva. It is said that after the war, Ram made Angad the chief of his army in Ayodhya.

The Manas devotes considerable space to the dialogue between Angad and Ravana. This dialogue takes place in Ravana's court, where Angad does his best to break the pride of Ravana, and convinces him that fighting against Ram was an act of futility. We have chosen three stanzas from this otherwise extensive dialogue.

These stanzas are remarkable for the wisdom that Tulsi displays through the dialogues he writes for his characters. In the first stanza, Angad says that be it love or hostility, it should be with an equal: *priti virodh saman sama kariya niti asi aahi.* The purpose was to convey to Ravana that Ram was far superior to him; but it is simultaneously a statement of worldly wisdom. Tulsi's illustration of this maxim is compelling. What would people say if a tiger, who is the king of the forest, were to spend his energies in killing frogs? The message is that in daily life, and in the secular realm, people should bear in mind their status before attempting to endear or attack another person. It can be said that Tulsi was seeking to reinforce the inequities of the prevailing social order when stating this, or to straitjacket the canvas of human interaction to a narrow spectrum, but, somewhere, there is, beyond larger issues of social hierarchies, an element of human realism too in his pronouncement. It is the kind of statement that, over time, acquires the pedestal of a verity, a quotable quote, enshrining the poet's earthy pragmatism in evaluating the efficacy of human relations.

In the second and third stanzas, Angad says that he could himself dash Ravana to the ground, destroy his army, lay waste to his city and carry off Sita along with all the ladies of his household, but this would hardly bring any credit since there is no valour in slaying the dead! At this point Tulsi steps in, and puts in Angad's mouth, his own views on the fourteen kinds of people who are 'no better than corpses'. These, according to Tulsi, are the secretive tantrics—the Vanamargis, those wholly given to lust, the miserly, the stupid, the destitute beggar, the disgraced, the very old, the perennially ill, the one always in the grip of passion, the enemy of Vishnu, the foe of the Vedas, the pathetically self-indulgent, the one given to slandering, and the thoroughly vicious by nature.

One may or may not agree with Tulsi's categorisation. But one has to concede, that our poet has very definitive views on life and people, and does not hesitate to voice them through the characters that inhabit the Manas.

37. Dialogue Between Shri Ram and Vibhishana

नाथ न रथ नहिं तन पद त्राना।
केहि बिधि जितब बीर बलवाना॥
सुनहु सखा कह कृपानिधाना।
जेहिं जय होइ सो स्यन्दन आना॥
सौरज धीरज तेहि रथ चाका।
सत्य सील दृढ़ धवजा पताका॥
बल बिबेक दस परहित घोरे।
छमा कृपा समता रजु जोरे॥[328]

nātha na ratha nahiṃ tana pada trānā ।
kehi bidhi jitaba bīra balavānā ।।
sunahu sakhā kaha kṛpānidhānā ।
jehiṃ jaya hoi so syaṃdana ānā ।।
sauraja dhīraja tehi ratha cākā ।
satya sīla dṛḍhaḍhvajā patākā ।।
bala bibeka dama parahita ghore ।
chamā kṛpā samatā raju jore ।।

(Vibhishana spoke to Shri Ram) 'My lord, You have no chariot nor any protection either for Your body (in the shape of armour) or for Your feet (in the shape of shoes). How, then, can You expect to conquer this mighty hero?' 'Listen, friend,' replied the all-merciful, 'the chariot which leads one to victory is quite another. Valour and fortitude are the wheels of that chariot, while truthfulness and good conduct are its enduring banner and standard. Even so strength, discretion, self-control and benevolence are its four horses, that have been joined to the chariot with the cords of forgiveness, compassion and evenness of mind.

ईस भजनु सारथी सुजाना।
बिरति चर्म संतोष कृपाना॥
दान परसु बुधि सक्ति प्रचंडा।
बर बिग्यान कठिन कोदंडा॥[329]

Isa bhajanu sārathī sujānā ।
birati carma saṃtoṣa kṛpānā ।।
dāna parasu budhi sakti pracaṃḍā ।
bara bigyāna kaṭhina kodaṃḍā ।।

'Adoration of god is the expert driver; dispassion, the shield and contentment, the sword. Again, charity is the axe; reason, the fierce lance and the highest wisdom, the relentless bow.

अमल अचल मन त्रोन समाना।
सम जम नियम सिलीमुख नाना॥
कवच अभेद बिप्र गुर पूजा।
एहि सम बिजय उपाय न दूजा॥[330]

amala acala mana trona samānā ।
sama jama niyama silīmukha nānā ।।
kavaca abheda bipra gura pūjā ।
ehi sama bijaya upāya na dūjā ।।

'A pure and steady mind is like a quiver; while quietude and the various forms of abstinence *(yamas)* and religious observances *(niyamas)* are a sheaf of arrows. Homage to the Brahmins and to one's own preceptor is an impenetrable coat of mail; there is no other equipment for victory as efficacious as this.

सखा धर्ममय अस रथ जाकें ।
जीतन कहँ न कतहुँ रिपु ताकें ।।[331]

sakhā dharmamaya asa ratha jākeṃ ।
jītana kahaṃ na katahuṃ ripu tākeṃ ।।

'My friend, he who owns such a chariot of piety shall have no enemy to conquer anywhere.'

These lines give Tulsi the opportunity of lauding the great strengths that come from righteousness. Evil may appear to be stronger, much better armed, with all the weapons at its command. Yet goodness has its own intrinsic power, and will always prevail over evil. The context for Tulsi to elaborate on this theme is this conversation between Vibhishana and Ram. Vibhishana expressed doubt. He is concerned about how Ram will take on the might of Ravana who, purely in conventional terms, appears to be much stronger with a well-organised army as against Ram's forces of monkeys and bears.

Tulsi draws up a powerful analogy of a chariot, and then gives to each of its parts, and to the bow and arrow of Ram, qualities that will allow good to triumph over evil. He specifically refers to the qualities of valour and fortitude, of truthfulness and virtuous conduct, of self-control, restraint and benevolence, of dispassion and charity, of a pure and steady mind, and a deeply religious disposition. His essential point is that righteousness is the most invincible weapon in itself, and cannot be defeated by instruments of conventional strength.

Is he being too idealistic in his assessment? Perhaps yes, but not in the case of Ram. Ram is the embodiment of righteousness. That is his strength, and his reason to be a source of inspiration as the maryada purushottam. Tulsi wants to make the point that Ram has the virtues that make a person invincible. These virtues are not acquired from external factors, but are a factor of internal disposition and resolve. They give to an individual the strength of character to overcome any adversity, even in situations where there is apparent asymmetry between the relative might of opposing forces. In this sense, Tulsi, through the medium of Ram, sets forth an ideal for every human being, often caught in situations where personal virtues appear to be dwarfed by the power of an opponent. His message is that, as in the case of Ram, it is precisely these virtues that will ensure the victory of good over evil.

38. Shri Ram's Adoration by Lord Shiva

जय राम रमारमनं समनं।
भवताप भयाकुल पाहि जनं ।।
अवधेस सुरेस रमेस बिभो।
सरनागत मागत पाहि प्रभो ।।[332]

jaya Rāma Ramāramnaṃ samanaṃ ।
bhava tāpa bhayākula pāhi janaṃ ।।
avadhesa suresa ramesa bibho ।
saranāgata māgata pāhi prabho ।।

Hail to You, Ram, Ram's (Sita's) spouse, reliever of the afflictions of worldly existence! Protect this servant, who is obsessed with the fear of transmigration. O King of Ayodhya, ruler of the gods, Lord of Lakshmi, all-pervading master! Having fled to You for refuge, I implore You: pray, extend Your protection to me.

दससीस बिनासन बीस भुजा।
कृत दूरि महा महि भूरि रुजा ।।
रजनीचर बृंद पतंग रहे।
सर पावक तेज प्रचंड दहे ।।[333]

dasasīsa bināsana bīsa bhujā ।
kṛta dūri mahā mahi bhūri rujā ।।
rajanīcara bṛṃda pataṃga rahe ।
sara pāvaka teja pracaṃḍa dahe ।।

By disposing of Ravana who possessed as many as ten heads and twenty arms, You rid the earth of many a severe scourge. The hosts of demons were a veritable swarm of moths that were reduced to ashes by the fierce glow of Your fire-like arrows.

महि मंडल मंडन चारुतरं ।
धृत सायक चाप निषंग बरं ॥
मद मोह महा ममता रजनी ।
तम पुंज दिवाकर तेज अनी ॥[334]

mahi maṃḍala maṃḍana cārutaraṃ ।
dhṛta sāyaka cāpa niṣaṃga baraṃ ॥
mada moha mahā mamatā rajanī ।
tama puṃja divākara teja anī ॥

An exceedingly beautiful jewel of the terrestrial globe, You have armed Yourself with an excellent bow, arrows and quiver. You are a radiant sun as it were to disperse the thick darkness prevailing in the night of pride, gross ignorance and attachment.

मनजात किरात निपात किए ।
मृग लोग कुभोग सरेन हिए ॥
हति नाथ अनाथनि पाहि हरे ।
बिषया बन पावँर भूलि परे ॥[335]

manajāta kirāta nipāta kie ।
mṛga loga kubhoga sarena hie ॥
hati nātha anāthani pāhi Hare ।
biṣayā bana pāvaṃra bhūli pare ॥

The hunter in the form of lust has laid low the human deer by piercing his heart with the shafts of evil desire: O Lord! pray, kill the hunter and thus save the life of these poor helpless creatures, lost as they are in the wilderness of sensuality, O Hari!

बहु रोग बियोगन्हि लोग हए।
भवदंघ्रि निरादर के फल ए॥
भव सिंधु अगाध परे नर ते।
पद पंकज प्रेम न जे करते॥[336]

bahu roga biyoganhi loga hae ।
bhavadaṃghri nirādara ke phala e ।।
bhava siṃdhu agādha pare nara te ।
pada paṃkaja prema na je karate ।।

People are stricken with a host of diseases and bereavements, which are surely the result of neglecting Your feet. Those men who cherish no love for your lotus-feet continue to drift in the fathomless ocean of mundane existence.

अति दीन मलीन दुखी नितहीं।
जिन्ह के पद पंकज प्रीति नहीं॥
अवलंब भवंत कथा जिन्ह के।
प्रिय संत अनंत सदा तिन्ह कें॥[337]

ati dīna malīna dukhī nitahīṃ ।
jinha ke pada paṃkaja prīti nahīṃ ।।
avalaṃba bhavaṃta kathā jinha ke ।।
priya saṃta anaṃta sadā tinha keṃ ।।

They are ever most wretched, impure and unhappy, who have no devotion to Your lotus-feet. On the other hand, they who derive their sustenance from Your stories hold the saints and the eternal Lord (Yourself) as constantly dear to them.

नहिं राग न लोभ न मान मदा॥
तिन्ह कें सम बैभव वा बिपदा॥
एहि ते तव सेवक होत मुदा।
मुनि त्यागत जोग भरोस सदा॥[338]

nahiṃ rāga na lobha na māna madā ||
tinha keṃ sama baibhava vā bipadā ||
ehi te tava sevaka hota mudā |
muni tyāgata joga bharosa sadā ||

They are free from passion, greed, pride and arrogance; prosperity and adversity are alike to them. That is why sages give up forever all faith in Yoga (mental discipline) and gladly become Your servants.

करि प्रेम निरंतर नेम लिएँ।
पद पंकज सेवत सुद्ध हिएँ॥
सम मानि निरादर आदरही।
सब संत सुखी बिचरंति मही॥[339]

kari prema niraṃtara nema lieṃ |
pada paṃkaja sevata suddha hieṃ ||
sama māni nirādara ādarahī |
saba saṃta sukhī bicaraṃti mahī ||

With a pure heart and under a solemn pledge, they constantly and lovingly adore Your lotus-feet. Regarding honour and ignominy alike, all such saints move about happily on earth.

मुनि मानस पंकज भृंग भजे।
रघुबीर महा रनधीर अजे॥
तव नाम जपामि नमामि हरी।
भव रोग महागद मान अरी॥[340]

muni mānasa paṃkaja bhṛṃga bhaje |
Raghubīra mahā ranadhīra aje ||
tava nāma japāmi namāmi harī |
bhava roga mahāgada māna arī ||

O Hero of Raghu's line, invincible and exceedingly staunch in battle, in dwelling as a bee the lotus heart of sages, I take refuge in You. I repeat

Your Name and bow to You, O Hari; You are a sovereign remedy for the disease of birth and death and an enemy of pride.

गुन सील कृपा परमायतनं।
प्रनमामि निरंतर श्रीरमनं॥
रघुनंद निकंदय द्वंद्वघनं।
महिपाल बिलोकय दीनजनं॥[341]

guna sīla kṛpā paramāyatanaṃ ।
pranamāmi niraṃtara Srīramnaṃ ।।
Raghunaṃda nikaṃdaya dvaṃdvaghanaṃ ।
mahipāla bilokaya dīna janaṃ ।।

I constantly greet You, Lakshmi's spouse, supreme abode of goodness, amiability and compassion. O delight of the Raghus, put an end to all pairs of contrary experiences (such as joy and sorrow, pleasure and pain, attraction and repulsion, etc.); O Ruler of the earth, just cast a glance on this humble servant.

This is one of most powerful prayers in praise of Ram in the Manas. The sheer flow of its rhyme and meter, its soaring devotional tempo, and the overwhelming mood of complete surrender and supplication that it invokes, makes it a truly fine poetic composition.

The fact that these stanzas are chanted by Shiva in praise of Ram is of great interest. After the other gods have made their praises of Ram, it is Shiva's turn, and as the Manas itself states, the Mahadeva uttered these lines with 'the hair on his body standing erect' and a voice quivering with emotion. It is clear that Tulsi wanted Shiva's ode to be the most pivotal recognition of Ram's unchallenged greatness.

Why would Tulsi reserve this place for Shiva? Because, as in several earlier stanzas, he wished to bury the false dichotomy between the followers of Vishnu and Shiva. Devotees could have their *isht devata,* their choice of deity, but the worship of Ram transcended these fault lines, since he was an incarnation of Vishnu and the beloved of Shiva, thereby synthesising in himself all devotees and sects.

It is to be noted that Shiva's praise for Ram is fully reciprocated. Ram, too, is a worshipper of Shiva. In fact, elsewhere, Ram says specifically that he is against anyone who does not revere Shiva. Thus, the legacy of Shiva is subsumed by the worship of Ram, and the adoration of Ram is incomplete without praise for Shiva. Both these deities become two sides of the same coin of devotion, and if Shiva accepts Ram as the Supreme Lord, Ram too believes in the divine omnipotence of Shiva. Devotion then moves away from man-made compartments to a larger bathos of total surrender, of which Shiva and Ram, given their mutual love, become joint icons.

But with this as the backdrop, Tulsi, it would appear, clearly wanted that the highest and most lyrical praise for Ram comes from Shiva. And these lines, which have become a prayer recited by millions of Hindus every day, are the consequence of his intention. No other god could so convincingly prove Ram's greatness, since the efficacy of praise depends on who is voicing it. Praise by the Lord of Lords, the Great God, Mahadeva,—and that too of this effulgent nature—was necessary, in the eyes of Tulsi, to establish once and for all the primacy of Ram in his devotional scheme of things. If Shiva himself sings the glory of Ram so evocatively, who can ever question the pedestal on which Tulsi sought to place Ram?

There are several points to be noted in this deeply moving hymn. Firstly, reverence is showered on Ram not only because he is the supreme deity, but because he uses his powers of benevolence to dispel the darkness of pride, ignorance and attachment. For human beings caught in the mire of attachment to objects, he is a deliverer. Thus, there is, in his divinity, a strong ethical character, which has the power to influence a devotee towards goodness. Secondly, redemption from him is guaranteed only to those who unconditionally surrender to the grace of his lotus-feet. Those who refuse to do so are condemned to live in the cycle of sorrow and sadness. Thirdly, it is this bhakti which is the most efficacious path.

Tulsi makes the point that even sages understand that any other path, including the path of ascetism, is of little value compared to the rewards that pure bhakti can reap. This thought is interesting since Shiva himself is often regarded as the Great Ascetic, smeared in ash with a garland of skulls around his neck and capable of long periods of meditation and abstinence. But here, Shiva is himself saying that ascetism or Yoga are of little consequence in comparison to the bhakti *marga* (path). Fourthly, Tulsi seeks to emphasise that bhakti to Ram is not only for conventional rewards in temporal terms, but for its transformative ability to make a person acquire greater joy and equilibrium. It liberates a person from the opposing polarities of joy and sorrow, prosperity and adversity, attraction and repulsion, and from the cycle of birth and death.

Thus, in Shiva's iconic ode, Ram is the great liberator, who both emancipates and transforms a devotee, provided the devotee fully surrenders to him. His powers are unlimited; his benevolence is boundless; his joys are unblemished; and, his transformative influence is for the creation of a better human being, better prepared to lead a life of bliss and balance.

39. Ramrajya

दैहिक दैविक भौतिक तापा।
राम राज नहिं काहुहि ब्यापा।
सब नर करहिं परस्पर प्रीती।
चलहिं स्वधर्म निरत श्रुति नीती ॥[342]

daihika daivika bhautika tāpā ।
Rāma rāja nahiṃ kāhuhi byāpā ।।
saba nara karahiṃ paraspara prītī ।
calahiṃ svadharma nirata śruti nītī ।।

Under the rule of Ram there was none who suffered from affliction of any kind whether of the body, or proceeding from divine or supernatural agencies or that caused by another living being. All men loved one another: each followed one's prescribed duty, conformably to the precepts of the Vedas.

चारिउ चरन धर्म जग माहीं।
पूरि रहा सपनेहुँ अघ नाहीं॥
राम भगति रत नर अरु नारी।
सकल परम गति के अधिकारी ॥[343]

cāriu carana dharma jaga māhīṃ ।
pūri rahā sapanehuṃ agha nāhīṃ ।।
rāma bhagati rata nara aru nārī ।
sakala param gati ke adhikārī ।।

Dharma with its four pillars (viz., truth, purity—both external and internal—compassion and charity) reigned everywhere throughout the world; no one even dreamt of sin. Men and women alike were devoted to Shri Ram's worship and all were qualified for final beatitude.

अल्पमृत्यु नहिं कवनिउ पीरा।
सब सुंदर सब बिरुज सरीरा॥
नहिं दरिद्र कोउ दुखी न दीना।
नहीं कोउ अबुध न लच्छन हीना॥[344]

alpamṛtyu nahiṃ kavaniu pīrā ।
saba suṃdara saba biruja sarīrā ।।
nahiṃ daridra kou dukhī na dīnā ।
nahiṃ kou abudha na lacchana hīnā ।।

There was no premature death nor suffering of any kind; everyone was comely and sound of body. No one was destitute, afflicted or miserable; no one was stupid or devoid of auspicious marks.

सब निर्दंभ धर्मरत पुनी।
नर अरु नारि चतुर सब गुनी॥
सब गुनग्य पंडित सब ग्यानी।
सब कृतग्य नहिं कपट सयानी॥[345]

saba nirdaṃbha dharmarata punī ।
nara aru nāri catura saba gunī ।।
saba gunagya paṃḍita saba gyānī ।
saba kṛtagya nahiṃ kapaṭa sayānī ।।

All were unaffectedly good, pious and virtuous; all were clever and accomplished—both men and women. Everyone recognised the merits of others and was learned and wise; nay, everyone acknowledged the services and benefits received from others and there was no guileful prudence.

राम राज नभगेस सुनु सचराचर जग माहिं ।
काल कर्म सुभाव गुन कृत दुख काहुहि नाहिं ॥[346]

Rāma rāja nabhagesa sunu sacarācara jaga māhīṃ ।।
kāla karma subhāva guna kṛta dukha kāhuhi nāhiṃ ।।

Listen, O king of the birds (continues Kakabhushundi), during Shri Ram's reign, there was not a creature in this world, animate or inanimate, that was liable to any of the sufferings attributable to time, past conduct, personal temperament and character.

भूमि सप्त सागर मेखला ।
एक भूप रघुपति कोसला ॥
भुअन अनेक रोम प्रति जासू ।
यह प्रभुता कछु बहुत न तासू ॥[347]

bhūmi sapta sāgara mekhalā ।
eka bhūpa Raghupati kosalā ।।
bhuana aneka roma prati jāsū ।
yaha prabhutā kachu bahuta na tāsū ।।

Shri Ram (the Lord of the Raghus), who reigned in Ayodhya, was the undisputed sovereign of the entire globe girdled by the seven oceans. This lordship (of the entire globe) was nothing great for Him every follicle in whose (cosmic) body contains myriads of universes.

सो महिमा समुझत प्रभु केरी ।
यह बरनत हीनता घनेरी ॥
सोउ महिमा खगेस जिन्ह जानी ।
फिरि एहिं चरित तिन्हहुँ रति मानी ॥[348]

so mahimā samujhata prabhu kerī ।
yaha baranata hīnatā ghanerī ।।
sou mahimā khagesa jinha jānī ।
phirī ehiṃ carita tinhahuṃ rati mānī ।।

To him who has realised such infinite greatness of the Lord, even this description (viz., to speak of Him as the sovereign of the entire globe) will sound highly disparaging. But even those, O king of the birds, (continues Kakabhushundi) who have realised the greatness of the Lord (as indicated above) have turned round and conceived a fondness for this story of the Lord.

सोउ जाने कर फल यह लीला।
कहहिं महा मुनिबर दमसीला॥
राम राज कर सुख संपदा।
बरनि न सकइ फनीस सारदा॥[349]

sou jāne kara phala yaha līlā ।
kahahiṃ mahā munibara damasīlā ।।
Rāma rāja kara sukha saṃpadā ।
barani na sakai phanīsa Sāradā ।।

For the immediate perception of such exploits of the Lord is the reward of knowing His infinite greatness; so declare the greatest of sages that have subdued their senses. The happiness and prosperity of Shri Ram's reign were more than even Shesh (the serpent-god) and Sharada (the Goddess of Learning) could describe.

सब उदार सब पर उपकारी।
बिप्र चरन सेवक नर नारी॥
एकनारि ब्रत रत सब झारी।
ते मन बच क्रम पति हितकारी॥[350]

saba udāra saba para upakārī ।
bipra carana sevaka nara nārī ।।
ekanāri brata rata saba jhārī ।
te mana baca kram pati hitakārī ।।

All were generous and all beneficent; men and women alike were devoted to the feet of the Brahmins. Every husband was pledged to a vow of monogamy and the wives too were devoted to their husband in thought, word and deed.

दंड जतिन्ह कर भेद जहँ नर्तक नृत्य समाज ।
जीतहु मनहि सुनिअ अस रामचंद्र कें राज ॥[351]

daṃḍa jatinha kara bheda jahaṃ nartaka nṛtya samāja ।
jītahu manahi sunia asa Rāmacaṃdra keṃ rāja ॥

Danda (stick) was never seen save in the hands of the recluse and *bhedai* (differences) too had ceased to exist except among the dancers in a dancing party. Even so the order 'Conquer!' was heard only with reference to the mind throughout the realm of Shri Ramchandra.

फूलहिं फरहिं सदा तरु कानन ।
रहहिं एक सँग गज पंचानन ॥
खग मृग सहज बयरु बिसराई ।
सबन्हि परस्पर प्रीति बढ़ाई ॥[352]

phūlahiṃ pharahiṃ sadā taru kānana ।
rahahi eka saṃga gaja paṃcānana ॥
khaga mṛga sahaja bayaru bisarāī ।
sabanhi paraspara prīti baḍhaāī ॥

Trees in the forest blossomed and bore fruit throughout the year; the elephant and the lion lived together as friends. Nay, birds and beasts of every description had forgotten their natural animosities and developed friendly relations with one another.

कूजहिं खग मृग नाना बृंदा ।
अभय चरहिं बन करहिं अनंदा ॥
सीतल सुरभि पवन बह मंदा ।
गुंजत अलि लै चलि मकरंदा ॥[353]

kūjahiṃ khaga mṛga nānā bṛṃdā ।
abhaya carahiṃ bana karahiṃ anaṃdā ।।
sītala surabhi pavana baha maṃdā ।
gūṃjata ali lai cali makaraṃdā ।।

Birds sang and beasts fearlessly moved about in the woods in distinct herds, making merry all the time. The air breathed cool, soft and fragrant; bees hummed even as they moved about laden with honey.

लता बिटप मागें मधु चवहीं ।
मनभावतो धेनु पय स्रवहीं ॥
ससि संपन्न सदा रह धरनी ।
त्रेताँ भइ कृतजुग कै करनी ॥[354]

latā biṭapa māgeṃ madhu cavahīṃ ।
manabhāvato dhenu paya stravahīṃ ।।
sasi saṃpanna sadā raha dharanī ।
tretāṃ bhai kṛtajuga kai karanī ।।

Creepers and trees dropped honey to those who asked for it; cows yielded milk to one's heart's content. The earth was ever clothed with crops; even in the Treta age the conditions of the Satyayuga prevailed.

प्रगटीं गिरिन्ह बिबिधि मनि खानी ।
जगदातमा भूप जग जानी ॥
सरिता सकल बहहिं बर बारी ।
सीतल अमल स्वाद सुखकारी ॥[355]

pragaṭīṃ girinha bibidha mani khānī ।
jagadātamā bhūpa jaga jānī ।।
saritā sakala bahahiṃ bara bārī ।
sītala amala svāda sukhakārī ।।

Conscious of the fact that the ruler of the earth was no other than the universal spirit, the mountains brought to light their mines containing jewels of every description. Every river carried in it excellent water—cool, limpid and pleasant to the taste.

सागर निज मरजादाँ रहहीं।
डारहिं रत्न तटन्हि नर लहहीं॥
सरसिज संकुल सकल तड़ागा।
अति प्रसन्न दस दिसा बिभागा॥[356]

sāgara nija marajādāṃ rahahīṃ ।
ḍārahiṃ ratna taṭanhi nara lahahīṃ ।।
sarasija saṃkula sakala taḍaāgā ।
ati prasanna dasa disā bibhāgā ।।

The oceans kept within their bounds and scattered jewels on their shores for men to gather. Ponds were all thick with lotuses and every quarter was clear and bright.

बिधु महि पूर मयूखन्हि रबि तप जेतनेहि काज।
मागें बारिद देहिं जल रामचंद्र के राज॥[357]

bidhu mahi pūra mayūkhanhi rabi tapa jetanehi kāja ।
māgeṃ bārida dehiṃ jala Rāmacaṃdra ke rāja ।।

The moon flooded the earth with her rays, while the sun shone just as much as was necessary. Similarly, clouds poured forth showers for the mere asking so long as Shri Ramchandra wielded the sceptre.

कोटिन्ह बाजिमेध प्रभु कीन्हे।
दान अनेक द्विजन्ह कहँ दीन्हे॥
श्रुति पथ पालक धर्म धुरंधर।
गुनातीत अरु भोग पुरंदर॥[358]

koṭinha bājimedha prabhu kīnhe ।
dāna aneka dvijanha kahaṃ dīnhe ।।

śruti patha pālaka dharma dhuraṃdhara ।
gunātīta aru bhoga puraṃdara ॥

The Lord performed myriads of horse sacrifices and bestowed innumerable gifts on the Brahmins. The defender of the Vedic usage and the champion of righteousness, He transcended the three modes of prakati (sattva, rajas and tamas) and was another Indra (the lord of paradise) so far as enjoyment was concerned.

पति अनुकूल सदा रह सीता।
सोभा खानि सुसील बिनीता॥
जानति कृपासिंधु प्रभुताई।
सेवति चरन कमल मन लाई॥[359]

pati anukūla sadā raha Sitā ।
sobhā khāni susīla binītā ॥
jānati kṛpāsiṃdhu prabhutāī ।
sevati carana kamala mana lāī ॥

A mine of beauty, virtuous and meek, Sita was ever devoted to Her lord. She knew the greatness of the all-merciful Lord and adored His lotus-feet with a devoted heart.

जद्यपि गृहँ सेवक सेवकिनी।
बिपुल सदा सेवा बिधि गुनी॥
निज कर गृह परिचरजा करई।
रामचंद्र आयसु अनुसरई॥[360]

jadyapi gṛhaṃ sevaka sevakinī ।
bipula sadā sevā bidhi gunī ॥
nija kara gṛha paricarajā karaī ।
Rāmacaṃdra āyasu anusaraī ॥

Although there were many manservants and maidservants in her palace, all expert in the art of service, She did all household work with her own hands and carried out the behests of Shri Ramchandra.

जेहि बिधि कृपासिंधु सुख मानइ।
सोइ कर श्री सेवा बिधि जानई॥
कौसल्यादि सासु गृह माहीं।
सेवइ सबन्हि मान मद नाहीं॥[361]

jehi bidhi kṛpāsiṃdhu sukha mānai ।
soi kara śrī sevā bidhi jānai ।।
kausalyādi sāsu gṛha māhīṃ ।
sevai sabanhi māna mada nāhīṃ ।।

Sita invariably did what would afford delight to the all-merciful, conversant as She was with the art of service. Devoid of pride and conceit, She waited upon Kaushalya and all the other mothers-in-law in the palace.

उमा रमा ब्रह्मादि बंदिता।
जगदंबा संततमनिंदिता॥[362]

Umā Ramā Brahmādi baṃditā ।
Jagadaṃbā saṃtatamaniṃditā ।।

Uma (continues Lord Shiva), Sita was no other than Goddess Ram (Lakshmi), the mother of the universe, who is adored even by Brahma and other gods and is ever flawless.

जासु कृपा कटाच्छु सुर चाहत चितव न सोइ।
राम पदारबिंद रति करति सुभावहि खोइ॥[363]

jāsu kṛpā kaṭācchu sura cāhata citava na soi ।
Rāma padārabiṃda rati karati subhāvahi khoi ।।

The same Lakshmi whose benign look is craved by the gods but who never casts a glance at them constantly loves Shri Ram's lotus-feet, forgetting Her natural majesty.

सेवहिं सानकूल सब भाई।
राम चरन रति अति अधिकाई॥
प्रभु मुख कमल बिलोकत रहहीं।
कबहुँ कृपाल हमहि कछु कहहीं॥[364]

sevahiṃ sānakūla saba bhāī ।
Rāma carana rati ati adhikāī ।।
prabhu mukha kamala bilokata rahahīṃ ।
kabahuṃ kṛpāla hamahi kachu kahahīṃ ।।

All the younger brothers served the Lord with great fidelity; for their love for Shri Ram knew no bounds. They ever kept gazing on His lotus-face in the hope that the benign Lord might give some order to them at any moment.

राम करहिं भ्रातन्ह पर प्रीती।
नाना भाँति सिखावहिं नीती॥
हरषित रहहिं नगर के लोगा।
करहिं सकल सुर दुर्लभ भोगा॥[365]

Rāma karahiṃ bhrātanha para prītī ।
nānā bhāṃti sikhāvahiṃ nītī ।।
haraṣita rahahiṃ nagara ke logā ।
karahiṃ sakala sura durlabha bhogā ।।

Shri Ram too loved His younger brothers and taught them wisdom of every kind. The citizens led a happy life and enjoyed all sorts of pleasures which even gods could scarcely obtain.

अहनिसि बिधिहि मनावत रहहीं।
श्री रघुबीर चरन रति चहहीं॥

दुइ सुत सुंदर सीताँ जाए।
लव कुस बेद पुरानन्ह गाए ॥[366]

ahanisi bidhihi manāvata rahahīṃ ।
Srīraghubīra carana rati cahahīṃ ।।
dui suta sundara Sītāṃ jāe ।
Lava Kusa Beda Purānanha gāe ।।

Day and night they prayed to god and sought the boon of devotion to the feet of Shri Ram (the Hero of Raghu's line). Sita gave birth to two pretty sons, Lava and Kusha by name, who have figured in the Vedas and Puranas.

दोउ बिजई बिनई गुन मंदिर।
हरि प्रतिबिंब मनहुँ अति सुंदर॥
दुइ दुइ सुत सब भ्रातन्ह केरे।
भए रूप गुन सील घनेरे॥[367]

dou bijaī binaī guna maṃdira ।
Hari pratibiṃba manahuṃ ati suṃdara ।।
dui dui suta saba bhrātanha kere ।
bhae rūpa guna sīla ghanere ।।

Both these boys were victorious in battle, modest, accomplished and handsome, the very images as it were, of Shri Hari (Ram). Shri Ram's other brothers too had two sons each, pre-eminent in comeliness of form, merit and virtue.

ग्यान गिरा गोतीत अज माया मन गुन पार।
सोइ सच्चिदानंद घन कर नर चरित उदार॥[368]

gyāna girā gotīta aja māyā mana guna pāra ।
soi Saccidānaṃda ghana kara nara carita udāra ।।

The same Brahma who is beyond all knowledge, speech and sense-perception, nay, who is unborn and transcends Maya (prakati or matter), the mind and the modes of prakati and is truth, knowledge and bliss solidified, exhibited the ideal behaviour of a human being.

प्रातकाल सरऊ करि मज्जन ।
बैठहिं सभाँ संग द्विज सज्जन ॥
बेद पुरान बसिष्ट बखानहिं ।
सुनहिं राम जद्यपि सब जानहिं ॥[369]

prātakāla Saraū kari majjana ।
baiṭhahiṃ sabhāṃ saṃga dvija sajjana ।।
Beda Purāna Basiṣṭa bakhānahiṃ ।
sunahiṃ Rāma jadyapi saba jānahiṃ ।।

After taking a bath in the Sarayu early in the morning, the Lord sat in an assembly of Brahmins and holy men. The sage Vasishtha expounded the Vedas and Puranas, while Shri Ram listened to the exposition, even though He knew everything Himself.

अनुजन्ह संजुत भोजन करहीं ।
देखि सकल जननीं सुख भरहीं ।
भरत सत्रुहन दोनउ भाई ।
सहित पवनसुत उपबन जाई ॥
बूझहिं बैठि राम गुन गाहा ।
कह हनुमान सुमति अवगाहा ॥
सुनत बिमल गुन अति सुख पावहिं ।
बहुरि बहुरि करि बिनय कहावहिं ॥[370]

anujanha saṃjuta bhojana karahīṃ ।
dekhi sakala jananīṃ sukha bharahīṃ ।।
Bharat Satruhana donau bhāī ।
sahita pavanasuta upabana jāī ।।
būjhahiṃ baiṭhi Rāma guna gāhā ।
kaha Hanumāna sumati avagāhā ।।

sunata bimala guna ati sukha pāvahiṃ ।
bahuri bahuri kari binaya kahāvahiṃ ।।

He took His meals with His younger brothers and the sight filled all the mothers with joy The two brothers, Bharat and Shatrughna, would accompany the son of the wind-god to some grove, where they would sit and ask Hanuman to expatiate on Shri Ram's virtues, and Hanuman would plunge his sound intellect into the ocean of His virtues and then recount them. The two brothers derived much joy from the discourse on His immaculate virtues and with much entreaty had it repeated again and again.

सब कें गृह गृह होहिं पुराना ।
राम चरित पावन बिधि नाना ।।
नर अरु नारि राम गुन गानहिं ।
करहिं दिवस निसि जात न जानहिं ।।[371]

saba keṃ gṛha gṛha hohiṃ Purānā ।
Rāmacarita pāvana bidhi nānā ।।
nara aru nāri Rāma guna gānahiṃ ।
karahiṃ divasa nisi jāta na jānahiṃ ।।

Everywhere—in every house—the people recited the Puranas and narrated Shri Ram's holy exploits of a diverse character. Men and women alike joined in hymning Shri Ram's praises and days and nights passed on unnoticed.

अवधपुरी बासिन्ह कर सुख संपदा समाज।
सहस सेष नहिं कहि सकहिं जहँ नृप राम बिराज ।।[372]

avadhapurī bāsinha kara sukha saṃpadā samāja ।
sahasa Seṣa nahiṃ kahi sakahiṃ jahaṃ nṛpa Rāma birāja ।।

Not a thousand Shesha could tell all the happiness and prosperity of the people of Ayodhya, where Shri Ram reigned as king.

नारदादि सनकादि मुनीसा ।
दरसन लागि कोसलाधीसा ॥
दिन प्रति सकल अजोध्या आवहिं ।
देखि नगरु बिरागु बिसरावहिं ॥
जातरूप मनि रचित अटारीं ।
नाना रंग रुचिर गच ढारीं ॥
पुर चहुँ पास कोट अति सुंदर ।
रचे कँगूरा रंग रंग बर ॥
नव ग्रह निकर अनीक बनाई।
जनु घेरी अमरावति आई ॥
लमहि बहु रंग रचित गच काँचा ।
जो बिलोकि मुनिबर मन नाचा ॥
धवल धाम ऊपर नभ चुंबत ।
कलस मनहुँ रबि ससि दुति निंदत ॥
बहु मनि रचित झरोखा भ्राजहिं ।
गृह गृह प्रति मनि दीप बिराजहिं ॥[373]

Nāradādi Sanakādi munīsā ।
darasana lāgi Kosalādhīsā ।।
dina prati sakala Ajodhyā āvahiṃ ।
dekhi nagaru birāgu bisarāvahiṃ ।।
jātarūpa mani racita aṭārīṃ ।
nānā raṃga rucira gaca ḍhārīṃ ।।
pura cahuṃ pāsa koṭa ati suṃdara ।
race kaṃgūrā raṃga raṃga bara ।।
nava graha nikara anīka banāī ।
janu gherī Amarāvati āī ।।
mahi bahu raṃga racita gaca kāṃcā ।
jo biloki munibara mana nācā ।।
dhavala dhāma ūpara nabha cuṃbata ।
kalasa manahuṃ rabi sasi duti niṃdata ।।
bahu mani racita jharokhā bhrājahiṃ ।
gṛha gṛha prati mani dīpa birājahiṃ ।।

All great sages like Narada, Sanaka and others came to Ayodhya everyday to have a sight of the Lord of Koshala, and forgot all their indifference to the world the moment they saw the city, with its attics built of gold and jewels and having splendid pavements laid in diverse colours. A most beautiful boundary wall with its battlements painted in different colours enclosed the city on all sides, as though the nine planets had mustered a large army and besieged Amaravati (Indra's capital). The ground (the streets and squares etc.,) was so beautifully paved with crystals of various colours that the mind of the greatest sages would be enraptured at the sight. The white palaces were so high as to reach the skies; their shining pinnacles put to shame as it were, the effulgence of the sun and the moon. Latticed windows made of diverse precious stones shone here and there; while every house was lit up with jewels that served as lamps.

मनि दीप राजहिं भवन भ्राजहिं देहरीं बिद्रुम रची।
मनि खंभ भीति बिरंचि बिरची कनक मनि मरकत खची ॥
सुंदर मनोहर मंदिरायत अजिर रुचिर फटिक रचे ।
प्रति द्वार द्वार कपाट पुरट बनाइ बहु बज्रन्हि खचे ॥[374]

mani dīpa rājahiṃ bhavana bhrājahiṃ deharīṃ bidruma racī ।
mani khaṃbha bhīti biraṃci biracī kanaka mani marakata khacī ।।
suṃdara manohara maṃdirāyata ajira rucira phaṭika race ।
prati dvāra dvāra kapāṭa puraṭa banāi bahu bajranhi khace ।।

The mansions were illumined by jewels that served as so many lamps had shining thresholds made of coral, pillars of jewels and walls of gold inlaid with emeralds, which were as lovely as though they had been built by the Creator (Brahma) himself. Beautiful, charming and commodious as the palaces were, they had their courtyards worked with crystal, and every gate thereof was provided with doors of gold embossed with diamonds.

चारु चित्रसाला गृह गृह प्रति लिखे बनाइ ।
राम चरित जे निरख मुनि ते मन लेहिं चोराइ ॥[375]

cāru citrasālā gṛha gṛha prati likhe banāi ।
Rāma carita je nirakha muni te mana lehiṃ corāi ।।

Every house equipped with a hall adorned with lovely frescos which had Shri Ram's exploits reproduced in such beautiful colours that they would ravish the soul of a sage who looked at them.

सुमन बाटिका सबहिं लगाईं।
बिबिध भाँति करि जतन बनाईं॥
लता ललित बहु जाति सुहाईं।
फूलहिं सदा बसंत कि नाईं॥[376]

sumana bāṭikā sabahiṃ lagāī ।
bibidha bhāṃti kari jatana banāī ।।
latā lalita bahu jāti suhāī ।
phūlahiṃ sadā baṃsata ki nāī ।।

Everyone had a flower garden planted in a characteristic design and trimmed with the greatest care, in which beautiful and lovely creepers of every variety blossomed all the year round as in the vernal season.

गुंजत मधुकर मुखर मनोहर।
मारुत त्रिबिधि सदा बह सुंदर॥
नाना खग बालकन्हि जिआए।
बोलत मधुर उड़ात सुहाए॥[377]

guṃjata madhukara mukhara manohara ।
māruta tribidha sadā baha suṃdara ।।
nānā khaga bālakanhi jiāe ।
bolata madhura uḍaāta suhāe ।।

Bees hummed in a pleasant strain and a delightful breeze breathed cool, soft and fragrant. Birds of all kinds, reared by the children, sang in melodious notes and looked graceful in their flight.

मोर हंस सारस पारावत।
भवननि पर सोभा अति पावत ॥
जहँ तहँ देखहिं निज परिछाहीं ।
बहु बिधि कूजहिं नृत्य कराहीं ॥[378]

mora haṃsa sārasa pārāvata ।
bhavanani para sobhā ati pāvata ।।
jahaṃ tahaṃ dekhahiṃ nija parichāhīṃ ।
bahu bidhi kūjahiṃ nṛtya karāhīṃ ।।

Peacocks, swans, cranes and pigeons presented a most lovely sight on the houses, warbling and dancing in a variety of ways at the sight of their own shadow reflected everywhere (on the glossy surface of the roofs and balconies etc.).

सुक सारिका पढ़ावहिं बालक ।
कहहु राम रघुपति जनपालक ॥
राज दुआर सकल बिधि चारू ।
बीथीं चौहट रुचिर बजारू ॥[379]

suka sārikā paḍhaāvahiṃ bālaka ।
kahahu Rāma Raghupati janapālaka ।।
rāja duāra sakala bidhi cārū ।
bīthīṃ cauhaṭa rūcira bajārū ।।

The children taught parrots and mynahs to repeat the words, 'Ram, Raghupati (the Lord of the Raghus), the Protector of His devotees.' The gates of the royal palace were magnificent in every way; the streets, crossroads and bazaars were all splendid.

बाजार रुचिर न बनइ बरनत बस्तु बिनु गथ पाइए ।
जहँ भूप रमानिवास तहँ की संपदा किमि गाइए ॥
बैठे बजाज सराफ बनिक अनेक मनहुँ कुबेर ते ।
सब सुखी सब सच्चरि सुंदर नारि नर सिसु जरठ जे ॥[380]

bājāra rucira na banai baranata bastu binu gatha pāie ।
jahaṃ bhūpa ramānivāsa tahaṃ kī saṃpadā kimi gāie ।।
baiṭhe bajāja sarāpha banika aneka manahuṃ Kubera te ।
saba sukhī saba saccarita suṃdara nāri nara sisu jaraṭha je ।।

The bazaars were splendid beyond description; things could be had without any consideration there. How can anyone describe the wealth of the city where the Abode of Lakshmi Himself reigned as king? The cloth-merchants, bankers and other dealers sat at their shops like so many Kuberas (gods of riches). All men and women, children and aged folk alike were happy, all of good conduct and comely in appearance.

उत्तर दिसि सरजू बह निर्मल जल गंभीर ।
बाँधे घाट मनोहर स्वल्प पंक नहिं तीर ।।[381]

uttara disi Sarajū baha nirmala jala gaṃbhīra ।
bāṃdhe ghāṭa manohara svalpa paṃka nahiṃ tīra ।।

To the north (of the city) flowed the deep and limpid stream of the Sarayu with a line of charming ghats and no trace of mud at the bank.

दूरि फराक रुचिर सो घाटा ।
जहँ जल पिअहिं बाजि गज ठाटा ।।
पनघट परम मनोहर नाना ।
तहाँ न पुरुष करहिं अस्नाना ।।[382]

dūri pharāka rucira so ghāṭā ।
jahaṃ jala piahiṃ bāji gaja ṭhāṭā ।।
panighaṭa param manohara nānā ।
tahāṃ na puruṣa karahiṃ asnānā ।।

Apart from the other ghat and situated at some distance from them was the fine ghat where multitudes of horses and elephants went to drink. There were numerous most charming ghats for women to take water from, where men did not bathe.

राजघाट सब बिधि सुंदर बर।
मज्जहिं तहाँ बरन चारिउ नर ॥
तीर तीर देवन्ह के मंदिर।
चहुँ दिसि तिन्ह के उपबन सुंदर ॥[383]

rājaghāṭa saba bidhi suṃdara bara ।
majjahiṃ tahāṃ barana cāriu nara ।।
tīra tīra devanha ke maṃdira ।
cahuṃ disi tinha ke upabana suṃdara ।।

The best of all and beautiful in every way was the royal ghat, where men of all the four castes could bathe. All along the bank stood temples sacred to the gods and surrounded by lovely groves.

कहुँ कहुँ सरिता तीर उदासी।
बसहिं ग्यान रत मुनि संन्यासी ॥
तीर तीर तुलसिका सुहाई।
बृंद बृंद बहु मुनिन्ह लगाई ॥[384]

kahuṃ kahuṃ saritā tīra udāsī ।
basahiṃ gyāna rata muni saṃnyāsī ।।
tīra tīra Tulsikā suhāī ।
bṛṃda bṛṃda bahu muninha lagāī ।।

Here and there on the river bank dwelt sages and recluses unconcerned with the world and devoted to spiritual wisdom. All along the bank stood in clusters many a lovely Tulsi plant reared by hermits.

पुर सोभा कछु बरनि न जाई।
बाहेर नगर परम रुचिराई ॥
देखत पुरी अखिल अघ भागा।
बन उपबन बापिका तड़ागा ॥[385]

pura sobhā kachu barani na jāī ।
bāhera nagara param rucirāī ।।

dekhata purī akhila agha bhāgā ।
bana upabana bāpikā taḍạāgā ॥

The splendour of the city defied all description; its outskirts too were most picturesque. The very sight of the city with its groves and gardens, wells and ponds, drove away all one's sins.

बापीं तड़ाग अनूप कूप मनोहरायत सोहहीं।
सोपान सुंदर नीर निर्मल देखि सुर मुनि मोहहीं॥
बहु रंग कंज अनेक खग कूजहिं मधुप गुंजारहीं।
आराम रम्य पिकादि खग रव जनु पथिक हंकारहीं॥[386]

bāpīṃ taḍaāgā anūpa kūpa manoharāyata sohahīṃ ।
sopāna suṃdara nīra nirmala dekhi sura muni mohahīṃ ॥
bahu raṃga kaṃja aneka khaga kūjahiṃ madhupa guṃjārahīṃ ।
ārāma ramya pikādi khaga rava janu pathika haṃkārahīṃ ॥

Its peerless ponds and tanks and charming and spacious wells looked so beautiful with their elegant flights of steps and limpid water that even gods and sages were fascinated by their sight. The lakes were adorned with many-coloured lotuses and resounded with the cooing of the numerous birds and the humming of the bees; and the delightful gardens seemed to invite the passers-by through the notes of the cuckoos and other birds.

रमानाथ जहँ राजा सो पुर बरनि कि जाइ।
अनिमादिक सुख संपदा रहीं अवध सब छाइ॥[387]

Ramānātha jahaṃ rājā so pura barani ki jāi ।
animādika sukha saṃpadā rahīṃ Avadha saba chāi ॥

Is it ever possible to describe the city of which Lord Ram was the king? *Anima* (the power of assuming atomic size) and all other superhuman powers and even so joys and riches of every kind stayed in Ayodhya forever.

जहँ तहँ नर रघुपति गुन गावहिं।
बैठि परसपर इहइ सिखावहिं ॥
भजहु प्रनत प्रतिपालक रामहि।
सोभा सील रूप गुन धामहि ॥
जलज बिलोचन स्यामल गातहि।
पलक नयन इव सेवक त्रातहि ॥
धृत सर रुचिर चाप तूनीरहि।
संत कंज बन रबि रनधीरहि ॥
काल कराल ब्याल खगराजहि।
नमत राम अकाम ममता जहि ॥
लोभ मोह मृगजूथ किरातहि।
मनसिज करि हरि जन सुखदातहि ॥
संसय सोक निबिड़ तम भानुहि।
दनुज गहन घन दहन कृसानुहि ॥
जनकसुता समेत रघुबीरहि।
कस न भजहु भंजन भव भीरहि ॥
बहु बासना मसक हिम रासिहि।
सदा एकरस अज अबिनासिहि ॥
मुनि रंजन भंजन महि भारहि।
तुलसिदास के प्रभुहि उदारहि ॥[388]

jahaṃ tahaṃ nara Raghupati guna gāvahiṃ ।
baiṭhi parasapara ihai sikhāvahiṃ ।।
bhajahu pranata pratipālaka rāmahi ।
sobhā sīla rūpa guna dhāmahi ।।
jalaja bilocana syāmala gātahi ।
palaka nayana iva sevaka trātahi ।।
dhṛta sara rucira cāpa tūnīrahi ।
saṃta kaṃja bana rabi ranadhīrahi ।।
kāla karāla byāla khagarājahi ।
namata Rāma akāma mamatā jahi ।।
lobha moha mṛgajūtha kirātahi ।
manasija kari Hari jana sukhadātahi ।।

saṃsaya soka nibiḍaṭama bhānuhi ।
danuja gahana ghana dahana kṛsānuhi ।।
janakasutā sameta Raghubīrahi ।
kasa na bhajahu bhaṃjana bhava bhīrahi ।।
bahu bāsanā masaka hima rāsihi ।
sadā ekarasa aja abināsihi ।।
muni raṃjana bhaṃjana mahi bhārahi ।
Tulsidāsa ke prabhuhi udārahi ।।

Everywhere men sang the praises of Shri Ram (the Lord of the Raghus), and even as they sat, this is how they exhorted one another: 'Worship Shri Ram, the Protector of the suppliant, the home of elegance, amiability, beauty and goodness, who has lotus-like eyes and swarthy limbs, who looks after His servants even as the eyelids guard the eyeballs, who is armed with a splendid bow, arrows and quiver and is staunch in battle, who delights the saints even as the sun brings joy to a bed of lotuses, who is a Garuda (the king of the birds) to devour the dreadful serpent in the form of Death, who destroys the feeling of mineness the moment a person bows to Him in a disinterested spirit, and who is a hunter to kill the herd of deer in the form of greed and infatuation, a lion to quell the elephant of concupiscence, the delight of His servants, a sun to scatter the thick darkness of doubt and sorrow, and a fire to consume the dense forest of the demon race. Oh, why should you not adore the Hero of Raghu's line, ever accompanied by Janak's daughter, who dispels the fear of transmigration, who plays the role of frost to destroy mosquitoes in the disguise of manifold latent desires, who is ever unchangeable, unborn and imperishable, the delight of the sages, the reliever of the earth's burdens, the munificent Lord of Tulsidas.'

एहि बिधि नगर नारि नर करहिं राम गुन गान ।
सानुकूल सब पर रहहिं संतत कृपानिधान ।।[389]

ehi bidhi nagara nāri nara karahiṃ Rāma guna gāna ।
sānukūla saba para rahahiṃ saṃtata kṛpānidhāna ।।

In this way, the men and women of the city sang Shri Ram's praises and the all-merciful was ever favourable to all.

जब ते राम प्रताप खगेसा।
उदित भयउ अति प्रबल दिनेसा॥
पूरि प्रकास रहेउ तिहुँ लोका।
बहुतेन्ह सुख बहुतन मन सोका॥[390]

jaba te Rāma pratāpa khagesā ।
udita bhayau ati prabala dinesā ।।
pūri prakāsa raheu tihuṃ lokā ।
bahutenha sukha bahutana mana sokā ।।

From the time, O king of the birds (continues Kakabhushundi), the most dazzling sun of Shri Ram's glory appeared on the horizon, the three spheres were all flooded with light, which brought delight to many and sorrow to many others.

जिन्हहि सोक ते कहउँ बखानी।
प्रथम अबिद्या निसा नसानी॥
अघ उलूक जहँ तहाँ लुकाने।
काम क्रोध कैरव सकुचाने॥[391]

jinhahi soka te kahauṃ bakhānī ।
prathama abidyā nisā nasānī ।।
agha ulūka jahaṃ tahāṃ lukāne ।
kāma krodha kairava sakucāne ।।

First, I enumerate at length those to whom it caused sorrow. To begin with, the night of ignorance terminated; the owl-like sins hid themselves wherever they could; the white lily in the form of lust and anger closed.

बिबिध कर्म गुन काल सुभाउ।
ए चकोर सुख लहहिं न काऊ॥

मत्सर मान मोह मद चोरा।
इन्ह कर हुनर न कवनिहुँ ओरा॥
धरम तड़ाग ग्यान बिग्याना।
ए पंकज बिकसे बिधि नाना॥
सुख संतोष बिराग बिबेका।
बिगत सोक ए कोक अनेका॥[392]

bibidha karma guna kāla subhāū ।
e cakora sukha lahahiṃ na kāū ॥
matsara māna moha mada corā ।
inha kara hunara na kavanihuṃ orā ॥
dharam taḍāga gyāna bigyānā ।
e paṃkaja bikase bidhi nānā ॥
sukha saṃtoṣa birāga bibekā ।
bigata soka e koka anekā ॥

Chakora birds in the shape of activities of various kinds, the phenomenal existence, time and nature never rejoiced; thieves like jealousy, pride, infatuation and arrogance had no occasion to display their skill in any quarter; lotuses of every description in the shape of knowledge and realisation opened in the pond of piety Happiness, contentment, dispassion and discernment, like so many Chakravaka birds, were rid of sorrow.

यह प्रताप रबि जाकें उर जब करइ प्रकास।
पछिले बाढ़हिं प्रथम जे कहे ते पावहिं नास॥[393]

yaha pratāpa rabi jākeṃ ura jaba karai prakāsa ।
pachile bāḍhahiṃ prathama je kahe te pāvahiṃ nāsa ॥

When the sun of Shri Ram's glory illumines the heart of an individual, the qualities enumerated in the end grow while those mentioned in the beginning die away.

Once Ram ascends the throne of Ayodhya, Tulsi waxes eloquent on the nature of his rule—Ramrajya. This was a deliberate elaboration of an utopia—an imagined place or state where everything is perfect and everyone happy. The concept of this Ramrajya has become a part of our cultural inheritance, a universally accepted goal to be aspired for society in every era by citizens, State and society. It is the benchmark of excellence, the touchstone of harmony, and the yardstick of prosperity and plenty.

In enumerating the elements of this utopia, Tulsi was not being original. He borrowed directly from Valmiki's Ramayana, where too such a description exists. Valmiki writes that in Ramrajya there are no widows lamenting, no fear of disease, no threat of violence, and no derogation from harmony. It is a State where virtue prevails, and nature's bounty is plenteous. Trees abound with flower and fruit, there is abundant rainfall, and the climate is soothing.

Mahatma Gandhi was greatly inspired with this ancient ideal. It is said that in his entire life he saw only one film. That film was titled *Ram Rajya,* directed by Vijay Bhatt. Gandhi visualised Ramrajya to be an ideal State, and he dwelt on different aspects of it—as he saw it—in his writings. According to him, Ramrajya was a democratic polity, where the ruler ruled with the consent of the people; in it, there were equal rights for everyone; it was bereft of violence of any kind; it dispensed quick and accessible justice; its government was guided by truth; and, it fostered the sovereignty of the people based on pure moral authority.

Gandhi did not see such a State in religious terms. While the best in every religion could inform the values of the citizens, the State itself was, for him, categorically secular. As he himself wrote: 'I do not mean Hindu Raj—I mean by Ramrajya divine raj.' In the Mahatma's notion of Ramrajya, respect for all faiths was a key ingredient. 'My Hinduism teaches me to respect all religions,' Gandhi wrote. 'In this lies the secret of Ramrajya.'

Was Tulsi's vision of Ramrajya also secular? In asking this question, are we using historical hindsight to judge the poet by the context of today's ideologies? Both of these are relevant questions. Tulsi wrote in the context of his times. He was writing the story of Ram; Ram was a Hindu king; the kingdom that he set up would—by extension of logic— be a Hindu kingdom. However, to a substantial extent, Tulsi rises above such a specifically narrow outlook. He does so by stressing on harmony as one of the essential elements of this Utopia. In a key line, he says: *sab nara karahin paraspar priti:* all people were bound by mutual love. This love was the basis of a larger unity that transcended a narrow sectarian outlook. It is true that in the very next line, Tulsi writes: *chalahin svadharma nirat Shruti riti:* all people followed the dharma as laid down by the Shrutis. The Shrutis normally connote the Vedas, which are a foundational text of Hinduism. But, Hinduism itself is eclectic and inclusive, as defined by the Vedas themselves. Mahatma Gandhi, who had immersed himself in the philosophy of Hinduism—as that of other religions—rightly, therefore, says that the Hinduism he knows teaches him to respect all religions.

Tulsi emphasises another pivotal aspect: righteousness. In his definition of Ramrajya, righteousness prevails, supported by the four pillars of truth, purity, compassion and charity. In fact, righteousness could not but prevail, because it was the key aspect of the persona of maryada purushottam Ram. Would such a kingdom, governed by such a notion of righteousness, which included compassion, be rigidly sectarian? I believe not. It would work to foster love among all its citizens, and create a harmonious society, respecting people of all faiths.

The remaining passages of the description of Ramrajya follow a predictable template, and are based largely on Valmiki's narrative. But the ethical notion of an ideal State as embodied in Ramrajya has become a key aspect of India's social, cultural and political heritage, and has gone much beyond merely the narrower definition of only an exclusively Hindu State.

40. Dialogue Between Bharat and Shri Ram

बिषय अलंपट सील गुनाकर।
पर दुख दुख सुख सुख देखे पर॥
सम अभूतरिपु बिमद बिरागी।
लोभामरष हरष भय त्यागी॥[394]

biṣaya alaṃpaṭa sīla gunākara ।
para dukha dukha sukha sukha dekhe para ।।
sama abhūtaripu bimada birāgī ।
lobhāmaraṣa haraṣa bhaya tyāgī ।।

Saints, as a rule, have no hankering for the pleasures of sense and are the very mines of amiability and other virtues. They grieve to see others in distress and rejoice at the sight of others' joy. They are even-minded and look upon none as their enemy. Free from vanity and passion, they are conquerers of greed, anger, joy and fear.

कोमलचित दीनन्ह पर दाया।
मन बच क्रम मम भगति अमाया॥
सबहि मानप्रद आपु अमानी।
भरत प्रान सम मम ते प्रानी॥[395]

komalacita dīnanha para dāyā ।
mana baca kram mama bhagati amāyā ।।
sabahi mānaprada āpu amānī ।
Bharat prāna sama mama te prānī ।।

Tender of heart and compassionate to the distressed, they cherish guileless devotion to me in thought, word and deed; and giving honour to all, they are modest themselves. Such souls, Bharat, are dear to me as life.

बिगत काम मम नाम परायन ।
सांति बिरति बिनती मुदितायन ॥
सीतलता सरलता मयत्री ।
द्विज पद प्रीति धर्म जनयत्री ॥[396]

bigata kāma mama nāma parāyana ।
sāṃti birati binatī muditāyana ।।
sītalatā saralatā mayatrī ।
dvija pada prīti dharma janayatrī ।।

Having no interested motive of their own, they are devoted to my name and are abodes of tranquillity, dispassion, humility and good humour. Again, know him for all time, dear brother, a genuine saint, whose heart is a home of all such noble qualities as placidity, guilelessness, friendliness and devotion to the feet of the Brahmins, which is the fountain of all virtues.

सुनहु असंतन्ह केर सुभाऊ ।
भूलेहुँ संगति करिअ न काऊ ॥
तिन्ह कर संग सदा दुखदाई ।
जिमि कपिलहि घालइ हरहाई ॥[397]

sunahu asaṃtanha kera subhāū ।
bhūlehuṃ saṃgati karia na kāū ।।
tinha kara saṃga sadā dukhadāī ।
jimi kalapahi ghālai harahāī ।।

Now hear the characteristics of the noble, association with whom should be scrupulously avoided; for their company ever brings woe, even as a wicked cow ruins by her company a cow of noble breed.

खलन्ह हृदयँ अति ताप बिसेषी।
जरहिं सदा पर संपति देखी॥
जहँ कहुँ निंदा सुनहिं पराई।
हरषहिं मनहुँ परी निधि पाई॥[398]

khalanha hṛdayaṃ ati tāpa biseṣī ।
jarahiṃ sadā para saṃpati dekhī ।।
jahaṃ kahuṃ niṃdā sunahiṃ parāī ।
harasahiṃ manahuṃ parī nidhi pāī ।।

The heart of the wicked suffers terrible agony; for they ever burn at the sight of others' prosperity Wherever they hear others reviled, they feel delighted as though they had stumbled upon a treasure lying on the road.

काम क्रोध मद लोभ परायन।
निर्दय कपटी कुटिल मलायन॥
बयरु अकारन सब काहू सों।
जो कर हित अनहित ताहू सों॥[399]

kāma krodha mada lobha parāyana ।
nirdaya kapaṭī kuṭila malāyana ।।
bayaru akārana saba kāhū soṃ ।
jo kara hita anahita tāhū soṃ ।।

Devoted to sensuality, anger, arrogance and greed, they are merciless, deceitful, crooked and impure. They bear enmity towards all without rhyme or reason; nay, they behave inimically even with those who are actively kind to them.

झूठइ लेना झूठइ देना।
झूठइ भोजन झूठ चबेना॥
बोलहिं मधुर बचन जिमि मोरा।
खाई महा अहि हृदय कठोरा॥[400]

jhūṭhai lenā jhūṭhai denā ।
jhūṭhai bhojana jhūṭha cabenā ।।
bolahiṃ madhura bacana jimi morā ।
khāi mahā ati hṛdaya kaṭhorā ।।

They are false in their dealings (lying is their stock-in-trade); nay, falsehood is their dinner and falsehood their breakfast (whatever they eat is intended to deceive others). They speak honeyed words just like the peacock, that has a stony heart and devours the most venomous snake.

पर हित सरिस धर्म नहिं भाई ।
पर पीड़ा सम नहिं अधमाई ॥
निर्नय सकल पुरान बेद कर ।
कहेउँ तात जानहिं कोबिद नर ॥[401]

para hita sarisa dharma nahiṃ bhāī ।
para pīḍā sama nahiṃ adhamāī ।।
nirnaya sakala Purāna Beda kara ।
kaheuṃ tāta jānahiṃ kobida nara ।।

Brother, there is no virtue like benevolence, and no meanness like oppressing others. I have declared to you, dear brother, the verdict of all the Vedas and Puranas; the wise also know it.

In these lines, Ram answers Bharat's question on the qualities that distinguish the good from the bad. Bharat probably was sufficiently qualified to know the answer himself, but the asking of the question, and Ram's extensive reply to it, provides Tulsi an opportunity to expound on one of his favourite subjects. Our poet had trenchant views on the wicked, and probably faced many of them, both in his personal life, and in the form of opponents to his literary profile. He, therefore, loses no opportunity to lash out against such people, and finds in Ram the most eloquent and authentic person to do so. This is because Ram was universally recognised to be righteousness personified. Although he was beyond the polarities of good and bad, and was intrinsically transcendent to human categories, the Lord dwells—through Tulsi's pen—at length on this matter.

The contrast that Ram draws is stark. The good are the very picture of virtue, free of greed, vanity and passion, tender-hearted and compassionate, humble and dispassionate, full of peace and joy, guileless, completely devoted to the lotus-feet of the Lord, and forever willing to rejoice in the achievements of others, and to be sorrowful when anyone suffers from affliction. The bad, on the other hand, indulge in slander, are lustful, wrathful and greedy, merciless, deceitful, crooked and utterly foul, cherishing causeless animosity against everyone, and returning evil for good.

In one of his chaupais, Tulsi compares the wicked to a peacock: *jhutai lena, jhutai dena, jhutai bhojan, jhuth chabena, bolahin madhur bachan jimi mora, khai maha ahi hridaya hathora.* The wicked speak falsehood, deal in falsehood, literally eat and chew falsehood, and are as duplicitous as the peacock, that is beautiful and speaks melodiously but is ruthless enough to devour the most venomous snake. Many commentators have found this analogy somewhat awkward, but Tulsi's intent appears to be to say that, just as a peacock in its beautiful plumage does not look harmful but can be vicious in attacking and killing a snake, so do the evil inflict grievous harm while appearing to be something entirely different.

The most significant lines in this selection are where Ram sums up the essence of dharma for Bharat: *para hita sarisa dharma nahiṃ bhai, para pida sama nahiṃ adhamai: there* is no religious duty higher than doing good to others, no greater evil than causing injury to others. This categorical statement by Ram emphasising the importance of treating others with benevolence, and stressing the importance of non-injury, is truly unique, and should work as a sharp reminder to the illiterate bigots who are today committing violence against the vulnerable in the name of Ram. There have been several incidents where mobs have attacked Muslims, and forced them to recite 'Jai Shri Ram', thereby demeaning the name of Ram, and shaming us both as Hindus and as citizens of a plural and composite democracy where people of many faiths have lived for centuries in peace and harmony. The biggest riposte to such ultra-Right fanatics comes from Ram himself, who tells Bharat that non-injury to others is the greatest dharma.

41. Shri Ram's Exhortation to the Citizens of Ayodhya

बड़े भाग मानुष तनु पावा ।
सुर दुर्लभ सब ग्रंथन्हि गावा ।।
साधन धाम मोच्छ कर द्वारा ।
पाइ न जेहिं परलोक सँवारा ।।[402]

baḍeṃ bhāga mānuṣa tanu pāvā ।
sura durlabha saba graṃthinha gāvā ।।
sādhana dhāma moccha kara dvārā ।
pāi na jehiṃ paraloka saṃvārā ।।

It is by good fortune that you have secured a human body, which as declared by all the scriptures is difficult even for the gods to attain. It is a tabernacle suitable for spiritual endeavours, gateway to liberation. He who fails to earn a good destiny hereafter even on attaining it.

सो परत्र दुख पावै सिर धुनि धुनि पछिताई ।
कालहि कर्महि ईस्वरहि मिथ्या दोस लगाइ ।।[403]

so paratra dukha pāvai sira dhuni dhuni pachitāi ।
kālahi karmahi īsvarahi mithyā doṣa lagāi ।।

He reaps torture in the other world and beats his head in remorse, wrongly attributing the blame to time, fate and god.

जौं परलोक इहाँ सुख चहहू ।
सुनि मम बचन हृदयँ दृढ़ गहहू ॥
सुलभ सुखद मारग यह भाई ।
भगति मोरि पुरान श्रुति गाई ॥[404]

jauṃ paraloka ihāṃ sukha cahahū ।
suni mama bacana hrṛdayaṃ dṛḍhagahahū ।।
sulabha sukhada māraga yaha bhāī ।
bhagati mori Purāna śruti gāī ।।

If you seek happiness here as well as hereafter, listen to my words and imprint them deeply in your heart. It is an easy and pleasant road, brethren, that of devotion to my feet, extolled in the Puranas and Vedas.

ग्यान अगम प्रत्यूह अनेका ।
साधन कठिन न मन कहुँ टेका ॥
करत कष्ट बहु पावइ कोऊ ।
भक्ति हीन मोहि प्रिय नहिं सोऊ ॥[405]

gyāna agama pratyūha anekā ।
sādhana kaṭhina na mana kahuṃ ṭekā ।।
karata kaṣṭa bahu pāvai koū ।
bhakti hīna mohi priya nahiṃ soū ।।

Knowledge is difficult to attain and beset with numerous obstacles. The path is rugged and there is no solid ground for the mind to rest on. Scarcely one attains it after a hard struggle; yet, lacking in devotion, the man fails to win my love.

भक्ति सुतंत्र सकल सुख खानी ।
बिनु सतसंक न पावहिं प्रानी ।
पुन्य पुंज बिनु मिलहिं न संता ।
सतसंगति संसृति कर अंता ॥[406]

bhakti sutaṃtra sakala sukha khānī ।
binu satasaṃga na pāvahiṃ prānī ।।
punya puṃja binu milahiṃ na saṃtā ।
satasaṃgati saṃsṛti kara aṃtā ।।

Devotion is independent and a mine of all blessings; men, however, cannot attain it except through the fellowship of saints. Saints for their part are inaccessible without a stock of merit; communion with the Lord's devotees in any case brings to an end the cycle of births and deaths.

औरउ एक गुपुत मत सबहि कहउँ कर जोरि।
संकर भजन बिना नर भगति न पावइ मोरि ॥[407]

aurau eka guputa mata sabahi kahauṃ kara jori ।
Saṃkara bhajana binā nara bhagati na pāvai mori ।।

With joined palms I lay before you all, another secret doctrine: without adoring Shankara (Lord Shiva) man cannot attain devotion to me.

कहहु भगति पथ कवन प्रयासा।
जोग न मख जप तप उपवासा॥
सरल सुभाव न मन कुटिलाई।
जथा लाभ संतोष सदाई ॥[408]

kahahu bhagati patha kavana prayāsā ।
joga na makha japa tapa upavāsā ।।
sarala subhāva na mana kuṭilāī ।
jathā lābha saṃtoṣa sadāī ।।

Tell me what pains are involved in treading the path of devotion: it requires neither Yoga (mind-control), nor sacrifices, nor japa (muttering of prayers), nor penance, nor fasting. A guileless disposition, a mind free from perversity and absolute contentment with whatever may be got is all that is needed.

मोर दास कहाइ नर आसा ।
करइ तौ कहहु कहा बिस्वासा ॥
बहुत कहउँ का कथा बढ़ाई ।
एहि आचरन बस्य मैं भाई ॥[409]

mora dāsa kahāi nara āsā ।
karai tau kahahu kahā bisvāsā ।।
bahuta kahauṃ kā kathā baḍhaāī ।
ehi ācarana basya maiṃ bhāī ।।

If he who is called a devotee yet counts upon man, tell me, what faith does he have in me? What use my dwelling on the subject further: I am won by the conduct of a man as depicted below, brethren.

बैर न बिग्रह आस न त्रासा।
सुखमय ताहि सदा सब आसा ॥
अनारंभ अनिकेत अमानी ।
अनघ अरोष दच्छ बिग्यानी ॥
प्रीति सदा सज्जन संसर्गा ।
तृन सम बिषय स्वर्ग अपबर्गा ॥
भगति पच्छ हठ नहिं सठताई ।
दुष्ट तर्क सब दूरि बहाई ॥[410]

baira na bigraha āsa na trāsā ।
sukhamaya tāhi sadā saba āsā ।।
anāraṃbha aniketa amānī ।
anagha aroṣa daccha bigyānī ।।
prīti sadā sajjana saṃsargā ।
tṛna sama biṣaya svarga apabargā ।।
bhagati paccha haṭha nahiṃ saṭhatāī ।
duṣṭa tarka saba dūri bahāī ।।

He who has no enmity or quarrel with anyone and is devoid of hope and fear—to such a man, all the quarters are ever full of joy. Undertaking nothing (with an interested motive), without home, without pride and without sin, free from wrath, clever and wise, ever loving the company of saints and accounting the enjoyments even of heaven as well as final beatitude as no more than a blade of grass, tenaciously adhering to the cult of devotion but avoiding bigotry, and giving up all sophistical reasoning.

A king must be in direct touch with his subjects, and this is the prime purpose behind this prasang, where Ram directly addresses the ordinary people of Ayodhya, after having returned victorious to his kingdom. The attempt here is to show a participatory polity, which may be a monarchy, but runs on the unqualified support and endorsement of the people at large, and is, thus, essentially democratic in nature.

Tulsi uses this occasion primarily to dwell on two points. Firstly, as has been his repeated refrain, he uses Ram to re-stress the primacy of bhakti, absolute devotion and surrender to the Lord, over all other means of spiritual and religious endeavours. Bhakti is the *sugam* or easy path to follow, and our poet cites the Puranas and the Vedas as proof of this assertion. By comparison, the jnana marga, or the path of knowledge, is encumbered by too many impediments; it entangles the mind, and an overburdened mind does not find the solace that comes so easily by the simplicity of bhakti. Knowledge does bestow wisdom to some, but that wisdom is of little consequence without the redemption of faith. Faith, reinforced by the company of saints, is an end in itself; it requires no supporting instruments, such as mind control, or yagna (sacrifices), japa or repetition of prayers, or ascetic penance. All it asks for is a guileless disposition, contentment of mind, and untiring effort to be a good human being.

This brings Tulsi to his second point. What kind of person is equipped to follow the path of bhakti? Such a person must have equilibrium; he should be detached, without desires; he should be above enmity; he must not wish to quarrel with anyone; he should be free from pride and wrath; forever seeking the company of the good, he should relinquish arrogance and infatuations; beyond the entanglements of the mind, he must avoid 'contentious arguments'; he should be free even from the desire to achieve the pleasures of heaven or the bliss of moksha or salvation; and, he should be fully and unconditionally devoted to Ram. Tulsi implies that to pursue such a path of idealised goodness, is the great opportunity that human beings have, for to be born as a human is something that even the gods envy. When such a great opportunity is given, why waste it in anything else?

It is no coincidence that many of these qualities also make for a good citizen, even an ideal citizen. The kingdom of Ram, Ramrajya, could only have ideal citizens. Thus, Tulsi, while espousing his strong belief in the efficacy of bhakti as the most ideal path to salvation, also profiles the qualities of a good citizen, the kind of citizen that would be a reflection of Ram, the repository of every form of goodness.

42. Narration of Kakabhushundi's Previous Lives in Garuda's Presence

कीट मनोरथ दारु सरीरा।
जेहि न लाग घुन को अस धीरा॥
सुत बित लोक ईषना तीनी।
केहि कै मति इन्ह कृत न मलीनी॥[411]

kīṭa manoratha dāru sarīrā ।
jehi na lāga ghuna ko asa dhīrā ।।
suta bita loka īṣanā tīnī ।
kehi ke mati inha kṛta na malīnī ।।

Again, is there anyone so resolute of mind, whose body is not being consumed by desire as a piece of wood is eaten away by a 'wooded-borer'? Whose mind has not been polluted by the threefold desire—the desire of progeny, the desire of wealth and the desire of fame?

सोई सच्चिदानंद घन रामा।
अज बिग्यान रूप बल धामा।
ब्यापक ब्याप्य अखंड अनंता।
अखिल अमकेघसक्ति भगवंता॥[412]

soi Saccidānaṃda ghana Rāmā ।
aja bigyāna rūpo bala dhāmā ।।
byāpaka byāpya akhaṃḍa anaṃtā ।
akhila amoghasakti bhagavaṃtā ।।

Such is Shri Ram, who is devoid of birth, the totality of existence, knowledge and bliss, wisdom personified, the home of beauty and strength. He is both pervading and pervaded, fractionless, infinite and integral, the Lord of unfailing power.

परबस जीव स्वबस भगवंता।
जीव अनेक एक श्रीकंता॥
मुधा भेद जद्यपि कृत माया।
बिनु हरि जाई न कोटि उपाया॥[413]

parabasa jīva svabasa bhagavaṃtā ।
jīva aneka eka Srīkaṃtā ।।
mudhā bheda jadyapi kṛta māyā ।
binu Hari jāi na koṭi upāyā ।।

The jivas are many, while the Beloved of Lakshmi is one (without a second). Even though this difference, which has been created by Maya, is false, it cannot disappear except by Shri Hari's grace, whatever you may do.

भगति हीन गुन सब सुख ऐसे।
लवन बिना बहु बिंजन जैसे॥
भजन हीन सुख कवने काजा।
अस बिचारि बोलेउँ खगराजा॥[414]

bhagati hīna guna saba sukha aise ।
lavana binā bahu biṃjana jaise ।।
bhajana hīna sukha kavane kājā ।
asa bicāri boleuṃ khagarājā ।।

Without such devotion, all sorts of virtues and blessings are like so many auxiliary dishes without salt. Of what avail is any blessing without adoration. Pondering thus, O king of the birds, I replied as follows.

मम माया संभव संसारा।
जीव चराचर बिबिधि प्रकारा॥
सब मम प्रिय सब मम उपजाए।
सब ते अधिक मनुज मोहि भाए॥[415]

mama māyā saṃbhava saṃsārā ।
jīva carācara bibidhi prakārā ।।
saba mama priya saba mama upajāe ।
saba te adhika manuja mohi bhāe ।।

'This world with all its varieties of life, both moving and motionless, is a creation of my Maya (delusive potency). I love them all, because all are my creatures. But human beings are the dearest to me of all.'

तिन्ह महँ द्विज द्विज महँ श्रुतिधारी।
तिन्ह महुँ निगम धरम अनुसारी॥
तिन्ह महँ प्रिय बिरक्त पुनि ग्यानी।
ग्यानिहु ते अति प्रिय बिग्यानी॥
तिन्हते पुनि मोहि प्रिय निज दासा।
जोहि गति मोरि न दूसरि आसा॥
पुनि पुनि सत्य करउँ तोहि पाहीं।
मोहि सेवक सम प्रिय कोउ नाहीं॥
भगति हीन बिरंचि किन होई।
सब जीवहु सम प्रिय मोहि सोई॥
भगतिवंत अति नीचउ प्रानी।
मोही प्रानप्रिय असि मम बानी॥[416]

tinha mahaṃ dvija dvija mahaṃ śrutidhārī ।
tinha mahuṃ nigama dharam anusārī ।।
tinha mahaṃ priya birakta puni gyānī ।
gyānihu te ati priya bigyānī ।।
tinha te puni mohi priya nija dāsā ।
jehi gati mori na dūsari āsā ।।
puni puni satya kahauṃ tohi pāhīṃ ।

mohi sevaka sama priya kou nāhīṃ ।।
bhagati hīna biraṃci kina hoī ।
saba jīvahu sama priya mohi soī ।।
bhagativaṃta ati nīcau prānī ।
mohi prānapriya asi mama bānī ।।

Of human beings, the Brahmins; of the Brahmins, those well-versed in the Vedas; of these, again, those that follow the course of conduct prescribed in the Vedas; of these latter, those who are averse to the pleasure of sense are dear to me, and yet more the wise; of the wise too I love a man of realisation all the more; more beloved to me even than these is my own servant (devotee), who solely depends on me and has no other hope. Again and again, I repeat to you the truth that no one is so dear to me as my devotee. If Viranchi (the Creator) too had no devotion to me, he would be only as dear to me as all the other creatures. And the humblest creature that breathes, if possessed of devotion, is dear to me as life: such is my nature.

जप तप मख सम दम ब्रत दाना।
बिरति बिबेक जोग बिग्याना।।
सब कर फल रघुपति पद प्रेमा।
तेहि बिनु कोउ न पावउ छेमा।।[417]

japa tapa makha sama dama brata dānā ।
birati bibeka joga bigyānā ।।
saba kara phala Raghupati pada premā ।
tehi binu kou na pāvai chemā ।।

The muttering of prayers, austere penance, performing sacrifices, subjugation of the mind and the senses, undertaking sacred vows, charity, dispassion, right judgement, Yoga and realisation—the fruit of all these is devotion to the feet of Shri Ram (the Lord of the Raghus); without this, no one can attain lasting peace.

The *Uttara Kanda* includes a very long dialogue between

Kakabhushundi and Garuda, the king of birds, which covers Kakabhushundi's remembrance of his former lives and his many avatars. From this extensive dialogue, we have taken a few stanzas that are notable for the expounding of the bhakti rasa. Kakabhushundi was a sage, who in his final incarnation was transformed into a crow by the curse of the saint, Lomas. As per Hindu texts, Kakabhushundi was a great devotee of Lord Ram, and was, it is believed, the first person to narrate the Ramayana, even before Valmiki, Shiva and Tulsidas. He enjoys a very venerable position in the mythology of Ram, and is regarded as one of the chiranjeevis, or immortal living beings in Hinduism.

Kakabhushundi was an ideal narrator of the story of Ram, because he could both stand outside time, and travel through it. He was thus the quintessential observer, and the mission of his life was to describe and participate in the life and exploits of Ram. In fact, it is said that he was able to see Ramayana played out as many as eleven times. The belief is that whenever Shri Ram takes an incarnation on earth in different *kalpas* or aeons, Kakabhushundi flies away and shifts to Ayodhya, because especially of his eagerness to watch the leela of the child Ram.

Tulsi, through Kakabhushundi, first speaks of the limitations of the ordinary mortal: the grip of desire. Desire is like termite, and the body is like wood. The termite eats into the wood, even as the individual continues to be obsessed with the three primary desires: for progeny, for wealth, and for fame. By contrast, Ram is unsullied perfection. He is described in decidedly nirguna terms, as self-existent, intelligence personified—*sarva pratyaya darshinin*—all-pervasive, indivisible or akhanda, infinite or *amatra,* and pure bliss.

Although all beings—animate and inanimate—are part of the all-encompassing divinity of Ram, Maya creates the illusion of separateness. The world then becomes inhabited by many jivas, or individuals, and one separate Absolute, which is a false distinction. There is only one way to see through the cosmic illusion created by Maya, and that is to surrender to the lotus-feet of Ram.

Without the elevating aspect of this faith and surrender, everything else is of devalued consequence, tasting like food does without the addition of salt. The only pursuit that can grant redemption is absolute devotion. Who then is dear to Ram? Is it those considered higher in the conventional social hierarchy? Or those who are well-versed in the Vedas? Is it those who embrace celibacy to worship the Lord single-mindedly, or those who acquire spiritual wisdom? Kakabhushundi says, that while the Lord's gaze is never exclusionist, and all of such people are dear, the ones whom he really loves are those who have surrendered their all to him, and have no other refuge except him. 'One without devotion, be he the Creator himself, is no dearer to me than any other creature, but the humblest creature that breathes, if he is possessed of devotion, is dear to me as my own life: such is my doctrine.'

The bhakti marga—so dear to Tulsi—is thus spelt out in crystal clear terms. In fact, Tulsi goes further to exclude all other alternatives. Not prayer, penance, sacred vows, austerities, dispassion or discernment (that come from the jnana marga) or mystic intuition (a hint at the Tantric school), are equal to the peace that comes from devotional surrender, which is the sum of what the other paths seek to achieve.

Kakabhushundi's unqualified praise for bhakti of Ram is understandable considering that he is himself one of the biggest bhakts of Ram. In the dialogue between Kakabhushundi and Garuda, Tulsi gets the space and the opportunity to fully expound on the efficacy of pure bhakti to the Lord.

43. The Glory of Kali Age Described by Kakabhushundi

बरन धर्म नहिं आश्रम चारी।
श्रुति बिरोध रत सब नर नारी॥
द्विज श्रुति बेचक भूप प्रजासन।
कोउ नहिं मान निगम अनुसासन॥[418]

barana dharma nahiṃ āśram cārī ।
śruti birodha rata saba nara nārī ।।
dvija śruti becaka bhūpa prajāsana ।
kou nahiṃ māna nigama anusāsana ।।

No one follows the duties of one's own caste, and the four ashrams or stages of life also disappear. Every man and woman takes delight in revolting against the Vedas. The Brahmins sell the Vedas; the kings bleed their subjects; no one respects the injunction of the Vedas.

मारग सोइ जा कहुँ जोइ भावा।
पंडित सोइ जो गाल बजावा॥
मिथ्यारंभ दंभ रत जोई।
ता कहूँ संत कहइ सब कोई॥[419]

māraga soi jā kahuṃ joi bhāvā ।
Paṃḍita soi jo gāla bajāvā ।।
mithyāraṃbha daṃbha rata joī ।
tā kahuṃ saṃta kahai saba koī ।।

The right course for every individual is that which one takes a fancy to; a man of erudition is he who plays the braggart. Whoever launches spurious undertakings and is given over to hypocrisy, him does everyone call a saint.

सोई सयान जो परधन हारी।
जो कर दंभ सो बड़ आचारी॥
जो कह झूठ मसखरी जाना।
कलिजुग सोइ गुनवंत बखाना॥[420]

soi sayāna jo paradhana hārī ।
jo kara daṃbha so baḍaācārī ।।
jau kaha jhūṃṭha masakharī jānā ।
kalijuga soi gunavaṃta bakhānā ।।

He alone is clever, who robs another of his wealth; he who puts up false appearances is an ardent follower of established usage. He who is given to lying and is clever at joking is spoken of as a man of parts in the Kali age.

निराचार जो श्रुति पथ त्यागी।
कलिजुग सोइ ग्यानी सो बिरागी॥
जाकें नख अरु जटा बिसाला।
सोइ तापस प्रसिद्ध कलिकाला॥[421]

nirācāra jo śruti patha tyāgī ।
Kalijuga soi gyānī so birāgī ।।
jākeṃ nakha aru jaṭā bisālā ।
soi tāpasa prasīddha kalikālā ।।

He alone who is a reprobate and has abandoned the path of the Vedas is a man of wisdom and dispassion in the Kali age. He alone who has grown big nails and long locks of matted hair is a renowned ascetic in the Kali age.

धनवंत कुलीन मलीन अपी ।
द्विज चिन्ह जनेउ उघार तपी ॥
नहिं मान पुरान न बेदहि जो ।
हरि सेवक संत सही कलि सो ॥[422]

dhanavaṃta kulīna malīna apī ।
dvija cinha janeu ughāra tapī ।।
nahiṃ māna Purāna na bedahi jo ।
Hari sevaka saṃta sahī kali so ।

The meanest churl, if he is rich, is accounted noble. A Brahmin is known only by his sacred thread, and an ascetic by his naked body. He who refuses to recognise the Vedas and Puranas is a true saint and servant of Shri Hari in the Kali age.

कवि बृंद उदार दुनी न सुनी ।
गुन दूषक ब्रात न कोपि गुनी ॥
कलि बारहिं बार दुकाल परै ।
बिनु अन्न दुखी सब लोग मरै ॥[423]

kabi bṛṃda udāra dunī na sunī ।
guna dūṣaka brāta na kopi gunī ।।
Kali bārahiṃ bāra dukāla parai ।
binu anna dukhī saba loga marai ।।

Poets are seen in large numbers; but the munificent (who reward them) are seldom heard of. Those who find fault with others' virtues can be had in any number, but no one possessing virtues. In the Kali age, famines are of frequent occurrence: for want of foodgrains people perish miserably *en masse.*

सुनु खगेस कलि कपट हठ दंभ द्वेष पाषंड ।
मान मोह मारादि मद ब्यापि रहे ब्रह्मंड ॥[424]

sunu khagesa kali kapaṭa haṭha daṃbha dveṣa pāṣaṃḍa ।
māna moha mārādi mada byāpi rahe brahmaṃḍa ।।

Listen, lord of the winged creatures: in the age of Kali, duplicity, perversity, hypocrisy, malice, heresy, pride, infatuation, concupiscence and arrogance etc., pervade the whole universe.

कृतजुग त्रेताँ द्वापर पूजा मख अरु जोग।
जो गति होइ सो कलि हरि नाम ते पावहिं लोग ।।[425]

kṛtajuga tretā dvāpara pūjā makha aru joga ।
jo gati hoi so kali Hari nāma te pāvahiṃ loga ।।

Moreover, the same goal which is reached through worship of god, performance of sacrifices or practice of Yoga in the Satyayuga, Treta and Dvapara, men are able to attain through the name of Shri Hari in the Kali age.

कलिजुग जोग न जग्य न ग्याना।
एक अधार राम गुन गाना।
सब भरोस तजि जो भज रामहि।
प्रेम समेत गाव गुन ग्रामहि ।।
सोइ भव तर कछु संसय नाहीं।
नाम प्रताप प्रगट कलि माहीं ।।
कलि भरोस तजि जो भज रामहि।
प्रेम समेत गाव गुन ग्रामहि ।।[426]

Kalijuga joga na jagya na gyānā ।
eka adhāra Rāma guna gānā ।।
saba bharosa taji jo bhaja Rāmahi ।
prema sameta gāva guna grāmahi ।।
soi bhava tara kachu saṃsaya nāhīṃ ।
nāma pratāpa pragaṭa kali māhīṃ ।।
kali bharosa tajijo bhaja rāmahi ।
prema sameta gāva guna grāmahi ।।

In the Kali age, however, men reach the end of mundane existence simply by singing Shri Hari's praises. In the age of Kali, neither Yoga (concentration of mind), nor the performance of sacrifices nor spiritual wisdom is of any avail; one's only hope lies in hymning Shri Ram's praises. Giving up all other hopes, whosoever worships Shri Ram and fondly chants His praises undoubtedly crosses the ocean of transmigration. The power of the name is thus manifest in the age of Kali. The Kali age possesses another sacred virtue: in this age, projected acts of virtuous nature are virtues but those of evil propensity are not sins.

कलिजुग सम जुग आन नहिं जौं नर कर बिस्वास ।
गाइ राम गुन गन बिमल भव तर बिनहिं प्रयास ।।[427]

Kalijuga sama juga āna nahiṃ jauṃ nara kara bisvāsa ।
gāi Rāma guna gana bimalaṃ bhava tara binahiṃ prayāsa ।।

No other age can compare with the Kali age, provided a man has faith (in its virtue); for in this age one can easily cross the ocean of transmigration simply by singing Shri Ram's holy praises.

An interesting part of the dialogue between Kakabhushundi and Garuda is the description by the former of Kaliyuga, the present era that we live in, which is the last of the four stages the world goes through as part of a cycle of *yugas,* after which there is *pralaya* or total destruction, which in turn is followed by *shrishti,* the dawn of new creation. In the previous yugas or aeons—Satya, Treta and Dvapara—there were redeeming qualities, but Tulsi makes a damning indictment of Kaliyuga, as can be witnessed in these selected stanzas.

However, even in what appears like a sweeping condemnation, there is a structure that our poet keeps in focus. He first laments the fact that the social order ceases to exist and unravels from its firm moorings of tradition and established practice. Thus, for instance, he says that there is no varna dharma, nor are the four ashrams—or stages of life—followed. A casteless society is today a desired goal, but for Tulsi the varna dharma was a sign of the structured working of society as sanctioned by religion and practice. He can be forgiven for his lack of progressive views, but his essential message is that the social order disintegrates. Secondly, all behavioural norms are upturned. He who does little else but brag is considered erudite; he who loots is considered honest; the hypocritical are considered saints; he who lies is considered accomplished. Thirdly—and this is dear to Tulsi's heart—the creative arts are sullied. Poets abound, but the numbers of those who have the discernment to judge good poetry, dwindle. Fourthly, the economy is destroyed. Famines occur with depressing frequency, and people suffer for the absence of food. And, lastly ethics are demolished. Duplicity, perversity, hypocrisy, malice, heresy, arrogance, infatuation, lust, pride and the like pervade the whole universe.

In such a depressing state of affairs, Tulsi adroitly manages to place the bhakti of Ram as the only means of salvation. Precisely because things are so bad, the only path to redemption is the complete and total surrender to the lotus-feet of the Lord. In earlier yugas, meditation, yagnas or sacrifices, and ritual worship could be an instrument to escape the suffering of the world. But, in Kaliyuga, our poet argues, no amount of austerity, sacrifices or spiritual wisdom are to any avail. The only instrument that is efficacious is devotion and worship of Ram.

Thus, in the lengthy description of Kaliyuga by Kakabhushundi, Tulsi premeditatedly brings the argument back to the unconditional and unqualified virtue of the total surrender to Lord Ram, the only path to salvation and redemption.

44. Rudrashtaka or a Hymn of Eight Verses Addressed to Lord Shiva by Shri Ram

करि दंडवत सप्रेम द्विज सिव सन्मुख कर जोरि।
बिनय करत गदगद स्वर समुझि घोर गति मोरि ॥[428]

kari daṃḍavata saprema dvija Siva sanmukha kara jori ।
binaya karata gadagada svara samujhi ghora gati mori ।।

Reflecting on my awful fate, the Brahmin prostrated himself before Lord Shiva and, with joined palms and his voice choked with emotion, he prayed as follows:

नमामीशमीशान निर्वाणरूपं।
विभुं व्यापकं ब्रह्म वेदस्वरूपं ॥
निजं निर्गुणं निर्विकल्पं निरीहं।
चिदाकाशमाकाशवासं भजेऽहं ॥[429]

namāmīśamīśāna nirvāṇarūpaṃ ।
viṃbhuṃ byāpakaṃ Brahma vedasvarūpaṃ ।
nijaṃ nirguṇaṃ nirvikalpaṃ nirīṃhaṃ ।
cidākāśamākāśavāsaṃ bhaje'haṃ ।।

'I adore You, the guardian of the south-east quarter and Ruler of the whole universe, eternal bliss personified, the omnipresent and all-pervading Brahma manifest in the form of the Vedas. I worship Lord Shiva, shining in His own glory, devoid of material attributes, undifferentiated, desireless, all-pervading consciousness, having nothing to wrap about Himself except ether (or enveloping ether itself).

निराकारमोंकारमूलं तुरीयं ।
गिरा ग्यान गोतीतमीशं गिरीशं ॥
करालं महाकाल कालं कृपालं ।
गुणागार संसारपारं नतोऽहं ॥[430]

nirākāramoṃkāramūlaṃ turīyaṃ ।
girā gyāna gotītamīśaṃ girīśaṃ ।।
karālaṃ mahākāla kālaṃ kṛpālaṃ ।
guṇāgāra saṃsārapāraṃ nato'haṃ ।।

'I bow to the supreme Lord, who is devoid of form, transcendent and extra-cosmic, beyond speech, understanding and sense perception, terrible yet gracious, the seed of the mystic syllable Om, the Ruler of Kailasha, the devourer even of the great Time-Spirit and the abode of virtues.

तुषाराद्रि संकाश गौरं गभीरं ।
मनोभूत कोटि प्रभा श्रीशरीरं ।
स्फुरन्मौलि कल्लोलिनी चारु गंगा ।
लसद्भालबालेन्दु कंठे भुजंगा ॥
चलत्कुण्डलं भ्रू सुनेत्रं विशालं ।
प्रसन्नाननं नीलकंठं दयालं ।
मृगाधीशचर्माम्बरं मुण्डमालं ।
प्रियं शंकरं सर्वनाथं भजामि ॥[431]

tuṣārādri saṃkāśa gauraṃ gabhīraṃ ।
manobhūta koṭi prabhā śrī śarīraṃ ।।
sphuranmauli kallolinī cāru gaṃgā ।
lasadbhālabālendu kaṃṭhe bhujaṃgā ।।
calatkuṃḍalaṃ bhrū sunetraṃ viśālaṃ ।
prasannānanaṃ nīlakaṃṭhaṃ dayālaṃ ।।

mṛgādhīśacarmāmbaraṃ muṇḍamālaṃ ।
priyaṃ Saṃkaraṃ sarvanāthaṃ bhajāmi ।।

'I adore the all-merciful Shankara, the universal Lord, who is loved by all and yet unfathomable, who is possessed of a form white as the snow-clad Himalaya, and radiant with the beauty of a myriad Cupids, whose head sparkles with the lovely stream of the Ganga, whose brow is adorned by the crescent moon and neck coiled by serpents, who has tremulous pendants hanging from His earlobes, is possessed of beautiful eyebrows and large eyes, who has a cheerful countenance and a blue speck on His throat, and who has a lion-skin wrapped round His waist and a garland of skulls round His neck.

प्रचंडं प्रकृष्टं प्रगल्भं परेशं ।
अखंडं अजं भानुकोटिप्रकाशं ।
त्रयः शूल निर्मूलनं शूलपाणिं ।
भजेऽहं भवानीपतिं भावगम्यं ।।[432]

pracaṃḍaṃ prakṛṣṭaṃ pragalbhaṃ pareśaṃ ।
akhaṃḍaṃ ajaṃ bhānukoṭiprakāśaṃ ।।
trayaḥśūla nirmūlanaṃ śūlapāṇiṃ ।
bhaje'haṃ Bhavānīpatiṃ bhāvagamyaṃ ।।

'I take my refuge in Bhavani's spouse, the supreme Lord, terrible, exalted, intrepid, indivisible, unborn and invested with the glory of a myriad suns, who roots out the threefold agony and holds a trident in His hand and who is accessible only through love.

कलातीत कल्याण कल्पान्तकारी ।
सदा सज्जनानन्ददाता पुरारी ।।
चिदानंद संदोह मोहापहारी ।
प्रसीद प्रसीद प्रभो मन्मथारी ।।[433]

kalātīta kalyāṇa kalpāntakārī ।
sadā sajjanāndadātā purārī ।।

cidānaṃdasaṃdoha mohāpahārī ।
prasīda prasīda prabho manmathārī ॥

'Beyond number, ever blessed, bringing about universal destruction at the end of each round of creation, a source of perpetual delight to the virtuous, slayer of the demon Tripura, consciousness and bliss personified, dispeller of delusion, be propitious, my lord, be propitious, O Destroyer of Cupid.

न यावद् उमानाथ पादारविंदं ।
भजंतीह लोके परे वा नराणां ।
न तावत्सुखं शान्ति सन्तापनाशं ।
प्रसीद प्रभो सर्वभूताधिवासं ॥[434]

na yāvad umānātha pādāravindaṃ ।
bhajaṃtīha loke pare vā narāṇāṃ ॥
na tāvatsukhaṃ śānti santāpanāśaṃ ।
prasīda prabho sarvabhūtādhivāsaṃ ॥

'So long as they worship not the lotus-feet of Uma's Lord, there is no happiness nor peace nor cessation of suffering for men either in this world or in the next. Therefore, be propitious, my Lord, dwelling as You do in the heart of all living beings.

न जानामि योगं जपं नैव पूजां ।
नतोऽहं सदा सर्वदा शंभु तुभ्यं ।
जरा जन्म दुःखौघ तातप्यमानं ॥
प्रभो पाहि आपन्नमामीश शंभो ॥[435]

na jānāmi yogaṃ japaṃ naiva pūjāṃ ।
nato'haṃ sadā sarvadā saṃbhu tubhyaṃ ॥
jarā janma duḥkhaugha tātapyamānaṃ ।
prabho pāhi āpannamāmīśa Saṃbho ॥

'I know not Yoga (concentration), nor japa (the muttering of prayers) nor ritual. I simply bow to you at all times and at every moment, O Shambhu! Pray, protect me, my lord, miserable and afflicted by sufferings attendant on old age and birth (and death) as I am, O Lord Shambhu!'

> श्लोक : रुद्राष्टकमिदं प्रोक्तं विप्रेण हरतोषये।
> ये पठन्ति नरा भक्त्या तेषां शम्भुः प्रसीदति॥ [436]

> Rudrāṣṭakamidaṃ proktaṃ vipreṇa Haratoṣaye ।
> ye paṭhanti narā bhaktyā teṣāṃ śambhuḥ prasīdati ।।

This hymn of eight verses was uttered by the Brahmin in order to propitiate Lord Hara. Shri Shambhu is pleased with those men who devoutly repeat it.

If Shiva himself pays tribute to Shri Ram in Tulsi's composition *'jaya Ram Ram Ramnang shamanang,'* discussed earlier, it is Tulsi's turn to pay fulsome tribute to Shiva, as is evidenced by this Rudrashtaka. A Rudrashtaka is an *ashtaka* or octet in the form of a prayer consisting of eight rhyming verses. It is dedicated to Rudra, which is Shiva in his fearsome form. Composed in Sanskrit, it is said that Tulsi wrote it while in the Vishwanath temple in Kashi, which is the most holy shrine dedicated to Shiva in the holy city. The lyrical intensity of this hymn, delineating every aspect of Mahadeva, and the total surrender it advocates to his will, could not have been achieved—so people believe—until the grace of Shiva himself had blessed Tulsidas.

The Rudrashtaka has become a widely popular evocation of Shiva, recited by devotees on a daily basis across India, and especially on Mondays, which is a day dedicated to Shambhu. The prayer profiles Shiva as the manifestation of Brahman—all-pervasive, intelligence personified, beyond form, timeless, beyond knowledge, speech and perception, self-contained, fearless, undifferentiated, unqualified, changeless, compassionate, and the harbinger of bliss and awareness that is the inferential experience of Brahma-*anubhav*, the experience of Brahman.

The Rudrashtaka is as much a tribute to the poetic dexterity of Tulsi, as it is a supremely powerful invocation of the divine plenitude of Shiva. Tulsi himself writes that Shiva will be pleased to shower his benediction on those who recite this ashtaka with devotion.

Endnotes

1. Characteristics of Saints and Salutations to Them

1. Shriramcharitmanas, Balakanda—1.3
2. Shriramcharitmanas, Balakanda—2.4
3. Shriramcharitmanas, Balakanda—2.5
4. Shriramcharitmanas, Balakanda—3 (s)

2. Characteristics of the Wicked and Salutations to Them

5. Shriramcharitmanas, Balakanda—3 (s).1
6. Shriramcharitmanas, Balakanda—3 (s).2
7. Shriramcharitmanas, Balakanda—3 (s).3
8. Shriramcharitmanas, Balakanda—3 (s).4

3. The Creation of Brahma and its Form

9. Shriramcharitmanas, Balakanda—5.2
10. Shriramcharitmanas, Balakanda—5.3–5

4. The Form of Shri Ram-Sita and Salutations to Them

11. Shriramcharitmanas, Balakanda— 18
12. Shriramcharitmanas, Balakanda—18.1

5. Glory of the Name and Character of Shri Ram

13. Shriramcharitmanas, Balakanda—22.1
14. Shriramcharitmanas, Balakanda—25
15. Shriramcharitmanas, Balakanda—27
16. Shriramcharitmanas, Balakanda—27.1
17. Shriramcharitmanas, Balakanda—31

6. The Glory, Creator and Form of Shri Ramcharitmanas

18. Shriramcharitmanas, Balakanda—34.4
19. Shriramcharitmanas, Balakanda—34.5
20. Shriramcharitmanas, Balakanda—34.6
21. Shriramcharitmanas, Balakanda—3 5
22. Shriramcharitmanas, Balakanda—35.1
23. Shriramcharitmanas, Balakanda—35.2
24. Shriramcharitmanas, Balakanda—36
25. Shriramcharitmanas, Balakanda—36.1
26. Shriramcharitmanas, Balakanda—36.2
27. Shriramcharitmanas, Balakanda—36.3

7. Dialogue Between Shiva and Sati

28. Shriramcharitmanas, Balakanda—59.4
29. Shriramcharitmanas, Balakanda—61.3
30. Shriramcharitmanas, Balakanda—76.2

8. The Spring Form of Kamadeva (the God of Love) and His Immolation by Shiva

31. Shriramcharitmanas, Balakanda—83
32. Shriramcharitmanas, Balakanda—83.1
33. Shriramcharitmanas, Balakanda—83.2
34. Shriramcharitmanas, Balakanda—83.3
35. Shriramcharitmanas, Balakanda—83.4
36. Shriramcharitmanas, Balakanda—83, quatrain
37. Shriramcharitmanas, Balakanda—84

38. Shriramcharitmanas, Balakanda—84.1
39. Shriramcharitmanas, Balakanda—84.2
40. Shriramcharitmanas, Balakanda—84.3–4
41. Shriramcharitmanas, Balakanda—84, quatrain
42. Shriramcharitmanas, Balakanda—85
43. Shriramcharitmanas, Balakanda—85.1
44. Shriramcharitmanas, Balakanda—85.2
45. Shriramcharitmanas, Balakanda—85.3
46. Shriramcharitmanas, Balakanda—85.4
47. Shriramcharitmanas, Balakanda—85, quatrain
48. Shriramcharitmanas, Balakanda—86
49. Shriramcharitmanas, Balakanda—86.1
50. Shriramcharitmanas, Balakanda—86.2
51. Shriramcharitmanas, Balakanda—86.3
52. Shriramcharitmanas, Balakanda—86.4
53. Shriramcharitmanas, Balakanda—86, quatrain
54. Shriramcharitmanas, Balakanda—87
55. Shriramcharitmanas, Balakanda—87.1

9. Dialogue Between Shiva and Parvati About Saguna-Nirguna

56. Shriramcharitmanas, Balakanda—115.1
57. Shriramcharitmanas, Balakanda—115.2
58. Shriramcharitmanas, Balakanda—115.3
59. Shriramcharitmanas, Balakanda—115.4
60. Shriramcharitmanas, Balakanda—117.3
61. Shriramcharitmanas, Balakanda—117.3

10. Incarnation of Shri Ram

62. Shriramcharitmanas, Balakanda—190
63. Shriramcharitmanas, Balakanda—190.1
64. Shriramcharitmanas, Balakanda—190.2
65. Shriramcharitmanas, Balakanda—190.3–4
66. Shriramcharitmanas, Balakanda—191

67. Shriramcharitmanas, Balakanda—191.1
68. Shriramcharitmanas, Balakanda—191.2
69. Shriramcharitmanas, Balakanda—191.3
70. Shriramcharitmanas, Balakanda—191.4
71. Shriramcharitmanas, Balakanda—192

11. A Visit to Janak's Garden by Shri Ram-Lakshman When Shri Ram-Sita Catch Sight of Each Other

72. Shriramcharitmanas, Balakanda—226.2
73. Shriramcharitmanas, Balakanda—226.3
74. Shriramcharitmanas, Balakanda—226.4
75. Shriramcharitmanas, Balakanda—227
76. Shriramcharitmanas, Balakanda—227.1
77. Shriramcharitmanas, Balakanda—227.2
78. Shriramcharitmanas, Balakanda—227.3
79. Shriramcharitmanas, Balakanda—227.4
80. Shriramcharitmanas, Balakanda—228
81. Shriramcharitmanas, Balakanda—228.1
82. Shriramcharitmanas, Balakanda—228.2
83. Shriramcharitmanas, Balakanda—229
84. Shriramcharitmanas, Balakanda—229.1
85. Shriramcharitmanas, Balakanda—229.2
86. Shriramcharitmanas, Balakanda—229.3
87. Shriramcharitmanas, Balakanda—229.4
88. Shriramcharitmanas, Balakanda—230
89. Shriramcharitmanas, Balakanda—230.1
90. Shriramcharitmanas, Balakanda—230.2
91. Shriramcharitmanas, Balakanda—230.3
92. Shriramcharitmanas, Balakanda—230.4
93. Shriramcharitmanas, Balakanda—231
94. Shriramcharitmanas, Balakanda—231.1
95. Shriramcharitmanas, Balakanda—232
96. Shriramcharitmanas, Balakanda—232.1
97. Shriramcharitmanas, Balakanda—232.2–3

98. Shriramcharitmanas, Balakanda—232.4
99. Shriramcharitmanas, Balakanda—234.1
100. Shriramcharitmanas, Balakanda—234.2
101. Shriramcharitmanas, Balakanda—234.3
102. Shriramcharitmanas, Balakanda—234.4

12. Description of Sita's Unique Beauty by Shri Ram

103. Shriramcharitmanas, Balakanda—236.4
104. Shriramcharitmanas, Balakanda—237
105. Shriramcharitmanas, Balakanda—237.1
106. Shriramcharitmanas, Balakanda—237.2

13. Shri Ram-Lakshman in Sita's Svayamwara

107. Shriramcharitmanas, Balakanda—239.3
108. Shriramcharitmanas, Balakanda—240.1
109. Shriramcharitmanas, Balakanda—240.2
110. Shriramcharitmanas, Balakanda—240.3
111. Shriramcharitmanas, Balakanda—240.4
112. Shriramcharitmanas, Balakanda—241
113. Shriramcharitmanas, Balakanda—241.1
114. Shriramcharitmanas, Balakanda—241.2
115. Shriramcharitmanas, Balakanda—241.3
116. Shriramcharitmanas, Balakanda—241.4
117. Shriramcharitmanas, Balakanda—246.1
118. Shriramcharitmanas, Balakanda—246.2
119. Shriramcharitmanas, Balakanda—246.3
120. Shriramcharitmanas, Balakanda—246.4
121. Shriramcharitmanas, Balakanda—247
122. Shriramcharitmanas, Balakanda—258.1
123. Shriramcharitmanas, Balakanda—258.2–3
124. Shriramcharitmanas, Balakanda—258.4
125. Shriramcharitmanas, Balakanda—260.2

14. The Ceremony of Jaimala and Marriage of Shri Ram-Sita

126. Shriramcharitmanas, Balakanda—262
127. Shriramcharitmanas, Balakanda—262.1
128. Shriramcharitmanas, Balakanda—262.2
129. Shriramcharitmanas, Balakanda—262.3
130. Shriramcharitmanas, Balakanda—262.4
131. Shriramcharitmanas, Balakanda—263
132. Shriramcharitmanas, Balakanda—263.1
133. Shriramcharitmanas, Balakanda—263.2
134. Shriramcharitmanas, Balakanda—263.3
135. Shriramcharitmanas, Balakanda—263.4
136. Shriramcharitmanas, Balakanda—264
137. Shriramcharitmanas, Balakanda—264.1
138. Shriramcharitmanas, Balakanda—264.2
139. Shriramcharitmanas, Balakanda—264.3
140. Shriramcharitmanas, Balakanda—264.4
141. Shriramcharitmanas, Balakanda—265
142. Shriramcharitmanas, Balakanda—308.1

15. Dialogue Between Dashrath and Kaikeyi

143. Shriramcharitmanas, Ayodhyakanda—22.3
144. Shriramcharitmanas, Ayodhyakanda—24, quatrain
145. Shriramcharitmanas, Ayodhyakanda—33.2

16. Dialogue Between Shri Ram and Kaikeyi

146. Shriramcharitmanas, Ayodhyakanda—39
147. Shriramcharitmanas, Ayodhyakanda—39.1
148. Shriramcharitmanas, Ayodhyakanda—39.2
149. Shriramcharitmanas, Ayodhyakanda—39.3–4
150. Shriramcharitmanas, Ayodhyakanda—40
151. Shriramcharitmanas, Ayodhyakanda—40.1–2
152. Shriramcharitmanas, Ayodhyakanda—40.3–4

153. Shriramcharitmanas, Ayodhyakanda—41
154. Shriramcharitmanas, Ayodhyakanda—41.1
155. Shriramcharitmanas, Ayodhyakanda—41.2
156. Shriramcharitmanas, Ayodhyakanda—41.3
157. Shriramcharitmanas, Ayodhyakanda—41.4
158. Shriramcharitmanas, Ayodhyakanda—42
159. Shriramcharitmanas, Ayodhyakanda—42.1
160. Shriramcharitmanas, Ayodhyakanda—42.2
161. Shriramcharitmanas, Ayodhyakanda—42.3
162. Shriramcharitmanas, Ayodhyakanda—42.4

17. Dialogue Between Lakshman and Nishadraja

163. Shriramcharitmanas, Ayodhyakanda—91.2
164. Shriramcharitmanas, Ayodhyakanda—91.3–4
165. Shriramcharitmanas, Ayodhyakanda—92
166. Shriramcharitmanas, Ayodhyakanda—92.1
167. Shriramcharitmanas, Ayodhyakanda—92.2
168. Shriramcharitmanas, Ayodhyakanda—92.3
169. Shriramcharitmanas, Ayodhyakanda—92.4
170. Shriramcharitmanas, Ayodhyakanda—93

18. The Form of Shri Ram-Sita and Lakshman in the Woods

171. Shriramcharitmanas, Ayodhyakanda—122.1
172. Shriramcharitmanas, Ayodhyakanda—122.2

19. Dialogue Between Shri Ram and Valmiki

173. Shriramcharitmanas, Ayodhyakanda—123.3
174. Shriramcharitmanas, Ayodhyakanda—123.4
175. Shriramcharitmanas, Ayodhyakanda—124
176. Shriramcharitmanas, Ayodhyakanda—124.1
177. Shriramcharitmanas, Ayodhyakanda—124.2
178. Shriramcharitmanas, Ayodhyakanda—124.3

179. Shriramcharitmanas, Ayodhyakanda—124.4
180. Shriramcharitmanas, Ayodhyakanda—125
181. Shriramcharitmanas, Ayodhyakanda—125.1
182. Shriramcharitmanas, Ayodhyakanda—125.2
183. Shriramcharitmanas, Ayodhyakanda—125.3
184. Shriramcharitmanas, Ayodhyakanda—125.4
185. Shriramcharitmanas, Ayodhyakanda—125, quatrain
186. Shriramcharitmanas, Ayodhyakanda—126
187. Shriramcharitmanas, Ayodhyakanda—126.1
188. Shriramcharitmanas, Ayodhyakanda—126.2
189. Shriramcharitmanas, Ayodhyakanda—126.3
190. Shriramcharitmanas, Ayodhyakanda—126.4
191. Shriramcharitmanas, Ayodhyakanda—127
192. Shriramcharitmanas, Ayodhyakanda—127.1
193. Shriramcharitmanas, Ayodhyakanda—127.2–4
194. Shriramcharitmanas, Ayodhyakanda—128
195. Shriramcharitmanas, Ayodhyakanda—128.1
196. Shriramcharitmanas, Ayodhyakanda—128.2
197. Shriramcharitmanas, Ayodhyakanda—128.3
198. Shriramcharitmanas, Ayodhyakanda—128.1–4
199. Shriramcharitmanas, Ayodhyakanda—129
200. Shriramcharitmanas, Ayodhyakanda—129.1
201. Shriramcharitmanas, Ayodhyakanda—129.2–4
202. Shriramcharitmanas, Ayodhyakanda—130
203. Shriramcharitmanas, Ayodhyakanda—130.1
204. Shriramcharitmanas, Ayodhyakanda—130.2
205. Shriramcharitmanas, Ayodhyakanda—130.3
206. Shriramcharitmanas, Ayodhyakanda—130.4
207. Shriramcharitmanas, Ayodhyakanda—131

20. Dialogue Between Sumantra and Dashrath

208. Shriramcharitmanas, Ayodhyakanda—149.3
209. Shriramcharitmanas, Ayodhyakanda—149.4

21. Dialogue Between Sage Vasishtha and Bharat

210. Shriramcharitmanas, Ayodhyakanda—171
211. Shriramcharitmanas, Ayodhyakanda—171.2–4
212. Shriramcharitmanas, Ayodhyakanda—172
213. Shriramcharitmanas, Ayodhyakanda—172.1
214. Shriramcharitmanas, Ayodhyakanda—172.2
215. Shriramcharitmanas, Ayodhyakanda—172.3
216. Shriramcharitmanas, Ayodhyakanda—172.4
217. Shriramcharitmanas, Ayodhyakanda—174
218. Shriramcharitmanas, Ayodhyakanda—174.1
219. Shriramcharitmanas, Ayodhyakanda—174.2
220. Shriramcharitmanas, Ayodhyakanda—174.3

22. Dialogue Between Bharat and the People of Ayodhya

221. Shriramcharitmanas, Ayodhyakanda—176.1
222. Shriramcharitmanas, Ayodhyakanda—176.2
223. Shriramcharitmanas, Ayodhyakanda—177.3

23. A Meeting Between Shri Ram and Janak in the Woods

224. Shriramcharitmanas, Ayodhyakanda—275
225. Shriramcharitmanas, Ayodhyakanda—276.2
226. Shriramcharitmanas, Ayodhyakanda—292.4
227. Shriramcharitmanas, Ayodhyakanda—301.4

24. Description of Spiritual Wisdom, Dispassion and Illusion Through Dialogue Between Shri Ram and Lakshman

228. Shriramcharitmanas, Aranyakanda—13.3
229. Shriramcharitmanas, Aranyakanda—13.4
230. Shriramcharitmanas, Aranyakanda—14
231. Shriramcharitmanas, Aranyakanda—14.1
232. Shriramcharitmanas, Aranyakanda—14.2

233. Shriramcharitmanas, Aranyakanda—14.3
234. Shriramcharitmanas, Aranyakanda—14.4
235. Shriramcharitmanas, Aranyakanda—15
236. Shriramcharitmanas, Aranyakanda—15.1
237. Shriramcharitmanas, Aranyakanda—15.2
238. Shriramcharitmanas, Aranyakanda—15.3
239. Shriramcharitmanas, Aranyakanda—15.4
240. Shriramcharitmanas, Aranyakanda—15.5
241. Shriramcharitmanas, Aranyakanda—15.6
242. Shriramcharitmanas, Aranyakanda—16
243. Shriramcharitmanas, Aranyakanda—16.1

25. Shri Ram's Lament in the Disassociation of Sita

244. Shriramcharitmanas, Aranyakanda—29
245. Shriramcharitmanas, Aranyakanda—29.1–2
246. Shriramcharitmanas, Aranyakanda—29.3
247. Shriramcharitmanas, Aranyakanda—29.4
248. Shriramcharitmanas, Aranyakanda—29.5–6
249. Shriramcharitmanas, Aranyakanda—29.7
250. Shriramcharitmanas, Aranyakanda—29.8
251. Shriramcharitmanas, Aranyakanda—29.9

26. Dialogue Between Shri Ram and Shabari

252. Shriramcharitmanas, Aranyakanda—33.3
253. Shriramcharitmanas, Aranyakanda—33.4
254. Shriramcharitmanas, Aranyakanda—33.5
255. Shriramcharitmanas, Aranyakanda—34
256. Shriramcharitmanas, Aranyakanda—34.1
257. Shriramcharitmanas, Aranyakanda—34.2
258. Shriramcharitmanas, Aranyakanda—34.3
259. Shriramcharitmanas, Aranyakanda—34.4
260. Shriramcharitmanas, Aranyakanda—35
261. Shriramcharitmanas, Aranyakanda—35.1

262. Shriramcharitmanas, Aranyakanda—35.2
263. Shriramcharitmanas, Aranyakanda—35.3
264. Shriramcharitmanas, Aranyakanda—35.4
265. Shriramcharitmanas, Aranyakanda—35.5
266. Shriramcharitmanas, Aranyakanda—35.6–7
267. Shriramcharitmanas, Aranyakanda—35, quatrain
268. Shriramcharitmanas, Aranyakanda—36

27. Dialogue Between Shri Ram and Lakshman

269. Shriramcharitmanas, Aranyakanda—36.2
270. Shriramcharitmanas, Aranyakanda—36.4–5

28. Dialogue Between Shri Ram and Sugriva

271. Shriramcharitmanas, Kishkindhakanda—6.1
272. Shriramcharitmanas, Kishkindhakanda—6.2–3
273. Shriramcharitmanas, Kishkindhakanda—6.4
274. Shriramcharitmanas, Kishkindhakanda—6.5

29. Dialogue Between Shri Ram and Bali

275. Shriramcharitmanas, Kishkindhakanda—8.3
276. Shriramcharitmanas, Kishkindhakanda—8.4
277. Shriramcharitmanas, Kishkindhakanda—10.2
278. Shriramcharitmanas, Kishkindhakanda—10.3
279. Shriramcharitmanas, Kishkindhakanda—10.4
280. Shriramcharitmanas, Kishkindhakanda—11.1

30. A Description of the Rainy Season

281. Shriramcharitmanas, Kishkindhakanda—12
282. Shriramcharitmanas, Kishkindhakanda—12.1
283. Shriramcharitmanas, Kishkindhakanda—12.2
284. Shriramcharitmanas, Kishkindhakanda—12.3

285. Shriramcharitmanas, Kishkindhakanda—12.4
286. Shriramcharitmanas, Kishkindhakanda—13
287. Shriramcharitmanas, Kishkindhakanda—13.1
288. Shriramcharitmanas, Kishkindhakanda—13.2
289. Shriramcharitmanas, Kishkindhakanda—13.3
290. Shriramcharitmanas, Kishkindhakanda—13.4
291. Shriramcharitmanas, Kishkindhakanda—14
292. Shriramcharitmanas, Kishkindhakanda—14.1
293. Shriramcharitmanas, Kishkindhakanda—14.2
294. Shriramcharitmanas, Kishkindhakanda—14.3
295. Shriramcharitmanas, Kishkindhakanda—14.4
296. Shriramcharitmanas, Kishkindhakanda—14.5
297. Shriramcharitmanas, Kishkindhakanda—14.6
298. Shriramcharitmanas, Kishkindhakanda—15 (s)
299. Shriramcharitmanas, Kishkindhakanda—15 (s)

31. A Description of the Winter Season

300. Shriramcharitmanas, Kishkindhakanda—15.1
301. Shriramcharitmanas, Kishkindhakanda—15.2
302. Shriramcharitmanas, Kishkindhakanda—15.3
303. Shriramcharitmanas, Kishkindhakanda—15.4
304. Shriramcharitmanas, Kishkindhakanda—15.5
305. Shriramcharitmanas, Kishkindhakanda—16
306. Shriramcharitmanas, Kishkindhakanda—16.1
307. Shriramcharitmanas, Kishkindhakanda—16.2
308. Shriramcharitmanas, Kishkindhakanda—16.3
309. Shriramcharitmanas, Kishkindhakanda—16.4
310. Shriramcharitmanas, Kishkindhakanda—17

32. A Description of Shri Hanuman

311. Shriramcharitmanas, Sundarakanda—19.2
312. Shriramcharitmanas, Sundarakanda—22.2
313. Shriramcharitmanas, Sundarakanda—33

33. Dialogue Between Ravana and Vibhishana

314. Shriramcharitmanas, Sundarakanda—37
315. Shriramcharitmanas, Sundarakanda—37.3
316. Shriramcharitmanas, Sundarakanda—38
317. Shriramcharitmanas, Sundarakanda—38.2
318. Shriramcharitmanas, S undarakanda—39 (s).3

34. Dialogue Between Shri Ram and Vibhishana

319. Shriramcharitmanas, Sundarakanda—45.4
320. Shriramcharitmanas, Sundarakanda—47.2–3
321. Shriramcharitmanas, Sundarakanda—47.4

35. Dialogue Between Ravana and Mandodari

322. Shriramcharitmanas, Lankakanda—14.1
323. Shriramcharitmanas, Lankakanda—14.2
324. Shriramcharitmanas, Lankakanda—14.3
325. Shriramcharitmanas, Lankakanda—14.4

36. Dialogue Between Angad and Ravana

326. Shriramcharitmanas, Lankakanda—23¼×½
327. Shriramcharitmanas, Lankakanda—30.1–2

37. Dialogue Between Shri Ram and Vibhishana

328. Shriramcharitmanas, Lankakanda—79.2–3
329. Shriramcharitmanas, Lankakanda—79.4
330. Shriramcharitmanas, Lankakanda—79.5
331. Shriramcharitmanas, Lankakanda—79.6

38. Shri Ram's Adoration by Lord Shiva

332. Shriramcharitmanas, Uttarakanda—13 (s).1

333. Shriramcharitmanas, Uttarakanda—13 (s).2
334. Shriramcharitmanas, Uttarakanda—13 (s).3
335. Shriramcharitmanas, Uttarakanda—13 (s).4
336. Shriramcharitmanas, Uttarakanda—13 (s).5
337. Shriramcharitmanas, Uttarakanda —13 (s). 6
338. Shriramcharitmanas, Uttarakanda—13 (s). 7
339. Shriramcharitmanas, Uttarakanda—13 (s).8
340. Shriramcharitmanas, Uttarakanda—13 (s).9
341. Shriramcharitmanas, Uttarakanda—13 (s).10

39. Ramrajya

342. Shriramcharitmanas, Uttarakanda—20.1
343. Shriramcharitmanas, Uttarakanda—20.2
344. Shriramcharitmanas, Uttarakanda—20.3
345. Shriramcharitmanas, Uttarakanda—20.4
346. Shriramcharitmanas, Uttarakanda—21
347. Shriramcharitmanas, Uttarakanda—21.1
348. Shriramcharitmanas, Uttarakanda—21.2
349. Shriramcharitmanas, Uttarakanda—21.3
350. Shriramcharitmanas, Uttarakanda—21.4
351. Shriramcharitmanas, Uttarakanda—22
352. Shriramcharitmanas, Uttarakanda—22.1
353. Shriramcharitmanas, Uttarakanda—22.2
354. Shriramcharitmanas, Uttarakanda—22.3
355. Shriramcharitmanas, Uttarakanda—22.4
356. Shriramcharitmanas, Uttarakanda—22.5
357. Shriramcharitmanas, Uttarakanda—23
358. Shriramcharitmanas, Uttarakanda—23.1
359. Shriramcharitmanas, Uttarakanda—23.2
360. Shriramcharitmanas, Uttarakanda—23.3
361. Shriramcharitmanas, Uttarakanda—23.4
362. Shriramcharitmanas, Uttarakanda—23.5
363. Shriramcharitmanas, Uttarakanda—24
364. Shriramcharitmanas, Uttarakanda—24.1

365. Shriramcharitmanas, Uttarakanda—24.2
366. Shriramcharitmanas, Uttarakanda—24.3
367. Shriramcharitmanas, Uttarakanda—24.4
368. Shriramcharitmanas, Uttarakanda—25
369. Shriramcharitmanas, Uttarakanda—25.1
370. Shriramcharitmanas, Uttarakanda—25.2–3
371. Shriramcharitmanas, Uttarakanda—25.4
372. Shriramcharitmanas, Uttarakanda—26
373. Shriramcharitmanas, Uttarakanda—26.1–4
374. Shriramcharitmanas, Uttarakanda—26, quatrain
375. Shriramcharitmanas, Uttarakanda—27
376. Shriramcharitmanas, Uttarakanda—27.1
377. Shriramcharitmanas, Uttarakanda—27.2
378. Shriramcharitmanas, Uttarakanda—27.3
379. Shriramcharitmanas, Uttarakanda—27.4
380. Shriramcharitmanas, Uttarakanda—27, quatrain
381. Shriramcharitmanas, Uttarakanda—28
382. Shriramcharitmanas, Uttarakanda—28.1
383. Shriramcharitmanas, Uttarakanda—28.2
384. Shriramcharitmanas, Uttarakanda—28.3
385. Shriramcharitmanas, Uttarakanda—28.4
386. Shriramcharitmanas, Uttarakanda—28, quatrain
387. Shriramcharitmanas, Uttarakanda—29
388. Shriramcharitmanas, Uttarakanda—29.1–5
389. Shriramcharitmanas, Uttarakanda—30
390. Shriramcharitmanas, Uttarakanda—30.1
391. Shriramcharitmanas, Uttarakanda—30.2
392. Shriramcharitmanas, Uttarakanda—30.3–4
393. Shriramcharitmanas, Uttarakanda—31

40. Dialogue Between Bharat and Shri Ram

394. Shriramcharitmanas, U ttarakanda—37.1
395. Shriramcharitmanas, Uttarakanda—37.2
396. Shriramcharitmanas, Uttarakanda—37.3

397. Shriramcharitmanas, Uttarakanda—38.1
398. Shriramcharitmanas, Uttarakanda—38.2
399. Shriramcharitmanas, Uttarakanda—38.3
400. Shriramcharitmanas, Uttarakanda—38.4
401. Shriramcharitmanas, Uttarakanda—40.1

41. Shri Ram's Exhortation to the Citizens of Ayodhya

402. Shriramcharitmanas, Uttarakanda—42.4
403. Shriramcharitmanas, Uttarakanda—43
404. Shriramcharitmanas, Uttarakanda—44.1
405. Shriramcharitmanas, Uttarakanda—44.2
406. Shriramcharitmanas, Uttarakanda—44.3
407. Shriramcharitmanas, Uttarakanda—45
408. Shriramcharitmanas, Uttarakanda—45.1
409. Shriramcharitmanas, Uttarakanda—45.2
410. Shriramcharitmanas, Uttarakanda—45.3–4

42. Narration of Kakabhushundi's Previous Lives in Garuda's Presence

411. Shriramcharitmanas, Uttarakanda—70 (s).3
412. Shriramcharitmanas, Uttarakanda—71 (s).2
413. Shriramcharitmanas, Uttarakanda—77 (s).4
414. Shriramcharitmanas, Uttarakanda—83 (s).3
415. Shriramcharitmanas, Uttarakanda—85 (s).2
416. Shriramcharitmanas, Uttarakanda—85 (s).3–5
417. Shriramcharitmanas, Uttarakanda—94 (s).3

43. The Glory of Kali Age Described by Kakabhushundi

418. Shriramcharitmanas, Uttarakanda—97 (s).1
419. Shriramcharitmanas, Uttarakanda—97 (s).2
420. Shriramcharitmanas, Uttarakanda—97 (s).3
421. Shriramcharitmanas, Uttarakanda—97 (s).4

422. Shriramcharitmanas, Uttarakanda—100 (s).4
423. Shriramcharitmanas, Uttarakanda—100 (s).5
424. Shriramcharitmanas, Uttarakanda—101 (s)
425. Shriramcharitmanas, Uttarakanda—102 (s)
426. Shriramcharitmanas, Uttarakanda—102 (s).3–4
427. Shriramcharitmanas, Uttarakanda—103 (s).l

44. Rudrashtaka or a Hymn of Eight Verses Addressed to Lord Shiva by Shri Ram

428. Shriramcharitmanas, Uttarakanda—107
429. Shriramcharitmanas, Uttarakanda—107.1
430. Shriramcharitmanas, Uttarakanda—107.2
431. Shriramcharitmanas, Uttarakanda—107.3–4
432. Shriramcharitmanas, Uttarakanda—107.5
433. Shriramcharitmanas, Uttarakanda—107.6
434. Shriramcharitmanas, Uttarakanda—107.7
435. Shriramcharitmanas, Uttarakanda—107.8
436. Shriramcharitmanas, Uttarakanda—107.9

APPENDIX

The Hindi Commentary

१. सन्त चरित्र एवं उनकी वन्दना

संतो का चरित्र कपास के चरित्र (जीवन) के समान शुभ होता है, जिसका फल नीरस, विशद और गुणमय होता है। (कपास की डोडी नीरस होती है, संत चरित्र में भी विषयासक्ति नहीं है, इससे वह भी नीरस हैय कपास उज्जवल होता है, संत का हृदय भी अज्ञान और पापरूपी अन्धकार से रहित होता है, इसलिए वह विशद है, और कपास में गुण (तन्तु) होते हैं, इसी प्रकार संत का चरित्र भी सद्गुणों का भण्डार होता है, इसलिए वह गुणमय होता है)। [जैसे कपास का धागा सूई के किये हुए छेद को अपना तन देकर ढक देता है, अथवा कपास जैसे लोढ़े जाने, काते जाने और बुने जाने का कष्ट सह कर भी वस्त्र के रूप में परिणत होकर दूसरों के गोपनीय स्थानों को ढकता है, उसी प्रकार] संत स्वयं दुःख सहकर दूसरों के छिद्रों (दोषों) को ढकता है, जिसके कारण उसने जगत् में वन्दनीय यश प्राप्त किया है

सत्संग के बिना विवेक नहीं होता और श्रीरामजी की कृपा के बिना वह सत्संग सहज में मिलता नहीं। सत्संगति आनन्द और कल्याण की जड़ है। सत्संग की सिद्धि (प्राप्ति) ही फल है और सब साधन तो फूल हैं।।

दुष्ट भी सत्संगति पाकर सुधर जाते हैं, जैसे पारस के स्पर्श से लोहा सुहावना हो जाता है (सुन्दर सोना बन जाता है)। किन्तु दैवयोग से यदि कभी सज्जन कुसंगति में पड़ जाते हैं, तो वे वहाँ भी साँप की मणि के समान अपने गुणों का ही अनुसरण करते हैं (अर्थात् जिस प्रकार साँप का संसर्ग पाकर भी मणि उसके विष को ग्रहण नहीं करती तथा अपने सहज

गुण प्रकाश को नहीं छोड़ती, उसी प्रकार साधु पुरुष दुष्टों के संग में रहकर भी दूसरों को प्रकाश ही देते हैं, दुष्टों का उनपर कोई प्रभाव नहीं पड़ता)।

मैं सन्तों को प्रणाम करता हूँ, जिनके चित्त में समता है, जिनका न कोई मित्र है और न शत्रु! जैसे अञ्जलि में रखे हुए सुन्दर फूल (जिस हाथ ने फूलों को तोड़ा और जिसने उनको रखा उन) दोनों ही हाथों को समान रूप से सुगन्धित करते हैं (वैसे ही सन्त शत्रु और मित्र दोनों का ही समान रूप से कल्याण करते हैं)।

२. दुष्ट चरित्र एवं उनकी वन्दना

अब मैं सच्चे भाव से दुष्टों को प्रणाम करता हूँ, जो बिना ही प्रयोजन अपना हित करने वाले के भी प्रतिकूल आचरण करते हैं। दूसरों के हित की हानि ही जिनकी दृष्टि में लाभ है, जिनको दूसरों के उजड़ने में हर्ष और बसने में विषाद होता है।

जो हरि और हर के यशरूपी पूर्णिमा के चन्द्रमा के लिए राहु के समान हैं (अर्थात् जहाँ कहीं भगवान् विष्णु या शंकर के यश का वर्णन होता है, उसी में वे बाधा देते हैं) और दूसरों की बुराई करने में सहस्रबाहु के समान वीर हैं। जो दूसरों के दोषों को हजार आँखों से देखते हैं और दूसरों के हितरूपी घी के लिए जिनका मन मक्खी के समान है (अर्थात् जिस प्रकार मक्खी घी में गिरकर उसे खराब कर देती है और स्वयं भी मर जाती है, उसी प्रकार दुष्ट लोग दूसरों के बने–बनाये काम को अपनी हानि कर के भी बिगाड़ देते हैं)।

जो तेज (दूसरों को जलाने वाले ताप) में अग्नि और क्रोध में यमराज के समान हैं, पाप और अवगुणरूपी धन में कुबेर के समान धनी हैं, जिनका उदय सभी के हित का नाश करने के लिए केतु (पुच्छल तारे) के समान है और जिनके कुम्भकर्ण की तरह सोते रहने में ही भलाई है।

जैसे ओले खेती का नाश करके स्वयं भी गल जाते हैं, वैसे ही वे (दुष्ट व्यक्ति) दूसरों का काम बिगाड़ने के लिए अपना शरीर तक छोड़ देते हैं। मैं दुष्टों को (हजार मुख वाले) शेषनाग के समान समझकर प्रणाम करता हूँ, जो पराये दोषों का हजार मुखों से बड़े रोष के साथ वर्णन करते हैं।

३. ब्रह्मा की सृष्टि एवं उसका स्वरूप

भले, बुरे सभी ब्रह्मा के पैदा किये हुए हैं, पर गुण और दोषों का विचार कर वेदों ने उनको

अलग–अलग कर दिया है। वेद, इतिहास और पुराण कहते हैं कि ब्रह्मा की यह सृष्टि गुण–अवगुणों से सनी हुई है।

दुःख–सुख, पाप–पुण्य, दिन–रात, साधु–असाधु, सुजाति–कुजाति, दानव–देवता, ऊँच–नीच, अमृत–विष, सुजीवन (सुन्दर जीवन), मृत्यु, माया–ब्रह्म, जीव–ईश्वर, सम्पत्ति–दरिद्रता, रंक–राजा, काशी–मगध, गङ्गा–कर्मनाशा, मारवाड़–मालवा, ब्राह्मण–कसाई, स्वर्ग–नरक, अनुराग–वैराग्य, [ये सभी पदार्थ ब्रह्मा की सृष्टि हैं] वेद–शास्त्रों ने उनके गुण–दोषों का विभाग कर दिया है।।

४. श्री सीता–राम का स्वरूप एवं उनकी वन्दना

जो वाणी और उसके अर्थ तथा जल और जल की लहर के समान कहने में अलग–अलग हैं, परन्तु वास्तव में अभिन्न (एक) हैं, उन श्रीसीतारामजी के चरणों की मैं वन्दना करता हूँ, जिन्हें दीन – दुःखी बहुत ही प्रिय हैं।।

मैं श्रीरघुनाथजी के नाम 'राम' की वन्दना करता हूँ, जो कृशानु (अग्नि), भानु (सूर्य) और हिमकर (चन्द्रमा) का हेतु अर्थात् 'र' 'आ' और 'म' रूप से बीज है। वह 'राम' नाम ब्रह्मा, विष्णु और शिवरूप है। वह वेदों का प्राण हैय निर्गुण, उपमा रहित और गुणों का भण्डार है।।

५. श्रीराम नाम एवं श्रीरामचरित की महिमा

निर्गुण और सगुण–ब्रह्म के दो स्वरूप हैं। ये दोनों ही अकथनीय, अथाह, अनादि और अनुपम हैं। मेरी सम्मति में (श्री राम) नाम इन दोनों से बड़ा है, जिसने अपने बल से दोनों को अपने वश में कर रखा है।।

इस प्रकार नाम [निर्गुण] ब्रह्म और [सगुण] राम दोनों से बड़ा है। यह वरदान देने वालों को भी वर देने वाला है। श्रीशिवजी ने अपने हृदय में यह जानकर ही सौ करोड़ रामचरित्र में से इस 'राम' नाम को [साररूप से चुनकर] ग्रहण किया है।।

रामनाम श्री नृसिंह भगवान् है, कलियुग हिरण्यकशिपु है और जप करने वाले जन प्रहलाद के समान है य यह रामनाम देवताओं के शत्रु (कलियुगरूपी दैत्य) को मार कर जप करने वालों की रक्षा करेगा।।

अच्छे भाव (प्रेम) से, बुरे भाव (वैर) से, क्रोध से या आलस्य से, किसी तरह से भी नाम जपने से दसों दिशाओं में कल्याण होता है। उसी (परम कल्याणकारी) रामनाम का

स्मरण करके और श्रीरघुनाथजी को मस्तक नवाकर मैं रामजी के गुणों का वर्णन करता हूँ।

तुलसीदासजी कहते हैं कि रामकथा मन्दाकिनी नदी है, सुन्दर (निर्मल) चित्त चित्रकूट है, और सुन्दर स्नेह ही वन है, जिसमें श्रीसीतारामजी विहार करते हैं।

६. श्रीरामचरितमानस की महिमा, रचनाकार एवं स्वरूप

इसका नाम रामचरितमानस है, जिसके कानों से सुनते ही शान्ति मिलती है। मनरूपी हाथी विषयरूपी दावानल में जल रहा है, वह यदि इस रामचरितमानस रूपी सरोवर में आ पड़े तो सुखी हो जाय।।

यह रामचरितमानस मुनियों का प्रिय है, इस सुहावने और पवित्र मानस की शिवजी ने रचना की। यह तीनों प्रकार के दोषों, दुःखों और दरिद्रता को तथा कलियुग की कुचालों और सब पापों का नाश करने वाला है।

श्री महादेवजी ने इसको रचकर अपने मन में रखा था और सुअवसर पाकर पार्वतीजी से कहा। इसी से शिवजी ने इसको अपने हृदय में देखकर और प्रसन्न होकर इसका सुन्दर 'रामचरितमानस' नाम रखा।

यह रामचरितमानस जैसा है, जिस प्रकार बना है और जिस हेतु से जगत् में इसका प्रचार हुआ, अब वही सब कथा मैं श्री उमा–महेश्वर का स्मरण करके कहता हूँ।

श्री शिव जी की कृपा से उसके हृदय में सुन्दर बुद्धि का विकास हुआ, जिससे यह तुलसीदास श्रीरामचरितमानस का कवि हुआ। अपनी बुद्धि के अनुसार तो वह इसे मनोहर ही बनाता है। किन्तु फिर भी हे सज्जनों! सुन्दर चित्त से सुनकर इसे आप सुधार लीजिए।

सुन्दर (सात्त्विकी) बुद्धि भूमि है, हृदय ही उसमें गहरा स्थान है, वेद–पुराण समुद्र हैं साधु–संत मेघ हैं। वे (साधुरूपी मेघ) श्रीरामजीके सुयशरूपी सुन्दर, मधुर, मनोहर और मङ्गलकारी जल की वर्षा करते हैं।।

इस कथा में बुद्धि से विचारकर जो चार अत्यन्त सुन्दर और उत्तम संवाद (भुशुण्डि – गरुड़, शिव–पार्वती, याज्ञवल्क्य–भरद्वाज और तुलसीदास और सन्त) रचे हैं, वही इस पवित्र और सुन्दर सरोवर के चार मनोहर घाट हैं।

सात काण्ड ही इस मानस सरोवर की सुन्दर सात सीढ़ियाँ हैं, जिनको ज्ञानरूपी नेत्रों से देखते ही मन प्रसन्न हो जाता है। श्री रघुनाथ जी निर्गुण (प्राकृतिक गुणों से अतीत) और निर्बाध (एकरस) महिमा का जो वर्णन किया जायेगा, वही इस सुन्दर जल की अथाह गहराई है

श्रीरामचन्द्रजी और सीताजी का यश अमृत के समान जल है। इसमें जो उपमाएँ दी गयी हैं वही तरंगों का मनोहर विलास है। सुन्दर चौपाइयाँ ही इसमें घनी फैली हुई पुरइन (कमलिनी) हैं और कविता की युक्तियाँ सुन्दर मणि (मोती) उत्पन्न करने वाली सुहावनी सीपियाँ हैं।।

जो सुन्दर छन्द, सोरठे और दोहे हैं, वही इसमें बहुरंगे कमलों के समूह सूशोभित हैं। अनुपम अर्थ, ऊँचे भाव और सुन्दर ही पराग (पुष्परज), मकरन्द (पुष्परस) और सुगन्ध हैं।।

७. शिव–सती संवाद

जब दक्ष ने इतना बड़ा अधिकार पाया तब उनके हृदय में अत्यन्त अभिमान आ गया। जगत् में ऐसा कोई नहीं पैदा हुआ जिसको प्रभुता पाकर मद न हो।।

यद्यपि इसमें सन्देह नहीं कि मित्र, स्वामी, पिता और गुरु के घर बिना बुलाये भी जाना चाहिये तो भी जहाँ कोई विरोध मानता हो, उसके घर जाने से कल्याण नहीं होता।

माता, पिता, गुरु और स्वामी की बात को बिना ही विचारे शुभ समझकर करना (मानना) चाहिये। फिर आप तो सब प्रकार से मेरे परम हितकारी हैं। हे नाथ! आपकी आज्ञा मेरे सिर पर है।।

८. कामदेव का वासन्तीय स्वरूप एवं भगवान् शिव के द्वारा भस्म होना

देवताओं ने कामदेव से अपनी सारी विपत्ति कही। सुनकर कामदेव ने मन में विचार किया और हँसकर देवताओं से यों कहा कि शिवजी के साथ विरोध करने में मेरी कुशल नहीं है।

तथापि मैं तुम्हारा काम तो करूँगा, क्योंकि वेद दूसरे के उपकार को परम धर्म कहते हैं। जो दूसरे के हित के लिये अपना शरीर त्याग देता है, संत सदा उसकी बड़ाई करते हैं।

यों कह और सबको सिर नवाकर कामदेव अपने पुष्प के धनुष को हाथ में लेकर [वसन्तादि] सहायकों के साथ चला। चलते समय कामदेव ने हृदय में ऐसा विचार किया कि शिव जी के साथ विरोध करने से मेरा मरण निश्चित है।

तब उसने अपना प्रभाव फैलाया और समस्त संसार को अपने वश में कर लिया। जिस समय उस मछली के चिह्न की ध्वजा वाले कामदेव ने कोप किया, उस समय क्षण भर में ही वेदों की सारी मर्यादा मिट गयी।

ब्रह्मचर्य, नियम, नाना प्रकार के संयम, धीरज, धर्म, ज्ञान–विज्ञान, सदाचार, जप, योग, वैराग्य आदि विवेक की सारी सेना डरकर भाग गयी।

विवेक अपने सहायकों सहित भाग गया, उसके योद्धा रणभूमि से पीठ दिखा गये। उस समय वे सब सद्ग्रन्थरूपी पर्वत की कन्दराओं में जा छिपे (अर्थात् ज्ञान, वैराग्य, संयम, नियम, सदाचारादि ग्रन्थों में ही लिखे रह गये; उनका आचरण छूट गया)। सारे जगत् में खलबली मच गयी [और सब कहने लगे–] हे विधाता! अब क्या होने वाला है, हमारी रक्षा कौन करेगा? ऐसा दो सिरवाला कौन है, जिसके लिये रति के पति कामदेव ने कोप करके हाथ में धनुष–बाण उठाया है?

जगत् में स्त्री–पुरुष संज्ञा वाले जितने चर–अचर प्राणी थे, वे सब अपनी–अपनी मर्यादा छोड़ कर काम के वश हो गये।।

सब के हृदय में काम की इच्छा हो गयी। लताओं (बेलों) को देखकर वृक्षों की डालियाँ झुकने लगीं। नदियाँ उमड़–उमड़ कर समुद्र की ओर दौड़ीं और ताल–तलैयाँ भी आपस में संगम करने (मिलने–जुलने) लगीं।।

जब जड (वृक्ष, नदी आदि) की यह दशा कही गयी, तब चेतन–जीवों की करनी कौन कह सकता है? आकाश, जल और पृथ्वी पर विचरने वाले सारे पशु–पक्षी (अपने संयोग का) समय भुला कर काम के वश हो गये।

सब लोग कामान्ध होकर व्याकुल हो गये। चकवा–चकवी रात–दिन नहीं देखते। देव, दैत्य, मनुष्य, किन्नर, सर्प, प्रेत, पिशाच, भूत, बेताल–ये तो सदा काम के गुलाम हैं, यह समझकर मैंने इनकी दशा का वर्णन नहीं किया। सिद्ध बिरक्त, महामुनि और महान् योगी भी काम के वश होकर योग रहित या स्त्री के विरही हो गये।

जब योगीश्वर और तपस्वी भी काम के वश हो गये, तब पामर मनुष्यों की कौन कहे? जो समस्त चराचर जगत् को ब्रह्ममय देखते थे, वे अब उसे स्त्रीमय देखने लगे। स्त्रियाँ सारे संसार को पुरुषमय देखने लगीं और पुरुष उसे स्त्रीमय देखने लगे। दो घड़ी तक सारे ब्रह्माण्ड के अंदर कामदेव का रचा हुआ यह कौतुक (तमाशा) रहा।

किसी ने भी हृदय में धैर्य नहीं धारण किया, कामदेव ने सबके मन हर लिये। श्री रघुनाथ जी ने जिनकी रक्षा की, केवल वे ही उस समय बचे रहे।।

दो घड़ी तक ऐसा तमाशा हुआ, जब तक कामदेव शिव जी के पास पहुँच गया। शिव जी को देखकर कामदेव डर गया, तब सारा संसार जैस–का–तैसा स्थिर हो गया।

तुरंत ही सब जीव वैसे ही सुखी हो गये जैसे मतवाले (नशा पिये हुए) लोग मद (नशा) उतर जाने पर सुखी होते हैं। दुराधर्ष (जिनको पराजित करना अत्यन्त ही कठिन है) और दुर्गम (जिनका पार पाना कठिन है) भगवान् (सम्पूर्ण ऐश्वर्य, धर्म, यश, श्री, ज्ञान और वैराग्य रूप छ: ईश्वरीय गुणों से युक्त) रुद्र (महाभयङ्कर) शिव जी को देखकर कामदेव भयभीत हो गया।।

लौट जाने में लज्जा मालूम होती है और करते कुछ बनता नहीं। आखिर मन में मरने का निश्चय करके उसने उपाय रचा। तुरंत ही सुन्दर ऋतुराज वसन्त को प्रकट किया। फूले नये–नये वृक्षों की कतारें सुशोभित हो गयीं।

वन–उपवन, बावली–तालाब और सब दिशाओं के विभाग परम सुन्दर हो गये। जहाँ–तहाँ मानो प्रेम उमड़ रहा है, जिसे देखकर मरे मनों में भी कामदेव जाग उठा।।

मरे हुए मन में भी कामदेव जागने लगा, वन की सुन्दरता कही नहीं जा सकती। काम रूपी सच्चा मित्र शीतल–मन्द–सुगन्धित पवन चलने लगा। सरोवरों में अनेकों कमल खिल गये, जिन पर सुन्दर भौरों के समूह गुंजार करने लगे। राजहंस, कोयल और तोते रसीली बोली बोलने लगे और अप्सराएँ गा–गाकर नाचने लगी।

कामदेव अपनी सेना समेत करोड़ों प्रकार की सब कलाएँ (उपाय) करके हार गया, पर शिव जी की अचल समाधि न डिगी। तब कामदेव क्रोधित हो उठा।।

आम के वृक्ष की एक सुन्दर डाली देख कर मन में क्रोध से भरा हुआ कामदेव उस पर चढ़ गया। उसने पुष्प–धनुष पर अपने [पाँचों] बाण चढ़ाये और अत्यन्त क्रोध से [लक्ष्य की ओर] ताक कर उन्हें कान तक तान लिया।

कामदेव ने तीक्ष्ण बाण छोड़े, जो शिव जी के हृदय में लगे। तब उनकी समाधि टूट गयी और वे जाग गये। ईश्वर (शिव जी) के मन में बहुत क्षोभ हुआ। उन्होंने आँखे खोलकर सब ओर देखा।

जब आम के पत्तों में [छिपे हुए] कामदेव को देखा तो उन्हें बड़ा क्रोध हुआ, जिससे तीनों लोक काँप उठे। तब शिव जी ने तीसरा नेत्र खोला, उनके देखते ही कामदेव जल कर भस्म हो गया।

जगत् में बड़ा हाहाकार मच गया। देवता डर गये, दैत्य सुखी हुए। भोगी लोग काम सुख को याद करके चिन्ता करने लगे और साधक योगी निष्कंटक हो गये।।

योगी निष्कंटक हो गये, कामदेव की स्त्री रति अपने पति की यह दशा सुनते ही मूर्छित हो गयी। रोती–चिल्लाती और भाँति–भाँति करुणा करती हुई वह शिव जी के पास गयी। अत्यन्त प्रेम के साथ अनेकों प्रकार से विनती करके हाथ जोड़कर सामने खड़ी हो गयी।

शीघ्र प्रसन्न होने वाली कृपालु शिव जी अबला (असहाया स्त्री) को देखकर सुन्दर (उसको सान्त्वना देने वाले) वचन बोले–

हे रति! अब से तेरे स्वामी का नाम अनङ्ग होगा। वह बिना ही शरीर सबको व्यापेगा। अब तू अपने पति से मिलने की बात सुन ।।

जब पृथ्वी के बड़े भारी भार को उतारने के लिए यदुवंश में श्रीकृष्ण का अवतार होगा, तब तेरा पति उनके पुत्र (प्रद्युम्न) के रूप में उत्पन्न होगा। मेरा यह वचन अन्यथा नहीं होगा।।

९. सगुण–निर्गुण विषयक शिव–पार्वती संवाद

सगुण और निर्गुण में कुछ भी भेद नहीं है–मुनि, पुराण, पण्डित और वेद सभी ऐसा कहते हैं। जो निर्गुण, अरूप (निराकार), अलख (अव्यक्त) और अजन्मा है, वही भक्तों के प्रेम वश सगुण हो जाता है।।

जो निर्गुण है, वही सगुण कैसे है? जैसे जल और ओले में भेद नहीं। (दोनों जल ही हैं, ऐसे ही निर्गुण और सगुण एक ही हैं) जिसका नाम भ्रमरूपी अन्धकार को मिटाने के लिये सूर्य है, उसके लिये मोह का प्रसंग भी कैसे कहा जा सकता है?।।

श्री रामचन्द्रजी सच्चिदानन्द स्वरूप सूर्य हैं। वहाँ मोहरूपी रात्रि का लवलेश भी नहीं है। वे स्वभाव से ही प्रकाशरूप और [षडैश्वर्ययुक्त, भगवान् हैं] वहाँ तो विज्ञानरूपी प्रात: काल भी नहीं होता। (अज्ञानरूपी रात्रि हो तब तो विज्ञानरूपी प्रातः काल होय भगवान् तो नित्य ज्ञानस्वरूप हैं।)

हर्ष, शोक, ज्ञान, अज्ञान, अहंता और अभिमान–ये सब जीव के धर्म हैं। श्रीरामचन्द्र जी तो व्यापक ब्रह्म, परमानन्दस्वरूप, परात्पर प्रभु और पुराण पुरुष हैं। इस बात को सारा जगत् जानता है।

वह (ब्रह्म) बिना ही पैर के चलता है, बिना ही कान के सुनता है, बिना ही हाथ के नाना प्रकार के काम करता है, बिना मुँह (जिह्वा) के ही सारे (छहों) रसों का आनन्द लेता है और बिना ही वाणी के बहुत योग्य वक्ता है।।

वह बिना ही शरीर (त्वचा) के स्पर्श करता है, बिना ही आँखों के देखता है और बिना ही नाक के सब गन्धों को ग्रहण करता है (सूँघता है)। उस ब्रह्म की करनी सभी प्रकार से ऐसी अलौकिक है कि जिसकी महिमा कही नहीं जा सकती।

१०. भगवान् श्रीराम का प्राकट्य

योग, लग्न, ग्रह, वार तिथि सभी अनुकूल हो गये। जड़ और चेतन सब हर्ष, से भर गये। [क्योंकि] श्रीराम का जन्म सुख का मूल है।।

पवित्र चौत्र का महीना था, नवमी तिथि थी। शुक्ल पक्ष और भगवान् का प्रिय अभिजित मुहूर्त्त था। दोपहर का समय था। न बहुत सरदी थी, न धूप (गरमी) थी। वह पवित्र समय सब लोकों को शान्ति देने वाला था।।

शीतल, मन्द और सुगन्धित पवन बह रहा था। देवता हर्षित थे और संतों के मन में [बड़ा] चाव था। वन फूले हुए थे, पर्वतों के समूह मणियों से जगमगा रहे थे और सारी नदियाँ अमृत की धारा बहा रही थीं।।

जब ब्रह्मा जी ने वह (भगवान् के प्रकट होने का) अवसर जाना तब [उनके समेत] सारे देवता विमान सजा–सजाकर चले। निर्मल आकाश देवताओं के समूहों से भर गया। गन्धर्वों के दल गुणों का गान करने लगे और सुन्दर अञ्जलियों में सजा–सजाकर पुष्प बरसाने लगे। आकाश में घमाधम नगाड़े बजने लगे। नाग, मुनि और देवता स्तुति करने लगे और बहुत प्रकार से अपनी–अपनी सेवा (उपहार) भेंट करने लगे।

देवताओं के समूह विनती करके अपने–अपने लोक में जा पहुँचे। समस्त लोकों को शान्ति देने वाले, जगदाधार प्रभु प्रकट हुए ।।

दीनों पर दया करने वाले, कौसल्याजी के हितकारी कृपालु प्रभु प्रकट हुए। मुनियों के मन को हरने वाले उनके अद्भुत रूप का विचार करके माता हर्ष से भर गई। नेत्रों को आनंद देने वाला मेघ के समान श्याम शरीर था, चारों भुजाओं में अपने (खास) आयुध (धारण किए हुए) थे, (दिव्य) आभूषण और वनमाला पहने थे, बड़े–बड़े नेत्र थे। इस प्रकार शोभा के समुद्र तथा खर राक्षस को मारने वाले भगवान प्रकट हुए।

दोनों हाथ जोड़कर माता कहने लगी–हे अनन्त! मैं किस प्रकार तुम्हारी स्तुति करूँ। वेद और पुराण तुमको माया, गुण और ज्ञान से परे और परिमाण रहित बतलाते हैं। श्रुतियाँ और संतजन दया और सुख का समुद्र, सब गुणों का धाम कह कर जिनका गान करते हैं, वही भक्तों पर प्रेम करने वाले लक्ष्मी पति भगवान् मेरे कल्याण के लिये प्रकट हुए हैं।।

वेद कहते हैं कि तुम्हारे प्रत्येक रोम में माया के रचे हुए अनेकों ब्रह्माण्डों के समूह [भरे] हैं। वे तुम मेरे गर्भ में रहे–इस हँसी की बात के सुनने पर धीर (विवेकी) पुरुषों की बुद्धि भी स्थिर नहीं रहती (विचलित हो जाती है)। जब माता को ज्ञान उत्पन्न हुआ, तब प्रभु मुसकराये। वे बहुत प्रकार के चरित्र करना चाहते हैं। अत: उन्होंने [पूर्वजन्म की] सुन्दर

कथा कह कर माता को समझाया, जिससे उन्हें पुत्र का (वात्सल्य) प्रेम प्राप्त हो (भगवान् के प्रति पुत्रभाव हो जाय)।।

माता की वह बुद्धि बदल गयी, तब वह फिर बोली– हे तात! यह रूप छोड़कर अत्यन्त प्रिय बललीला करो, [मेरे लिये] यह सुख परम अनुपम होगा। [माता का] चह वचन सुनकर देवताओं के स्वामी सुजान भगवान् ने बालक [रूप] होकर रोना शुरू कर दिया। [तुलसीदास जी कहते हैं–] जो इस चरित्र का गान करते हैं, वे श्रीहरिका पद पाते हैं– और [फिर] संसाररूपी कूप में नहीं गिरते।

ब्राह्मण, गौ, देवता और संतो के लिये भगवान् ने मनुष्य का अवतार लिया। वे [अज्ञानमयी, मलिना] माया और उसके गुण (सत्, रज, तम) और [बाहरी तथा भीतरी] इन्द्रियों से परे हैं। उनका [दिव्य] शरीर अपनी इच्छा से ही बना है [किसी कर्मबन्धन से परवश होकर त्रिगुणात्मक भौतिक पदार्थों के द्वारा नहीं]।

११. श्री राम–लक्ष्मण द्वारा राजा जनक की पुष्पवाटिका का निरीक्षण, सीता–राम का परस्पर दर्शन

उन्होंने (श्रीराम–लक्षमण ने) जाकर राजा का सुन्दर बाग देखा, जहाँ वसन्त ऋतु लुभाकर रह गयी है। मन को लुभाने वाले अनेक वृक्ष लगे हैं। रंग–बिरंगी उत्तम लताओं के मण्डप छाये हुए हैं।।

नये पत्तों, फलों और फूलों से युक्त सुन्दर वृक्ष अपनी सम्पत्ति से कल्पवृक्ष को भी लजा रहे हैं। पपीहे, कोयल, तोते, चकोर आदि पक्षी मीठी बोली बोल रहे हैं और मोर सुन्दर नृत्य कर रहे हैं।

बाग के बीचो–बीच सुहावना सरोवर सुशोभित है, जिसमें मणियों की सीढ़ियाँ बिचित्र ढंग से बनी हैं। उसका जल निर्मल है, जिसमें अनेक रंगों के कमल खिले हुए हैं, जल के पक्षी कलरव कर रहे हैं और भ्रमर गुंजार कर रहे हैं।

बाग और सरोवर को देखकर प्रभु श्री रामचन्द्रजी भाई लक्ष्मण सहित हर्षित हुए। यह बाग (वास्तव में) परम रमणीय है, जो (जगत् को सुख देने वाले) श्रीरामचन्द्रजी को सुख दे रहा है।

चारों ओर दृष्टि डालकर और मालियों से पूछकर वे प्रसन्न मन से पत्र–पुष्प लेने लगे। उसी समय सीताजी वहाँ आई। माता ने उन्हें गिरिजाजी (पार्वती) की पूजा करने के लिए भेजा था।

साथ में सब सुंदरी और सयानी सखियाँ हैं, जो मनोहर वाणी से गीत गा रही हैं। सरोवर के पास गिरिजाजी का मंदिर सुशोभित है, जिसका वर्णन नहीं किया जा सकता, देखकर मन मोहित हो जाता है।

सखियों सहित सरोवर में स्नान करके सीताजी प्रसन्न मन से गिरिजाजी के मंदिर में गईं। उन्होंने बड़े प्रेम से पूजा की और अपने योग्य सुंदर वर माँगा।

एक सखी सीताजी का साथ छोड़कर फुलवाड़ी देखने चली गई थी। उसने जाकर दोनों भाइयों को देखा और प्रेम में विह्वल होकर वह सीताजी के पास आई।

सखियों ने उसकी दशा देखी कि उसका शरीर पुलकित है और नेत्रों में जल भरा है। सब कोमल वाणी से पूछने लगीं कि अपनी प्रसन्नता का कारण बता।

उसने कहा–) दो राजकुमार बाग देखने आए हैं। किशोर अवस्था के हैं और सब प्रकार से सुंदर हैं। वे साँवले और गोरे (रंग के) हैं, उनके सौंदर्य को मैं कैसे बखान कर कहूँ। वाणी बिना नेत्र की है और नेत्रों के वाणी नहीं है।।

यह सुनकर और सीताजी के हृदय में बड़ी उत्कंठा जानकर सब सयानी सखियाँ प्रसन्न हुईं। तब एक सखी कहने लगी– हे सखी! ये वही राजकुमार हैं, जो सुना है कि कल विश्वामित्र मुनि के साथ आए हैं।।

नारद जी के वचनों का स्मरण करके सीता जी के मन में पवित्र प्रीति उत्पन्न हुई। वे चकित होकर सब ओर इस तरह देख रही हैं मानो डरी हुई मृगछौनी इधर–उधर देख रही हो।

कंकण (हाथों के कड़े), करधनी और पायजेब के शब्द सुनकर श्रीरामचन्द्रजी हृदय में विचार कर लक्ष्मण से कहते हैं–[यह ध्वनि ऐसी आ रही है] मानो कामदेव ने विश्व को जीतने का संकल्प करके डंके पर चोट मारी।।

ऐसा कह कर श्रीराम जी ने फिरकर उस ओर देखा। श्री सीता जी के मुख रूपी चन्द्रमा ख्को निहारने के लिये उनके नेत्र चकोर बन गये। सुन्दर नेत्र स्थिर हो गये (टकटकी लग गयी)। मानो निमि (जनकजी के पूर्वज) ने [जिनका सबकी पलकों में निवास माना गया है, लड़की – दामाद के मिलन–प्रसङ्ग को देखना उचित नहीं, इस भाव से] सकुचाकर पलके छोड़ दीं, (पलकों में रहना छोड़ दिया, जिससे पलकों का गिरना रुक गया)।।

सीता जी की शोभा देखकर श्रीरामजी ने बड़ा सुख पाया। हृदय में वे उसकी सराहना करते हैं, किन्तु मुख से वचन नहीं निकलते। [वह शोभा ऐसी अनुपम है] मानो ब्रह्मा ने अपनी सारी निपुणता को मूर्तिमान् कर संसार को प्रकट करके दिखा दिया हो।

वह (सीताजी की शोभा) सुन्दरता को भी सुन्दर करने वाली हैं [वह ऐसी मालूम होती है] मानो सुन्दरतारूपी घर में दीपक की लौ जल रही हो। (अब तक सुन्दरतारूपी भवन में अन्धेरा था, वह भवन मानो सीता जी की सुन्दरतारूपी दीपशिखा को पाकर जगमगा उठा है, पहले से भी अधिक सुन्दर हो गया है।) सारी उपमाओं को तो कवियों ने जूँठा कर रखा है। मैं जनकनन्दिनी श्रीसीताजी की किससे उपमा दूँ।

इस प्रकार) हृदय में सीताजी की शोभा का वर्णन करके और अपनी दशा को विचारकर प्रभु श्रीरामचन्द्रजी पवित्र मन से अपने छोटे भाई लक्ष्मण से समयानुकूल वचन बोले–।।

हे तात! यह वही जनकजी की कन्या है जिसके लिये धनुषयज्ञ हो रहा है। सखियाँ इसे गौरी पूजन के लिये ले आयी हैं। यह फुलवाड़ी में प्रकाश करती हुई फिर रही है।।

जिसकी अलौकिक सुंदरता देखकर स्वभाव से ही पवित्र मेरा मन क्षुब्ध हो गया है। वह सब कारण (अथवा उसका सब कारण) तो विधाता जानें, किन्तु हे भाई! सुनो, मेरे मंगलदायक (दाहिने) अंग फड़क रहे हैं।।

रघुवंशियों का यह सहज (जन्मगत) स्वभाव है कि उनका मन कभी कुमार्ग पर पैर नहीं रखता। मुझे तो अपनेमन का अत्यन्त ही विश्वास है कि जिसने (जाग्रत की कौन कहे) स्वप्न में भीपराई स्त्री पर दृष्टि नहीं डाली है।।

रण में शत्रु जिनकी पीठ नहीं देख पाते (अर्थात् जो लड़ाई के मैदान से भागते नहीं), पराई स्त्रियाँ जिनके मन और दृष्टि को नहीं खींच पातीं और भिखारी जिनके यहाँ से 'नाहीं' नहीं पाते (खाली हाथ नहीं लौटते), ऐसे श्रेष्ठ पुरुष संसार में थोड़े हैं।।

यों श्री रामजी छोटे भाई से बातें कर रहे हैं, पर मन सीताजी के रूप में लुभाया हुआ उनके मुख रूपी कमल के छबि रूप मकरंद रस को भौंरे की तरह पी रहा है।।

सीताजी चकित होकर चारों ओर देख रही हैं। मन इस बात की चिन्ता कर रहा है कि राजकुमार कहाँ चले गए। बाल मृगनयनी (मृग के छौने की सी आँख वाली) सीताजी जहाँ दृष्टि डालती हैं, वहाँ मानो श्वेत कमलों की कतार बरस जाती है।।

उसी समय दोनों भाई लता मंडप (कुंज) में से प्रकट हुए। मानो दो निर्मल चन्द्रमा बादलों के परदे को हटाकर निकले हों।।

दोनों सुन्दर भाई शोभा की सीमा हैं। उनके शरीर की आभा नीले और पीले कमल की–सी है। सिर पर सुन्दर मोर पंख सुशोभित हैं। उनके बीच–बीच में फूलों की कलियों के गुच्छे लगे हैं।।

माथे पर तिलक और पसीने की बूँदें शोभायमान हैं। कानों में सुन्दर भूषणों की छबि छायी है। टेढ़ी भौंहें और घुंघराले बाल हैं। नये लाल कमल के समान रतनारे (लाल) नेत्र हैं ।। ठोड़ी, नाक और गल बड़े सुन्दर हैं, और हँसी की शोभा मन को मोल लिये लेती है। मुख की छबि तो मुझसे कही ही नहीं जाती, जिसे देखकर बहुत–से कामदेव लजा जाते हैं।।

वक्ष:स्थल पर मणियों की माला है। शंख के सदृश सुंदर गला है। कामदेव के हाथी के बच्चे की सूँड के समान (उतार–चढ़ाव वाली एवं कोमल) भुजाएँ हैं, जो बल की सीमा हैं। जिसके बाएँ हाथ में फूलों सहित दोना है, हे सखि! वह साँवला कुँअर तो बहुत ही सलोना है।।

शिवजी के धनुष को कठोर जानकर वे विसूरती (मन में विलाप करती) हुई हृदय में श्री रामजी की साँवली मूर्ति को रखकर चलीं। (शिवजी के धनुष की कठोरता का स्मरण आने से उन्हे चिंता होती थी कि ये सुकुमार रघुनाथजी उसे कैसे तोड़ेंगे, पिता के प्रण की स्मृति से उनके हृदय में क्षोभ था ही, इसलिए मन में विलाप करने लगीं। प्रेम वश ऐश्वर्य की विस्मृति हो जाने से ही ऐसा हुआ, फिर भगवान के बल का स्मरण आते ही वे हर्षित हो गईं और साँवली छबि को हृदय में धारण करके चलीं।)

प्रभु श्री रामजी ने जब सुख, स्नेह, शोभा और गुणों की खान श्री जानकीजी को जाती हुई जाना। तब परम प्रेम की कोमल स्याही बनाकर उनके स्वरूप को अपने सुंदर चित्त रूपी भित्ति पर चित्रित कर लिया। सीताजी पुनः भवानीजी के मंदिर में गईं और उनके चरणों की वंदना करके हाथ जोड़कर बोलीं–।

हे श्रेष्ठ पर्वतों के राजा हिमाचल की पुत्री पार्वती! आपकी जय हो, जय हो, हे महादेवजी के मुख रूपी चन्द्रमा की (ओर टकटकी लगाकर देखने वाली) चकोरी! आपकी जय हो, हे हाथी के मुख वाले गणेशजी और छह मुख वाले स्वामि कार्तिकजी की माता! हे जगज्जननी! हे बिजली की सी कान्तियुक्त शरीर वाली! आपकी जय हो!।।

आपका न आदि है, न मध्य है और न अंत है। आपके असीम प्रभाव को वेद भी नहीं जानते। आप संसार को उत्पन्न, पालन और नाश करने वाली हैं। विश्व को मोहित करने वाली और स्वतंत्र रूप से विहार करने वाली हैं।।

१२. श्रीराम द्वारा सीता के अनुपम सौन्दर्य का वर्णन

उधर) पूर्व दिशा में सुंदर चन्द्रमा उदय हुआ। श्री रामचन्द्रजी ने उसे सीता के मुख के समान देखकर सुख पाया। फिर मन में विचार किया कि यह चन्द्रमा सीताजी के मुख के समान नहीं है।।

खारे समुद्र में तो इसका जन्म, फिर (उसी समुद्र से उत्पन्न होने के कारण) विष इसका भाई, दिन में यह मलिन (शोभाहीन, निस्तेज) रहता है, और कलंकी (काले दाग से युक्त) है। बेचारा गरीब चन्द्रमा सीताजी के मुख की बराबरी कैसे पा सकता है? ।।

फिर यह घटता–बढ़ता है और विरहिणी स्त्रियों को दुःख देने वाला है, राहु अपनी संधि में पाकर इसे ग्रस लेता है। चकवे को (चकवी के वियोग का) शोक देने वाला और कमल का बैरी (उसे मुरझा देने वाला) है। हे चन्द्रमा! तुझमें बहुत से अवगुण हैं (जो सीताजी में नहीं हैं।)।।

अतः जानकीजी के मुख की तुझे उपमा देने में बड़ा अनुचित कर्म करने का दोष लगेगा। इस प्रकार चन्द्रमा के बहाने सीताजी के मुख की छबि का वर्णन करके, बड़ी रात हो गई जान, वे गुरुजी के पास चले।।

१३. सीताजी के स्वयम्वर में श्रीराम–लक्ष्मण

दोनों भाई रंग भूमि में आए हैं, ऐसी खबर जब सब नगर निवासियों ने पाई, तब बालक, जवान, बूढ़े, स्त्री, पुरुष सभी घर और काम–काज को भुलाकर चल दिए।।

उसी समय राजकुमार (राम और लक्ष्मण) वहाँ आए। (वे ऐसे सुंदर हैं) मानो साक्षात् मनोहरता ही उनके शरीरों पर छा रही हो। सुंदर साँवला और गोरा उनका शरीर है। वे गुणों के समुद्र, चतुर और उत्तम वीर हैं

वे राजाओं के समाज में ऐसे सुशोभित हो रहे हैं, मानो तारा गणों के बीच दो पूर्ण चन्द्रमा हों। जिनकी जैसी भावना थी, प्रभु की मूर्ति उन्होंने वैसी ही देखी।।

महान् रणधीर (राजा लोग) श्री रामचन्द्रजी के रूप को ऐसा देख रहे हैं, मानो स्वयं वीर रस शरीर धारण किए हुए हों। कुटिल राजा प्रभु को देखकर डर गए, मानो बड़ी भयानक मूर्ति हो।।

छल से जो राक्षस वहाँ राजाओं के वेष में (बैठे) थे, उन्होंने प्रभु को प्रत्यक्ष काल के समान देखा। नगर निवासियों ने दोनों भाइयों को मनुष्यों के भूषण रूप और नेत्रों को सुख देने वाला देखा।।

स्त्रियाँ हृदय में हर्षित होकर अपनी–अपनी रुचि के अनुसार उन्हें देख रही हैं। मानो शृंगार रस ही परम अनुपम मूर्ति धारण किए सुशोभित हो रहा हो।।

विद्वानों को प्रभु विराट रूप में दिखाई दिए, जिसके बहुत से मुँह, हाथ, पैर, नेत्र और सिर हैं। जनकजी के सजातीय (कुटुम्बी) प्रभु को किस तरह (कैसे प्रिय रूप में) देख रहे हैं, जैसे सगे सजन (संबंधी) प्रिय लगते हैं।

जनक समेत रानियाँ उन्हें अपने बच्चे के समान देख रही हैं, उनकी प्रीति का वर्णन नहीं किया जा सकता। योगियों को वे शांत, शुद्ध, सम और स्वतः प्रकाश परम तत्व के रूप में दिखे।।

हरि भक्तों ने दोनों भाइयों को सब सुखों के देने वाले इष्ट देव के समान देखा। सीताजी जिस भाव से श्री रामचन्द्रजी को देख रही हैं, वह स्नेह और सुख तो कहने में ही नहीं आता।।

उस (स्नेह और सुख) का वे हृदय में अनुभव कर रही हैं, पर वे भी उसे कह नहीं सकतीं। फिर कोई कवि उसे किस प्रकार कह सकता है। इस प्रकार जिसका जैसा भाव था, उसने कोसलाधीश श्री रामचन्द्रजी को वैसा ही देखा।।

रूप और गुणों की खान जगज्जननी जानकीजी की शोभा का वर्णन नहीं हो सकता। उनके लिए मुझे (काव्य की) सब उपमाएँ तुच्छ लगती हैं, क्योंकि वे लौकिक स्त्रियों के अंगों से अनुराग रखने वाली हैं (अर्थात् वे जगत की स्त्रियों के अंगों को दी जाती हैं)। (काव्य की उपमाएँ सब त्रिगुणात्मक, मायिक जगत से ली गई हैं, उन्हें भगवान की स्वरूपा शक्ति श्री जानकीजी के अप्राकृत, चिन्मय अंगों के लिए प्रयुक्त करना उनका अपमान करना और अपने को उपहासास्पद बनाना है)।।

सीताजी के वर्णनमें उन्हीं उपमाओं को देकर कौन कुकवि कहलाए और अपयश का भागी बने (अर्थात सीताजी के लिए उन उपमाओं का प्रयोग करना सुकवि के पद से च्युत होना और अपकीर्ति मोल लेना है, कोई भी सुकवि ऐसी नादानी एवं अनुचित कार्य नहीं करेगा।) यदि किसी स्त्री के साथ सीताजी की तुलना की जाए तो जगत में ऐसी सुंदर युवती है ही कहाँ (जिसकी उपमा उन्हें दी जाए)।।

पृथ्वी की स्त्रियों की तो बात ही क्या, देवताओं की स्त्रियों को भी यदि देखा जाए तोहमारी अपेक्षा कहीं अधिक दिव्य और सुंदर हैं, तो उनमें) सरस्वती तो बहुत बोलने वाली हैं, पार्वती अंर्द्धांगिनी हैं (अर्थात अर्ध– नारी नटेश्वर के रूप में उनका आधा ही अंग स्त्री का है, शेष आधा अंग पुरुष–शिवजी का है), कामदेव की स्त्री रति पति को बिना शरीर का (अनंग) जानकर बहुत दुःखी रहती है और जिनके विष और मद्य–जैसे (समुद्र से उत्पन्न होने के नाते) प्रिय भाई हैं, उन लक्ष्मी के समान तो जानकीजी को कहा ही कैसे जाए ।।

जिन लक्ष्मीजी की बात ऊपर कही गई है, वे निकली थीं खारे समुद्र से, जिसको मथने के लिए भगवान ने अति कर्कश पीठ वाले कच्छप का रूप धारण किया, रस्सी बनाई गई

महान विषधरवासुकि नाग की, मथानी का कार्य किया अतिशय कठोर मंदराचल पर्वत ने और उसे मथा सारे देवताओं और दैत्यों ने मिलकर। जिन लक्ष्मी को अतिशय शोभा की खान और अनुपम सुंदरी कहते हैं, उनको प्रकट करने में हेतु बने ये सब असुंदर एवं स्वाभाविक ही कठोर उपकरण। ऐसे उपकरणों से प्रकट हुई लक्ष्मी श्री जानकीजी की समता को कैसे पा सकती हैं। हाँ, (इसके विपरीत) यदि छबि रूपी अमृत का समुद्र हो, परम रूपमय कच्छप हो, शोभा रूप रस्सी हो, शृंगार (रस) पर्वत हो और (उस छबि के समुद्र को) स्वयं कामदेव अपने ही करकमल से मथे।।

इस प्रकार (का संयोग होने से) जब सुंदरता और सुख की मूल लक्ष्मी उत्पन्न हो, तो भी कवि लोग उसे (बहुत) संकोच के साथ सीताजी के समान कहेंगे।।

(जिस सुंदरता के समुद्र को कामदेव मथेगा वह सुंदरता भी प्राकृत, लौकिक सुंदरता ही होगी, क्योंकि कामदेव स्वयं भी त्रिगुणमयी प्रकृति का ही विकार है। अतः उस सुंदरता को मथकर प्रकट की हुई लक्ष्मी भी उपर्युक्त लक्ष्मी की अपेक्षा कहीं अधिक सुंदर और दिव्य होने पर भी होगी प्राकृत ही, अतः उसके साथ भी जानकीजी की तुलना करना कवि के लिए बड़े संकोच की बात होगी। जिस सुंदरता से जानकीजी का दिव्याति दिव्य परम दिव्य विग्रह बना है, वह सुंदरता उपर्युक्त सुंदरता से भिन्न अप्राकृत है– वस्तुत: लक्ष्मीजी का अप्राकृत रूप भी यही है। वह कामदेव के मथने में नहीं आ सकती और वह जानकीजी का स्वरूप ही है, अतः उनसे भिन्न नहीं और उपमा दी जाती है भिन्न वस्तु के साथ। इसके अतिरिक्त जानकीजी प्रकट हुई हैं स्वयं अपनी महिमा से, उन्हें प्रकट करने के लिए किसी भिन्न उपकरण की अपेक्षा नहीं है। अर्थात शक्तिशक्तिमान से अभिन्न, अद्वैत तत्व है, अतएव अनुपमेय है, यही गूढ़ दार्शनिकतत्व भक्त शिरोमणि कवि ने इस अभूतोपमालंकार के द्वारा बड़ी सुंदरता से व्यक्त किया है।)

सीताजी की वाणी रूपी भ्रमरी को उनके मुख रूपी कमल ने रोक रखा है। लाज रूपी रात्रि को देखकर वह प्रकट नहीं हो रही है। नेत्रों का जल नेत्रों के कोने (कोये) में ही रह जाता है। जैसे बड़े भारी कंजूस का सोना कोने में ही गड़ा रह जाता है।।

अपनी बढ़ी हुई व्याकुलता जानकर सीताजी सकुचा गईं और धीरज धरकर हृदय में विश्वास ले आई कि यदि तन, मन और वचन से मेरा प्रण सच्चा है और श्री रघुनाथजी के चरण कमलों में मेरा चित्त वास्तव में अनुरक्त है तो सबके हृदय में निवास करने वाले भगवान मुझे रघु श्रेष्ठ श्री रामचन्द्रजी की दासी अवश्य बनाएँगे। जिसका जिस पर सच्चा स्नेह होता है, वह उसे मिलता ही है, इसमें कुछ भी संदेह नहीं है।।

प्रभु की ओर देखकर सीता जी ने शरीर के द्वारा प्रेम ठान लिया (अर्थात् यह निश्चय कर लिया कि यह शरीर इन्हीं का होकर रहेगा या रहेगा या रहेगा ही नहीं)। कृपा निधान श्रीरामजी सब जान गये। उन्होंने सीताजी को देखकर धनुष की ओर कैसे ताका, जैसे गरुड़ जी छोटे से साँप की ओर देखते हैं।

सारी खेती के सूख जाने पर वर्षा किस काम की? समय बीत जाने पर फिर पछताने से क्या लाभ? जी में ऐसा समझकर श्रीरामजी ने जानकीजी की ओर देखा और उनका और उनका विशेष प्रेम लखकर वे पुलकित हो गये।।

१४. श्रीराम–सीता जयमाल एवं विवाह

धीर बुद्धि वाले, भाट, मागध और सूत लोग विरुदावली (कीर्ति) का बखान कर रहे हैं। सब लोग घोड़े, हाथी, धन, मणि और वस्त्र निछावर कर रहे हैं।।

झाँझ, मृदंग, शंख, शहनाई, भेरी, ढोल और सुहावने नगाड़े आदि बहुत प्रकार के सुंदर बाजे बज रहे हैं। जहाँ–तहाँ युवतियाँ मंगल गीत गा रही हैं।।

सखियों सहित रानी अत्यन्त हर्षित हुई, मानो सूखते हुए धान पर पानी पड़ गया हो। जनकजी ने सोच त्याग कर सुख प्राप्त किया। मानो तैरते–तैरते थके हुए पुरुष ने थाह पा ली हो।।

धनुष टूट जाने पर राजा लोग ऐसे श्रीहीन (निस्तेज) हो गए, जैसे दिन में दीपक की शोभा जाती रहती है। सीताजी का सुख किस प्रकार वर्णन किया जाए, जैसे चातकी स्वाती का जल पा गई हो।।

श्री रामजी को लक्ष्मणजी किस प्रकार देख रहे हैं, जैसे चन्द्रमा को चकोर का बच्चा देख रहा हो। तब शतानंदजी ने आज्ञा दी और सीताजी ने श्री रामजी के पास गमन किया।।

साथ में सुंदर चतुर सखियाँ मंगलाचार के गीत गा रही हैं, सीताजी बाल हंसिनी की चाल से चलीं। उनके अंगों में अपार शोभा है।।

सखियों के बीच में सीताजी कैसी शोभित हो रही हैं, जैसे बहुत सी छवियों के बीच में महाछवि हो। करकमल में सुंदर जयमाला है, जिसमें विश्व विजय की शोभा छाई हुई है।।

सीताजी के शरीर में संकोच है, पर मन में परम उत्साह है। उनका यह गुप्त प्रेम किसी को जान नहीं पड़ रहा है। समीप जाकर, श्री रामजी की शोभा देखकर राजकुमारी सीताजी जैसे चित्र में लिखी सी रह गई।।

चतुर सखी ने यह दशा देखकर समझाकर कहा–सुहावनी जयमाला पहनाओ। यह सुनकर सीताजी ने दोनों हाथों से माला उठाई, पर प्रेम में विवश होने से पहनाई नहीं जाती।।

(उस समय उनके हाथ ऐसे सुशोभित हो रहे हैं) मानो डंडियों सहित दो कमल चन्द्रमा को डरते हुए जयमाला दे रहे हों। इस छवि को देखकर सखियाँ गाने लगीं। तब सीताजी ने श्री रामजी के गले में जयमाला पहना दी।।

श्री रघुनाथजी के हृदय पर जयमाला देखकर देवता फूल बरसाने लगे। समस्त राजागण इस प्रकार सकुचा गए मानो सूर्य को देखकर कुमुदों का समूह सिकुड़ गया हो।।

नगर और आकाश में बाजे बजने लगे। दुष्ट लोग उदास हो गए और सज्जन लोग सब प्रसन्न हो गए। देवता, किन्नर, मनुष्य, नाग और मुनीश्वर जय–जयकार करके आशीर्वाद दे रहे हैं।

देवताओं की स्त्रियाँ नाचती गाती हैं। बार–बार हाथों से पुष्पों की अंजलियाँ छूट रही हैं। जहाँ–तहाँ ब्रह्म वेद ध्वनि कर रहे हैं और भाट लोग विरुदावली (कुलकीर्ति) बखान रहे हैं।

पृथ्वी, पाताल और स्वर्ग तीनों लोकों में यश फैल गया कि श्री रामचन्द्रजी ने धनुष तोड़ दिया और सीताजी को वरण कर लिया। नगर के नर–नारी आरती कर रहे हैं और अपनी पूँजी (हैसियत) को भुलाकर (सामर्थ्य से बहुत अधिक) निछावर कर रहे हैं।।

श्री सीता–रामजी की जोड़ी ऐसी सुशोभित हो रही है मानो सुंदरता और शृंगार रस एकत्र हो गए हों। सखियाँ कह रही हैं–सीते! स्वामी के चरण छुओ, किन्तु सीताजी अत्यन्त भयभीत हुई उनके चरण नहीं छूतीं।।

गौतमजी की स्त्री अहल्या की गति का स्मरण करके सीताजी श्री रामजी के चरणों को हाथों से स्पर्श नहीं कर रही हैं। सीताजी की अलौकिक प्रीति जानकर रघुकुल मणि श्री रामचन्द्रजी मन में हँसे।।

श्रीरामचन्द्रजी को देखकर बारात शीतल हुई (राम के वियोग में सबके हृदय में जो आग जल रही थी, वह शान्त हो गयी)। प्रीति की रीतिका बखान नहीं हो सकता। राजा के पास चारों पुत्र ऐसी शोभा पा रहे हैं मानो धर्म, अर्थ, काम और मोक्ष शरीर धारण किये हुए हों।।

१५. दशरथ–कैकेयी संवाद

विपत्ति (कलह) बीज है, दासी वर्षा दृऋतु है, कैकेयी की कुबुद्धि [उस बीज के बोने के

लिये] जमीन हो गयी। उसमें कपटरूपी जल पाकर अंकुर फूट निकला। दोनों वरदान उस अंकुर के दो पत्ते हैं और अन्त में इसके दुःख रूपी फल होगा।।

'हे रानी किसलिये रूठी हो?' यह कहकर राजा उसे हाथ से स्पर्श करते हैं तो वह उनके हाथ को [झटककर] हटा देती है और ऐसे देखती है मानो क्रोध में भरी हुई नागिन क्रूर दृष्टि से देख रही हो। दोनों [वरदानों की] वासनाएँ उस नागिन की दो जीभें हैं और दोनों वरदान दाँत हैंय वह काटने के लिये मर्म स्थान देख रही है। तुलसीदास जी कहते हैं कि राजा दशरथ होनहार के वश में होकर इसे (इस प्रकार हाथ झटकने और नागिन की भाँति देखने को) कामदेव की क्रीडा ही समझ रहे हैं।

दोनों वरदान उस नदी के दो किनारे हैं, कैकेयी का कठिन हठ ही उसकी [तीव्र] धारा है और कुबरी (मन्थरा) के वचनों की प्रेरणा ही भँवर है। [वह क्रोधरूपी नदी] राजा दशरथ रूपी वृक्ष को जड़–मूल से ढहाती हुई विपत्ति रूपी समुद्र की ओर [सीधी] चली है।

१६. श्रीराम–कैकेयी संवाद

रघुवंशमणि श्री रामचन्द्रजी ने जाकर देखा कि राजा अत्यन्त ही बुरी हालत में पड़े हैं, मानो सिंहनी को देखकर कोई बूढ़ा गजराज सहमकर गिर पड़ा हो।।

राजा के होठ सूख रहे हैं और सारा शरीर जल रहा है, मानो मणि के बिना साँप दुःखी हो रहा हो। पास ही क्रोध से भरी कैकेयी को देखा, मानो (साक्षात) मृत्यु ही बैठी (राजा के जीवन की अंतिम) घड़ियाँ गिन रही हो।।

श्री रामचन्द्रजी का स्वभाव कोमल और करुणामय है। उन्होंने (अपने जीवन में) पहली बार यह दुःख देखा, इससे पहले कभी उन्होंने दुःख सुना भी न था। तो भी समय का विचार करके हृदय में धीरज धरकर उन्होंने मीठे वचनों से माता कैकेयी से पूछा–।।

हे माता! मुझे पिताजी के दुःख का कारण कहो, ताकि उसका निवारण हो (दुःख दूर हो) वह यत्न किया जाए। (कैकेयी ने कहा–) हे राम! सुनो, सारा कारण यही है कि राजा का तुम पर बहुत स्नेह है, इन्होंने मुझे दो वरदान देने को कहा था। मुझे जो कुछ अच्छा लगा, वही मैंने माँगा। उसे सुनकर राजा के हृदय में सोच हो गया, क्योंकि ये तुम्हारा संकोच नहीं छोड़ सकते।।

इधर तो पुत्र का स्नेह है और उधर वचन (प्रतिज्ञा), राजा इसी धर्मसंकट में पड़ गए हैं। यदि तुम कर सकते हो, तो राजा की आज्ञा शिरोधार्य करो और इनके कठिन क्लेश को मिटाओ।।

कैकेयी बेधड़क बैठी ऐसी कड़वी वाणी कह रही है, जिसे सुनकर स्वयं कठोरता भी अत्यन्त व्याकुल हो उठी। जीभ धनुष है, वचन बहुत से तीर हैं और मानो राजा ही कोमल निशाने के समान हैं।। (इस सारे साज–समान के साथ) मानो स्वयं कठोरपन श्रेष्ठ वीर का शरीर धारण करके धनुष विद्या सीख रहा है। श्री रघुनाथजी को सब हाल सुनाकर वह ऐसे बैठी है, मानो निष्ठुरता ही शरीर धारण किए हुए हो।।

सूर्यकुल के सूर्य, स्वाभाविक ही आनंद निधान श्री रामचन्द्रजी मन में मुस्कुराकर सब दूषणों से रहित ऐसे कोमल और सुंदर वचन बोले जो मानो वाणी के भूषण ही थे–हे माता! सुनो, वही पुत्र बड़ भागी है, जो पिता–माता के वचनों का अनुरागी (पालन करने वाला) है। (आज्ञा पालन द्वारा) माता–पिता को संतुष्ट करने वाला पुत्र, हे जननी! सारे संसार में दुर्लभ है।।

वन में विशेष रूप से मुनियों का मिलाप होगा, जिसमें मेरा सभी प्रकार से कल्याण है। उसमें भी, फिर पिताजी की आज्ञा और हे जननी! तुम्हारी सम्मति है।।

और प्राण प्रिय भरत राज्य पावेंगे। (इन सभी बातों को देखकर यह प्रतीत होता है कि) आज विधाता सब प्रकार से मुझे सम्मुख हैं (मेरे अनुकूल हैं)। यदि ऐसे काम के लिए भी मैं वन को न जाऊँ तो मूर्खों के समाज में सबसे पहले मेरी गिनती करनी चाहिए।।

जो कल्पवृक्ष को छोड़कर रेंड की सेवा करते हैं और अमृत त्याग कर विष माँग लेते हैं, हे माता! तुम मन में विचार कर देखो, वे (महामूर्ख) भी ऐसा मौका पाकर कभी न चूकेंगे।।

हे माता! मुझे एक ही दुःख विशेष रूप से हो रहा है, वह महाराज को अत्यन्त व्याकुल देखकर। इस थोड़ी सी बात के लिए ही पिताजी को इतना भारी दुःख हो, हे माता! मुझे इस बात पर विश्वास नहीं होता।।

क्योंकि महाराज तो बड़े ही धीर और गुणों के अथाह समुद्र हैं। अवश्य ही मुझसे कोई बड़ा अपराध हो गया है, जिसके कारण महाराज मुझसे कुछ नहीं कहते। तुम्हें मेरी सौगंध है, माता! तुम सच–सच कहो ।।

रघुकुल में श्रेष्ठ श्री रामचन्द्रजी के स्वभाव से ही सीधे वचनों को दुर्बुद्धि कैकेयी टेढ़ा ही करके जान रही है, जैसे यद्यपि जल समान ही होता है, परन्तु जोंक उसमें टेढ़ी चाल से ही चलती है।।

रानी कैकेयी श्री रामचन्द्रजी का रुख पाकर हर्षित हो गई और कपटपूर्ण स्नेह दिखाकर

बोली– तुम्हारी शपथ और भरत की सौगंध है, मुझे राजा के दुःख का दूसरा कुछ भी कारण विदित नहीं है।।

हे तात! तुम अपराध के योग्य नहीं हो (तुमसे माता–पिता का अपराध बन पड़े यह संभव नहीं)। तुम तो माता–पिता और भाइयों को सुख देने वाले हो। हे राम! तुम जो कुछ कह रहे हो, सब सत्य है। तुम पिता–माता के वचनों (के पालन) में तत्पर हो।।

मैं तुम्हारी बलिहारी जाती हूँ, तुम पिता को समझाकर वही बात कहो, जिससे चौथेपन (बुढ़ापे) में इनका अपयश न हो। जिस पुण्य ने इनको तुम जैसे पुत्र दिए हैं, उसका निरादर करना उचित नहीं।।

कैकेयी के बुरे मुख में ये शुभ वचन कैसे लगते हैं जैसे मगध देश में गया आदिक तीर्थ! श्री रामचन्द्रजी को माता कैकेयी के सब वचन ऐसे अच्छे लगे जैसे गंगाजी में जाकर (अच्छे–बुरे सभी प्रकार के) जल शुभ, सुंदर हो जाते हैं।।

१७. लक्ष्मण–निषादराज संवाद

लक्ष्मण जी ज्ञान, वैराग्य और भक्ति के रस से सनी हुई मीठी और कोमल वाणी बोले–हे भाई! कोई किसी को सुख–दुःख देने वाला नहीं है। सब अपने ही किये हुए कर्मों का फल भोगते हैं।

संयोग (मिलना), वियोग (बिछुड़ना), भले–बुरे भोग, शत्रु, मित्र और उदासीन–ये सभी भ्रम के फंदे हैं। जन्म–मृत्यु, सम्पति–विपत्ति, कर्म और काल– जहाँ तक जगत् के जंजाल हैंय धरती, घर, धन, नगर, परिवार, स्वर्ग और नरक आदि जहाँ तक व्यवहार हैं जो देखने, सुनने और मन के अंदर विचारने में आते हैं, इन सबका मूल मोह (अज्ञान) ही है। परमार्थतः ये नहीं हैं।।

जैसे स्वप्न में राजा भिखारी हो जाए या कंगाल स्वर्ग का स्वामी इन्द्र हो जाए, तो जागने पर लाभ या हानि कुछ भी नहीं है, वैसे ही इस दृश्य–प्रपंच को हृदय से देखना चाहिए।।

ऐसा विचारकर क्रोध नहीं करना चाहिए और न किसी को व्यर्थ दोष ही देना चाहिए। सब लोग मोह रूपी रात्रि में सोने वाले हैं और सोते हुए उन्हें अनेकों प्रकार के स्वप्न दिखाई देते हैं।।

इस जगत रूपी रात्रि में योगी लोग जागते हैं, जो परमार्थी हैं और प्रपंच (मायिक जगत) से छूटे हुए हैं। जगत में जीव को जागा हुआ तभी जानना चाहिए, जब सम्पूर्ण भोग–विलासों से वैराग्य हो जाए।।

विवेक होने पर मोहरूपी भ्रम भाग जाता है, तब (अज्ञान का नाश होने पर) श्रीरघुनाथ जी के चरणों में प्रेम होता है। हे सखा! मन, वचन और कर्म से श्रीराम जी के चरणों में प्रेम होना, यही सर्वश्रेष्ठ परमार्थ (पुरुषार्थ) है।।

श्री रामजी परमार्थ स्वरूप (परम वस्तु) पर ब्रह्म हैं। वे अविगत (जानने में न आने वाले) अलख (स्थूल दृष्टि से देखने में न आने वाले), अनादि (आदि रहित), अनुपम (उपमा रहित) सब विकारों से रहति और भेद शून्य हैं, वेद जिनका नित्य 'नेति नेति' कहकर निरूपण करते हैं।।

वही कृपालु श्री रामचन्द्रजी भक्त, भूमि, ब्राह्मण, गो और देवताओं के हित के लिए मनुष्य शरीर धारण करके लीलाएँ करते हैं, जिनके सुनने से जगत के जंजाल मिट जाते हैं।।

१८. वनगमन करते श्री सीता–राम एवं लक्ष्मण का स्वरूप

आगे श्रीरामजी हैं, पीछे लभ्मणजी सुशोभित हैं। तपस्वियों के वेष बनाये दोनों बड़ी ही शोभा पा रहे हैं। दोनों के बीच में सीता जी कैसी सुशोभित हो रही हैं, जैसे ब्रह्म और जीव के बीच में माया!।।

फिर जैसी छबि मेरे मन में बस रही है, उसको कहता हूँ – मानो वसन्त ऋतु और कामदेव के बीच में रति (कामदेव की स्त्री) शोभित हो। फिर अपने हृदय में खोजकर उपमा कहता हूँ कि मानो बुध (चन्द्रमा के पुत्र) और चन्द्रमा के बीच में रोहिणी (चन्द्रमा की स्त्री) सुशोभित हो रही हो।।

१९. श्रीराम–वाल्मीकि संवाद

सुंदर वन, तालाब और पर्वत देखते हुए प्रभु श्री रामचन्द्रजी वाल्मीकिजी के आश्रम में आए। श्री रामचन्द्रजी ने देखा कि मुनि का निवास स्थान बहुत सुंदर है, जहाँ सुंदर पर्वत, वन और पवित्र जल है।।

सरोवरों में कमल और वनों में वृक्ष फूल रहे हैं और मकरन्द रस में मस्त हुए भौंरे सुंदर गुंजार कर रहे हैं। बहुत से पक्षी और पशु कोलाहल कर रहे हैं और वैर से रहित होकर प्रसन्न मन से विचर रहे हैं।।

पवित्र और सुंदर आश्रम को देखकर कमल नयन श्री रामचन्द्रजी हर्षित हुए। रघु श्रेष्ठ श्री रामजी का आगमन सुनकर मुनि वाल्मीकिजी उन्हें लेने के लिए आगे आए।।

श्री रामचन्द्रजी ने मुनि को दण्डवत किया। विप्रश्रेष्ठ मुनि ने उन्हें आशीर्वाद दिया। श्री रामचन्द्रजी की छबि देखकर मुनि के नेत्र शीतल हो गए। सम्मान पूर्वक मुनि उन्हें आश्रम में ले आए।।

श्रेष्ठ मुनि वाल्मीकिजी ने प्राण प्रिय अतिथियों को पाकर उनके लिए मधुर कंद, मूल और फल मँगवाए। श्री सीताजी, लक्ष्मणजी और रामचन्द्रजी ने फलों को खाया। तब मुनि ने उनको (विश्राम करने के लिए) सुंदर स्थान बतला दिए।।

(मुनि श्री रामजी के पास बैठे हैं और उनकी) मंगल मूर्ति को नेत्रों से देखकर वाल्मीकिजी के मन में बड़ा भारी आनंद हो रहा है। तब श्री रघुनाथजी कमल सदृश हाथों को जोड़कर, कानों को सुख देने वाले मधुर वचन बोले–।।

हे मुनिनाथ! आप त्रिकाल दर्शी हैं। सम्पूर्ण विश्व आपके लिए हथेली पर रखे हुए बेर के समान है। प्रभु श्री रामचन्द्रजी ने ऐसा कहकर फिर जिस–जिस प्रकार से रानी कैकेयी ने वनवास दिया, वह सब कथा विस्तार से सुनाई।।

(और कहा–) हे प्रभो! पिता की आज्ञा (का पालन), माता का हित और भरत जैसे (स्नेही एवं धर्मात्मा) भाई का राजा होना और फिर मुझे आपके दर्शन होना, यह सब मेरे पुण्यों का प्रभाव है।।

हे मुनिराज! आपके चरणों का दर्शन करने से आज हमारे सब पुण्य सफल हो गए (हमें सारे पुण्यों का फल मिल गया)। अब जहाँ आपकी आज्ञा हो और जहाँ कोई भी मुनि उद्वेग को प्राप्त न हो– ।।

क्योंकि जिनसे मुनि और तपस्वी दुःख पाते हैं, वे राजा बिना अग्नि के ही (अपने दुष्ट कर्मों से ही) जलकर भस्म हो जाते हैं। ब्राह्मणों का संतोष सब मंगलों की जड़ है और भूदेव ब्राह्मणों का क्रोध करोड़ों कुलों को भस्म कर देता है।।

ऐसा हृदय में समझकर– वह स्थान बतलाइए जहाँ मैं लक्ष्मण और सीता सहित जाऊँ और वहाँ सुंदर पत्तों और घास की कुटी बनाकर, हे दयालु! कुछ समय निवास करूँ।।

श्री रामजी की सहज ही सरल वाणी सुनकर ज्ञानी मुनि वाल्मीकि बोले– धन्य! धन्य! हे रघुकुल के ध्वजास्वरूप! आप ऐसा क्यों न कहेंगे? आप सदैव वेद की मर्यादा का पालन (रक्षण) करते हैं।।

हे राम! आप वेद की मर्यादा के रक्षक जगदीश्वर हैं और जानकीजी (आपकी स्वरूप भूता) माया हैं, जो कृपा के भंडार आपका रुख पाकर जगत का सृजन, पालन और संहार

करती हैं। जो हजार मस्तक वाले सर्पों के स्वामी और पृथ्वी को अपने सिर पर धारण करने वाले हैं, वही चराचर के स्वामी शेषजी लक्ष्मण हैं। देवताओं के कार्य के लिए आप राजा का शरीर धारण करके दुष्ट राक्षसों की सेना का नाश करने के लिए चले हैं।

हे राम! आपका स्वरूप वाणी के अगोचर, बुद्धि से परे, अव्यक्त, अकथनीय और अपार है। वेद निरंतर उसका 'नेति–नेति' कहकर वर्णन करते हैं।।

हे राम! जगत् दृश्य है, आप उसके देखने वाले हैं। आप ब्रह्मा, विष्णु और शंकर को भी नचाने वाले हैं। जब वे भी आपके मर्म को नहीं जानते, तब और कौन आपको जानने वाला है?

वही आपको जानता है, जिसे आप जना देते हैं और जानते ही वह आपका ही स्वरूप बन जाता है। हे रघुनंदन! हे भक्तों के हृदय को शीतल करने वाले चंदन! आपकी ही कृपा से भक्त आपको जान पाते हैं।।

आपकी देह चिदानन्दमय है (यह प्रकृतिजन्य पंच महाभूतों की बनी हुई कर्म बंधनयुक्त, त्रिदेह विशिष्ट मायिक नहीं है) और (उत्पत्ति–नाश, वृद्धि–क्षय आदि) सब विकारों से रहित है, इस रहस्य को अधिकारी पुरुष ही जानते हैं। आपने देवता और संतों के कार्य के लिए (दिव्य) नर शरीर धारण किया है और प्राकृत (प्रकृति के तत्वों से निर्मित देह वाले, साधारण) राजाओं की तरह से कहते और करते हैं।।

हे राम! आपके चरित्रों को देख और सुनकर मूर्ख लोग तो मोह को प्राप्त होते हैं और ज्ञानीजन सुखी होते हैं। आप जो कुछ कहते, करते हैं, वह सब सत्य (उचित) ही है, क्योंकि जैसा स्वाँग भरे वैसा ही नाचना भी तो चाहिए (इस समय आप मनुष्य रूप में हैं, अतः मनुष्योचित व्यवहार करना ठीक ही है।)।।

आपने मुझसे पूछा कि मैं कहाँ रहूँ? परन्तु मैं यह पूछते सकुचाता हूँ कि जहाँ आप न हों, वह स्थान बता दीजिए। तब मैं आपके रहने के लिए स्थान दिखाऊँ।।

मुनि के प्रेम रस से सने हुए वचन सुनकर श्री रामचन्द्रजी रहस्य खुल जाने के डर से सकुचाकर मन में मुस्कुराए। वाल्मीकिजी हँसकर फिर अमृत रस में डुबोई हुई मीठी वाणी बोले–

हे रामजी! सुनिए, अब मैं वे स्थान बताता हूँ, जहाँ आप, सीताजी और लक्ष्मणजी समेत निवास कीजिए। जिनके कान समुद्र की भाँति आपकी सुंदर कथा रूपी अनेक सुंदर नदियों से निरंतर भरते रहते हैं, परन्तु कभी पूरे (तृप्त) नहीं होते, उनके हृदय आपके लिए सुंदर घर हैं और जिन्होंने अपने नेत्रों को चातक बना रखा है, जो आपके दर्शन रूपी मेघ के लिए सदा लालायित रहते हैं तथा जो भारी–भारी नदियों, समुद्रों और झीलों का निरादर

करते हैं और आपके सौंदर्य (रूपी मेघ) की एक बूँद जल से सुखी हो जाते हैं (अर्थात आपके दिव्य सच्चिदानन्दमय स्वरूप के किसी एक अंग की जरा सी भी झाँकी के सामने स्थूल, सूक्ष्म और कारण तीनों जगत के अर्थात पृथ्वी, स्वर्ग और ब्रह्मलोक तक के सौंदर्य का तिरस्कार करते हैं), हे रघुनाथजी! उन लोगों के हृदय रूपी सुखदायी भवनों में आप भाई लक्ष्मणजी और सीताजी सहित निवास कीजिए ॥

आपके यश रूपी निर्मल मानसरोवर में जिसकी जीभ हंसिनी बनी हुई आपके गुण समूह रूपी मोतियों को चुगती रहती है, हे रामजी! आप उसके हृदय में बसिए ॥

जिसकी नासिका प्रभु (आप) के पवित्र और सुगंधित (पुष्पादि) सुंदर प्रसाद को नित्य आदर के साथ ग्रहण करती (सूँघती) है और जो आपको अर्पण करके भोजन करते हैं और आपके प्रसाद रूप ही वस्त्राभूषण धारण करते हैं, जिनके मस्तक देवता, गुरु और ब्राह्मणों को देखकर बड़ी नम्रता के साथ प्रेम सहित झुक जाते हैं, जिनके हाथ नित्य श्री रामचन्द्रजी (आप) के चरणों की पूजा करते हैं और जिनके हृदय में श्री रामचन्द्रजी (आप) का ही भरोसा है, दूसरा नहीं तथा जिनके चरण श्री रामचन्द्रजी (आप) के तीर्थों में चलकर जाते हैं, हे रामजी! आप उनके मन में निवास कीजिए। जो नित्य आपके (राम नाम रूप) मंत्रराज को जपते हैं और परिवार (परिकर) सहित आपकी पूजा करते हैं।। जो अनेक प्रकार से तर्पण और हवन करते हैं तथा ब्राह्मणों को भोजन कराकर बहुत दान देते हैं तथा जो गुरु को हृदय में आपसे भी अधिक (बड़ा) जानकर सर्वभाव से सम्मान करके उनकी सेवा करते हैं।।

और ये सब कर्म करके सबका एक मात्र यही फल माँगते हैं कि श्री रामचन्द्रजी के चरणों में हमारी प्रीति हो, उन लोगों के मन रूपी मंदिरों में सीताजी और रघुकुल को आनंदित करने वाले आप दोनों बसिए ॥

जिनके न तो काम, क्रोध, मद, अभिमान और मोह हैं, न लोभ है, न क्षोभ है, न राग है, न द्वेष है और न कपट, दम्भ और माया ही है– हे रघुराज! आप उनके हृदय में निवास कीजिए ॥

जो सबके प्रिय और सबका हित करने वाले हैं, जिन्हें दुःख और सुख तथा प्रशंसा (बड़ाई) और गाली (निंदा) समान है, जो विचारकर सत्य और प्रिय वचन बोलते हैं तथा जो जागते–सोते आपकी ही शरण हैं और आपको छोड़कर जिनके दूसरे कोई गति (आश्रय) नहीं है, हे रामजी! आप उनके मन में बसिए। जो पराई स्त्री को जन्म देने वाली माता के समान जानते हैं और पराया धन जिन्हें विष से भी भारी विष है जो दूसरे की सम्पत्ति देखकर हर्षित

होते हैं और दूसरे की विपत्ति देखकर विशेष रूप से दुःखी होते हैं और हे रामजी! जिन्हें आप प्राणों के समान प्यारे हैं, उनके मन आपके रहने योग्य शुभ भवन हैं।।

हे तात! जिनके स्वामी, सखा, पिता, माता और गुरु सब कुछ आप ही हैं, उनके मन रूपी मंदिर में सीता सहित आप दोनों भाई निवास कीजिए ।।

जो अवगुणों को छोड़कर सबके गुणों को ग्रहण करते हैं, ब्राह्मण और गो के लिए संकट सहते हैं, नीति–निपुणता में जिनकी जगत में मर्यादा है, उनका सुंदर मन आपका घर है।।

जो गुणों को आपका और दोषों को अपना समझता है, जिसे सब प्रकार से आपका ही भरोसा है और राम भक्त जिसे प्यारे लगते हैं, उसके हृदय में आप सीता सहित निवास कीजिए ।।

जाति, पाँति, धन, धर्म, बड़ाई, प्यारा परिवार और सुख देने वाला घर, सबको छोड़कर जो केवल आपको ही हृदय में धारण किए रहता है, हे रघुनाथजी! आप उसके हृदय में रहिए।।

स्वर्ग, नरक और मोक्ष जिसकी दृष्टि में समान हैं, क्योंकि वह जहाँ–तहाँ (सब जगह) केवल धनुष–बाण धारण किए आपको ही देखता है और जो कर्म से, वचन से और मन से आपका दास है, हे रामजी! आप उसके हृदय में डेरा कीजिए ।।

जिसको कभी कुछ भी नहीं चाहिए और जिसका आपसे स्वाभाविक प्रेम है, आप उसके मन में निरंतर निवास कीजिए, वह आपका अपना घर है।।

२०. सुमन्त्र–दशरथ संवाद

जन्म–मरण, सुख–दुःख के भोग, हानि–लाभ, प्यारों का मिलना–बिछुड़ना, ये सब हे स्वामी! काल और कर्म के अधीन रात और दिन की तरह बरबस होते रहते हैं।।

मूर्ख लोग सुख में हर्षित होते हैं और दुःख में रोते हैं, पर धीर पुरुष अपने मन में दोनों को समान समझते हैं। हे सबके हितकारी (रक्षक)! आप विवेक विचार कर धीरज धरिये और शोक का परित्याग कीजिए।

२१. वशिष्ठ–भरत संवाद

मुनिनाथ ने विलखकर (दुःखी होकर) कहा गृहे भरत! सुनों, भावी (होनहार) बड़ी बलवान्है । हानि–लाभ, जीवन–मरण और यश–अपयश, ये सब विधाता के हाथ हैं।।

सोच उस ब्राह्मण का करना चाहिये जो वेद नहीं जानता और जो अपना धर्म छोड़कर विषय – भोग में ही लीन रहता है। उस राजा का सोच करना चाहिये जो नीति नहीं जानता और जिसको प्रजा प्राणों के समान प्यारी नहीं हैं।। उस वैश्य का सोच करना चाहिये जो धनवान होकर भी कंजूस है, और जो अतिथि सत्कार तथा शिव जी की भक्ति करने में कुशल नहीं हैं। उस शूद्र का सोच करना चाहिए जो ब्रह्मणों का अपमान करने वाला, बहुत बोलने वाला मान–बड़ाई चाहने वाला और ज्ञान का घमंड रखने वाला है।। पुनः उस स्त्री का सोच करना चाहिये जो पति को छलने वाली, कुटिल, कलह प्रिय और स्वेच्छा चारिणी है। उस ब्रह्मचारी का सोच करना चाहिये जो अपने ब्रह्मचर्य–व्रत को छोड़ देता है और गुरु की आज्ञा के अनुसार नहीं चलता।।

उस गृहस्थ का सोच करना चाहिए, जो मोह वश कर्म मार्ग का त्याग कर देता है, उस संन्यासी का सोच करना चाहिए, जो दुनिया के प्रपंच में फँसा हुआ और ज्ञान–वैराग्य से हीन है।।

वानप्रस्थ वही सोच करने योग्य है, जिसको तपस्या छोड़कर भोग अच्छे लगते हैं। सोच उसका करना चाहिए जो चुगलखोर है, बिना ही कारण क्रोध करने वाला है तथा माता, पिता, गुरु एवं भाई–बंधुओं के साथ विरोध रखने वाला।।

सब प्रकार से उसका सोच करना चाहिए, जो दूसरों का अनिष्ट करता है, अपने ही शरीर का पोषण करता है और बड़ा भारी निर्दयी है और वह तो सभी प्रकार से सोच करने योग्य है, जो छल छोड़कर हरि का भक्त नहीं होता।।

कोसलराज दशरथजी सोच करने योग्य नहीं हैं, जिनका प्रभाव चौदहों लोकों में प्रकट। हे भरत! तुम्हारे पिता जैसा राजा तो न हुआ, न है और न अब होने का ही है।।

ब्रह्मा, विष्णु, शिव, इन्द्र और दिक्पाल सभी दशरथजी के गुणों की कथाएँ कहा करते हैं।

जो अनुचित और उचित का विचार छोड़कर पिता के वचनों का पालन करते हैं, वे (यहाँ) सुख और सुयश के पात्र होकर अंत में इन्द्रपुरी (स्वर्ग) में निवास करते हैं।।

राजा का वचन अवश्य सत्य करो। शोक त्याग दो और प्रजा का पालन करो। ऐसा करने से स्वर्ग में राजा संतोष पावेंगे और तुम को पुण्य और सुंदर यश मिलेगा, दोष नहीं लगेगा ।।

यह वेद में प्रसिद्ध है और (स्मृति–पुराणादि) सभी शास्त्रों के द्वारा सम्मत है कि पिता

जिसको दे वही राजतिलक पाता है, इसलिए तुम राज्य करो, ग्लानि का त्याग कर दो। मेरे वचन को हित समझकर मानो।।

इस बात को सुनकर श्री रामचन्द्रजी और जानकीजी सुख पावेंगे और कोई पंडित इसे अनुचित नहीं कहेगा। कौसल्याजी आदि तुम्हारी सब माताएँ भी प्रजा के सुख से सुखी होंगी।

२२. भरत–प्रजा संवाद

गुरुजी ने मुझे सुन्दर उपदेश दिया (फिर), प्रजा, मन्त्री आदु सभी को यही सम्मत है। माता ने भी उचित समझकर ही आज्ञा दी है और मैं भी अवश्य उसको सिर चढ़ाकर वैसा ही करना चाहता हूँ।

[क्योंकि] गुरु, पिता, माता, स्वामी और सुहृद् (मित्र) की वाणी सुनकर प्रसन्न मन से उसे अच्छी समझकर करना (मानना) चाहिये। उचित–अनुचित का विचार करने से धर्म जाता है और सिर पर पाप का भार चढ़ता है।।

रोगी शरीर के लिए नाना प्रकार के भोग व्यर्थ हैं। श्री हरि की भक्ति बिना जप और योग व्यर्थ है। जीव के बिना सुन्दर देह व्यर्थ है। वैसे ही श्री रघुनाथ जी के बिना मेरा सब कुछ व्यर्थ है।

२३. वनगमन के समय श्रीराम–जनक मिलाप

श्रीरामजी का आश्रम शान्त रस रूपी पवित्र जल से परिपूर्ण समुद्र है। जनकजीकी सेना (समाज) मानो करुणा (करुण रस) की नदी है, जिसे श्रीरघुनाथ जी [उस आश्रम रुपी शान्त रस के समुद्र में मिलाने के लिये] लिये जा रहे हैं।

विषयी, साधक और ज्ञानवान् सिद्ध पुरुष–जगत् में ये तीन प्रकार के जीव वेदों ने बताये हैं। इन तीनों में जिसका चित्त श्रीरामजी के स्नेह से सरस (सराबोर) रहता है, साधुओं की सभा में उसी का बड़ा आदर होता है।।

वेद, शास्त्र और पुराणों में प्रसिद्ध है और जगत् जानता है कि सेवा धर्म बड़ा कठिन है। स्वामी धर्म में (स्वामी के प्रति कर्तव्य पालन में) और स्वार्थ में विरोध है (दोनों एक साथ नहीं निभ सकते)। वैर अंधा होता है और प्रेम को ज्ञान नहीं रहता [मैं स्वार्थ वश कहूँगा या प्रेम वश, दोनों में ही भूल होने का भय है]।

चित्त दो तरफा हो जाने से वे कहीं सन्तोष नहीं पाते और एक दूसरे से अपना मर्म भी नहीं कहते। कृपा निधान श्रीरामचन्द्र जी यह दशा देखकर हृदय में हँसकर कहने लगे– कुत्ता, इन्द्र

और नवयुवक (कामी पुरुष) एक – सरीखे एक (एक ही स्वभाव के हैं। [पाणिनीय व्याकरण के अनुसार श्वन्, युवन् और मघवन् शब्दों के रूप भी एक–सरीखे होते हैं]।

२४. श्री राम–लक्ष्मण संवाद के माध्यम से ज्ञान, वैराग्य और माया का प्रतिपादन

एक बार प्रभु श्री रामजी सुख से बैठे हुए थे। उस समय लक्ष्मणजी ने उनसे छल रहित (सरल) वचन कहे– हे देवता, मनुष्य, मुनि और चराचर के स्वामी! मैं अपने प्रभु की तरह (अपना स्वामी समझकर) आपसे पूछता हूँ।।

हे देव! मुझे समझाकर वही कहिए, जिससे सब छोड़कर मैं आपकी चरणरज की ही सेवा करूँ। ज्ञान, वैराग्य और माया का वर्णन कीजिए और उस भक्ति को कहिए, जिसके कारण आप दया करते हैं।।

हे प्रभो! ईश्वर और जीव का भेद भी सब समझाकर कहिए, जिससे आपके चरणों में मेरी प्रीति हो और शोक, मोह तथा भ्रम नष्ट हो जाएँ।।

(श्रीरामजी ने कहा–) हे तात! मैं थोड़े ही में सब समझाकर कहे देता हूँ। तुम मन, चित्त और बुद्धि लगाकर सुनो! मैं और मेरा, तू और तेरा– यही माया है, जिसने समस्त जीवों को वश में कर रखा है।।

इंद्रियोंके विषयों को और जहाँ तक मन जाता है, हे भाई! उन सबको माया जानना। उसके भी एक विद्या और दूसरी अविद्या, इन दोनों भेदों को तुम सुनो– ।।

एक (अविद्या) दुष्ट (दोषयुक्त) है और अत्यंत दुःखरूप है, जिसके वश होकर जीवसंसार रूपी कुएँ में पड़ा हुआ है और एक (विद्या) जिसके वश में गुण है और जो जगत् की रचना करती है, वह प्रभु से ही प्रेरित होती है, उसके अपना बल कुछ भी नही है।।

ज्ञान वह है, जहाँ (जिसमें) मान आदि एक भी (दोष) नहीं है और जो सबसे समान रूप से ब्रह्म को देखता है। हे तात! उसी को परम वैराग्यवान् कहना चाहिए, जो सारी सिद्धियों को और तीनों गुणों को तिनके के समान त्याग चुका हो।

(जिसमें मान, दम्भ, हिंसा, क्षमाराहित्य, टेढ़ापन, आचार्य सेवा का अभाव, अपवित्रता, अस्थिरता, मन का निगृहीत न होना, इंद्रियों के विषय में आसक्ति, अहंकार, जन्म–मृत्यु–जरा–व्याधिमय जगत् में सुख–बुद्धि, स्त्री–पुत्र–घर आदि में आसक्ति तथा ममता, इष्ट और अनिष्ट की प्राप्ति में हर्ष–शोक, भक्ति का अभाव, एकान्त में मन न लगना, विषयी मनुष्यों के संग में प्रेम– ये अठारहन हों और नित्य अध्यात्म (आत्मा) में स्थिति

तथा तत्त्व ज्ञान के अर्थ (तत्त्व ज्ञान के द्वारा जानने योग्य) परमात्मा का नित्य दर्शन हो, वही ज्ञान कहलाता है। देखिए गीता अध्याय १३ / ७ से ११)

जो माया को, ईश्वर को और अपने स्वरूप को नहीं जानता, उसे जीव कहना चाहिए। जो (कर्मानुसार) बंधन और मोक्ष देने वाला, सबसे परे और माया का प्रेरक है, वह ईश्वर है।।

धर्म (के आचरण) से वैराग्य और योग से ज्ञान होता है तथा ज्ञान मोक्ष का देनेवाला है– ऐसा वेदों ने वर्णन किया है। और हे भाई! जिससे मैं शीघ्र ही प्रसन्न होता हूँ, वह मेरी भक्ति है जो भक्तों को सुख देने वाली है।।

वह भक्ति स्वतंत्र है, उसको (ज्ञान–विज्ञान आदि किसी) दूसरे साधन का सहारा (अपेक्षा) नहीं है। ज्ञान और विज्ञान तो उसके अधीन हैं। हे तात! भक्ति अनुपम एवं सुख मूल है और वह तभी मिलती है, जब संत अनुकूल (प्रसन्न) होते हैं।।

अब मैं भक्ति के साधन को विस्तार से कहता हूँ– यह सुगम मार्ग है, जिससे जीव की मुझको सहज ही पा जाते हैं। पहले तो ब्राह्मणों के चरणों में अत्यंत प्रीति हो और वेद की रीति के अनुसार अपने–अपने (वर्णाश्रम के) कर्मों में लगा रहे।।

इसका फल, फिर विषयों से वैराग्य होगा। तब (वैराग्य होने पर) मेरे धर्म (भागवत धर्म) में प्रेम उत्पन्न होगा। तब श्रवण आदि नौ प्रकार की भक्तियाँ दृढ होंगी और मन में मेरी लीलाओं के प्रति अत्यंत प्रेम होगा ।।

जिसका संतों के चरण कमलों में अत्यंत प्रेम हो, मन, वचन और कर्म से भजन का दृढ नियम हो और जो मुझको ही गुरु, पिता, माता, भाई, पति और देवता सब कुछ जाने और सेवा में दृढ़ हो ।।

मेरा गुण गाते समय जिसका शरीर पुलकित हो जाए, वाणी गदगद हो जाए और नेत्रों से (प्रेमाश्रुओं का) जल बहने लगे और काम, मद और दम्भ आदि जिसमें न हों, हे भाई! मैं सदा उसके वश में रहता हूँ।।

जिनको कर्म, वचन और मन से मेरी ही गति है और जो निष्काम भाव से मेरा भजन करते हैं, उनके हृदय कमल में मैं सदा विश्राम किया करता हूँ।।

इस भक्ति योग को सुनकर लक्ष्मणजी ने अत्यंत सुख पाया और उन्होंने प्रभु श्रीरामचंद्रजी के चरणों में सिर नवाया। इस प्रकार वैराग्य, ज्ञान, गुण और नीति कहते हुए कुछ दिन बीत गए।।

२५. सीता वियोग में श्रीराम विलाप

जिस प्रकार कपट मृग के साथ श्री रामजी दौड़ चले थे, उसी छवि को हृदय में रखकर वे हरिनाम (रामनाम) रटती रहती हैं।।

(इधर) श्री रघुनाथजी ने छोटे भाई लक्ष्मणजी को आते देखकर बाह्य रूप में बहुत चिंता की (और कहा–) हे भाई! तुमने जानकी को अकेली छोड़ दिया और मेरी आज्ञा का उल्लंघन कर यहाँ चले आए!। राक्षसों के झुंड वन में फिरते रहते हैं। मेरे मन में ऐसा आता है कि सीता आश्रम में नहीं है। छोटे भाई लक्ष्मणजी ने श्री रामजी के चरणकमलों को पकड़कर हाथ जोड़कर कहा– हे नाथ! मेरा कुछ भी दोष नहीं है।

लक्ष्मणजी सहित प्रभु श्री रामजी वहाँ गए, जहाँ गोदावरी के तट पर उनका आश्रम था। आश्रम को जानकीजी से रहित देखकर श्री रामजी साधारण मनुष्य की भाँति व्याकुल और दीन (दुःखी) हो गए।।

(वे विलाप करने लगे–) हा गुणों की खान जानकी! हा रूप, शील, व्रत और नियमों में पवित्र सीते! लक्ष्मणजी ने बहुत प्रकार से समझाया। तब श्री रामजी लताओं और वृक्षों की पंक्तियों से पूछते हुए चले।।

हे पक्षियों! हे पशुओं! हे भौंरों की पंक्तियों! तुमने कहीं मृगनयनी सीता को देखा है? खंजन, तोता, कबूतर, हिरन, मछली, भौंरों का समूह, प्रवीण कोयल, कुन्दकली, अनार, बिजली, कमल, शरद् का चंद्रमा और नागिनी, अरुण का पाश, कामदेव का धनुष, हंस, गज और सिंह– ये सब आज अपनी प्रशंसा सुन रहे हैं।।

बेल, सुवर्ण और केला हर्षित हो रहे हैं। इनके मन में जरा भी शंका और संकोच नहीं है। हे जानकी! सुनो, तुम्हारे बिना ये सब आज ऐसे हर्षित हैं, मानो राज पा गए हों। (अर्थात् तुम्हारे अंगों के सामने ये सब तुच्छ, अपमानित और लज्जित थे। आज तुम्हें न देखकर ये अपनी शोभा के अभिमान में फूल रहे हैं)।।

तुमसे यह अनख (स्पर्धा) कैसे सही जाती है? हे प्रिये! तुम शीघ्र ही प्रकट क्यों नहीं होती? इस प्रकार (अनन्त ब्रह्माण्डों के अथवा महा महिमा मयी स्वरूपाशक्ति श्री सीताजी के) स्वामी श्री रामजी सीताजी को खोजते हुए (इस प्रकार) विलाप करते हैं, मानो कोई महाविरही और अत्यंत कामी पुरुष हो।

पूर्णकाम, आनंद की राशि, अजन्मा और अविनाशी श्री रामजी मनुष्यों के चरित्र कर रहे हैं।

२६. श्रीराम–शबरी संवाद

उदार श्री रामजी उसे गति देकर शबरीजी के आश्रम में पधारे। शबरीजी ने श्री रामचंद्रजी को घर में आए देखा, तब मुनि मतंगजी के वचनों को याद करके उनका मन प्रसन्न हो गया।।

कमल सदृश नेत्र और विशाल भुजाओं वाले, सिर पर जटाओं का मुकुट और हृदय पर वनमाला धारण किए हुए सुंदर, साँवले और गोरे दोनों भाइयों के चरणों में शबरीजी लिपट पड़ीं ।।

वे प्रेम में मग्न हो गईं, मुख से वचन नहीं निकलता। बार–बार चरण–कमलों में सिर नवा रही हैं। फिर उन्होंने जल लेकर आदर पूर्वक दोनों भाइयों के चरण धोए और फिर उन्हें सुंदर आसनों पर बैठाया।।

उन्होंने अत्यंत रसीले और स्वादिष्ट कन्द, मूल और फल लाकर श्री रामजी को दिए। प्रभु ने बार–बार प्रशंसा करके उन्हें प्रेम सहित खाया।।

फिर वे हाथ जोड़कर आगे खड़ी हो गईं। प्रभु को देखकर उनका प्रेम अत्यंत बढ़ गया। (उन्होंने कहा–) मैं किस प्रकार आपकी स्तुति करूँ? मैं नीच जाति की और अत्यंत मूढ़ बुद्धि हूँ।।

जो अधम से भी अधम हैं, स्त्रियाँ उनमें भी अत्यंत अधम हैं, और उनमें भी हे पापनाशन! मैं मंदबुद्धि हूँ। श्री रघुनाथजी ने कहा– हे भामिनि! मेरी बात सुन! मैं तो केवल एक भक्ति ही का संबंध मानता हूँ।।

जाति, पाँति, कुल, धर्म, बड़ाई, धन, बल, कुटुम्ब, गुण और चतुरता– इन सबके होने पर भी भक्ति से रहित मनुष्य कैसा लगता है, जैसे जलहीन बादल (शोभाहीन) दिखाई पड़ता है।।

मैं तुझसे अब अपनी नवधा भक्ति कहता हूँ। तू सावधान होकर सुन और मन में धारण कर। पहली भक्ति है संतों का सत्संग। दूसरी भक्ति है मेरे कथा प्रसंग में प्रेम।।

तीसरी भक्ति है अभिमान रहित होकर गुरु के चरण कमलों की सेवा और चौथी भक्ति यह है कि कपट छोड़कर मेरे गुण समूहों का गान करें।।

मेरे (राम) मंत्र का जाप और मुझमें दृढ़ विश्वास– यह पाँचवीं भक्ति है, जो वेदों में प्रसिद्ध है। छठी भक्ति है इंद्रियों का निग्रह, शील (अच्छा स्वभाव या चरित्र), बहुत कार्यों से वैराग्य और निरंतर संत पुरुषों के धर्म (आचरण) में लगे रहना।।

सातवीं भक्ति है जगत् भर को समभाव से मुझमें ओतप्रोत (राममय) देखना और संतों

को मुझसे भी अधिक करके मानना। आठवीं भक्ति है जो कुछ मिल जाए, उसी में संतोष करना और स्वप्न में भी पराए दोषों को न देखना।।

नवीं भक्ति है सरलता और सबके साथ कपटरहित बर्ताव करना, हृदय में मेरा भरोसा रखना और किसी भी अवस्था में हर्ष और दैन्य (विषाद) का न होना। इन नवों में से जिनके एक भी होती है, वह स्त्री–पुरुष, जड़–चेतन कोई भी हो–।।

हे भामिनि! मुझे वही अत्यंत प्रिय है। फिर तुझ में तो सभी प्रकार की भक्ति दृढ़ है। अतएव जो गति योगियों को भी दुर्लभ है, वही आज तेरे लिए सुलभ हो गई है।।

मेरे दर्शन का परम अनुपम फल यह है कि जीव अपने सहज स्वरूप को प्राप्त हो जाता है। हे भामिनि! अब यदि तू गजगामिनी जानकी की कुछ खबर जानती हो तो बता।।

(शबरी ने कहा–) हे रघुनाथजी! आप पंपा नामक सरोवर को जाइए। वहाँ आपकी सुग्रीव से मित्रता होगी। हे देव! हे रघुवीर! वह सब हाल बतावेगा। हे धीरबुद्धि! आप सब जानते हुए भी मुझसे पूछते हैं!।। बार–बार प्रभु के चरणों में सिर नवाकर, प्रेम सहित उसने सब कथा सुनाई।।

सब कथा कहकर भगवान् के मुख के दर्शन कर, उनके चरणकमलों को धारण कर लिया और योगाग्नि से देह को त्याग कर (जलाकर) वह उस दुर्लभ हरिपद में लीन हो गई, जहाँ से लौटना नहीं होता। तुलसीदासजी कहते हैं कि अनेकों प्रकार के कर्म, अधर्म और बहुत से मत– ये सब शोकप्रद हैं, हे मनुष्यों! इनका त्याग कर दो और विश्वास करके श्री रामजी के चरणों में प्रेम करो।

जो नीच जाति की और पापों की जन्मभूमि थी, ऐसी स्त्री को भी जिन्होंने मुक्त कर दिया, अरे महादुर्बुद्धि मन! तू ऐसे प्रभु को भूलकर सुख चाहता है?।।

२७. श्रीराम–लक्ष्मण संवाद

हे लक्ष्मण! जरा वन की शोभा तो देखो। इसे देखकर किसका मन क्षुब्ध नहीं होगा? पक्षी और पशुओं के समूह सभी स्त्रीसहित हैं। मानो वे मेरी निन्दा कर रहे हैं।

हाथी हथिनियों को साथ लगा लेते हैं। वे मानो मुझे शिक्षा देते हैं (कि स्त्री को कभी अकेली नहीं छोड़नी चाहिए)। भली भाँति चिन्तन किये हुए शास्त्र को भी बार–बार देखते रहना चाहिए। अच्छी तरह सेवा किए हुए भी राजा को वश में नहीं समझना चाहिए। और स्त्री को चाहे हृदय में ही क्यों न रखा जायय परन्तु युवती स्त्री, शास्त्र और राजा किसी के वश में नहीं रहते। हे तात! इस सुन्दर वसन्त को देखो। प्रिया के बिना मुझको यह भय उत्पन्न कर रहा है।

२८. श्रीराम–सुग्रीव संवाद

जो लोग मित्र के दुःख से दुःखी नहीं होते, उन्हें देखने से ही बड़ा पाप लगता है। अपने पर्वत के समान दुःख को धूल के समान और मित्र के धूल के समान दुःख को सुमेरु (बड़े भारी पर्वत) के समान जाने।।

जिन्हें स्वभाव से ही ऐसी बुद्धि प्राप्त नहीं है, वे मूर्ख हठ करके क्यों किसी से मित्रता करते हैं? मित्र का धर्म है कि वह मित्र को बुरे मार्ग से रोककर अच्छे मार्ग पर चलावे। उसके गुण प्रकट करे और अवगुणों को छिपावे। देने–लेने में मन में शंका न रखे। अपने बल के अनुसार सदा हित ही करता रहे। विपत्ति के समय तो सदा सौगुना स्नेह करे। वेद कहते हैं कि संत (श्रेष्ठ) मित्र के गुण (लक्षण) ये हैं।

जो सामने तो बना–बनाकर कोमल वचन कहता है और पीठ–पीछे बुराई करता है तथा मन में कुटिलता रखता है दृ हे भाई! [इस तरह] जिसका मन साँप की चाल के समान टेढ़ा है, ऐसे कुमित्र को त्यागने में ही भलाई है।।

मूर्ख सेवक, कंजूस राजा, कुलटा स्त्री और कपटी मित्र – ये चारों शूल के समान [पीड़ा देने वाले] हैं। हे सखा! मेरे बल पर अब तुम चिन्ता छोड़ दो। मैं सब प्रकार से तुम्हारे काम आऊँगा (तुम्हारी सहायता करूँगा)।।

२९. श्रीराम–बालि संवाद

हे गोसाई! आपने धर्म की रक्षा के लिए अवतार लिया है और मुझे व्याध की तरह (छिपकर) मारा? मैं वैरी और सुग्रीव प्यारा? हे नाथ! किस दोष से आपने मुझे मारा?

[श्रीरामजी ने कहा–] हे मूर्ख! सुन, छोटे भाई की स्त्री, बहिन, पुत्र की स्त्री और कन्या – ये चारों समान हैं। इनको जो कोई बुरी दृष्टि से देखता है, उसे मारने में कुछ भी पाप नहीं होता।

तारा को व्याकुल देखकर श्री रघुनाथजी ने उसे ज्ञान दिया और उसकी माया (अज्ञान) हर ली। (उन्होंने कहा–) पृथ्वी, जल, अग्नि, आकाश और वायु– इन पाँच तत्वों से यह अत्यंत अधम शरीर रचा गया है।।

वह शरीर तो प्रत्यक्ष तुम्हारे सामने सोया हुआ है, और जीव नित्य है। फिर तुम किसके लिए रो रही हो? जब ज्ञान उत्पन्न हो गया, तब वह भगवान् के चरणों लगी और उसने परम भक्ति का वर माँग लिया।।

(शिवजी कहते हैं–) हे उमा! स्वामी श्री रामजी सबको कठपुतली की तरह नचाते हैं। तदनन्तर श्री रामजी ने सुग्रीव को आज्ञा दी और सुग्रीव ने विधि पूर्वक बालि का सब मृतक कर्म किया।।

हे पार्वती! जगत में श्री रामजी के समान हित करने वाला गुरु, पिता, माता, बंधु और स्वामी कोई नहीं है। देवता, मनुष्य और मुनि सबकी यह रीति है कि स्वार्थ के लिए ही सब प्रीति करते हैं।

३०. वर्षा वर्षा ऋतु वर्णन

देवताओं ने पहले से ही उस पर्वत की एक गुफा को सुंदर बना (सजा) रखा था। उन्होंने सोच रखा था कि कृपा की खान श्री रामजी कुछ दिन यहाँ आकर निवास करेंगे।।

सुंदर वन फूला हुआ अत्यंत सुशोभित है। मधु के लोभ से भौंरों के समूह गुंजार कर रहे हैं।। जब से प्रभु आए, तब से वन में सुंदर कन्द, मूल, फल और पत्तों की बहुतायत हो गई।।

मनोहर और अनुपम पर्वत को देखकर देवताओं के सम्राट् श्री रामजी छोटे भाई सहित वहाँ रह गए। देवता, सिद्ध और मुनि भौंरों, पक्षियों और पशुओं के शरीर धारण करके प्रभु की सेवा करने लगे।।

जब से रमापति श्री रामजी ने वहाँ निवास किया तब से वन मंगल स्वरूप हो गया। सुंदर स्फटिक मणि की एक अत्यंत उज्ज्वल शिला है, उस पर दोनों भाई सुख पूर्वक विराजमान हैं।।

श्री राम छोटे भाई लक्ष्मणजी से भक्ति, वैराग्य, राजनीति और ज्ञान की अनेकों कथाएँ कहते हैं। वर्षाकाल में आकाश में छाए हुए बादल गरजते हुए बहुत ही सुहावने लगते हैं।।

(श्री रामजी कहने लगे–) हे लक्ष्मण! देखो, मोरों के झुंड बादलों को देखकर नाच रहे हैं जैसे वैराग्य में अनुरक्त गृहस्थ किसी विष्णु भक्त को देखकर हर्षित होते हैं।।

आकाश में बादल घुमड़–घुमड़कर घोर गर्जना कर रहे हैं, प्रिया (सीताजी) के बिना मेरा मन डर रहा है। बिजली की चमक बादलों में ठहरती नहीं, जैसे दुष्ट की प्रीति स्थिर नहीं रहती।।

बादल पृथ्वी के समीप आकर (नीचे उतरकर) बरस रहे हैं, जैसे विद्या पाकर विद्वान नम्र हो जाते हैं। बूँदों की चोट पर्वत कैसे सहते हैं, जैसे दुष्टों के वचन संत सहते हैं।।

छोटी नदियाँ भरकर (किनारों को) तुड़ाती हुई चलीं, जैसे थोड़े धन से भी दुष्ट इतरा जाते हैं। (मर्यादा का त्याग कर देते हैं)। पृथ्वी पर पड़ते ही पानी गंदला हो गया है, जैसे श्रुद्ध जीव को माया लिपट गई हो ।।

जल एकत्र हो–होकर तालाबों में भर रहा है, जैसे सद्गुण (एक–एककर) सज्जन के पास चले आते हैं। नदी का जल समुद्र में जाकर वैसे ही स्थिर हो जाता है, जैसे जीव श्री हरि को पाकर अचल (आवागमन से मुक्त) हो जाता है।।

पृथ्वी घास से परिपूर्ण होकर हरी हो गई है, जिससे रास्ते समझ नहीं पड़ते। जैसे पाखंड मत के प्रचार से सद्ग्रंथ गुप्त (लुप्त) हो जाते हैं।।

चारों दिशाओं में मेंढकों की ध्वनि ऐसी सुहावनी लगती है, मानो विद्यार्थियों के समुदाय वेद पढ़ रहे हों। अनेकों वृक्षों में नए पत्ते आ गए हैं, जिससे वे ऐसे हरे–भरे एवं सुशोभित हो गए हैं जैसे साधक का मन विवेक (ज्ञान) प्राप्त होने पर हो जाता है।।

मदार और जवासा बिना पत्ते के हो गए (उनके पत्ते झड़ गए)। जैसे श्रेष्ठ राज्य में दुष्टों का उद्यम जाता रहा (उनकी एक भी नहीं चलती)। धूल कहीं खोजने पर भी नहीं मिलती, जैसे क्रोध धर्म को दूर कर देता है। (अर्थात् क्रोध का आवेश होने पर धर्म का ज्ञान नहीं रह जाता)।।

अन्न से युक्त (लहराती हुई खेती से हरी–भरी) पृथ्वी कैसी शोभित हो रही है, जैसी उपकारी पुरुष की संपत्ति। रात के घने अंधकार में जुगनू शोभा पा रहे हैं, मानो दम्भयों का समाज आ जुटा हो।।

भारी वर्षा से खेतों की क्यारियाँ फूट चली हैं, जैसे स्वतंत्र होने से स्त्रियाँ बिगड़ जाती हैं। चतुर किसान खेतों को निरा रहे हैं (उनमें से घास आदि को निकालकर फेंक रहे हैं।) जैसे विद्वान् लोग मोह, मद और मान का त्याग कर देते हैं।।

चक्रवाक पक्षी दिखाई नहीं दे रहे हैं, जैसे कलियुग को पाकर धर्म भाग जाते हैं। ऊसर में वर्षा होती है, पर वहाँ घास तक नहीं उगती। जैसे हरिभक्त के हृदय में काम नहीं उत्पन्न होता।।

पृथ्वी अनेक तरह के जीवों से भरी हुई उसी तरह शोभायमान है, जैसे सुराज्य पाकर प्रजा की वृद्धि होती है। जहाँ–तहाँ अनेक पथिक थककर ठहरे हुए हैं, जैसे ज्ञान उत्पन्न होने पर इंद्रियाँ (शिथिल होकर विषयों की ओर जाना छोड़ देती हैं)।।

कभी–कभी वायु बड़े जोर से चलने लगती है, जिससे बादल जहाँ–तहाँ गायब हो जाते हैं। जैसे कुपुत्र के उत्पन्न होने से कुल के उत्तम धर्म (श्रेष्ठ आचरण) नष्ट हो जाते हैं।।

कभी (बादलों के कारण) दिन में घोर अंधकार छा जाता है और कभी सूर्य प्रकट हो जाते हैं। जैसे कुसंग पाकर ज्ञान नष्ट हो जाता है और सुसंग पाकर उत्पन्न हो जाता है।।

३१. शरद ऋतु वर्णन

हे लक्ष्मण! देखो, वर्षा बीत गई और परम सुंदर शरद् ऋतु आ गई। फूले हुए कास से सारी पृथ्वी छा गई। मानो वर्षा ऋतु ने (कास रूपी सफेद बालों के रूप में) अपना बुढ़ापा प्रकट किया है।।

अगस्त्य के तारे ने उदय होकर मार्ग के जल को सोख लिया, जैसे संतोष लोभ को सोख लेता है। नदियों और तालाबों का निर्मल जल ऐसी शोभा पा रहा है जैसे मद और मोह से रहित संतों का हृदय!।।

नदी और तालाबों का जल धीरे–धीरे सूख रहा है। जैसे ज्ञानी (विवेकी) पुरुष ममता का त्याग करते हैं। शरद ऋतु जानकर खंजन पक्षी आ गए। जैसे समय पाकर सुंदर सुकृत आ सकते हैं। (पुण्य प्रकट हो जाते हैं)।।

न कीचड़ है न धूल? इससे धरती (निर्मल होकर) ऐसी शोभा दे रही है जैसे नीति निपुण राजा की करनी! जल के कम हो जाने से मछलियाँ व्याकुल हो रही हैं, जैसे मूर्ख (विवेक शून्य) कुटुम्बी (गृहस्थ) धन के बिना व्याकुल होता है।।

बिना बादलों का निर्मल आकाश ऐसा शोभित हो रहा है जैसे भगवद् भक्त सब आशाओं को छोड़कर सुशोभित होते हैं। कहीं–कहीं (विरले ही स्थानों में) शरद् ऋतु की थोड़ी–थोड़ी वर्षा हो रही है। जैसे कोई विरले ही मेरी भक्ति पाते हैं।।

(शरद् ऋतु पाकर) राजा, तपस्वी, व्यापारी और भिखारी (क्रमशः विजय, तप, व्यापार और भिक्षा के लिए) हर्षित होकर नगर छोड़कर चले। जैसे श्री हरि की भक्ति पाकर चारों आश्रम वाले (नाना प्रकार के साधन रूपी) श्रमों को त्याग देते हैं।।

जो मछलियाँ अथाह जल में हैं, वे सुखी हैं, जैसे श्री हरि के शरण में चले जाने पर एक भी बाधा नहीं रहती। कमलों के फूलने से तालाब कैसी शोभा दे रहा है, जैसे निर्गुण ब्रह्म सगुण होने पर शोभित होता है।।

भौंरे अनुपम शब्द करते हुए गूँज रहे हैं तथा पक्षियों के नाना प्रकार के सुंदर शब्द हो रहे हैं। रात्रि देखकर चकवे के मन में वैसे ही दुःख हो रहा है, जैसे दूसरे की संपत्ति देखकर दुष्ट को होता है।।

पपीहा रट लगाए है, उसको बड़ी प्यास है, जैसे श्री शंकरजी का द्रोही सुख नहीं पाता (सुख के लिए झीखता रहता है) शरद् ऋतु के ताप को रात के समय चंद्रमा हर लेता है, जैसे संतों के दर्शन से पाप दूर हो जाते हैं।।

चकोरों के समुदाय चंद्रमा को देखकर इस प्रकार टकटकी लगाए हैं जैसे भगवद् भक्त भगवान् को पाकर उनके (निर्निमेष नेत्रों से) दर्शन करते हैं। मच्छर और डाँस जाड़े के डर से इस प्रकार नष्ट हो गए जैसे ब्राह्मण के साथ वैर करने से कुल का नाश हो जाता है।।

(वर्षा ऋतु के कारण) पृथ्वी पर जो जीव भर गए थे, वे शरद् ऋतु को पाकर वैसे ही नष्ट हो गए जैसे सद्गुरु के मिल जाने पर संदेह और भ्रम के समूह नष्ट हो जाते हैं।।

३२. हनुमान् प्रसंग

[शिव जी कहते हैं–] हे भवानी! सुनों, जिनका नाम जपकर ज्ञानी (विवेकी) मनुष्य संसार (जन्म–मरण) के बन्धन को काट डालते हैं, उनका दूत कहीं बन्धन में आ सकता है? किन्तु प्रभु के कार्य के लिये हनुमानजी ने स्वयं अपने को बँधा लिया।।

राम नाम के बिना वाणी शोभा नहीं पाती, मद–मोह को छोड़, विचार कर देखो। हे देवताओं के शत्रु! सब गहनों से सजी हुई सुन्दरी स्त्री भी कपड़ों के बिना (नंगी) शोभा नहीं पाती।

हे प्रभु! जिस पर आप प्रसन्न हो, उसके लिये कुछ भी कठिन नहीं है। आप के प्रभाव रूई [जो स्वयं बहुत जल्दी जल जाने वाली वस्तु है] बड़वानल को निश्चय ही जला सकती है (अर्थात् असम्भव भी सम्भव हो सकता है)।

३३. रावण–विभीषण संवाद

मन्त्री, वैद्य और गुरु–ये तीन यदि ख्अप्रसन्नता के, भय या [लाभ की] आशा से [हितकी बात न कहकर] प्रिय बोलते हैं (ठकुरसुहाती कहने लगते हैं) य तो [क्रमशः] राज्य, शरीर और धर्म– इन तीन का शीघ्र ही नाश हो जाता है।

जो मनुष्य अपना कल्याण, सुन्दर यश, सुबुद्धि, शुभ गति और नाना प्रकार के सुख चाहता हो, वह हे स्वामी! परस्त्री के ललाट को चौथ के चन्द्रमा की तरह त्याग दे (अर्थात् जैसे लोग चौथ के चन्द्रमा को नहीं देखते, उसी प्रकार पर स्त्री का मुख ही न देखे।

हे नाथ! काम, क्रोध, मद और लोभ–ये सब नरक के रास्ते हैं। इन सब को छोड़कर श्रीरामचन्द्रजी को भजिये, जिन्हें संत (सत्पुरुष) भजते हैं।।

उन कृपा के समुद्र भगवान् ने पृथ्वी, ब्राह्मण, गौ और देवताओं का हित करने के लिये ही मनुष्य – शरीर धारण किया है। हे भाई! सुनिये, वे सेवकों को आनन्द देने वाले, दुष्टों के समूह का नाश करने वाले और वेद तथा धर्म की रक्षा करने वाले हैं।

हे नाथ! पुराण और वेद ऐसा कहते हैं कि सुबुद्धि (अच्छी बुद्धि) और कुबुद्धि (खोटी बुद्धि) सबके हृदय में रहती हैं, जहाँ सुबुद्धि है, वहाँ नाना प्रकार की सम्पदाएँ (सुख की स्थिति) रहती हैं। और जहाँ कुबुद्धि है, वहाँ परिणाम में विपति (दुःखः रहती है।।

३४. श्रीराम–विभीषण संवाद

हे तात! नरक में रहना अच्छा है, परन्तु विधाता दुष्ट का संग [कभी] न दे। [विभीषण जी ने कहा–] हे रघुनाथ जी! अब आपके चरणों का दर्शन कर कुशल से हूँ, जो आपने अपना सेवक जानकर मुझ पर दया की है।

(श्रीराम जी ने विभीषण से कहा–) हे सखा! सुनो, मैं तुम्हें अपना स्वभाव बतलाता हूँ, जिसे काकभुशुण्डि, शिवजी और पार्वतीजी भी जनती हैं। कोई मनुष्य (जो सम्पूर्ण) जड़–चेतन का द्रोही हो, यदि वह भी भयभीत होकर मेरी शरण में आ जाय और मद, मोह तथा नाना प्रकार के छल–कपट त्याग दे तो मैं उसे बहुत श्रीघ्र साधु के समान कर देता हूँ। माता, पिता, भाई, पुत्र, स्त्री, शरीर, धन, घर, मित्र और परिवार इन सबके ममत्व रूपी तागों को बटोर कर और उन सबकी एक डोरी बटकर उसके द्वारा जो अपने मन को मेरे चरणों में बाँध देता है (सारे सांसारिक सम्बन्धों का केन्द्र मुझे बना लेता है), जो समदर्शी है, जिसे कुछ इच्छा नहीं है और जिसके मन में हर्ष, श्रोक और भय नहीं है।

ऐसा सज्जन मेरे हृदय में कैसे बसता है, जैसे लोभी के हृदय में धन बसा करता है। तुम–सरीखे संत ही मुझे प्रिय हैं। मैं और किसी के निहोरे से (कृतज्ञता वश) देह धारण नहीं करता।

३५. रावण–मन्दोदरी संवाद

पाताल [जिन विश्वरूप भगवान् का] चरण है, ब्रह्मलोक सिर है, अन्य (बीच के सब) लोकों का विश्राम (स्थिति) जिनके अन्य भिन्न–भिन्न अङ्गों पर है। भयङ्कर काल जिनका भृकुटि संचालन (भौहों का चलना) है। सूर्य नेत्र है, बादलों का समूह बाल है।

अश्विनी कुमार जिनकी नासिका हैं, रात और दिन जिनके अपार निमेष (पलक मारना और खोलना) हैं। दसों दिशाएँ कान हैं, वेद ऐसा कहते हैं। वायु श्वास है और वेद जिनकी अपनी वाणी है।

लोभ जिनका अधर (होठ) है, यमराज भयानक दाँत है। माया हँसी है, दिक्पाल भुजाएँ हैं। अग्नि मुख है, वरुण जीभ है। उत्पत्ति, पालन और प्रलय जिनकी चेष्टा (क्रिया) है।

अठारह प्रकार की असंख्य वनस्पतियाँ जिनकी रोमावली हैं, पर्वत अस्थियाँ है, नदियाँ नसों का जाल हैं, समुद्र पेट है और नरक जिनकी नीचे की इन्दियाँ है। इस प्रकार प्रभु विश्वमय हैं, अधिक कल्पना (ऊहापोह) क्या की जाय?।

३६. अंगद–रावण संवाद

प्रीति और वैर बराबरी वाले से ही करना चाहिये, नीति ऐसी ही है। सिंह यदि मेढकों को मारे, तो क्या उसे कोई भला कहेगा?

वाममार्गी, कामी, कंजूस, अत्यन्त मूढ, अति दरिद्र, बदनाम, बहुत बूढा, नित्य का रोगी, निरन्तर क्रोध युक्त रहने वाला, भगवान् विष्णु से विमुख, वेद और संतों का विरोधी, अपना ही शरीर पोषण करने वाला, परायी निन्दा करने वाला और पाप की खान (महान् पापी) – ये चौदह प्राणी जीते ही मुरदे के समान हैं।

३७. श्रीराम–विभीषण संवाद

(रावण से युद्ध के समय विभीषण श्रीराम जी से बोले –) हे नाथ! आपके न रथ है, तन की रक्षा करने वाला कवच है और न जूते ही हैं। वह बलवान् वीर रावण किस प्रकार जीता जायेगा? कृपा निधान श्रीरामजी ने कहा– हे सखे! सुनो, जिससे जय होती है, वह रथ दूसरा ही है। शौर्य और धैर्य उस रथ के पहिये हैं। सत्य और शील (सदाचार) उसकी मजबूत ध्वजा और पताका हैं। बल, विवेक, दम (इन्दियों का वश में होना) और परोपकार– ये चार उसके घोड़े हैं, जो क्षमा, दया और समता रूपी डोरी से रथ में जुड़े हुए हैं।

ईश्वर का भजन ही [उस रथ को चलाने वाला] चतुर सारथि है। वैराग्य ढाल है और सन्तोष तलवार है। दान फरसा है, बुद्धि प्रचण्ड शक्ति है, श्रेष्ठ विज्ञान कठिन धनुष है।

निर्मल (पापरहित) और अचल (स्थिर) मन तरकस के समान है। शम (मन का वश में होना), [अहिंसादि] यम और [शौचादि] नियम–ये बहुत–से बाण हैं। ब्राह्मणों और गुरु का पूजन अभेद्य कवच है। इसके समान विजय का दूसरा उपाय नहीं है।।

हे सखे! ऐसा धर्ममय रथ जिसके पास हो उसके लिये जीतने को कहीं शत्रु ही नहीं है।

३८. शिव द्वारा श्रीराम स्तुति

हे राम! हे रमारमण (लक्ष्मीकान्त)! हे जन्म–मरण के संताप का नाश करने वाले! आपकी जय होय आवागमन के भय से व्याकुल इस सेवक की रक्षा कीजिये। हे अवधपति! हे

देवताओं के स्वामी! हे रमापति! हे विभो! मैं शरणागत आपसे यही माँगता हूँ कि हे प्रभों! मेरी रक्षा कीजिये।

हे दस सिर और भुजाओं वाले रावण का विनाश करके पृथ्वी के सब महान् रोगों (कष्टों) को दूर करने वाले श्रीरामजी! राक्षस समूह रूपी जो पतंगे थे, वे सब आपके बाण रूपी अग्नि के प्रचण्ड तेज से भस्म हो गये।।

आप पृथ्वी मण्डल के अत्यन्त सुन्दर आभूषण हैंय आप श्रेष्ठ बाण, धनुष और तरकस धारण किये हुए हैं। महान् मद, मोह और ममता रूपी रात्री के अन्धकार समूह के नाश करने के लिये आप सूर्य के तेजोमय किरण समूह हैं।

कामदेव रूपी भीलने मनुष्य रूपी हिरनों के हृदय में कुभोग रूपी बाण मारकर उन्हें गिरा दिया है। हे नाथ! हे [पाप – ताप का हरण करने वाले] हरे! उसे मारकर विषय रूपी वन में भूले पड़े हुए इन पामर अनाथ जीवों की रक्षा कीजिये।

लोग बहुत से रोगों और वियोगों (दुःखों) से मारे हुए हैं। ये सब आपके चरणों के निरादर के फल हैं। जो मनुष्य आपके चरण कमलों में प्रेम नहीं करते, वे अथाह भवसागर में पड़े हैं।।

जिन्हें आपके चरण कमलों में प्रीति नहीं है वे नित्य ही अत्यन्त दीन, मलिन (उदास) और दुःखी रहते हैं। और जिन्हें आपकी लीला – कथा का आधार है, उनको संत और भगवान् सदा प्रिय लगने लगते हैं।

उनमें न राग (आसक्ति) है, न लोभय न मान है, न मद। उनको सम्पति (सुख) और विपक्ति (दुःख) समान है। इसी से मुनि लोग योग (साधन) का भरोसा सदा के लिये त्याग देते हैं और प्रसन्नता के साथ आपके सेवक बन जाते हैं।।

वे प्रेम पूर्वक नियम लेकर निरन्तर शुद्ध हृदय से आपके चरणकमलों की सेवा करते रहते हैं और निरादर और आदर को समान मानकर वे सब संत सुखी होकर पृथ्वी पर विचरते हैं।

हे मुनियों के मनरूपी कमल के भ्रमर! हे महान् रणधीर एवं अजेय श्रीरघुवीर! मैं आपको भजता हूँ (आपकी शरण ग्रहण करता हूँ। हे हरि! आपका नाम जपता हूँ और आपको नमस्कार करता हूँ। आप जन्म दृमरण रूपी रोग की महान् औषध और अभिमान के शत्रु हैं।

आप गुण, शील और कृपा के परम स्थान हैं। आप लक्ष्मीपति हैं, मैं आपको निरन्तर प्रणाम करता हूँ। हे रघुनन्दन! [आप जन्म–मरण, सुख–दुःख, राग–द्वेषादि]

द्वन्द्व–समूहों का नाश कीजिये। हे पृथ्वी की पालन करने वाले राजन्! इस दीन जनकी ओर भी दृष्टि डालिये।

३९. रामराज्य

'रामराज्य' में दैहिक, दैविक और भौतिक ताप किसी को नहीं व्यापते। सब मनुष्य परस्पर प्रेम करते हैं और वेदों में बतायी हुई नीति (मर्यादा) में तत्पर रहकर अपने – अपने धर्म का पालन करते हैं।

धर्म अपने चारों चरणों (सत्य, शौच, दया और दान) से जगत् में परिपूर्ण हो रहा हैय स्वप्न में भी कहीं पाप नहीं है। पुरुष और स्त्री सभी रामभक्ति के परायण हैं और सभी परमगति (मोक्ष) के अधिकारी हैं।

छोटी अवस्था में मृत्यु नहीं होती, न किसी को कोई पीड़ा होती है। सभी के शरीर सुन्दर और नीरोग हैं। न कोई दरिद्र है, न दुःखी है और न दीन ही है। न कोई मूर्ख है और न शुभ लक्षणों से हीन ही है।

सभी दम्भरहित हैं, धर्म परायण हैं और पुण्यात्मा हैं। पुरुष और स्त्री सभी चतुर और गुणवान् हैं। सभी गुणों का आदर करने वाले और पण्डित हैं तथा सभी ज्ञानी हैं। सभी कृतज्ञ (दूसरे के किये हुए उपकार को मानने वाले) हैं, कपट–चतुराई (धूर्तता) किसी में नहीं है।

(काकभुशुण्डिजी कहते हैं–) हे पक्षीराज गुरुड़जी! सुनिए। श्री राम के राज्य में जड़, चेतन सारे जगत में काल, कर्म स्वभाव और गुणों से उत्पन्न हुए दुःख किसी को भी नहीं होते (अर्थात् इनके बंधन में कोई नहीं है)।।

अयोध्या में श्री रघुनाथजी सात समुद्रों की मेखला (करधनी) वाली पृथ्वी के एक मात्र राजा हैं। जिनके एक–एक रोम में अनेकों ब्रह्मांड हैं, उनके लिए सात द्वीपों की यह प्रभुता कुछ अधिक नहीं है।

बल्कि प्रभु की उस महिमा को समझ लेने पर तो यह कहने में (कि वे सात समुद्रों से घिरी हुई सप्त द्वीपमयी पृथ्वी के एकच्छत्र सम्राट हैं) उनकी बड़ी हीनता होती है, परंतु हे गरुड़जी! जिन्होंने वह महिमा जान भी ली है, वे भी फिर इस लीला में बड़ा प्रेम मानते हैं।।

क्योंकि उस महिमा को भी जानने का फल यह लीला (इस लीला का अनुभव) ही है, इन्द्रियों का दमन करने वाले श्रेष्ठ महामुनि ऐसा कहते हैं। रामराज्य की सुख सम्पत्ति का वर्णन शेषजी और सरस्वतीजी भी नहीं कर सकते।।

सभी नर–नारी उदार हैं, सभी परोपकारी हैं और ब्राह्मणों के चरणों के सेवक हैं। सभी पुरुष मात्र एक पत्नीव्रती हैं। इसी प्रकार स्त्रियाँ भी मन, वचन और कर्म से पति का हित करने वाली हैं।।

श्री रामचंद्रजी के राज्य में दण्ड केवल संन्यासियों के हाथों में है और भेद नाचने वालों के नृत्य समाज में है और 'जीतो' शब्द केवल मन के जीतने के लिए ही सुनाई पड़ता है। (अर्थात् राजनीति में शत्रुओं को जीतने तथा चोर–डाकुओं आदि को दमन करने के लिए साम, दान, दण्ड और भेद–ये चार उपाय किए जाते हैं। रामराज्य में कोई शत्रु है ही नहीं, इसलिए 'जीतो' शब्द केवल मन के जीतने के लिए कहा जाता है। कोई अपराध करता ही नहीं, इसलिए दण्ड किसी को नहीं होता, दण्ड शब्द केवल संन्यासियों के हाथ में रहने वाले दण्ड के लिए ही रह गया है तथा सभी अनुकूल होने के कारण भेदनीति की आवश्यकता ही नहीं रह गई। भेद, शब्द केवल सुर–ताल के भेद के लिए ही कामों में आता है।)।।

वनों में वृक्ष सदा फूलते और फलते हैं। हाथी और सिंह (वैर भूलकर) एक साथ रहते हैं। पक्षी और पशु सभी ने स्वाभाविक वैर भुलाकर आपस में प्रेम बढ़ा लिया है।।

पक्षी कूजते (मीठी बोली बोलते) हैं, भाँति–भाँति के पशुओं के समूह वन में निर्भय विचरते और आनंद करते हैं। शीतल, मन्द, सुगंधित पवन चलता रहता है। भौंरे पुष्पों का रस लेकर चलते हुए गुंजार करते जाते हैं।

बेलें और वृक्ष माँगने से ही मधु (मकरन्द) टपका देते हैं। गायें मनचाहा दूध देती हैं। धरती सदा खेती से भरी रहती है। त्रेता में सत्ययुग की करनी (स्थिति) हो गई ।।

समस्त जगत के आत्मा भगवान् को जगत् का राजा जानकर पर्वतों ने अनेक प्रकार की मणियों की खानें प्रकट कर दीं। सब नदियाँ श्रेष्ठ, शीतल, निर्मल और सुखप्रद स्वादिष्ट जल बहाने लगीं।।

समुद्र अपनी मर्यादा में रहते हैं। वे लहरों द्वारा किनारों पर रत्न डाल देते हैं, जिन्हें मनुष्य पा जाते हैं। सब तालाब कमलों से परिपूर्ण हैं। दसों दिशाओं के विभाग (अर्थात् सभी प्रदेश) अत्यंत प्रसन्न हैं।।

श्री रामचंद्रजी के राज्य में चंद्रमा अपनी (अमृतमयी) किरणों से पृथ्वी को पूर्ण कर देते हैं। सूर्य उतना ही तपते हैं, जितने की आवश्यकता होती है और मेघ माँगने से (जब जहाँ जितना चाहिए उतना ही) जल देते हैं।।

प्रभु श्री रामजी ने करोड़ों अश्वमेध यज्ञ किए और ब्राह्मणों को अनेकों दान दिए। श्री रामचंद्रजी वेदमार्ग के पालने वाले, धर्म की धुरी को धारण करने वाले, (प्रकृति जन्य सत्व, रज और तम) तीनों गुणों से अतीत और भोगों (ऐश्वर्य) में इन्द्र के समान हैं।।

शोभा की खान, सुशील और विनम्र सीताजी सदा पति के अनुकूल रहती हैं। वे कृपासागर श्री रामजी की प्रभुता (महिमा) को जानती हैं और मन लगाकर उनके चरण कमलों की सेवा करती हैं।।

यद्यपि घर में बहुत से (अपार) दास और दासियाँ हैं और वे सभी सेवा की विधि में कुशल हैं, तथापि (स्वामी की सेवा का महत्व जानने वाली) श्री सीताजी घर की सब सेवा अपने ही हाथों से करती हैं और श्री रामचंद्रजी की आज्ञा का अनुसरण करती हैं।।

कृपा सागर श्री रामचंद्रजी जिस प्रकार से सुख मानते हैं, श्री जी वही करती हैं, क्योंकि वे सेवा की विधि को जानने वाली हैं। घर में कौसल्या आदि सभी सासुओं की सीताजी सेवा करती हैं, उन्हें किसी बात का अभिमान और मद नहीं है।।

(शिवजी कहते हैं–) हे उमा जगज्जननी रमा (सीताजी) ब्रह्मा आदि देवताओं से वंदित और सदा अनिंदित (सर्वगुण संपन्न) हैं ।।

देवता जिनका कृपा कटाक्ष चाहते हैं, परंतु वे उनकी ओर देखती भी नहीं, वे ही लक्ष्मीजी (जानकीजी) अपने (महामहिम) स्वभाव को छोड़कर श्री रामचंद्रजी के चरणारविन्द में प्रीति करती हैं।।

सब भाई अनुकूल रहकर उनकी सेवा करते हैं। श्री रामजी के चरणों में उनकी अत्यंत अधिक प्रीति है। वे सदा प्रभु का मुखारविन्द ही देखते रहते हैं कि कृपालु श्री रामजी कभी हमें कुछ सेवा करने को कहें।।

श्री रामचंद्रजी भी भाइयों पर प्रेम करते हैं और उन्हें नाना प्रकार की नीतियाँ सिखलाते हैं। नगर के लोग हर्षित रहते हैं और सब प्रकार के देव दुर्लभ (देवताओं को भी कठिनता से प्राप्त होने योग्य) भोग भोगते हैं।।

वे दिन–रात ब्रह्माजी को मनाते रहते हैं और (उनसे) श्री रघुवीर के चरणों में प्रीति चाहते हैं। सीताजी के लव और कुश ये दो पुत्र उत्पन्न हुए, जिनका वेद–पुराणों ने वर्णन किया है।।

वे दोनों ही विजयी (विख्यात योद्धा), नम्र और गुणों के धाम हैं और अत्यंत सुंदर हैं, मानो श्री हरि के प्रतिबिम्ब ही हों। दो–दो पुत्र सभी भाइयों के हुए, जो बड़े ही सुंदर, गुणवान और सुशील थे।।

जो (बौद्धिक) ज्ञान, वाणी और इंद्रियों से परे और अजन्मा है तथा माया, मन और गुणों के परे है, वही सच्चिदानन्दघन भगवान् श्रेष्ठ नरलीला करते हैं ।।

प्रात:काल सरयूजी में स्नान करके ब्राह्मणों और सज्जनों के साथ सभा में बैठते हैं। वशिष्ठजी वेद और पुराणों की कथाएँ वर्णन करते हैं और श्री रामजी सुनते हैं, यद्यपि वे सब जानते हैं।।

वे भाइयों को साथ लेकर भोजन करते हैं। उन्हें देखकर सभी माताएँ आनंद से भर जाती हैं। भरतजी और शत्रुघ्नजी दोनों भाई हनुमान्जी सहित उपवनों में जाकर, वहाँ बैठकर श्री रामजी के गुणों की कथाएँ पूछते हैं और हनुमान्जी अपनी सुंदर बुद्धि से उन गुणों में गोता लगाकर उनका वर्णन करते हैं। श्री रामचंद्रजी के निर्मल गुणों को सुनकर दोनों भाई अत्यंत सुख पाते हैं और विनय करके बार–बार कहलवाते है।।

सबके यहाँ घर–घर में पुराणों और अनेक प्रकार के पवित्र रामचरित्रों की कथा होती है। पुरुष और स्त्री सभी श्री रामचंद्रजी का गुणगान करते हैं और इस आनंद में दिन–रात का बीतना भी नहीं जान पाते।।

जहाँ भगवान् श्री रामचंद्रजी स्वयं राजा होकर विराजमान हैं, उस अवधपुरी के निवासियों के सुख–संपत्ति के समुदाय का वर्णन हजारों शेषजी भी नहीं कर सकते।।

नारद आदि और सनक आदि मुनीश्वर सब कोसलराज श्री रामजी के दर्शन के लिए प्रतिदिन अयोध्या आते हैं और उस (दिव्य) नगर को देखकर वैराग्य भुला देते हैं।। दिव्य) स्वर्ण और रत्नों से बनी हुई अटारियाँ हैं। उनमें (मणि–रत्नों की) अनेक रंगों की सुंदर ढली हुई फर्शें हैं। नगर के चारों ओर अत्यंत सुंदर परकोटा बना है, जिस पर सुंदर रंग–बिरंगे कँगूरे बने हैं।। मानो नवग्रहों ने बड़ी भारी सेना बनाकर अमरावती को आकर घेर लिया हो। पृथ्वी (सड़कों) पर अनेकों रंगों के (दिव्य) काँचों (रत्नों) की गच बनाई (ढाली) गई है, जिसे देखकर श्रेष्ठ मुनियों के भी मन नाच उठते हैं।। उज्ज्वल महल ऊपर आकाश को चूम (छू) रहे हैं। महलों पर के कलश (अपने दिव्य प्रकाश से) मानो सूर्य, चंद्रमा के प्रकाश की भी निंदा (तिरस्कार) करते हैं। (महलों में) बहुत सी मणियों से रचे हुए झरोखे सुशोभित हैं और घर–घर में मणियों के दीपक शोभा पा रहे हैं।।

घरों में मणियों के दीपक शोभा दे रहे हैं। मूँगों की बनी हुई देहलियाँ चमक रही हैं। मणियों (रत्नों) के खम्भे हैं। मरकतमणियों (पन्नों) से जड़ी हुई सोने की दीवारें ऐसी सुंदर हैं मानो ब्रह्मा ने खास तौर से बनाई हों। महल सुंदर, मनोहर और विशाल हैं। उनमें सुंदर स्फटिक के आँगन बने हैं। प्रत्येक द्वार पर बहुत से खरादे हुए हीरों से जड़े हुए सोने के किंवाड़ हैं।।

घर–घर में सुंदर चित्रशालाएँ हैं, जिनमें श्री रामचंद्रजी के चरित्र बड़ी सुंदरता के साथ सँवारकर अंकित किए हुए हैं। जिन्हें मुनि देखते हैं, तो वे उनके भी चित्त को चुरा लेते हैं।।

सभी लोगों ने भिन्न–भिन्न प्रकार की पुष्पों की वाटिकाएँ यत्न करके लगा रखी हैं, जिनमें बहुत जातियों की सुंदर और ललित लताएँ सदा वसंत की तरह फूलती रहती हैं।।

भौंरे मनोहर स्वर से गुंजार करते हैं। सदा तीनों प्रकार की सुंदर वायु बहती रहती है। बालकों ने बहुत से पक्षी पाल रखे हैं, जो मधुर बोली बोलते हैं और उड़ने में सुंदर लगते हैं।।

मोर, हंस, सारस और कबूतर घरों के ऊपर बड़ी ही शोभा पाते हैं। वे पक्षी (मणियों की दीवारों में और छत में) जहाँ–तहाँ अपनी परछाई देखकर (वहाँ दूसरे पक्षी समझकर) बहुत प्रकार से मधुर बोली बोलते और नृत्य करते हैं।।

बालक तोता–मैना को पढ़ाते हैं कि कहो–'राम' 'रघुपति' 'जनपालक'। राजद्वार सब प्रकार से सुंदर है। गलियाँ, चौराहे और बाजार सभी सुंदर हैं।।

सुंदर बाजार है, जो वर्णन करते नहीं बनता, वहाँ वस्तुएँ बिना ही मूल्य मिलती हैं। जहाँ स्वयं लक्ष्मीपति राजा हों, वहाँ की संपत्ति का वर्णन कैसे किया जाए? बजाज (कपड़े का व्यापार करने वाले), सराफ (रुपए–पैसे का लेन–देन करने वाले) आदि वणिक् (व्यापारी) बैठे हुए ऐसे जान पड़ते हैं मानो अनेक कुबेर हों, स्त्री, पुरुष बच्चे और बूढ़े जो भी हैं, सभी सुखी, सदाचारी और सुंदर हैं।।

नगर के उत्तर दिशा में सरयूजी बह रही हैं, जिनका जल निर्मल और गहरा है। मनोहर घाट बँधे हुए हैं, किनारे पर जरा भी कीचड़ नहीं है।।

अलग कुछ दूरी पर वह सुंदर घाट है, जहाँ घोड़ों और हाथियों के ठट्ट के ठट्ट जल पिया करते हैं। पानी भरने के लिए बहुत से (जनाने) घाट हैं, जो बड़े ही मनोहर हैं। वहाँ पुरुष स्नान नहीं करते।।

राजघाट सब प्रकार से सुंदर और श्रेष्ठ है, जहाँ चारों वर्णों के पुरुष स्नान करते हैं। सरयूजी के किनारे–किनारे देवताओं के मंदिर हैं, जिनके चारों ओर सुंदर उपवन (बगीचे) हैं।।

नदी के किनारे कहीं–कहीं विरक्त और ज्ञानपरायण मुनि और संन्यासी निवास करते हैं। सरयूजी के किनारे–किनारे सुंदर तुलसीजी के झुंड के झुंड बहुत से पेड़ मुनियों ने लगा रखे हैं।।

नगर की शोभा तो कुछ कही नहीं जाती। नगर के बाहर भी परम सुंदरता है। श्री अयोध्यापुरी के दर्शन करते ही संपूर्ण पाप भाग जाते हैं। (वहाँ) वन, उपवन, बावलिया और तालाब सुशोभित हैं।।

अनुपम बावलियाँ, तालाब और मनोहर तथा विशाल कुएँ श्रोभा दे रहे हैं, जिनकी सुंदर (रत्नों की) सीढ़ियाँ और निर्मल जल देखकर देवता और मुनि तक मोहित हो जाते हैं। (तालाबों में) अनेक रंगों के कमल खिल रहे हैं, अनेकों पक्षी कूज रहे हैं और भौंरे गुंजार कर रहे हैं। (परम) रमणीय बगीचे कोयल आदि पक्षियों की (सुंदर बोली से) मानो राह चलने वालों को बुला रहे हैं।

स्वयं लक्ष्मीपति भगवान् जहाँ राजा हों, उस नगर का कहीं वर्णन किया जा सकता है? अणिमा आदि आठों सिद्धियाँ और समस्त सुख–संपत्तियाँ अयोध्या में छा रही हैं।।

लोग जहाँ–तहाँ श्री रघुनाथजी के गुण गाते हैं और बैठकर एक–दूसरे को यही सीख देते हैं कि शरणागत का पालन करने वाले श्री रामजी को भजो, शोभा, शील, रूप और गुणों के धाम श्री रघुनाथजी को भजो।। कमलनयन और साँवले शरीर वाले को भजो। पलक जिस प्रकार नेत्रों की रक्षा करती हैं उसी प्रकार अपने सेवकों की रक्षा करने वाले को भजो। सुंदर बाण, धनुष और तरकस धारण करने वाले को भजो । संत रूपी कमलवन के (खिलाने के) सूर्य रूप रणधीर श्री रामजी को भजो।। काल रूपी भयानक सर्प के भक्षण करने वाले श्री राम रूप गरुड़जी को भजो। निष्काम भाव से प्रणाम करते ही ममता का नाश कर देने वाले श्री रामजी को भजो। लोभ–मोह रूपी हरिनों के समूह के नाश करने वाले श्री राम किरात को भजो। कामदेव रूपी हाथी के लिए सिंह रूप तथा सेवकों को सुख देने वाले श्री राम को भजो।। संशय और शोक रूपी घने अंधकार का नाश करने वाले श्री राम रूप सूर्य को भजो। राक्षस रूपी घने वन को जलाने वाले श्री राम रूप अग्नि को भजो। जन्म–मृत्यु के भय को नाश करने वाले श्री जानकी समेत श्री रघुवीर को क्यों नहीं भजते?।। बहुत सी वासनाओं रूपी मच्छरों को नाश करने वाले श्री राम रूप हिमराशि (बर्फ के ढेर) को भजो। नित्य एक रस, अजन्मा और अविनाशी श्री रघुनाथजी को भजो। मुनियों को आनंद देने वाले, पृथ्वी का भार उतारने वाले और तुलसीदास के उदार (दयालु) स्वामी श्री रामजी को भजो।।

इस प्रकार नगर के स्त्री–पुरुष श्री रामजी का गुण–गान करते हैं और कृपा निधान श्री रामजी सदा सब पर अत्यंत प्रसन्न रहते हैं।।

काकभुशुण्डिजी कहते हैं–) हे पक्षीराज गरुड़जी! जब से रामप्रताप रूपी अत्यंत प्रचण्ड सूर्य उदित हुआ, तब से तीनों लोकों में पूर्ण प्रकाश भर गया है। इससे बहुतों को सुख और बहुतों के मन में शोक हुआ।।

जिन–जिन को शोक हुआ, उन्हें मैं बखानकर कहता हूँ (सर्वत्र प्रकाश छा जाने से)

पहले तो अविद्या रूपी रात्रि नष्ट हो गई। पाप रूपी उल्लू जहाँ–तहाँ छिप गए और काम–क्रोध रूपी कुमुद मुँद गए।।

भाँति–भाँति के (बंधनकारक) कर्म, गुण, काल और स्वभाव– ये चकोर हैं, जो (रामप्रताप रूपी सूर्य के प्रकाश में) कभी सुख नहीं पाते। मत्सर (डाह), मान, मोह और मद रूपी जो चोर हैं, उनका हुनर (कला) भी किसी ओर नहीं चल पाता।। धर्म रूपी तालाब में ज्ञान, विज्ञान– ये अनेकों प्रकार के कमल खिल उठे। सुख, संतोष, वैराग्य और विवेक– ये अनेकों चकवे शोक रहित हो गए।।

यह श्री रामप्रताप रूपी सूर्य जिसके हृदय में जब प्रकाश करता है, तब जिनका वर्णन पीछे से किया गया है, वे (धर्म, ज्ञान, विज्ञान, सुख, संतोष, वैराग्य और विवेक) बढ़ जाते हैं और जिनका वर्णन पहले किया गया है, वे (अविद्या, पाप, काम, क्रोध, कर्म, काल, गुण, स्वभाव आदि) नाश को प्राप्त होते (नष्ट हो जाते) हैं।।

४०. भरत–राम संवाद

संत विषयों में लम्पट (लिप्त) नहीं होते, शील और सद्गुणों की खान होते हैं। उन्हें पराया दुःख देखकर दुःख और सुख देखकर सुख होता है। वे [सब में, सर्वत्र, सब समय] समता रखते हैं, उनके मन में कोई उनका शत्रु नहीं है, वे मद से रहित और वैराग्यवान् होते हैं तथा लोभ, क्रोध, हर्ष और भय का त्याग किये हुए रहते हैं।

उनका चित्त बड़ा कोमल होता है। वे दीनों पर दया करते हैं तथा मन, वचन और कर्म से मेरी निष्कपट (विशुद्ध) भक्ति करते हैं। सबको सम्मान देते हैं, पर स्वयं मानरहित होते हैं। हे भरत! वे प्राणी (संतजन) मेरे प्राणों के समान हैं।

उनको कोई कामना नहीं होती। वे मेरे नाम के परायण होते हैं। शान्ति, वैराग्य, विनय और प्रसन्नता के घर होते हैं। उनमें शीतलता, सरलता, सबके प्रति मित्र भाव और ब्राह्मण के चरणों में प्रीति होती है, जो धर्मों को उत्पन्न करने वाली है।

अब असंतों (दुष्टों) का स्वभाव सुनोय कभी भूलकर भी उनकी संगति नहीं करनी चाहिये। उनका संग सदा दुःख देने वाला होता है। जैसे हरहाई (बुरी जाति की) गाय कपिला (सीधी और दुधार) गाय को अपने संग से नष्ट कर डालती है।।

दुष्टों के हृदय में बहुत अधिक संताप रहता है। वे परायी सम्पत्ति (सुख) देखकर सदा जलते रहते हैं। वे जहाँ कहीं दूसरे की निन्दा सुन पाते हैं, वहाँ ऐसे हर्षित होते हैं मानो रास्ते में पड़ी निधि (खजाना) पा ली हो।।

वे काम, क्रोध, मद और लोभ के परायण तथा निर्दयी, कपटी, कुटिल और पापों के घर होते हैं। वे बिना ही कारण सब किसी से वैर किया करते हैं। जो भलाई करता है उसके साथ भी बुराई करते हैं।

उनका झूठा ही लेना और झूठा ही देना होता है। झूठा ही भोजन होता है और झूठा ही चबेना होता है (अर्थात् वे लेने–देने के व्यवहार में झूठ का आश्रय लेकर दूसरों का हक मार लेते हैं अथवा झूठी डींग हाँका करते हैं कि हमने लाखों रुपये ले लिये, करोड़ों का दान कर दिया। इसी प्रकार खाते हैं चने की रोटी और कहते हैं कि आज खूब माल खाकर आये। अथवा चबेना चबाकर रह जाते हैं और कहते हैं हमें बढ़िया भोजन से वैराग्य है, इत्यादि। मतलब यह कि वे सभी बातों में झूठ ही बोला करते हैं।) जैसे मोर [बहुत मीठा बोलता है, परन्तु उस] का हृदय ऐसा कठोर होता है कि वह महान् विषैले साँपों को भी खा जाता है। वैसे ही वे भी ऊपर मीठे वचन बोलते हैं [परन्तु हृदय के बड़े ही निर्दयी होते हैं]।।

हे भाई! दूसरों की भलाई के समान कोई धर्म नहीं है और दूसरों को दुःख पहुँचाने के समान कोई नीचता (पाप) नहीं है। हे तात! समस्त पुराणों और वेदों का यह निर्णय (निश्चित सिद्धान्त) मैंने तुमसे कहा है, इस बात को पण्डित लोग जानते हैं।

४१. श्रीराम द्वारा अयोध्यावासियों को उपदेश

बड़े भाग्य से यह मनुष्य शरीर मिला है। सब ग्रन्थों ने यही कहा है कि यह शरीर देवताओं को भी दुर्लभ है (कठिनता से मिलता है)। यह साधन का धाम और मोक्ष का दरवाजा है। इसे पाकर भी जिसने परलोक न बना लिया,।

वह परलोक में दुःख पाता है, सिर पीट–पीटकर पछताता है तथा (अपना दोष न समझकर) काल पर, कर्म पर और ईश्वर पर मिथ्या दोष लगाता है।

यदि परलोक में और यहाँ दोनों जगह सुख चाहते हो, तो मेरे वचन सुनकर उन्हें हृदय में दृढ़ता से पकड़ रखो। हे भाई! यह मेरी भक्ति का मार्ग सुलभ और सुखदायक है, पुराणों और वेदों ने इसे गाया है।।

ज्ञान अगम (दुर्गम) है (और) उसकी प्राप्ति में अनेकों विघ्न हैं। उसका साधन कठिन है और उसमें मन के लिए कोई आधार नहीं है। बहुत कष्ट करने पर कोई उसे पा भी लेता है, तो वह भी भक्ति रहित होने से मुझको प्रिय नहीं होता।।

भक्ति स्वतन्त्र है और सब सुखों की खान है। परन्तु सत्संग (संतों के संग) के बिना प्राणी इसे नहीं पा सकते। और पुण्य समूह के बिना संत नहीं मिलते। सत्संगति ही संसृति (जन्म–मरण के चक्र) का अन्त करती है।

और भी एक गुप्त मत है, मैं उसे सबसे हाथ जोड़कर कहता हूँ कि शंकरजी के भजन बिना मनुष्य मेरी भक्ति नहीं पाता।।

कहो तो, भक्ति मार्ग में कौन–सा परिश्रम है? इसमें न योग की आवश्यकता है, न यज्ञ, जप, तप और उपवास की! (यहाँ इतना ही आवश्यक है कि) सरल स्वभाव हो, मन में कुटिलता न हो और जो कुछ मिले उसी में सदा संतोष रखे।।

मेरा दास कहलाकर यदि कोई मनुष्यों की आशा करता है, तो तुम्हीं कहो, उसका क्या विश्वास है? (अर्थात् उसकी मुझ पर आस्था बहुत ही निर्बल है।) बहुत बात बढ़ाकर क्या हूँ? हे भाइयों! मैं तो इसी आचरण के वश में हूँ।

न किसी से वैर करे, न लड़ाई–झगड़ा करे, न आशा रखे, न भय ही करे। उसके लिए सभी दिशाएँ सदा सुखमयी हैं। जो कोई भी आरंभ (फल की इच्छा से कर्म) नहीं करता, जिसका कोई अपना घर नहीं है (जिसकी घर में ममता नहीं है), जो मानहीन, पापहीन और क्रोधहीन है, जो (भक्ति करने में) निपुण और विज्ञानवान् है।।

संतजनों के संसर्ग (सत्संग) से जिसे सदा प्रेम है, जिसके मन में सब विषय यहाँ तक कि स्वर्ग और मुक्ति तक (भक्ति के सामने) तृण के समान हैं, जो भक्ति के पक्ष में हठ करता है, पर (दूसरे के मत का खण्डन करने की) मूर्खता नहीं करता तथा जिसने सब कुतर्कों को दूर बहा दिया है।।

४२. काकभुशुण्डि द्वारा पक्षिराज गरुड़ के समक्ष सुनायी गयी पूर्वजन्म की कथा

मनोरथ कीड़ा है, शरीर लकड़ी है। ऐसा धैर्यवान् कौन है, जिसके शरीर में यह कीड़ा न लगा हो? पुत्र की, धन की और लोकप्रतिष्ठा की इन तीन प्रबल इच्छाओं ने किसकी बुद्धि को मलिन नहीं कर दिया (बिगाड़ नहीं दिया)? ।

श्रीराम जी वही सच्चिदानन्दघन हैं जो अजन्मा, विज्ञानस्वरूप, रूप और बल के धाम, सर्वव्यापक एवं व्याप्य (सर्वरूप), अखण्ड, अनन्त, सम्पूर्ण, अमोघशक्ति (जिसकी शक्ति व्यर्थ नहीं होती), और छः एश्वर्यों से युक्त भगवान् हैं।।

जीव परतन्त्र है, भगवान् स्वतन्त्र हैंय जीव अनेक हैं, श्रीपति भगवान् एक हैं। यद्यपि माया का किया हुआ यह भेद असत् है तथापि वह भगवान् के भजन बिना करोड़ों उपाय करने पर भी नहीं जा सकता।।

भक्ति से रहित सब गुण और सब सुख वैसे ही (फीके) हैं जैसे नमक के बिना बहुत प्रकार के भोजन के पदार्थ। भजन से रहित सुख किस काम के? हे पक्षिराज! ऐसा विचार कर मैं बोला।

(श्रीरामजी ने काकभुशुण्डि से कहा) यह सारा संसार मेरी माया से उत्पन्न है। [इसमें] अनेकों प्रकार के चराचर जीव हैं। वे सभी मुझे प्रिय हैंय क्योंकि सभी मेरे उत्पन्न किये हुए हैं। [किन्तु] मनुष्य मुझको सबसे अधिक अच्छे लगते हैं।।

उन मनुष्यों में भी द्विज, द्विजों में भी वेदों को [कण्ठ में] धारण करने वाले, उनमें भी वेदोक्त धर्म पर चलने वाले, उनमें भी विरक्त (वैराग्यवान्) मुझे प्रिय हैं। वैराग्यवानों में फिर ज्ञानी और ज्ञानियों से भी अत्यन्त प्रिय विज्ञानी हैं। विज्ञानियों से भी प्रिय मुझे अपना दास है, जिसे मेरी ही गति (आश्रय) है, कोई दूसरी आशा नहीं है। मैं तुझसे बार–बार सत्य ('निज सिद्धान्त' कहता हूँ कि मुझे अपने सेवक केसमान प्रिय कोई भी नहीं है। भक्तिहीन ब्रह्मा ही क्यों न हो, वह मुझे सब जीवों के समान ही प्रिय है। परन्तु भक्तिमान् अत्यन्त नीच भी प्राणी मुझे प्राणों के समान प्रिय है, यह मेरी घोषणा है।।

(काकभुशुण्डि ने पक्षिराज गरुड से कहा) अनेक जप, तप, यज्ञ, शम (मन को रोकना), दम (इन्द्रियों को रोकना), व्रत, दान, वैराग्य, विवेक, योग, विज्ञान आदि सबका फल श्रीरघुनाथ जी के चरणों में प्रेम होना है। इसके बिना कोई कल्याण नहीं पा सकता।

४३. काकभुशुण्डी द्वारा कलिमहिमा का प्रतिपादन

कलियुग में न वर्ण धर्म रहता है, न चारों आश्रम रहते हैं। सब पुरुष–स्त्री वेद के विरोध में लगे रहते हैं। ब्राह्मण वेदों के बेचने वाले और राजा प्रजा को खा डालने वाले होते हैं। वेद की आज्ञा कोई नहीं मानता।

जिसको जो अच्छा लग जाय, वही मार्ग है, जो डींग मारता है, वही पण्डित है। जो मिथ्या आरम्भ करता (आडम्बर रचता) है और जो दम्भ में रत है, उसी को सब कोई संत कहते हैं।।

जो [जिस किसी प्रकार से] दूसरे का धन हरण कर ले, वही बुद्धिमान्न् है। जो दम्भ करता है, वही बड़ा आचारी है। जो झूठ बोलता है और हँसी–दिल्लगी करना जानता है, कलियुग में वही गुणवान् कहा जाता है।।

जो आचारहीन है और वेदमार्ग को छोड़े हुए है, कलियुग में वही ज्ञानी और वही वैराग्यवान् है। जिसके बड़े–बड़े नख और लंबी जटाएँ है, वही कलियुग में प्रसिद्ध तपस्वी है।।

धनी लोग मलिन (नीच जाति के) होने पर भी कुलीन माने जाते हैं। द्विज का चिह्न जनेऊमात्र रह गया और नंगे बदन रहना तपस्वी का। जो वेदों और पुराणों को नहीं मानते, कलियुग में वे ही हरिभक्त और सच्चे संत कहलाते हैं।

कवियों के तो झुंड हो गये, पर दुनिया में उदार (कवियों का आश्रय दाता) सुनायी नहीं पड़ता। गुण में दोष लगाने वाले बहुत हैं, पर गुणी कोई भी नहीं है। कलियुग में बार–बार अकाल पड़ते हैं। अन्न के बिना सब लोग दुःखी होकर मरते हैं।

हे पक्षिराज गरुड़जी! सुनिये, कलियुग में कपट, हठ (दुराग्रह), दम्भ, द्वेष, पाखण्ड, मान, मोह और काम आदि (अर्थात् काम, क्रोध और लोभ) और मद ब्रह्माण्ड भर में व्याप्त हो गये (छा गये)।

सत्ययुग, त्रेता और द्वापर में जो गति पूजा, यज्ञ और योग से प्राप्त होती है, वही गति कलियुग में लोग केवल भगवान् के नाम से पा जाते हैं।

कलियुग में न तो योग और यज्ञ है, और न ज्ञान ही है। श्रीरामजी का गुणगान ही एकमात्र आधार है। अतएव सारे भरोसे त्याग कर जो श्रीराम जी को भजता है और प्रेम सहित उनके गुण समूहों को गाता हैं, वही भवसागर से तर जाता है, इसमें कुछ भी सन्देह नहीं है। नाम का प्रताप कलियुग में प्रत्यक्ष है। कलियुग का एक पवित्र प्रताप है कि मानसिक पुण्य तो होते हैं, पर (मानसिक) पाप नहीं होते।

यदि मनुष्य विश्वास करे, तो कलियुग के समान दूसरा युग नहीं है। [क्योंकि] इस युग में श्रीरामजी के निर्मल गुण समूहों को गा–गाकर मनुष्य बिना ही परिश्रम संसार [रूपी समुद्र] से तर जाता है।

४४. रुद्राष्टक

प्रेम सहित दण्डवत् करके वे ब्राह्मण श्री शिवजी के सामने हाथ जोड़कर मेरी भयंकर गति (दण्ड) का विचार कर गदगद वाणी से विनती करने लगे–॥

हे मोक्ष स्वरूप, विभु, व्यापक, ब्रह्म और वेद स्वरूप, ईशान दिशा के ईश्वर तथा सबके स्वामी श्री शिवजी मैं आपको नमस्कार करता हूँ। निज स्वरूप में स्थित (अर्थात् मायादिरहित), (मायिक) गुणों से रहित, भेदरहित, इच्छारहित, चेतन आकाश रूप एवं आकाश को ही वस्त्र रूप में धारण करने वाले दिगम्बर (अथवा आकाश को भी आच्छादित करने वाले) आपको मैं भजता हूँ।

निराकार, ओंकार के मूल, तुरीय (तीनों गुणों से अतीत), वाणी, ज्ञान और इन्द्रियों से परे, कैलासपति, विकराल, महाकाल के भी काल, कृपालु, गुणोंके धाम, संसार से परे आप परमेश्वर को मैं नमस्कार करता हूँ।

जो हिमाचल के समान गौरवर्ण तथा गंभीर हैं, जिनके शरीर में करोड़ों काम देवों की ज्योति एवं शोभा है, जिनके सिर पर सुंदर नदी गंगाजी विराजमान हैं, जिनके ललाट पर द्वितीया का चंद्रमा और गले में सर्प सुशोभित है। जिनके कानों में कुण्डल हिल रहे हैं, सुंदर भ्रुकुटी और विशाल नेत्र हैं, जो प्रसन्न मुख, नीलकण्ठ और दयालु हैं, सिंह चर्म का वस्त्र धारण किए और मुण्डमाला पहने हैं, उन सबके प्यारे और सबके नाथ (कल्याण करने वाले) श्री शंकरजी को मैं भजता हूँ।

प्रचण्ड (रुद्ररूप), श्रेष्ठ, तेजस्वी, परमेश्वर, अखण्ड, अजन्मे, करोड़ों सूर्यों के समान प्रकाश वाले, तीनों प्रकार के शूलों (दुःखों) कोनिर्मूल करने वाले, हाथ में त्रिशूल धारण किए, भाव (प्रेम) के द्वारा प्राप्त होने वाले भवानी के पति श्री शंकरजी को मैं भजता हूँ।

कलाओं से परे, कल्याण स्वरूप, कल्प का अंत (प्रलय) करने वाले, सज्जनों को सदा आनंद देने वाले, त्रिपुर के शत्रु, सच्चिदानंदघन, मोह को हरने वाले, मन को मथ डालने वाले कामदेव के शत्रु, हे प्रभो! प्रसन्न होइए, प्रसन्न होइए।

जब तक पार्वती के पति आपके चरण कमलों को मनुष्य नहीं भजते, तब तक उन्हें न तो इह लोक और परलोक में सुख–शांति मिलती है और न उनके तापों का नाश होता है। अतः हे समस्त जीवों के अंदर (हृदय में) निवास करने वाले हे प्रभो! प्रसन्न होइए।

मैं न तो योग जानता हूँ, न जप और न पूजा ही। हे शम्भो! मैं तो सदा–सर्वदा आपको ही नमस्कार करता हूँ। हे प्रभो! बुढ़ापा तथा जन्म (मृत्यु) के दुःख समूहों से जलते हुए मुझ दुःखी की दुःख से रक्षा कीजिए। हे ईश्वर! हे शम्भो! मैं आपको नमस्कार करता हूँ।

भगवान्‌रुद्र की स्तुति का यह अष्टक उन शंकरजी की तुष्टि (प्रसन्नता) के लिए ब्राह्मण द्वारा कहा गया। जो मनुष्य इसे भक्ति पूर्वक पढ़ते हैं, उन पर भगवान् शम्भु प्रसन्न होते हैं।

www.ingramcontent.com/pod-product-compliance
Lightning Source LLC
Chambersburg PA
CBHW071136130626
46553CB00004B/1391
* 9 7 8 9 3 5 7 7 6 4 7 4 2 *